OXFORD PAPERBACK REFERENCE

A Century of New Words

John Ayto is one of Britain's most established dictionary writers, the editor of *Brewer's Dictionary of Phrase and Fable*, and the author of several books about the English language.

A Century of New Words

JOHN AYTO

OXFORD
UNIVERSITY PRESS

Great Clarendon Street, Oxford OX2 6DP

Oxford University Press is a department of the University of Oxford.
It furthers the University's objective of excellence in research, scholarship, and education by publishing worldwide in

Oxford New York

Auckland Cape Town Dar es Salaam Hong Kong Karachi
Kuala Lumpur Madrid Melbourne Mexico City Nairobi
New Delhi Shanghai Taipei Toronto

With offices in

Argentina Austria Brazil Chile Czech Republic France Greece
Guatemala Hungary Italy Japan Poland Portugal Singapore
South Korea Switzerland Thailand Turkey Ukraine Vietnam

Oxford is a registered trade mark of Oxford University Press in the UK and in certain other countries

Published in the United States
by Oxford University Press Inc., New York

First published 1999 as 20th Century Words
Revised edition published 2006 as Movers and Shakers
First published in paperback 2007

British Library Cataloguing in Publication Data
Data available

Library of Congress Cataloging in Publication Data
Data available

Typeset by SPI Publisher Services, Pondicherry, India
Printed in Great Britain
by Clays Ltd, Bungay, Suffolk

ISBN 978–0–19–921369–6

1

Contents

Introduction 1

The 1990s 7
The 1910s 33
The 1920s 57
The 1930s 81
The 1940s 109
The 1950s 135
The 1960s 157
The 1970s 181
The 1980s 203
The 1990s and 2000s 227

Index 245

Introduction

Do words shape an age or are they shaped by it? Are our actions and modes of thought channelled by the vocabulary available to us for giving expression to them, or do we continually create our lexicon anew to reflect a changing world? The two propositions are far from mutually exclusive, but no doubt the rationalist would wish to emphasize the second of them. Every year that passes throws up new ideas, experiences, and inventions for which no name has hitherto existed, and since names are indispensable cogs in the machinery of communication, our natural human propensity for coining them soon plugs most gaps.

Take the development of powered flight in the first two decades of the 20th century, for example. Aeronautical technology evolved very fast and, since people needed to describe and discuss it, its vocabulary had to expand at a similar rate, and from almost a standing start. Using various strategies (borrowing words from French, for instance—the French were early leaders in the field—and cannibalizing nautical terminology) the English language cobbled together a serviceable lexicon for the new air age, many elements of which (*airliner*, *fuselage*, *pilot*, and so on) are still in place today.

So, at a purely practical level, words are language's response to circumstances. But—certainly when viewed in retrospect—can we not see the words of an era as giving shape to and summing up their time? They can be our terms of reference for a period—a decade, a crucial year, a whole century, perhaps a less easily definable stretch of history—which we constantly reinforce by usage, and which unfailingly conjure up their temporal origins. There are some words that possess that power to a high degree, and it is those lexical touchstones that form the subject matter of this collection.

Mention *ice cubes* and *air conditioning*, *surrealism* and *totalitarianism*, *hunger marches* and *rat-races*, *terrorists* and *paparazzi*, and there is nowhere else we could be but the 20th century. The fabric of our environment (*nylon*, *plastic*), how we get around (*motorways*, *traffic jams*, *spacecraft*), how we entertain ourselves (*cinema*, *movies*, *radio*, *television*), how we communicate with each other (*cyberspace*, *Internet*, *mobile*), how we fight each other (*world war*, *air raid*, *genocide*)—all these elements of human life, and many more, have produced certain key words that instantly locate themselves as post-1900. Other terms pinpoint a more precise period: *angry young man*, *beatnik*, *skiffle*, *sputnik*, *Teddy boy*, for instance, could be nothing other than the 1950s; *front line*, *mustard gas*, *shell shock*, and *tank* are a lexical short cut to World War I; and those who lived through them would find their minds directed instantaneously to the 1970s by *flying picket*, *industrial action* and *loony left*, by *green* 'environmentally concerned' and by *streaking*. *Fatwa* conjures up a moment in time, when the Ayatollah Khomeini promulgated a death sentence on the British writer Salman Rushdie in 1989.

The words of each decade are given a chapter to themselves (the final chapter extends the 1990s into the early years of the 21st century). They are listed alphabetically, with a brief introduction bringing together the main strands of lexical development within that period (including some items that did not make it to the final alphabetical listing) or setting them against their historical background. Each entry word has a date after it. I cannot emphasize too strongly that this represents the earliest date from which a printed or other written record of the word exists in the *Oxford English Dictionary* or its files—nothing more and nothing less. It is not meant to suggest that the word necessarily 'entered' the language in that year. It is not uncommon for words to escape immediate notice if they slip unobtrusively into the language rather than being announced with a fanfare; and slang and other colloquial items routinely take some time to find their way into the written record. Sometimes English is slow to adopt a term for a phenomenon, movement, etc. which to modern eyes seems the obvious one, and sometimes, no doubt, the record of an earlier adoption has yet to come to light (for example, Max Planck originated his quantum theory in 1900, but the terms *quantum* and *quantum theory* are not recorded in English until the second decade of the century; *art nouveau* was an important style of art of the last decade of the 19th century, but the term is not recorded as an English word until 1901). So, unless specifically documented details of a word's coinage are given, the date should be regarded simply as an indication of when a particular usage first appeared. The explanation of the word is followed by one or more examples of it in use, which often put further flesh on the bones of the definition. One of them may be the earliest recorded instance of the word in print, but that is not necessarily always the case.

By looking at the areas in which the vocabulary of a language is expanding fastest in a given period, we can form a fairly accurate impression of the chief preoccupations of society at that time and the points at which the boundaries of human endeavour are being advanced. Table 1 summarizes the semantic fields which grew most rapidly in the succeeding decades of the 20th century. The new technology of cars, aircraft, radio, and film dominated lexical innovation in the 1900s (*dashboard, aerodrome, wireless, cinema*), along with the vocabulary of psychology and psychoanalysis (*libido, psychoanalysis*). These last two were not so dominant after the 1910s, but the others continued to be major sources of neologisms well into the 1930s. However, in the decade of World War I they were not surprisingly overshadowed by the broad spectrum of military vocabulary (*gas mask, shell hole, U-boat*), and in the 1920s the lexicon of national post-war relief, the bright young things and the Jazz Age, dominated the scene (*Charleston, Oxford bags*). Then in the 1930s the build-up to and start of a new war (*dive-bomb, Blitzkrieg, black-out*) put such frivolities in their place. In the first half of the 1940s, World War II was again providing the majority of new usages (*doodlebug, gas chamber, kamikaze*), but the return of peace

TABLE 1: LEXICAL GROWTH-AREAS BY DECADE

1900s	Cars Aviation Radio Film Psychology
1910s	War Aviation Film Psychology
1920s	Clothes/dance/youth Transport Radio Film
1930s	War/build-up to war Transport Film/entertainment
1940s	War Post-war society/international affairs Nuclear power Computers Space
1950s	Media Nuclear power Space Computers Youth culture
1960s	Computers Space Youth culture/music Media Drugs
1970s	Computers Media Business Environment Political correctness
1980s	Media Computers Finance/money Environment Political correctness Youth culture/music
1990s & 2000s	Politics Media Internet and other electronic communication

brought other concerns to the fore: reconstruction, national and international (*National Health*, *Marshall Plan*, *superpower*), and the nuclear threat (*the bomb*). A small trickle of computer terminology (*electronic brain*, *hardware*) was to become a flood in the second half of the 20th century. Similar small beginnings for the vocabulary of space exploration (*booster*, *re-entry*) reached their apogee in the 1960s.

The 1950s saw the first significant burgeoning youth culture (*beatnik*, *teen*), which in its various manifestations continued to be a prolific contributor to the English language throughout the rest of the century. It was also the decade in which television combined with other forms of communication and entertainment in a new vocabulary of the media (*hi-fi*, *transistor radio*, *videotape*) that would dominate the next fifty years. Both had particular offshoots in the psychedelic 1960s in the language of music (*the twist*, *Merseybeat*) and the language of drugs (*acid*, *speed*). In the 1970s, concerns about the destruction of the environment became a long-term source of new vocabulary (*green*, *global warming*), and the language of political correctness and its proponents began to get into its stride (*chairperson*, *s/he*). The 1980s were the decade of money, typified both by financial jargon (*dawn raid*, *white knight*) and by the lifestyle terminology of those who made and enjoyed it (*yuppie*, *dinky*). The major new players on the 1990s lexical scene were the Internet and other electronically mediated methods of communication (*blog*, *cybernaut*, *website*), and their influence continued to be felt into the 2000s (*podcasting*).

Movements and trends in human affairs do not necessarily fit neatly into a particular decade, of course, and the terms we associate with them sometimes anticipate their high-water mark. We tend to think of *appeasement*, for instance, as essentially a phenomenon of the 1930s, and that was indeed the decade in which the negative connotations the word has today began to gather around it; but in fact the concept originated in the second decade of the century. Similarly that quintessentially Cold War expression *iron curtain* can be traced back to the 1920s. It is not at all uncommon for a new term to potter along for decades in obscurity (often as a piece of jargon known only to specialists), and then to find itself suddenly thrust into the spotlight: *greenhouse effect*, for example, was coined in the 1920s, but few non-climatologists had heard of it until the 1980s. Bear in mind, too, that one of the chief characteristics of human language is that it enables us to talk about things which do not exist yet: it can still cause a frisson to read H. G. Wells discussing the *atomic bomb* in 1914.

So although it may at first sight seem odd that some terms that are central to 20th-century life, and particularly to its technological culture (such as *car* and *aircraft*), are not represented in this collection, the answer in most cases is that they are pre-20th-century coinages. Table 2 gives a selection of high-profile or striking examples of this phenomenon, in chronological order.

TABLE 2: PRE-20TH-CENTURY COINAGES

flying machine (1736)
parachute (1785)
aircraft (1850)
Communist (1850)
acid rain (1859)
commuter (1865)
aeroplane (1873)
biplane (1874)
Venusian (1874)
benefit 'financial assistance' (1875)
relativity (1876)
phonograph (1877)
old-age pension (1879)
Labour party (1886)
department store (1887)
contact lens (1888)
milk shake (1889)
Mother's Day (1890)
electron (1891)
ouija (1891)
spaceship (1894)
automobile (1895)
feminism (1895)
modern art (1895)
motor car (1895)
car (1896)
motion picture (1896)
motor (verb) (1896)
moving picture (1896)
bad 'good' (slang) (1897)
photosynthesis (1898)
radioactive (1898)
aspirin (1899)
auto 'car' (1899)
motor 'car' (1899)

So what does the shape of our age turn out to be, when scrutinized through this retrospective lexical telescope? As amorphous as any other age, probably, and resistant to a trite summing up in a few words. Its vocabulary of science and technology gives it its glamorous gloss of human progress; its proliferation of acronyms and snappy contractions suggest a life lived at a faster pace; its embracing of colloquial speech patterns (which a collection such as this can do no more than hint at) implies a less formal, hierarchical society; its euphemisms (military/political and otherwise) and other circumlocutory devices show us to be more practised and systematic than ever in exploiting language's infinite capacity to mislead. An age, perhaps, when humanity can do more things and go more places than it could before, but underneath remains much the same.

JOHN AYTO
London, 2006

The 1900s

It is 1900. In Britain, Queen Victoria is still on the throne. At the start of the Victorian era, over sixty years before, the railways were a novelty; the only means of taking to the air was the balloon; the voting franchise was still biased towards the landed classes; and the crinoline had not been heard of. Now, the motor car has made its first noisy appearance on the roads; in the US, Orville and Wilbur Wright are planning the first powered flight in an aeroplane; women are agitating for the vote; and the coming thing in female fashion is the *motor veil*. The scientific and technical advances of the late 19th century are about to transform the world, especially in terms of speed of movement. We are shortly to be introduced to *atomic energy* and *hydroelectricity*, *gamma rays* and *hormones*, and the concept of the *world war*. Welcome to the 20th century.

The first decade of the century laid down the basic pattern of transportation that was to be elaborated over the succeeding ninety years, particularly on the roads and in the air. Motor vehicles had become commercially available in the 1890s, but not until the new century did they establish themselves as a serious alternative (and soon successor) to the horse (by the start of World War I, over 130,000 cars were registered in the UK). As automotive technology developed and the infrastructure of motoring began to be put in place, English had to evolve and absorb an enormous amount of new vocabulary. There were all the various bits and pieces of a car, the components and spare parts: *accelerators* and *sumps*, *big ends* and *dashboards*, *radiators* and *chassis*, *speedometers* and *windscreens* (or in the US, *windshields*). There were various sorts and styles of vehicle: *landaulettes*, *limousines*, and *saloons*, not to mention *motor-bikes* and *autocycles*. Roads made for the 19th century's *hippomobiles* (an ephemeral term for a horse-drawn vehicle) needed to be upgraded into *motor roads*, *motorways*, or *speedways*, with *flyovers*, *underpasses*, and *loop roads*. The basic terminology of *automobile*, *motor*, *motor car*, *car*, *auto*, and the short-lived *horseless carriage* had been established in the 1890s, but the first decade of the new century transformed it into everyday vocabulary.

Having put on his *motor coat*, taken his *Rolls-Royce* out of its *garage* (or *motor stable*), and *petrolled* it (or given it some *juice*), the *autoist* (or his *chauffeur*) could set off for a *day trip* (or perhaps indulge in some *week-ending*).

To ensure that his passengers did not get *car-sick* (and that he did not attract the attention of the *traffic police*), he would need to avoid *speeding* (or *overspeeding*). *Road signs* would guide him to his destination. Those unwilling to take to the wheel themselves might prefer to get a *taxi*.

Powered flight was born at Kittyhawk in 1903, when the Wright brothers' biplane took to the air; the *heavier-than-air* aircraft had come to stay. Expansion was rapid, and a new terminology needed to be assembled in a hurry (a lot of it—such as *aileron*, *fuselage*—was borrowed from French; and much, too, was already in place—*aeroplane*, *biplane*—thanks to the extended late-19th-century period of development that led to that first momentous take-off). A lot has proved durable (*aerofoil*, *airliner* (originally applied to airships), *pilot*); other coinages have fallen by the wayside (*aerial liner*, *aeroplanist* 'pilot', *hydroaeroplane* 'seaplane'). *Aerodromes* are still around; *flying grounds* are no more. Aircraft are still kept in *hangars* (another French borrowing), but no longer in *harbours* or *sheds*. From over the horizon in Germany there loomed the *Zeppelin*.

Meanwhile, below ground, *electrification* was making underground railways a practical proposition. In London, the *tube* was beginning its 20th-century expansion. Amongst the amenities were *escalators* to carry its passengers into the depths. *Straphangers* who suffered from claustrophobia might contemplate the alternative of the *motor bus* or even the *electrobus*.

Scientists were unlocking the secrets of the atom (*splitting the atom* was the colloquial phrase that has stuck), probing the foundations of life, developing new materials. *Electronic*, *half-life*, and radioactive *decaying* entered the language, as did *adrenaline* and *antibody*, *clone* and *genetics*. The transforming material of the 20th century, *plastic*, made its first appearance, initially in the form of *bakelite*. The *stratosphere* was named, and the potentiality of *solar power* and *wind power* examined. But the most momentous theoretical advance of the decade, if not of the century, was marked by the publication in 1905 of Albert Einstein's special theory of relativity. The term *relativity* itself was not a new one—the Scottish physicist James Clerk Maxwell is on record as using it in this same general sense in 1876, and it crops up sporadically in the last quarter of the 19th century—but its elucidation revolutionized our view of the universe and its laws.

In 1901, Guglielmo Marconi succeeded in transmitting a radio signal across the Atlantic Ocean; the era of modern communication media had begun. Both *radio* and *wireless*, which would enjoy a keen terminological rivalry in the ensuing decades, made their first appearance in the language, as did *aerial* and *antenna*. Understandably, a lot of early radio vocabulary—*Marconigram* 'telegram', *Marconist* 'radio operator'—eponymized its pioneer; you could even *marconi* a message to someone. But the fame was short-lived. The way of the future could already be seen. The *cathode-ray tube* had been invented, and people were discussing the possibility of *television*.

In 1902 the South African War (Boer War) came to an end (it had produced the jokey gerund *mafficking*, a punning coinage inspired by the relief of Mafeking in 1900 and capturing a mixture of national relief and celebration, but also the ominous *concentration camp*), but before the decade was over Britain was building its *dreadnoughts* in preparation for a forthcoming contest. Several terms that were to become all too familiar in World War I made their debut in the language: *dug-out* and *tin hat*, *no man's land* and *firing squad*, *Lee-Enfield* and *surprise attack*. *Gas* was now something for killing people with; and *bomb* was being used as a verb, anticipating the sort of aerial bombardment that was to drag civilian populations into the inferno of 20th-century warfare.

It was the decade in which the concepts *pacifism*, *war crime*, and *détente* first found a word, but it was also the decade of *expansionism*, *propaganda*, and new *pogroms*. The radical unrest of the 19th century was still in the air, and the world first heard of *palace revolutions* and *revisionism*. In Britain, though, a *Lib-Lab* pact offered hope of political stability.

The upper classes may have been starting to worry about the *servant problem*, but it was also the decade of the *bread-line*, the *hunger march*, and the *poverty line*. The beginnings of a state response to such problems are reflected in such terms as *welfare* and *social security*. That 20th-century Aunt Sally the *social worker* made her (or his) first appearance. The *women's movement* was becoming increasingly impatient in its search for female enfranchisement, and *suffragettes* were chaining themselves to railings. It was a decade in which more 'advanced' views on the relationship between the sexes were taking hold, particularly in Bohemian circles: the era of *mixed bathing* and the *trial marriage*. Relationships between the races were appearing on the agenda, too: the term *racialism* entered the language, along with *colour prejudice*, *ethnocentric*, *segregation*, and *white supremacy*.

If one man above all others dictated the way in which the 20th century viewed the workings of the human mind, it was the Austrian psychologist Sigmund Freud (1856–1939). Somewhat under a cloud by the end of the century, in this its first decade he was becoming more widely known in the English-speaking world, through translations of his works, and his terminology was beginning to make its way into the English language, notably *psychoanalysis* and its shortened form *analysis*, and also *libido*. The science of the mind was expanding on all fronts, bringing with it expressions like *neurosis* and *manic depressive*, *masochistic* and *repressed*, *complex* and *depression*, and *narcissism*, against which the introspective, anxious 20th century could examine itself. And as if they were not enough, *sexology* took its bow.

For the escapist there was the *cinema*. What better way to forget your anxiety neurosis than going to see a *film*—silent, of course (although someone in the pit might be producing *sound effects*). The first public film performance had taken place in 1895, but it was not until the first decade of the 20th century that the industry became organized on a serious footing. Entrepreneurs built *cinematograph theatres* (or *picture palaces*, or *nickelodeons*); the words *cameraman* and *subtitle* entered the language; and *Kinemacolor* offered an intriguing glimpse of the future. The *bioscope* had come to stay (although that particular term for 'cinema' did not stay long, except in South Africa). If music was more your thing, there were the latest products of *Tin Pan Alley*, or the more genteel strains emanating from the *palm court*, or you could do it (almost) yourself with a *Pianola*. To dance to there were the *cake walk* and the *veleta*. The sportingly inclined could choose between *ping-pong* and *table football*.

Models (or *mannequins*) were showing off the latest fashions (but not, as yet, *panties*, *brassières*, or other *undies*). *Cloche hats* were in, as were *beehives* (dome-shaped hats). For men, the *lounge suit* put in its first appearance. Tonsorially, waves were the thing: women wanted a *permanent wave*, and the *marcel* (named after the French hairdresser François Marcel Grateau (1852–1936)) was the market leader. If your own hair was not quite up to it, you could always try a *transformation* (a wig). Other *beauty culture* services available at the *beauty shop* included *electrolysis*.

In the home, the first of the 20th century's mod cons were making their appearance, including *central heating* and the *vacuum cleaner*. *Home helps* were no doubt enormously grateful for the advent of *floor polish* and *Jeyes fluid* (a household disinfectant), while upstairs the mistress of the house luxuriated in her *bath-salts*-scented bath. For breakfast there were *cornflakes*, and to spread on your toast, *Oxford marmalade* and the improbably named *Nutter*, a butter-substitute made from nut-oil. The canning industry gave the world *pineapple chunks*, and fast food made significant advances with *hot dogs* and the *club sandwich* (probably washed down with *Coke* or its new rival, *Pepsi-Cola*). There were *meat-lozenges* for the carnivore, while vegetarians could enjoy *Marmite* and the ineffable *nut cutlet*. Chinese food began its 20th-century infiltration of Western cuisine with the *chow mein*.

In the US, *big business* was gearing itself up for its decades of dominance. In *filing-cabinet*-lined offices, *executives* dictated to *shorthand typists* (or to a *Dictaphone*).

Western science 'discovered' the *okapi* (a relative of the giraffe) and unearthed the much more mediagenic *tyrannosaurus*. But undoubtedly the animal of the decade was the *teddy bear*.

addict *n* (1909) someone who is addicted to a drug. The 20th century was to find ample use for this noun, converted from the verb *addict.*

> 1924 *Westminster Gazette*: People who ... get into the habit of going to the chemist for drugs to induce sleep, and often end up by becoming opium, morphine, or heroin addicts.

adrenaline *n* (1901) a hormone secreted by the adrenal glands and affecting circulation, muscular action, etc. The discovery of the hormone and the coining of its name are both disputed; they may have been the work of Dr Jokichi Takamine (see the quote below), or of Dr Norton L. Wilson.

> 1901 *American Journal of Physiology*: The most important contribution to our knowledge of the active principle of the suprarenal gland ... is from Dr. Jokichi Takamine who has isolated the blood-pressure-raising principle of the gland in a stable and pure crystalline form ... To this body ... he has given the name 'Adrenalin'.

aerial *n* (1902) a wire or other device for transmitting or receiving radio waves. The term is a shortening of either *aerial conductor* (coined by Guglielmo Marconi, the inventor of radio, in 1899) or *aerial wire.*

aerodrome *n* (1909) an area with runways where aircraft can take off and land. The word was originally coined (from Greek *aerodromos* 'traversing the air') in the early 1890s by S. P. Langley. He used it to denote an aeroplane ('An actual working aerodrome model with its motor', *Experimental Aerodynamics* (1891)). This usage did not survive beyond the first decade of the 20th century, losing out to the much longer established *aeroplane* (1873).

An entirely new word *aerodrome* appeared in 1902, meaning 'a hangar for a balloon or other aircraft'. This was borrowed from French *aerodrome,* which had been coined from Greek *dromos* 'course, racecourse' on the model of such words as *hippodrome.* It persisted into the 1920s ('The building ... was easily recognisable as a huge aerodrome', Marie Corelli, *The Secret Power* (1921)), but then faded from the scene.

The application to an airfield developed towards the end of the decade, and at first was not universally well received (see the first quote below). It established itself in the 1910s, but as such facilities became bigger it gradually lost out to **airport (1919)**. US English preferred the variant **airdrome (1917)**.

> 1909 F. W. Lanchester: I regret to see that the misuse of the word 'aerodrome' is receiving support in your [i.e. *Flight* magazine's] columns ... I suppose because a hippodrome is a big open space for horses, you think that an aerodrome should be a big open space for flying machines.

> 1917 E. N. Fales: The airdrome ... is used exclusively for flying, and may be as large as a mile square.

airliner *n* (1908) a passenger aircraft. Comparatively rare in early use, the term has now largely taken the place of **liner (1905)** in the same sense. In the first recorded example, below, it refers to an airship (as did the contemporary *aerial liner* (1909)), and this was its main early application (German airships were the pioneers of commercial passenger air transport). The first unequivocal record of *airliner* for an aeroplane is in the 1929 edition of the *Concise Oxford Dictionary,* but it had a forerunner (soon to be defunct) in *aero-liner* (1908).

> 1908 *Daily Mail*: The cost of working the air-liner was represented as small.

> 1908 *Daily Mail*: The Aero-Liner. The future liner, the giant aeroplane.

> 1955 *Times*: Another important French 'first' was the arrival of the Caravelle, the country's first jet airliner.

anorexic *adj, n* (1907) (someone) suffering from anorexia nervosa. English acquired Latin *anorexia* in the 16th century in the anglicized form *anorexy,* meaning broadly 'lack of appetite'. Its specialized medical usage did not develop until the mid 19th century. Its original adjectival derivative was *anorectic,* but this is mainly used in technical contexts; *anorexic* has become the preferred general adjective and (along with *anorexia*) became much more familiar in the last quarter of the 20th century, as increasing numbers of adolescent girls were being diagnosed with the condition. See also **bulimia (1976)**.

> 1907 Pierre Janet: If food is introduced by force . . . into the stomach of the most anorexic hysterical . . . you will recognize that the digestion . . . comes to be completely effected.
>
> 1983 *Listener*: Compulsive runners share the same symptoms as anorexics.

art nouveau *n* (1901) a style of art developed in the last decade of the 19th century, characterized by the free use of ornament based on organic or foliate forms and by its flowing (i.e. non-geometrical) lines and curves. It was in and out of fashion throughout the 20th century: reviled between the wars, idolized in the late 1960s. The term is a borrowing from French, literally 'new art'.

> 1901 *Times*: It is much to be regretted that the authorities of South Kensington have introduced into the Museum specimens of the work styled, 'L'Art nouveau'.
>
> 1909 Joseph Thorp: The *art nouveau*, with its meandering tulips and inconsequent squirms and dots.

atomic energy *n* (1906) the energy released by the fission of the atomic nuclei of certain heavy elements such as uranium 235 or plutonium or by the fusion of light nuclei. 1906 was the year in which Ernest Rutherford discovered the atomic nucleus. A synonymous formulation is **atomic power (1914)**. The alternative *nuclear energy* is first recorded in 1930.

> 1906 *Nature*: Nevertheless, there is a sense in which it may be said that we are profiting by atomic energy.
>
> 1914 H. G. Wells: Holsten . . . was destined to see atomic energy dominating every other source of power.
>
> 1952 *Literary Guide*: Ours is the age of atomic energy . . . of psycho-analysis and abstractionism in the arts.

ballyhoo *n* (1901) a flamboyant performance outside a circus or carnival tent, intended to encourage people to enter. The word is first encountered in American English, but its precise origins are unclear. There is an obsolete nautical slang term *ballyhoo* meaning 'an unseaworthy vessel', which apparently comes from Spanish *balahú* 'schooner'; there is a village called *Ballyhooly* in Ireland; and there is an isolated reference in 1880 to a *ballyhoo bird*, a facetious name given to an artificial bird put together from wood and pasteboard to fool a bird-hunter: but none of these is particularly relevant to attracting custom to a show. The wider meaning 'sensational or vulgar (self-)advertising', which is more familiar in present-day English, had developed before the end of the decade.

> 1901 *World's Work*: First there is the ballyhoo—any sort of a performance outside the show, from the coon songs of the pickaninnies in front of the Old Plantation, to the tinkling tamborines of the dancers on the stage of 'Around the World'.
>
> 1908 *Saturday Evening Post*: It is the practice of almost every statesman to prepare the country for his performance by beating the drum and blatting a few lines of ballyhoo.

beauty shop *n* (1901), **beauty parlour** *n* (1908) an establishment where cosmetic and other treatments are given to improve personal beauty. The terms originated in the US. The synonymous **beauty salon** is not recorded until 1922.

> 1908 *Harper's Week*: The 'beauty parlors' of a large department store. There are a number of booths divided off by wooden partitions.

big business *n* (1905) large-scale commercial operations, especially when regarded as (excessively) powerful. The term is of US origin.

> 1913 Theodore Roosevelt: We demand that big business give the people a square deal; in return we must insist that when any one engaged in big business honestly endeavors to do right he shall himself be given a square deal.

birthday card *n* (1902) a greetings card sent to someone on their birthday.

> 1902 *Little Folks*: Miss Shaw seemed to appreciate Moya's birthday card very much.

bomb *v* (1909) to attack with bombs. *Bomb* had been used as a verb since the late 17th century, but it referred to the firing of mortar shells (Lord Nelson wrote in 1797 'The intention of bombing us still goes on'). The application (of the noun as well as the verb) to an explosive device placed by hand or dropped from an aircraft is an early 20th-century development (in the early months of World War I *The Times* reported 'A German aeroplane flew over the outskirts of Paris early this morning and threw several bombs' (9 October 1914); and such tactics had been practised before the war: 'There have been many contests by aviators in "bomb-dropping" ', Richard Ferris, *How it Flies* (1910)). The term *air bomb*, distinguishing such devices from other sorts of bomb, is first recorded in 1914; it continued in use for some years: 'And most murderous of all devices Are poison gases and air-bombs Refinements of evil', D. H. Lawrence, *Last Poems* (1930). The first quote below refers to terrorist activities in British India.

> 1909 *Daily Chronicle*: Attempts had been made to blow up Sir Andrew Fraser, to bomb trains known to contain Europeans, and to murder policemen and officials.

> *a*1917 E. A. Mackintosh: He turned to bomb the big dug-out.

boy scout *n* (1908) a member of a boys' organization founded by Robert Baden-Powell in 1908 and intended to develop character and self-reliance. Baden-Powell seems to have got the inspiration for the name from a corps of boys which was formed to help in the defence of Mafeking in the Boer War. Since 1992 the organization has been known simply as the *Scouts*, and has admitted girls. By the end of the 20th century there were over 25 million Scouts of various kinds throughout the world. See also **girl guide (1909)**.

> 1908 *Scout*: Although the Boy Scouts have only been set going within the last two months, they are rapidly increasing all over the country.

> 1909 *Daily Mail*: The following message from the King was read at Lieutenant-General Baden-Powell's review of the Boy Scouts at the Crystal Palace on Saturday… 'The King is glad to know that the Boy Scouts are holding their first annual parade. Please assure the boys that [etc.]'.

brassière, brassiere *n* (1909) a woman's undergarment worn to support the breasts. The term is a euphemistic borrowing of French *brassière* in its decidedly dated sense 'bodice' (in 20th-century French it has mainly been used, in the plural, to mean 'leading-strings'; the French word for a 'brassière' is *soutien-gorge*). The shortened form *bra* dates from the 1930s (see **bra (1936)**). The general idea for the brassière dates from the second half of the **19**th century (it is usually said to have been invented by Herminie Cadolle, a Parisian corsetière who exhibited an undergarment incorporating breast-support at the Great Exposition of **1900**, but garments serving a similar purpose have been identified in American sources going as far back as the **1860**s).

> 1909 *Vogue*: A brassière for dressy occasions.

> 1912 *Queen* (advert): The Stylish Figure of To-Day requires a Brassiere.

bread-line *n* (1900) a queue of destitute people waiting to receive bread. The term first occurs in, and as the title of, a magazine story by A. B. Paine. The shift in meaning in British English to 'subsistence level' (probably occasioned by a misunderstanding of American English *line* 'queue', and also perhaps by an association with **poverty line (1901)**) seems to have become established by the 1920s.

> 1900 *Lippincott's Magazine*: That's the bread line. They get a cup of coffee and a loaf of bread every night at twelve o'clock.

> 1959 *New Statesman*: The average African family in the urban areas lived calamitously below the bread-line.

buck *n* ***the buck*** (1908) the responsibility. The term occurred originally in the phrase *pass the buck*, and usually still does, but there are other variations (notably *the buck stops here*, attributed to US President Harry Truman (see the second quote below)). The expression seems to come from earlier US slang *buck* denoting an object passed round during a game of poker to indicate the dealer—but the origins of this are unknown.

> 1912 Will Irwin: The Big Commissioner will get roasted by the papers and hand it to the Deputy Comish, and the Deputy will pass the buck down to me, and I'll have to report how it happened.
>
> 1952 Harry Truman: When the decision is up before you—and on my desk I have a motto which says 'The buck stops here'—the decision has to be made.

cameraman *n* (1908) a man who uses or operates a camera professionally. The term has latterly been applied only to film or television cameramen.

> 1908 *Westminster Gazette*: After both had posed to the inevitable camera-men.
>
> 1920 *Quarterly Review*: The camera-man will film you anything.

canned *adj* (1904) of music, laughter, etc.: mechanically or artificially reproduced: a dismissive epithet coined while recording technology was still in its infancy.

> 1908 *Westminster Gazette*: The latest invention is the 'canned speech' delivered by a gramophone.

cathode-ray tube *n* (1905) a vacuum tube in which cathode rays are projected on a fluorescent screen (as used throughout the 20th century in television sets). The term is first recorded in an article called 'Some Applications of the Braun Cathode-Ray Tube' in the journal *The Electrician.*

central heating *n* (1906) (apparatus for) heating a building from a central heat source. It is mainly a British term. The idea dates from Roman times, but the terminology is 20th-century.

chauffeur *n* (1902) a paid driver of a private motor vehicle. English first borrowed *chauffeur* from French at the very end of the 19th century in the broader sense 'motorist' ('All the members of the Italian Royal Family are enthusiastic chauffeurs', *Lady's Realm* (1903)), but this was soon elbowed aside by the current meaning. The French word is derived from *chauffer* 'to heat', and originally denoted a 'stoker'.

> 1902 *Westminster Gazette*: As to the driver, 'chauffeur' seems at present to hold the field.

cinema *n* (1909) a shorter alternative to *cinematograph* (1896). English originally acquired the word at the end of the 19th century from French, as *cinéma*, and it is not clear whether the present-day form is an anglicization of this (itself an abbreviation of *cinématographe*) or an independent English formation. The earliest record of its use in the sense 'a building where films are shown' (short for *cinema hall, cinema theatre*, etc.) is from 1913. A later variant was *kinema* (1914), with an initial /k/ reintroduced from the original Greek *kinema* 'movement', but it does not seem to have survived beyond the 1930s.

> 1910 *Daily Chronicle*: 'Cinematograph'–which has just been cut down in a glaring advertisement to 'cinema'.
>
> 1913 Valentia Steer: The so-called 'comic' films from France which one sees on the cinema.

city centre *n* (1904) the central (often largely non-residential) part of a city. The first example is an early occurrence of a term which did not come into common use until after World War II.

> 1904 George Bernard Shaw: In city centres . . . the [housing] schemes are commercially hopeless.
>
> 1957 John Braine: The maze of side-streets off the city centre.

clone *n* (1903) originally, in botanical terminology, a group of cultivated plants the individuals of which are transplanted parts of one original stock; later used more broadly to denote any group of cells or organisms produced asexually from a single sexually produced ancestor. The form of the word as originally proposed by H. J. Webber in the journal *Science* was *clon*; the amendment to *clone* was put forward by C. L. Pollard in the same journal, on the grounds that it better represents its Greek source *klōn* 'twig, slip'. The noun was turned into a verb, meaning 'to cause to reproduce so as to form a clone', in the late 1950s.

> 1968 *Observer Colour Supplement*: One of the most extraordinary of the possibilities now being explored . . . is referred to as 'cloning people'—the creation of genetically identical individuals from body cells.

closed shop *n* (1904) a shop, factory, trade, etc. in which normally only trade-union members are employed. The term originated in the US, and established a salient place for itself in the vocabulary of 20th-century industrial relations.

> 1904 *New York Evening Post*: An increase in wages, recognition of the union, and 'closed shops' are demanded.

coke *n* (1908) A colloquial name, originally US, for the drug cocaine.

> 1908 R. S. Baker: They buy the 'coke' in the form of powder and snuff it up the nose.

Coke *n* (1909) Coca-Cola. A colloquial abbreviation, registered as a trademark by the Coca-Cola Company. The original name *Coca-Cola* dates from 1887.

> 1909 *Coca-Cola Bottler* (Philadelphia): If you . . . asked to be served with 'Ice Cold Cokes' you will be presented with a very good bottle of carbonated Coca-Cola.

colour prejudice *n* (1905) prejudice on the grounds of racial difference.

> 1905 William Baucke: In the case of the Maori, this is deterred by a colour prejudice.

complex *n* (1907) a connected group of repressed ideas which give rise to particular patterns of thought, feeling, and action. The use of the term was established by C. G. Jung in 1907 (*Ueber die Psychologie der Dementia Praecox*), but it originated with Neisser in 1906 (*Individualität und Psychose*). It is commonly used with a qualifying term (e.g. *inferiority complex, Oedipus complex*).

> 1907 Petersen & Jung: The complex robs the ego of light and nourishment, just as a cancer robs the body of its vitality.

concentration camp *n* (1901) a camp where non-combatants are incarcerated during a war. The term was originally applied to the camps set up by Lord Kitchener during the South African War (Boer War) of 1899–1902, the underlying idea being that the inmates were 'concentrated' in one place (see the first quote below), where they could not give help to the fighting forces. It gained even further notoriety when it was applied to camps for the internment, brutalization, extermination, etc. of Jews, gypsies, and political prisoners organized by the Nazi regime in Germany before and during World War II.

> 1901 *Hansard*: The policy of placing the women and children confined in the concentration camps in South Africa, whose husbands and fathers are in the field, on reduced rations.

> 1940 H. G. Wells: The White Paper of Nazi atrocities in the concentration camps and elsewhere.

conspiracy theory *n* (1909) the theory that an event or phenomenon occurs as a result of a conspiracy between interested parties. Originally it was a neutral term, but more recent usage (dating from around the mid 1960s) is often somewhat derogatory, implying a paranoid tendency to see the hand of some malign covert agency in any unexplained event. The derivative *conspiracy theorist* is first recorded in the 1960s.

> 1975 *New York Times*: Conspiracy theorists contend that two of the men have strong resemblances to E. Howard Hunt Jr. and Frank A. Sturgis, convicted in the Watergate break-in.

conveyor belt *n* (1906) an endless belt of rubber, canvas, etc., running over rollers, on which objects or material can be conveyed. It became a key element in the mass production which characterized 20th-century industry, and in due time the term came to connote conformist and mindless repetition of a process.

> 1948 J. B. Priestley: I don't admire the mass production and conveyor-belt system of education.

cornflakes *n* (1907) a kind of breakfast cereal made from flaked and flavoured maize: the archetypal 20th-century manufactured breakfast cereal (the second quote below refers to the World War I period). The term originated in the US.

> 1908 *Saturday Evening Post*: There are 13 imitations of Kellogg's Toasted Corn Flakes.

> 1960 John Betjeman: And, in the morning, cornflakes, bread and tea, Cook's Farm Eggs and a spoon of marmalade.

depression *n* (1905) a melancholic state often accompanied by feelings of inadequacy and lack of energy. In use since the 17th century as a general word for 'dejection', but in the 20th century it was adopted as a clinical term.

> 1905 *Psychological Review*: If these symptoms of depression—the motor retardation, the difficulty of apprehension and of association—become aggravated, one finds various forms of melancholia.

détente *n* (1908) the easing of strained relations, especially in a political situation. The word was borrowed from French, where it means literally 'loosening, relaxation'. It was quite common in the language of international diplomacy throughout the 20th century, but not generally familiar until the Cold War period, when it referred to a hoped-for relaxation of tension between East and West.

> 1908 *Times*: A change in the European situation . . . had . . . set in . . . The characteristic feature of this transformation may be called a détente.

> 1976 *National Observer* (US): All that detente brings the United States, Reagan says, is 'the right to sell Pepsi-Cola in Siberia'.

dreadnought *n* (1906) any of a class of British battleships having their main armament entirely of big guns of one calibre. These formidable firing-platforms were the keystone of Britain's pre-World War I arms build-up. The name (which originally belonged to a naval ship of Drake's era) was given to the first of the class to be launched (on 18 February 1906), and later generalized to its sister-ships.

> 1906 *Outlook*: The Atlantic Fleet will consist of three Dreadnoughts and five of the Canopus class.

> 1909 *Daily Chronicle*: Our Dreadnought strength and our strength in pre-Dreadnought ships, in comparison with those of Germany.

electrify *v* (1900) to introduce electric power into (a system of railways, a factory, etc.). The derivative *electrification* is first recorded in 1900. Alternative terms that were canvassed contemporaneously were *electralize* [sic] and *electrolization* or *electrilization* ('The electrolisation of the inner circle, with its twenty-six stations', *Westminster Gazette* (1900)), but these completely failed to catch on.

> 1900 *Westminster Gazette*: It is not very astonishing that the directors of the District Railway should be in no violent hurry to start upon the electrifying of their line.

electrocute *v* (1909) to kill accidentally by means of electricity. This is a generalized use of a verb which was coined in the late 1880s with the specific meaning 'to execute with electricity', denoting the action of the newly invented electric chair ('Kemmler, the murderer sentenced to be "electrocuted" ', *Voice* (New York) (1889)).

> 1913 *Daily Mail*: The horse . . . was struck by the wire and instantly electrocuted.

electronic *adj* (1902) originally, relating to electrons. The word's main present-day application, to the control of a device by the conduction of electrons in a vacuum, a gas, or a semiconductor, seems to have emerged in the late 1920s, and to have been originally used in the context of musical instruments and the music made by them. Its wider employment followed on the development of computers after World War II. Similarly, *electronics* (first recorded in 1910) initially denoted simply the study of the behaviour of electrons, and was not used in the context of electronically controlled systems until the 1940s.

1902 J. A. Fleming (title): The electronic theory of electricity.

1910 *Chemical Abstracts*: Radio activity and electronics.

1930 *Electronics*: Electronic Musical Instruments . . . Examples of such instruments are the electronic organ of M. Coupleaux of Paris.

1962 Marshall McLuhan: As we experience the new electronic and organic age with ever stronger indications of its main outlines, the preceding mechanical age becomes quite intelligible.

empathy *n* (1904) the power of mentally identifying oneself with (and so fully comprehending) a person or object. The word was introduced as a technical term in the field of aesthetics as in effect a translation of the parallel German term *Einfühlung*, which had been coined by T. Lipps in 1903. This in turn was based on Greek *empatheia*, literally 'in-feeling'. Around the middle of the century it escaped from the jargon of aestheticians and began to be used almost synonymously with sympathy. The derived verb *empathize* is first recorded in 1924.

1928 Rebecca West: The active power of empathy which makes the creative artist, or the passive power of empathy which makes the appreciator of art.

escalator *n* (1900) a moving staircase made on the endless-chain principle, so that the steps ascend or descend continuously, for carrying passengers (especially those using an underground railway) up or down. The word was originally a US trademark. It was familiar enough by the 1920s to have a verb *escalate* back-formed from it ('I dreamt I saw a Proctor "escalating", Rushing up a quickly moving stair', *Granta* (1922)), but its later much vilified metaphorical use was far in the future.

1923 *Spectator*: Three escalators will serve the Bakerloo Tube.

exclusive *adj* (1901) of clothing, furniture, etc.: of a pattern or model exclusively belonging to or claimed by a particular establishment or firm. The first quote below is the earliest recorded appearance of a usage which was to become a cliché of 20th-century marketing terminology.

1901 *Tatler*: Some very charming artistic novelties in exclusive and original designs are now ready for inspection.

1924 *Queen*: The absurdly low prices of the most exclusive gowns in London . . . Practical designs for golfing, country and travelling wear. Exclusive but inexpensive.

executive *n* (1902) someone holding an executive position in a business organization; a business person. The term originated in the US, and by the latter part of the 20th century its useful lack of sexual specificity had ensured it widespread usage, verging almost on cliché.

1902 G. H. Lorimer: They will never climb over the railing that separates the clerks from the executives.

1960 *Guardian*: There are three types [of private patients]—the snobs . . . the queue-jumpers . . . and the business executive.

expansionism *n* (1900) advocacy of, or furtherance of, a policy of expansion, especially territorial expansion. This particular sense of *expansion* dates from the 1880s.

1900 *Daily News*: By Imperialism British Liberals ought not to understand militarism or even expansionism.

expressionism *n* (1908) a style of painting in which the artist seeks to express emotional experience rather than impressions of the physical world. Initially a descriptive term, it does not seem to have evolved into a (capitalized) name for a specific school of painters until the second decade of the century, in the wake of abstract expressionists such as Kandinsky. (The term *expressionist* in this general sense dates from around 1850.)

1921 John Galsworthy: Expression! Ah, they were all Expressionists now, he had heard, on the Continent . . . He wondered where this—this Expressionism—had been hatched. The thing was a regular disease!

film *n* (1905) a cinematographic representation of a story, drama, episode, event, etc.; a movie. The term has become standard in British English, in preference to *motion picture* (1890s) and **movie (1912)**.

> 1905 *Westminster Gazette*: A firm who took cinematograph films of his operations . . . The films once obtained have been sold and even exhibited at country fairs.

> 1911 *Times*: The great majority of heroic and patriotic films shown here make United States sailors and roughriders the heroes.

firing squad *n* (1904) a squad of soldiers detailed to fire shots. In early use the term seems quite often to have been synonymous with *firing party* (i.e. 'a squad detailed to fire over the grave of someone buried with military honours'), but during World War I, when such things were much in use, the current sense 'a squad detailed to shoot someone sentenced to death by a court-martial' became firmly established.

> 1959 T. S. Eliot: The ones who don't get out in time Find themselves in gaol . . . Or before a firing squad.

floating voter *n* (1905) a voter not committed to one particular political party. The term *floating vote* dates from the mid 19th century.

> 1958 *Economist*: That now well-known and inoffensive favourite of the touchy floating voter, Mr. Aneurin Bevan.

futurism *n* (1909) an art movement, originating in Italy, characterized by violent departure from traditional forms, the avowed aim being to express movement and growth in objects, not their appearance at some particular moment. The term is also applied to similar tendencies in literature and music. It was modelled on Italian *futurismo* and French *futurisme.*

> 1937 Nicolas Slonimsky: Futurism was proclaimed in a manifesto published in the Paris *Figaro* on 20 February 1909. It aimed at complete annihilation of all accepted forms in favor of a future music created according to some imagined law of machine-like perfection.

gamma ray *n* (1903) a stream of electromagnetic radiation emitted by atomic nuclei, shorter in wavelength than X-rays. It was so named because it was originally regarded as the third and most penetrating kind of radiation emitted by radium (gamma (γ) being the third letter of the Greek alphabet), but it is now known to be identical with very short X-rays.

> 1903 Ernest Rutherford: The γ rays, which are non-deviable by a magnetic field, and which are of a very penetrating character.

garage *n* (1902) a building for the storage and shelter of motor vehicles while not in use. To begin with the term was mainly applied to a large commercially owned building accommodating many cars, a usage which by natural evolution soon came to cover an establishment offering repair and refuelling facilities. It was borrowed from French, where it was derived from *garer* 'to shelter'. An early but unsuccessful synonym, harking back to the horse age, was *motor stable* (1907).

> 1902 *Daily Mail*: The new 'garage' founded by Mr. Harrington Moore, hon. secretary of the Automobile Club . . . The 'garage', which is situated at the City end of Queen Victoria-street, . . . has accommodation for eighty cars.

> 1934 P. A. Reynolds: The third type of garage is . . . the Full Service business, which caters, in addition to the services already mentioned, for repairs of every description.

genetics *n* (1905) the scientific study of heredity and variation. The word (based on the adjective *genetic*, which had itself been coined in the 1830s from *genesis*) had already been used in the late 19th century, to mean 'the principles or laws of origination' and 'the branch of biology concerned with the study of natural development when not complicated by human interference', but neither of these usages caught on.

> 1905 William Bateson: The best title would, I think, be 'The Quick Professorship of the study of Heredity'. No single word in common use quite gives this meaning.., and if it were desirable to coin one, 'Genetics' might do.

geriatrics *n* (1909) the branch of medicine dealing with the health of old people. The term was coined from Greek *geras* 'old age' and *iatrikos* 'of a physician', on the model of *paediatrics*. It made a slow start (the derived adjective *geriatric* is not recorded until the mid 1920s), but more than made up for it in the latter part of the century.

> 1909 I. L. Nascher: Geriatrics, from *geras*, old age, and *iatrikos*, relating to the physician, is a term I would suggest as an addition to our vocabulary, to cover the same field in old age that is covered by the term paediatrics in childhood.

girl guide *n* (1909) a girl who is a member of the Girl Guides Association, an organization of girls, established in 1910, corresponding to the boy scouts. The abbreviated *Guide* is first recorded in 1912; in 1994 it became the official designation. See also **boy scout (1908)**.

> 1909 *Boy Scouts' Headquarters' Gazette*: Where it is desired to start 'Girl Guides' it would be best for ladies interested to form a Committee.

half-life *n* (1907) the time in which the quantity of a radioactive substance in a sample decreases by half. In earliest usage it occurs in the expression *half-life period*; it is not recorded on its own until the early 1950s, but thereafter it soon established a niche for itself in the half-understood but chilling vocabulary of nuclear power.

hip *adj* (1904) well-informed, knowledgeable, aware. The word originated in US slang, probably as a variant of the synonymous *hep*, which is not recorded in print until 1908: but the antecedents of that are unknown.

> 1904 G. V. Hobart: At this rate it'll take about 629 shows to get us to Jersey City, are you hip?

hormone *n* (1905) a chemical substance produced in an endocrine gland which is transported in the blood to a particular organ or tissue and has an effect on its function. The term was formed from the present participle of the Greek verb *horman* 'to stir up, urge on'.

> 1905 E. H. Starling: These chemical messengers, however, or 'hormones'... as we might call them.

> 1930 R. A. Fisher: The investigation of the influence of the sex hormones has shown how genetic modifications of the whole species can be made to manifest themselves in one sex only.

hospitalize *v* (1901) to place or accommodate in a hospital. This useful coinage attracted little adverse comment at first, but latterly has come to be viewed as objectionable by language purists.

> 1901 *Daily Chronicle*: The disease was spreading rapidly owing to the people refusing to hospitalise first cases.

> 1918 Alexander Woollcott: My present brief hospitalization is traceable to eye-strain.

hunger march *n* (1908) a march by the unemployed and poor to protest about their condition. The term is remembered with particular poignancy by those who lived through the 1920s and 30s.

> 1922 *Westminster Gazette*: Unemployed hunger marchers are persisting in their determination to see the Prime Minister.

> 1972 Mervyn Jones: Among the older people, there was grave talk of the days of mass unemployment and the Hunger Marches.

identity card *n* (1900), **identification card** *n* (1908) a card which gives personal particulars. Both terms survive, but *identity card* much more vigorously (the smart cards, the introduction of which is proposed in early 21st-century Britain, are so termed—when not abbreviated to simply *ID card*).

> 1900 *Westminster Gazette*: When troops are going on service each man has issued to him what is known as a field dressing and an identity card.

> 1969 *New Yorker*: Residents will show identification cards to gain admittance.

2005 news.bbc.co.uk: The latest Identity Cards Bill was published on Wednesday, but it contains only 'minor amendments' to the plans which were dropped when the election was called.

industrial relations *n* (1904) relationships between employers and employees. The first quotation below is an isolated early example of a term which did not become established until after World War II (since when its usage, usually in the context of bad relationships, has tended towards the euphemistic).

1904 S. A. Barnett: Luxury... leads to cruelty in our industrial relations.

1958 *Economist*: Both employers and unions are to blame for the dogfight that at present passes for industrial relations at BOAC.

intelligentsia *n* (1907) the part of a nation, originally in pre-revolutionary Russia, that aspires to intellectual activity; the class of society regarded as possessing culture and political initiative. The word is a borrowing of Russian *intelligéntsiya*, which itself was adapted from Latin *intelligentia* 'intelligence'.

1907 Maurice Baring: [The revolutionaries] fear that if the question of a Republic is brought forward there will be a general massacre of the educated bourgeoisie, the so-called 'Intelligenzia'.

1921 Aldous Huxley: The English colony [at Florence] is a queer collection; a sort of decayed provincial intelligentsia.

Lebensraum *n* (1905) territory which the Germans believed was needed for their natural development. A borrowing from German, literally 'life's space', it did not become widely known and used in English until the 1930s, when the Nazis began to put the idea into practice.

1957 *Encyclopedia Britannica*: Hitler was convinced that... Germany... needed Russian territory for Lebensraum.

libido *n* (1909) psychic drive or energy, especially that associated with the sexual instinct. The word (from Latin *libido* 'desire, lust') was in the vanguard of the new 20th-century vocabulary of psychology and sexology.

1909 A. A. Brill, translating Freud's *Selected Papers on Hysteria*: The anxiety neurosis goes along with the most distinct diminution of the sexual libido or the psychic desire.

1972 *Scientific American*: It has also been observed that removal of the ovaries does not reduce the libido of human females.

liner *n* (1905) a passenger aircraft. The term was originally adopted from the world of maritime transport. The first quote below is from Rudyard Kipling's 'With the Night Mail', a futuristic story about air travel set in the year 2000. Kipling envisaged airships as having conquered the skies, their pilots navigating by means of huge beams of light shone up from the ground, and aeroplanes having only a very minor role. *Liner* in the first quote refers to an airship, and Kipling uses other ship nomenclature in the same way (*war-boat, yacht, mail packet*). It survived to be applied to real aircraft of this type, but has been superseded as the main term by **airliner (1908)**.

1905 Rudyard Kipling: A Planet liner, east bound, heaves up in a superb spiral and takes the air of us humming.

1933 *Boys' Magazine*: Mile after mile of seemingly endless country unfurled itself beneath the flying wings of the giant liner.

manic depressive *adj* (1902) denoting a psychosis in which periods of manic elation alternate with depression. The related noun *manic depression* is not recorded until the 1950s.

1958 Michael Argyle: The upper and middle classes have higher rates for manic depression and neurosis.

Marmite *n* (1902) the British proprietary term (registered in 1920) for an extract made from fresh brewer's yeast, which has remained a popular comestible into the 21st century. A *marmite* was originally a type of cooking pot used for rich stews (a picture of which appears on the label of Marmite jars), so there is a subliminal suggestion of meat extract.

massage parlour *n* (1906) an establishment offering massage and usually also various sexual services for payment. From the beginning the word's connotation, 'brothel', was widely recognized (see the quote below).

> 1913 *Collier's*: Along with them go the announcements of 'massage parlors' (an all-too-obvious euphemism), free whiskies, and other agencies of public injury.

Meccano *n* (1907) the proprietary name (registered in 1907 by Frank Hornby) of a set of metal pieces, nuts, bolts, etc., and tools, specially designed for constructing small models of buildings, machines, or other engineering apparatus. It was a staple toy of British boys (and their fathers) in the middle years of the 20th century.

> 1930 J. B. Priestley: It seemed only yesterday when he was . . . putting the Meccano set by the boy's bedside.

model *n* (1904) someone, typically a woman, who is employed to display clothes by wearing them, or to appear in displays of other goods. It was an extension of the earlier sense 'someone who poses for an artist'. It competed with and eventually defeated the contemporary *mannequin* (1902), a borrowing from French. See also **supermodel (1977)**.

> 1911 D. G. Phillips: She was dressed in the sleek tight-fitting trying-on robe of the professional model.
>
> 1958 *Woman's Own*: The first lesson every model learns is to stand and walk correctly.

motor-bike *n* (1903) a cycle with a petrol engine. The term is a colloquial version of the earlier *motor-bicycle* (1894). Other broadly contemporary variations on the theme were *motor-cycle* (1896) and the short-lived *motor-cyclette* (1898).

> 1927 H. G. Wells: I remember my wild rush on my motor-bike to London.

motorway *n* (1903) a specially designated class of highway with two or more lanes in each direction, designed and regulated for use by fast motor traffic. As the quotations below suggest, motorways were thought of and named long before they were built, at any rate in the UK (the first stretch of motorway in Britain was the Preston by-pass, opened in 1958).

> 1903 *Car*: The Motor-way is bound to come!
>
> 1955 *Times*: Motorways, 345 miles in total length, for motor traffic only, are to be built by the Government.

muck-raker *n* (1906) someone who looks for and exposes scandal in a sensationalist way. The word was inspired by a reference by US President Theodore Roosevelt in 1906 to 'the Man with a Muck-rake', a character in John Bunyan's *Pilgrim's Progress* who was actually intended as an emblem not of unsavoury scandal-mongering but of absorption in the pursuit of worldly gain: 'The men with the muck-rakes are often indispensable to the well-being of society; but only if they know when to stop raking the muck' (the original literal muck-rake was a rake for moving and spreading manure). The derived *muck-raking* is first recorded in 1911.

> 1911 *New York Evening Post*: The same articles brought President Roosevelt to the defence of the Senate, and led him to apply the word 'muck-raking' to the literature of higher exposure.

multiracial *adj* (1903) of or comprising several races, peoples, or ethnic groups, especially as living in the same community on amicable and equal terms.

> 1923 *Overseas*: The interests of modern civilisation and, I think, Christian ethics, are better expressed in large, bi-racial or multi-racial States, . . . where racialism is accounted a public curse rather than a civic virtue.

narcissism *n* (1905) self-love and admiration that find emotional satisfaction in self-contemplation. It was originally a technical term in psychology, but over the century it has found its way into general English (there is actually an isolated instance of the general use recorded from 1822 in one of Samuel Taylor Coleridge's letters ('Of course, I am glad to be able to correct my fears as far as public Balls, Concerts, and Time-murder in Narcissism'), but it does not seem to have caught on). The sexologist Havelock Ellis suggested in 1898 the analogy with the beautiful Greek youth Narcissus who fell in love with his own reflection in a fountain, but the term itself was coined by Paul Näcke in German as *Narcissismus* in 1899.

neon *n* (1900) used in designating light sources using fluorescent neon-filled tubes, which became a characteristic feature of 20th-century urban nightscapes.

> 1913 *Transactions of the Illuminating Engineers' Society* (US): The neon light is physiologically excellent on account of its dull luminescence.

> 1940 Louis MacNeice: And the neon-lamps of London Stain the canals of night.

neurosis *n* (1904) a mental illness or disorder characterized by anxiety, fear, depression, etc. The word *neurosis* had been used in English since the 18th century to mean simply 'a nervous disease', and the contrast with *psychosis* was established in the late 19th century, but this specific usage reflects Sigmund Freud's terminology. Before the end of the 1920s it was being used colloquially for any sort of anxiety or malaise.

> 1967 J. R. Ackerley: One more neurosis, shared with my mother: I was worried about bad teeth.

news flash *n* (1904) a brief item of news, especially as broadcast in other than a regular bulletin. Originally applied to telegraphic news dispatches, the term came into its own with the advent of the broadcast media.

> 1974 Eric Ambler: There was a television news flash. The announcer didn't get your father's name quite right.

no man's land *n* (1908) the terrain between the front lines of armies entrenched opposite one another. The term was made notorious during World War I, but it was foreshadowed in earlier conflicts. It originally, in the 14th century, denoted a plot of ground lying outside the north wall of London which was used as a place of execution, and thereafter it was used for any piece of unclaimed ground lying between two others.

> 1915 George Adam: Perilous work it is repairing wire in the No Man's Land between trenches.

opinion-former *n* (1906) someone whose views shape the opinions of others. The term was not widely in use until the 1960s, and then often with a slight curl of sarcasm.

> 1977 *Private Eye*: He has a fine independence of outlook and a contemptuous disregard for whatever is smart or fashionable among opinion-formers.

pacifism *n* (1902) the policy or doctrine of rejecting war and every form of violent action as a means of solving disputes, especially in international affairs. The term was a direct adaptation of French *pacifisme.* The derivative *pacifist* is first recorded in 1906. At first a neutral word, it acquired decidedly contemptuous overtones during World War I.

> 1919 George Bernard Shaw: There was only one virtue, pugnacity: only one vice, pacifism. That is an essential condition of war.

> 1930 Winston Churchill: I have always been against the Pacifists during the quarrel, and against the Jingoes at its close.

paedophilia, pedophilia *n* (1906) an abnormal (sexual) love of young children. The derivative *paedophile* is not recorded until the late 1940s (see **paedophile (1949)**).

> 1906 Havelock Ellis: Paidophilia or the love of children ... may be included under this head [i.e. abnormality].

palace revolution *n* (1904) the overthrowing of a sovereign etc. without civil war, usually by other members of the ruling group. The term may be a translation of German *Palastrevolution.*

1907 Jack London: They will be like the guards of the palace in old Rome, and there will be palace revolutions whereby the labour castes will seize the reins of power.

Palestinian *n* (1905) a native or inhabitant of Palestine. *Palestine* (an ancient name from biblical times) was revived as an official political title for the land west of the Jordan mandated to Britain in 1920, but *Palestinian* preceded it as a term for Jews who wished to go and live there. At the beginning of the 21st century it denotes Arab peoples who have a measure of self-rule in Israeli-held territories in the Gaza Strip and on the West Bank.

1909 *Daily Chronicle*: Those who are for a mass return to the country of their origin . . . are termed 'Palestinians'.

1979 *Time*: The Administration's first goal then, would be to bring Palestinians, perhaps even some P.L.O. officials, into the talks between the Israelis and the Egyptians on the future of the West Bank and Gaza.

panties *n* (1908) knickers worn by women and girls. Originally *panties* (a cute diminutive of *pants*) was a somewhat dismissive term for men's trousers or shorts, and it continued to be used in this sense until around 1930 ('Panties for boys and skirts for girls . . . are being made very short', *Weekly Dispatch* (1928)). The earliest reference to it as a female garment comes in a book on dolls' clothing, and it does not seem to have been widely used for women's knickers until the 1930s. See also **underpants (1931)**.

1908 Mary Morgan: The under-garment is . . . easily made, for the little waist and panties are cut in one piece.

1932 *New Yorker*: There is a lace brassière top on a circular satin slip, and panties . . . are built in underneath.

paper handkerchief *n* (1907) a disposable handkerchief made from soft tissue paper—an early harbinger of the throwaway age.

1907 *Yesterday's Shopping*: Handkerchiefs, Paper (Medicated)—These soft, silky papers are specially prepared for invalids, and are invaluable to sufferers from bronchial affections, catarrh, &c.

Pepsi-Cola *n* (1903) the proprietary name (filed in the US in 1903) of a popular soft drink. Pepsi's great rival *Coca-Cola* dates from the 1880s.

1903 *New Bern* (North Carolina) *Journal*: Pepsi-Cola. At Soda Fountains . . . Aids Digestion.

physiotherapy *n* (1905) the treatment of disease, injury, or deformity by physical methods such as massage, exercise, and the application of heat, light, fresh air, and other external influences. The derivative *physiotherapist* is first recorded in 1923, its abbreviation *physio* in 1962.

1962 *Times*: They should, like the orthopaedic physiotherapists, also be nurses . . . I tell my physios: 'Keep your hands off, keep your minds on.'

pilot *n* (1907) someone who controls an aeroplane in flight. It is an adaptation of the earlier usage 'someone who controls an airship or balloon', which dates from the mid 19th century, and which in turn goes back ultimately to 'someone who steers a ship' (still current, of course; in early use, it was often necessary to specify *air pilot*). It has become the standard term, despite competition from the somewhat broader *aviator* (coined in the 1880s in deliberate contrast to *aeronaut* 'someone who flies a balloon'), the short-lived *aeroplanist* (1906), and the later, briefly popular *flyer* (1934). *Pilot* is first recorded as a verb in 1911.

1907 *Navigating the Air* (Aero Club of America): In order to qualify as a pilot one must make ten ascensions, one of which must be made at night, and two of which must be made alone.

1911 *Daily News*: The Dutch aviator has decided to pilot a . . . monoplane . . . instead of a . . . biplane.

1923 J. W. Simpson: The confident courage that inspires air-pilots.

plane *n* (1908) a shortening of *aeroplane* (1873). Condemned periodically as excessively colloquial, it has survived more vigorously than *aeroplane*.

> 1908 *Times*: Mr. Wright refused to give any details on the propeller employed, but on the general construction of the plane he said it was full of movable diversely articulated parts.

> 1910 *Daily Mail*: To the builders of aeroplanes he cries: 'Construct me planes capable of the maximum speed.'

plastic *n* (1909) any of a range of mouldable materials based on polymerized organic compounds. The original meaning of *plastic* is 'pliable' (it is derived ultimately from Greek *plassein* 'to mould'). It was being applied as a noun to mouldable substances as early as 1905 ('Models sufficiently perfect cannot be made from impressions taken in modelling compound or other of the plastics', E. H. Angle in *American Text-book of Operative Dentistry*), but the first reference in print to the specific type of material now known as plastic comes in 1909, from Leo Baekeland, the inventor of the type of plastic known as *bakelite*. Plastic went on to become, one might almost say, the substance from which the 20th century was made.

> 1909 L. H. Baekeland: As an insulator... [bakelite] is far superior to hard rubber, casein, celluloid, shellac and in fact all plastics... It can be used for similar purposes like knobs, buttons, knife handles, for which plastics are generally used.

plastic explosive *n* (1906) an explosive of putty-like consistency that can be shaped by hand and so placed in close contact with its target. One of the main weapons of terrorism in the latter part of the 20th century.

> 1906 C. E. Bichel: Add to the trinitrotoluol liquid resins... in such wise that... the crystalline trinitrotoluol with or without warming is worked in suitable mixing machines into a plastic explosive that detonates well.

plug *n* (1902) an advertisement; an instance of publicity; a method of drawing attention to a product, an entertainment, etc., especially by repeatedly referring to it. The colloquialism originated in the US. The related verb is first recorded in 1906.

> 1902 George Ade: They were friendly to the prosperous Bachelor and each one determined to put in a few quiet Plugs for Sis.

> 1906 Helen Green: I ain't got any music, so you kin plug any publisher's stuff an' play what you wanter.

pogrom *n* (1905) originally, an organized massacre in Russia for the destruction or annihilation of any body or class, especially the Jews. Hence, an organized, officially tolerated, attack on any community or group. The word was borrowed from Russian, where it means literally 'devastation, destruction'. There had been pogroms in Russia since 1881, but a new wave of them in 1903 propelled the word into English; it remains particularly associated with eastern and central Europe.

> 1931 *Times Literary Supplement*: Refugees to England from pogrom-haunted Russia.

poll *n* (1902) a canvassing of the opinion of a number of people on a particular topic. The usage was an adaptation of the earlier sense, 'vote'. The term did not begin to become common (usually in the form (*public*) *opinion poll*) until the late 1930s.

> 1939 George Gallup: The development during the last few years of the public-opinion survey or unofficial poll has raised... a host of new and far-reaching questions.

poverty line *n* (1901) a minimum level of income consistent with a decent standard of living. The word was first used as a socio-economic term by B. S. Rowntree in his 1901 book *Poverty*. See also **bread-line (1900)**.

> 1901 Winston Churchill: Families who cannot provide this necessary sum, or who, providing it, do not select their food with like discrimination are underfed and come below the 'poverty' line.

power station *n* (1901) an establishment where electricity is generated.

> 1901 *Daily Express*: The development of power-stations all over the country.

progressive *adj* (1908) characterized by (the desire to promote) change, innovation, or experiment; avant-garde. The usage is a more generalized employment of a term which had been in vogue in politics since the 1880s, in the sense 'favouring reform'.

1949 Josephine Tey: The great house in the park was a boarding-school for the unmanageable children of parents with progressive ideas and large bank accounts.

propaganda *n* (1908) the systematic dissemination of a particular doctrine by circulating polemical material. The term originally denoted a committee of Roman Catholic cardinals responsible for overseeing the propagation of the faith. It came to be used in English from the late 18th century for any association or movement for the propagation of a particular doctrine or practice ('a propaganda'). The shift to the modern connotation of spreading partisan material intended to indoctrinate was a gradual one. The first quote below still contains echoes of its religious origins, but as the century progressed propaganda became a key weapon of oppression and warfare.

1908 Lilley & Tyrrell: The Church... soon felt a need of new methods of propaganda and government.

1937 Arthur Koestler: One of the most effective propaganda campaigns launched by the rebels was that relating to the alleged shooting of hostages by the Madrid Government.

psychoanalysis *n* (1906) a therapeutic method originated by Sigmund Freud for treating disorders of the personality or behaviour by bringing into a patient's consciousness his or her unconscious conflicts and fantasies. Freud's original term for this was *psychische Analyse* (rendered in English as *psychic analysis* in 1898) or *klinischpsychologische Analyse*, but in a paper in the *Revue Neurologique* in 1896 he used the French word *psychoanalyse*, which formed the basis of the English term. See also **psychoanalyse (1911)**.

1906 *Journal of Abnormal Psychology*: Their importance with relation to treatment (by the method of 'psycho-analysis') is made clear.

questionnaire *n* (1901) a (printed) set of questions designed to elicit information, as in a survey. This borrowing from French was at first strongly resisted in some quarters, apparently on the grounds that the anglicized form *questionary* already existed. Henry Fowler, in his *Dictionary of Modern English Usage* (1940), called it 'too recent an importation to be in the *OED*'. Other diehards for a long time insisted on pronouncing it as a French word, with an initial /k/ rather than /kw/. However, it has gone from strength to strength, and *questionary* is now virtually unknown except in medical usage.

1920 *Glasgow Herald*: Valuable information, never previously collected, is being obtained through a questionnaire by the Federation of British Industries concerning the fuel requirements of the great industrial centres.

racialism *n* (1907) belief in the superiority of a particular race leading to prejudice and antagonism towards people of other races. In early use, the term tended to occur in a South African context. *Racism*, which has come to be used synonymously with *racialism* and to some extent superseded it, dates from the 1930s (see **racist (1932)**).

1910 *Westminster Gazette*: What appears to me to be the greatest results of the Botha-Smuts Government is the abolition of Racialism and the construction of roads.

radio *n* (1907) the transmission of speech and other uncoded signals by means of electromagnetic waves, without the use of a wire. Radio (ultimately from Latin *radius* 'ray') began life in English as a prefix, in such words as *radiotelegraphy* and *radiotelephony*, in the late 1890s. Its first known use as an independent form was in *radio receiver* (1903), but even here it was only part of a compound noun. The quote from 1907 shows it for the first time in a more free-ranging role, while the first 1917 quote is the first known instance of its not preceding another noun. 1917 is also the first year in which it is recorded in the sense 'radio set'.

At first, **wireless (1903)** was much more widespread in general use, and it remained so until World War II (although *radio* was far from uncommon—Edward VIII referred to it, for instance, in his abdication broadcast). From then on, however, perhaps partly from a preference for *radio* in military terminology, their relative frequency has steadily reversed, and at the end of the 20th century few of even the oldest or most conservative English-speakers talked unironically about the *wireless*.

> 1907 Lee de Forest: This factor, damping, is of far more vital import than any regulation of wave-lengths . . . Radio chaos will certainly be the result until . . . regulation is enforced.

> 1917 *Electrical Experimenter* (heading): Election returns flashed by radio to 7,000 amateurs.

> 1917 *Electrical Experimenter*: When the German spies . . . found that it was not very healthy to operate their outfits in attics or in house chimneys . . . they simply put their radios in touring cars, cleverly concealing the aerial wires inside of the car bodies.

> 1936 King Edward VIII: Science has made it possible for me . . . to speak to you all over the radio.

> 1968 *New Society*: Non-U radio/U wireless is no longer true; the U call it a radio too.

reinforced concrete *n* (1902) concrete strengthened with steel bars or metal netting, the building material par excellence of the 20th century. Its technical name, *ferro-concrete*, is first recorded in 1900.

> 1906 *Daily Chronicle*: There is undoubtedly a great future for reinforced concrete.

remote control *n* (1904) control of an apparatus at a distance. By the 1920s the term was being applied to a device used for remote control. The abbreviated form *remote* is first recorded in this sense in 1966.

repress *v* (1909) of a patient or person who is the object of study: to keep (unacceptable memories or desires) out of the conscious mind, or suppress them into the unconscious. The verb is an English translation of Sigmund Freud's term *verdrängen*. The derived noun *repression* was introduced into English in the same year.

> 1909 A. A. Brill, translating Freud's *Selected Papers on Hysteria*: The patient has not reacted to psychic traumas because the nature of the trauma . . . concerned things which the patient wished to forget and which he therefore intentionally inhibited and repressed from the conscious memory . . . If I could now make it probable that the idea became pathogenic in consequence of the exclusion and repression, the chain would seem complete.

Rolls-Royce *n* (1908) a Rolls-Royce car. The trademark, incorporating the names of the car's first designers, C. S. Rolls (1877–1910) and Sir Henry Royce (1863–1933), was registered in 1908, and has since become synonymous with luxury, expensiveness, and purringly smooth travel. The colloquial abbreviation *Rolls* is first recorded in 1928.

> 1928 Edgar Wallace: Dick knew the gentleman very well by name; indeed, he had recognised his big yellow Rolls standing outside the hotel.

> 1974 *Daily Telegraph*: Vintage port—the Rolls-Royce end of the trade—accounts for only about one per cent of port production.

segregation *n* (1903) the enforced separation of different racial groups in a country, community, or institution. Through the century the term was mainly applied to discriminatory practices against blacks in South Africa and the southern states of the US. Compare **apartheid (1947)**.

> 1903 T. T. Fortune: The Afro-American people have been held together rather by the segregation decreed by law . . . than by ties of consanguinity.

> 1957 *Times*: The ruling of the Supreme Court that racial segregation in public schools [in South Africa] was unconstitutional.

shadow cabinet *n* (1906) a group of members of an opposition party nominated as counterparts of the government cabinet. By the 1920s the use of *shadow* had broadened out to designate any opposition counterpart, although it does not seem to have become widespread or to any extent institutionalized until after World War II.

> 1906 A. J. Balfour: If we are to have, as you suggest, a Committee consisting of members selected from the Front Bench in both Houses, . . . what we should really have would be a shadow Cabinet once a week.

> 1953 Earl Winterton: I was in Mr. Churchill's 'Shadow Cabinet' from 1945 to 1950.

> 1958 *Spectator*: The Chancellors and Shadow-Chancellors.

shorthand typist *n* (1901) someone who takes down dictation in shorthand and then types out the text.

> 1901 *Phonetic Journal*: To a large extent the occupation of the shorthand-typist has hitherto been synonymous with the lady typist.

smog *n* (1905) fog intensified by smoke. In Britain the term is particularly associated with the very severe smog that afflicted London in the early 1950s, resulting in many deaths.

> 1905 *Daily Graphic*: In the engineering section of the Congress Dr. H. A. des Vœux, hon. treasurer of the Coal Smoke Abatement Society, read a paper on 'Fog and Smoke'. He said it required no science to see that there was something produced in great cities which was not found in the country, and that was smoky fog, or what was known as 'smog'.

social security *n* (1908) a system of state financial assistance for those citizens whose income is inadequate or non-existent owing to disability, unemployment, old age, etc. The term was coined by Winston Churchill, but did not come into widespread use until the 1930s.

> 1908 Winston Churchill: If we were able to underpin the whole existing social security apparatus with a foundation of comparatively low-grade state safeguards, we should in the result obtain something that would combine the greatest merits both of the English & the German systems.

> 1942 *Times*: Social security as envisaged in this report is a plan to secure to each citizen an income adequate to satisfy a national minimum standard . . . As regards unification, Sir William Beveridge suggests that there should be a Ministry of Social Security.

social worker *n* (1904) someone professionally trained to provide help and advice to the poor, the aged, and those with domestic problems. The term was derived from *social work*, which dates from around 1890. By the end of the 20th century its connotations were not altogether positive.

> 1904 *Annual Register of the University of Chicago*: A training center for social workers.

> 1977 Barbara Pym: A real bossy social-worker type.

speeding *n* (1908) driving a motor vehicle fast, especially at an illegal speed. *Speed* itself is not recorded as a verb until the 1930s (presumably as a back-formation from *speeding*). Both quickly overtook the now defunct *overspeed* (1906).

> 1931 John Galsworthy: 'I'm going to speed,' said Jean, looking back. The speedometer rose rapidly.

split the atom (1909) to cause atomic nuclei to undergo fission (see **fission (1939)**). The British physicist Sir Joseph Thomson, referred to in the first quote below, discovered the electron, but it is John Cockroft and Ernest Walton, who in 1932 used a particle accelerator to split an atomic nucleus of lithium, who at the beginning of the 21st century are more usually thought of as the men 'who split the atom'.

> 1909 *Busy Man's Magazine*: [Professor J. J. Thomson] is known both as 'The Man of Ion', and as the man 'who split the atom'.

> 1964 Margaret Gowing: [Cockroft and Walton] bombarded a foil of the metal lithium, disrupting the lithium nuclei which, after combining with incident protons, split into two alpha particles. The experimenters had 'split' atoms by artificial means.

standardize *v* (1900) to make uniform. *Standardize* in its literal sense 'to bring to a standard size, composition, etc.' dates from the 1850s, but this metaphorical use is a 20th-century development.

> 1911 Frederic Harrison: Life and Society have been standardised.

stratosphere *n* (1909) the region of the atmosphere extending from the top of the troposphere up to a height of about 50 km (the *stratopause*), in the lower part of which there is little temperature variation with height in temperate latitudes and in the higher part the temperature increases with height. In early use, the term was applied to the lower part of this region only (up to a height of about 20 km). It is based on *stratum*, from the idea of a 'layer' of the atmosphere.

streamline *adj* (1907) having or being a shape such that the flow of a fluid round it is smooth; hence, more widely, shaped so as to reduce air or water resistance—a key design-goal of the 20th century. The synonymous **streamlined** is not recorded before 1913.

> 1914 *Automobile Topics*: That beautiful stream-line Car.

student *n* (1900) someone attending a place of primary or secondary education. Originally a US usage, it took a long time to spread to British English, where *student* remained exclusively in the realm of tertiary education until quite late in the 20th century.

> 1976 *Times*: We have primary school students, presumably working for BAs in Plasticine; the National Union of School Students; and graduation day for high school students . . . Formerly people were schoolboys or schoolgirls until they became undergraduates.

suffragette *n* (1906) a female supporter of the cause of women's political enfranchisement, especially one of a violent or militant type. Coined from *suffrage* 'the right to vote', the term has the advantage of succinctness over *woman suffragist*, which had been in use since the mid 1880s. In the years when such campaigners were in the news (roughly, until World War I), the word spun off various derivatives, including *suffragettism*, *suffragetty*, and even a verb *suffragette*. See also **women's movement (1902)**.

> 1906 *Daily Mail*: Mr. Balfour and the 'Suffragettes' . . . It was not surprising that Mr. Balfour should receive a deputation of the Suffragettes.

> 1909 H. G. Wells: And her straight hair was out demonstrating and suffragetting upon some independent notions of its own.

> 1912 Clementine Churchill: Amy is kind, but more Suffragetty, Christian Sciency and Yankee Doodle than ever.

Sunday supplement *n* (1905) an illustrated section issued with a Sunday newspaper, sometimes characterized by the portrayal of voguish living.

> 1905 Edith Wharton: The photographer whose portraits of her formed the recurring ornament of 'Sunday Supplements'.

> 1971 Alan Bennett: Since then N.W.1 has been used as a catchphrase to indicate Sunday supplement trendiness which people now find rather suspect.

superman *n* (1903) an ideal superior man conceived by the German philosopher Friedrich Nietzsche (1844–1900) as being evolved from the normal human type; hence, more loosely, a man of extraordinary power or ability, a superior being. The word is a translation of German *Übermensch*. Earlier versions had been *overman* (1895) and *beyond-man* (1896), but the success of *superman* was no doubt assured by the title of George Bernard Shaw's play *Man and Superman* (1903) (and later reinforced by the name of the superhuman American comic-strip hero, created in the late 1930s).

> 1903 *Speaker*: It is possible by breeding, by education, by social reconstruction, that the Superman may be attained.

tabloid journalism *n* (1901) journalism featuring newspapers in a small format which handle stories in an easily assimilable and often sensational way. *Tabloid* was originally a trademark (registered in 1884) for a small medicinal tablet, but subsequently took off as a metaphor for anything produced in small or concentrated form (during World War I it was used as the nickname of a type of small Sopwith biplane, and as late as the 1930s the term *tabloid cruiser* was coined for a small cruising yacht). The use of *tabloid* as a noun to denote a newspaper of this sort is not recorded before 1918.

tanker *n* (1900) a sea-going vessel fitted with tanks for carrying oil or other liquids in bulk. The idea of such a ship dates from the late 19th century (see the following quote), but the word appears to be 20th-century. The earliest record of the compound noun *oil tanker* dates from 1920.

> 1950 *Sun* (Baltimore): It was in 1878 that [Gustav Conrad Hansen] first put his idea into practice, converting two sailing ships into tankers.

tape record *n* (1905) a recording on tape. With the introduction of steel tape in the 1930s, and later plastic tape, *tape-recording* came to be the preferred term. See also **tape recorder (1932)**.

> 1905 *Talking Machine News*: A tape record could be made to be reproduced by either the cylinder or disc type of machine.

taxi, taxi-cab *n* (1907) a passenger-conveyance with a fare calculated by a device called a *taximeter*. The word is short for *taximeter* (1898), an adaptation of French *taximètre*, which was based on *taxe* 'tax, charge'. In early usage it was sometimes spelled *taxy*.

> 1907 *Daily Chronicle*: Every journalist . . . has his idea of what the vehicle should be called. It has been described as the (1) taxi, (2) motor-cab, (3) taxi-cab, (4) taximo, . . . (7) taximeter-cab.

> 1907 *Daily Chronicle*: The 'taxicab', as the new taximeter motor-cab is called, is fast becoming a familiar feature in the streets of London.

> 1908 *Daily News*: Many ladies . . . now take a 'taxy' regularly for the morning's shopping. There are about 350 horsed 'taxies' on the road.

teddy bear *n* (1906) a stuffed figure of a bear, made of rough plush, used as a toy. It was so called in humorous allusion to Theodore Roosevelt (President of the US 1901–1909). Roosevelt's bear-hunting expeditions occasioned a celebrated comic poem, accompanied by cartoons, in the *New York Times* of 7 January 1906, concerning the adventures of two bears named 'Teddy B' and 'Teddy G'; these names were transferred to two bears (also known as the 'Roosevelt bears') presented to Bronx Zoo in the same year; finally in 1907 the fame of these bears was turned to advantage by toy dealers, whose toy 'Roosevelt bears', imported from Germany, became an instant fashion in the US.

> 1907 *New England Magazine*: The Teddy-bear has come, and one suspects that he has come to stay.

television *n* (1907) a system for reproducing an image at a distance on a screen by radio transmission. Theoretical discussion of such a system long preceded its implementation. The first name proposed for it appears to have been *televista* ('Dr. Low talks very modestly of the "televista" (the name he has given to his "seeing by wire" invention', *Daily News* (1904))). *Television* proved much more durable, although for many decades it was widely condemned by purists for being a 'hybrid' word—*tele-* being ultimately of Greek origin and *-vision* of Latin origin. The colloquial shortening to *telly* or *tellie* is first recorded in 1940. See also **TV (1948)**.

> 1907 *Scientific American*: Now that the photo-telegraph invented by Prof. Korn is on the eve of being introduced into general practice, we are informed of some similar inventions in the same field, all of which tend to achieve some step toward the solution of the problem of television.

> 1926 *Glasgow Herald*: Mr. John L. Baird, a native of Helensburgh, . . . recently invented an apparatus which makes television possible.

> 1942 T. S. Eliot: There are words which are ugly because of foreignness or ill-breeding (e.g. television): but I do not believe that any word well-established in its own language is either beautiful or ugly.

third degree *n* (1900) an interrogation of a prisoner by the police involving the infliction of mental or physical suffering in order to bring about a confession or to secure information. The colloquialism originated in the US; the underlying idea seems to be of the 'third or highest degree' of severity.

> 1900 *Everybody's Magazine*: From time to time a prisoner . . . claims to have had the Third Degree administered to him.

town planning *n* (1906) designing of urban areas so that houses, roads, and public amenities are planned as an integrated whole.

1906 *A National Housing Policy: Official Report of the Housing Deputation to the Prime Minister [by the] National Housing and Town Planning Council* (subheading): Town Planning and Village Development Commission.

tractor *n* (1903) a rugged powerful motor vehicle for drawing farm machinery, especially one with large rear wheels and an elevated driving seat. The word (in Latin literally 'puller') was originally applied to a traction-engine for supplying power to machinery (it is first recorded in that sense in 1901), but the 'vehicle' sense soon ousted this.

1903 *Motor Annual*: Rhodesia has appealed to motor manufacturers to supply motor-wagons or tractors for use specially in hilly country.

tube *n* (1900) an underground railway. The word is usually applied specifically to the London underground railway system. As early as 1847 Queen Victoria was referring in her journal to a 'tube' for trains to run through ('We passed the famous Swilly Rocks, and saw the works they are making for the tube for the railroad'), but London's first underground railways (in the 1860s) were built by the 'cut-and-cover' method. The first genuine 'tube' was the electric City to Stockwell line, opened in 1890. The actual term *tube* seems to have originated with the so-called 'Twopenny Tube', the Central London Railway, opened in 1900.

1903 *Westminster Gazette*: Thousands of Tube travellers.

1905 Rider Haggard: The first part of my journey . . . was by Tube.

tyrannosaurus *n* (1906) a large carnivorous dinosaur of the Cretaceous period. The name (literally 'tyrant lizard' in Greek) was coined in 1905 by H. F. Osborn, and first appeared in a 1906 issue of the *Bulletin of the American Museum of Natural History*. The species name *Tyrannosaurus rex* is also first recorded in 1906.

vacuum cleaner *n* (1903) an electrical appliance for removing dust (from carpets and other flooring, soft furnishings, etc.) by suction. The earliest known record of the term is in the name of a commercial company, the 'Vacuum Cleaner Company'. The abbreviated form *vacuum* is first recorded in 1910. A very short-lived alternative designation was *vacuum cleanser* (1903). See also **Hoover (1926)**.

1903 *Westminster Gazette*: There is a machine at work, called the 'vacuum cleanser', which gives them all, in turn, a thorough 'spring cleaning'.

1907 *Yesterday's Shopping* (1969): The 'Witch' Dust Extractor is a vacuum cleaner suitable alike for carpets, upholstery, clothing, &c.

1922 *Hotel World*: I have three vacuums going all day.

vet *v* (1904) to examine carefully and critically for deficiencies or errors. The verb is often applied specifically to investigating the suitability of someone for a post that requires loyalty and trustworthiness. The usage originated as a facetious adaptation of an earlier (and now little used) sense 'to examine (an animal) medically'.

1963 *Times*: He asked whether Vassall had been vetted as necessary for his special post, and was told that he would be revetted before he went.

voyeur *n* (1900) someone who gains sexual satisfaction from observing others' sex organs or sexual activities. The word was borrowed from French, where it was derived from *voir* 'to see'. See also **voyeurism (1924)**.

1900 Henry Blanchamp: The houses of ill-fame have a clientèle of 'voyeurs' of both sexes.

war crime *n* (1906) an act committed during a war which contravenes the conventions of warfare. The term *war criminal* is also first recorded in 1906. See also **war trial (1949)**.

1945 *Daily Express*: The United Nations War Crimes Commission announced last night: Hermann Goering's name was placed . . . on the first list of persons charged with war crimes.

welfare *n* (1903) maintenance or improvement of the social and economic conditions of a particular group of people. In early usage the term usually refers to provision made by firms for their employees, but from the 1930s onwards it increasingly connotes help for the poor and other disadvantaged members of society, especially as provided for by the government. The word initially appears only in compound forms, such as *welfare work* and *welfare manager*; it is not recorded in isolation until 1918.

> 1904 *Century Magazine*: The welfare manager... who may be either a man or a woman, is a recognized intermediary between the employers and employees of mercantile houses and manufacturing plants.

> 1918 Arnold Bennett: Canteens, and rest-rooms, and libraries, and sanitation, and all this damned 'welfare'.

white supremacy *n* (1902) the theory that white people are inherently superior to and therefore entitled to rule over black people. The term lay relatively dormant until the late 1950s, when events in southern Africa and the southern states of the US brought it to the surface.

> 1967 *Freedomways*: The black student is being educated in this country as if he were being programmed in white supremacy and self-hatred.

wind of change *n* (1905) change thought of metaphorically as a wind. It was institutionalized as a phrase by its use by British prime minister Harold Macmillan in a speech to the South African parliament in Cape Town on 3 February 1960.

> 1905 Sarojini Naidu: The wind of change for ever blows Across the tumult of our way.

> 1960 Harold Macmillan: The wind of change is blowing through the continent.

wireless *n* (1903) the transmission of speech and other uncoded signals by means of radio waves. *Wireless* began life as an adjective in the early 1890s, when it was used in such expressions as *wireless telegraphy* and *wireless telephony* to talk about the new systems being developed by Marconi and others to transmit signals through the air by electromagnetic waves, without the aid of wires. Below is the first known example of its being used as a noun in print. It was first used in the sense 'a radio receiver' in the 1920s. Its replacement by **radio (1907)** was a long but inexorable process which got properly under way around the time of World War II.

> 1903 *New York Commercial Advertiser*: First in this great field of making the 'wireless' a handmaid of commerce is the de Forrest system, which has won the approval also of the United States government.

> 1927 T. E. Lawrence: We have no wireless, and I don't look at papers.

women's movement *n* (1902) the movement promoting women's political and other rights. The term was relatively little used until the 1960s. See also **suffragette (1906)**, **women's liberation (1966)**.

> 1902 Helen Blackburn: The Married Women's Property Bill occupied the main attention of those engaged in the women's movement.

> 1968 *Ramparts*: The most active of the new radical women's movements is in Berkeley—which should surprise no one.

world war *n* (1909) a war involving all or many of the most powerful nations in the world. Initially a theoretical term (probably translated from German *Weltkrieg*), it was being applied to the 1914–18 war in its first year.

> 1914 Bernard Vaughan: What the South African War failed to teach I really believe this world-war will bring home to us.

The 1910s

In the second decade of the 20th century the world was convulsed by four years of terrible war. By the time the armistice was signed in November 1918, all the major English-speaking nations of the world had become embroiled in the conflict, and over 8.5 million lives had been lost in action. The massive scale of the slaughter, the appalling conditions on the Western Front, and detailed coverage in the press combined to impress the *Great War* deeply on contemporary minds, and not surprisingly a large proportion of the new vocabulary coming into English during the decade arose from it. There was plenty of demand for neologisms, too: new methods of warfare, new types of weapon, the advent of military aircraft, not to mention the unprecedented levels of civilian involvement, all played their part in expanding the English lexicon.

In the trenches of the *Western Front* the troops were *strafed* by *creeping barrages*, *trench mortars* (also known colloquially as *toc emmas*, or *Minnies*), and by *pipsqueaks* and *whizzbangs* (various types of small shell). At the battle of Ypres in 1915 the Germans used *poison gas* for the first time, and *gas attack* became the great fear; *gas masks* were developed to protect against the deadly *mustard gas*. Trench life was a matter of waiting, in a wilderness of mud and *shell holes*, for the moment to go *over the top* into a hail of machine-gun fire—purveyed on the Allied side by the *Lewis gun*. The incidence of *shell shock* was high. Horrendous injuries—not to mention afflictions such as *gas gangrene* and *trench foot*—left the field hospitals and *clearing stations* full of *amputees* and potential *basket cases*. The *walking wounded* could consider themselves lucky if they had an injury serious enough to warrant a return to *Blighty*. In 1916, German troops peering over the parapet with their equivalent of the *trenchoscope* (a type of periscope) would have seen *tanks* advancing towards them for the first time.

In the skies above the battlefields, the principles of *air warfare* were being laid down by the *air forces* of both sides. The *dogfights* (air battles) and the air *aces* (crack pilots) had the high profile, but *aerial reconnaissance* had an important part to play too. The distinction between *fighters* and *bombers* was established (the latter equipped in due course with *bomb bays*). Although protected by *camouflage*, they had *anti-aircraft* fire (colloquially *Archibald*) and *tracer* to deal with. Both the *Allies* and the Germans knew that in the new warfare of the 20th century, *air supremacy* was becoming a prerequisite of victory.

At sea, the new shape on the horizon might be a *battle cruiser*, a *carrier*, or even a *Q ship* (or *mystery ship*—an armed and camouflaged merchant ship). To counter the threat of German *U-boats* (and indeed Allied *subs*), *depth charges* were being developed.

On the *home front*, meanwhile, the *war effort* was being pursued by other means. *Munitioneers* and *munitionettes* toiled day and night in the factories, turning out the weapons and ammunition needed at the front, while others in *reserved occupations* kept the home fires burning. *Salvage* recycled valuable materials. There was *rationing* to put up with (although *food parcels* could still be sent to the troops), and the predations of the *profiteers*. *Coupons* ruled people's lives, as they would again during World War II, and in the US people were encouraged to *Hooverize* 'to be sparing or economical'. For the first time in a war, civilians were subjected to *air raids*; German *Zeps* were flying over England, and towns had to be *blacked out*. In France, cities were bombarded by the Germans' *Big Berthas* (large artillery guns). Anti-German feeling was whipped up to fever pitch—the *Hun* (or *Boche*, or *Fritzes*, or *Jerry*, or *krauts*) had become baby-bayoneting hate figures, and German shepherd dogs had to be renamed *Alsatians*—and the animus was scarcely less against the *conscientious objectors*, or *conchies*, who refused to fight, and received contemptuous nick-names such as *Cuthbert* and *Percy*. Anything that smacked of *defeatism* had to be ruthlessly suppressed. Meanwhile there was a steady demand for new recruits to *join up* (or to be conscripted into *national service*, or in the US *selective service*). When they got to France, they would have encountered several mangled French expressions that had infiltrated the argot of the trenches, a few of which (*napoo*, *san fairy ann* 'it doesn't matter', *toot sweet* 'straightaway') found their way home and survived for several decades.

The *ceasefire* came on 11 November 1918, a day commemorated thereafter as *Armistice Day*. Those who had survived for the *duration* (sometimes as *P.O.W.s*) would return to a very different world from the one they left. Plans for a *League of Nations* were put in place, and *appeasement* was not yet a dirty word. But in Russia there had been a revolution, bringing such terms as *Bolshevik* and *commissar*, *Leninist* and *Trotskyite*, *Comintern* and *soviet* into the English language, not to mention the portentous monosyllable *red* 'Communist'. *Spanish flu* killed more than had died during the war. And already the possibility of an *atomic bomb* existed in the minds of scientists.

The exigencies of war had advanced aeronautical technology by leaps and bounds, and aeronautical terminology was keeping pace. Pilots could *land* their aircraft (at an *airport* or *air station*) and *taxi*, and also, alas, *crash* (hopefully wearing a *crash helmet*—but your plane would be a *write-off*). They could do *aerobatics* in their *bus* (a colloquial term for an aircraft). The commercial possibilities of flying began to be exploited, with terms like *airmail* (or *air-post*), *airbus* (or *aerial bus*), and *airline* coming into the language. We first became acquainted with *cockpits* and *undercarriages*, with *test pilots* and *automatic pilots*.

The commercial development of the private motor car, on the other hand, had to take a back seat during the war years, and the terminology of *motorism* 'the use of motor vehicles' expanded far more slowly than it had in the previous decade. The *convertible* appeared, complete with *hubcaps*, and the sound of the *klaxon* was heard for the first time. Traffic arrangements developed, with *one-way* streets, *traffic signals* (ignored by *jaywalkers*), and *parks* for leaving your vehicle in; on the downside, however, the *traffic jam* appeared.

In the world of science, Albert Einstein followed up his special theory of relativity (see p. 8) with the general theory of relativity, and the concept of *space-time* made its first appearance. The *isotope* and the atomic *nucleus* were named, as were *radon*, the *curie*, and *superconductors*. The biological sciences gained *chromosomes*, *genes*, and *vitamins*.

The trickle of Freudian terminology which began in the 1900s increased to a flood, including *Freudian* itself; we learned about the *Oedipus complex* and *anal eroticism*, *fixation*, *denial*, *repression*, and the *unconscious*. It was joined by a new set of terms introduced by the Swiss psychologist Carl Gustav Jung, who had been a colleague of Freud but split with him in 1912: *extrovert* and *introvert*, *collective unconscious*, *persona*, and *psyche*. It was a productive time for the science of the mind, whose other new lexical contributions included *autism*, *behaviourism*, *schizophrenia*, and *sex drive*. On the subject of sex, it was also the decade that saw the first recorded use of *homosexual* as a noun. *Bisexual* and *cross-dressing* made their debut too, but the time for advanced *homo-erotic* views could scarcely be said to have arrived when they were joined by *faggot*, *poofter*, and the use of *normal* to mean 'heterosexual'. The latest euphemism for 'contraception' was *birth control*.

The development of radio for public entertainment was put on hold for World War I, although new terms like *cat's whisker*, *crystal receiver*, and *static* would become familiar when it got under way in the next decade. In its absence, you could always do a *crossword puzzle*. But by far the most popular form of public entertainment was the *cinema*. The *movies* were all silent, of course (although there was talk of *talkies*), but none the less eagerly devoured for that. Down at the local cinema (or *picturedrome* or, in the US, *movie theater*), fans could see the latest *feature film* (or *picture play*)—perhaps a *western*—and swoon over their favourite *film stars* (or *movie stars*, or *cinema stars*). Additionally they would probably be able to watch a *newsreel* (or a *topical*—much the same thing) or a *cartoon*. Terms like *director* and *script-writer* became familiar, as did *location*, *scenario*, *pan*, and *studio*. The appearance of the terms *Cinephone* and *Technicolor* gave promise of developments to come.

Dance crazes of the time included the *bunny hug*, the *cooch*, the *shimmy*, and the *tango*. The *foxtrot* also made its debut. But in the long run it would be *jazz* and the *blues* that made a permanent mark on 20th-century music.

Cellophane-wrapped *instant* foodstuffs bought in the local *self-service* store (or *cash-and-carry*, or *groceteria*) could be stored in the *kitchenette* of your *double-glazed maisonette*—where you might also have a shiny new *toaster*, some *stainless steel* cutlery (no more need for those old-fashioned knife polishers), a *pressure cooker*, some *Pyrex* dishes, and an *immersion heater* for constant hot water.

Fashion from the *front line* introduced the *trench coat*, but at home it was the era of the *hobble skirt* and the *split skirt*, and the *liberty bodice*. The *scarf* became a head-covering (so necessary for those breezy motor-car journeys—although not, perhaps, if you had had your hair boyishly *bobbed*).

In the visual arts, the defining 20th-century term *abstract* made its bow. The *avant-garde* proclaimed the arrival of *Cubism* and *Fauvism*, *post-impressionism* and *vorticism*.

abstract *adj* (1915) of painting, sculpture, etc.: dealing with abstract form; non-representational. It became a key term in 20th-century fine art, both as a technical label and—perhaps particularly—as a put-down by those out of sympathy with such work.

> 1921 Aldous Huxley: His work . . . [is] frightfully abstract now—frightfully abstract and frightfully intellectual.

adviser *n* (1915) a soldier sent to advise or help the government or army of a foreign country. The word is often a euphemism for a combatant soldier—a usage which became particularly notorious during the Vietnam War.

> 1915 *Handbook of the Turkish Army* (Intelligence Dept, Cairo): No attempts to form reserve divisions were noted at Constantinople during the mobilization, but there is every reason to believe that it was the policy of the Turkish military authorities and their German military advisers to form a certain number.

> 1972 *Guardian*: If the Australian Labour Party wins the election and the troops come home—there are only 150 'advisers' left in Vietnam—no one doubts that ANZUK would break up.

air force *n* (1917) that branch of a country's armed forces which is concerned with air warfare. The term was apparently originally applied to the newly formed Royal Air Force in Britain, but soon became the general term for any such organization.

> 1917 *Act of Parliament*: An Act to make provision for the establishment, administration, and discipline of an Air Force, the establishment of an Air Council, and for purposes connected therewith.

airline *n* (1914) (an organization offering) a service of scheduled (passenger) flights. The term represented a re-application of the earlier sense of *line*, '(a company operating) a shipping service over particular routes', which dates from the mid 19th century. Despite the early Australian example, it does not seem to have come into its own before the 1930s.

> 1914 *Argus* (Melbourne): The Defence flying school at Point Cook has been inaccessible . . . except by air line.

airport *n* (1919) a place where civil aircraft take off and land, usually with surfaced runways and passenger facilities. The term was fairly well established by the middle of the 1920s.

> 1919 *Aerial Age Weekly*: There is being established at Atlantic City the first 'air port' ever established, the purposes of which are . . . to provide a municipal aviation field, . . . to supply an air port for trans-Atlantic liners, whether of the seaplane, land aeroplane or dirigible balloon type.

air raid *n* (1914) an attack by hostile aircraft, especially with bombs. It was one of the key terms of 20th-century warfare. The alternative *aerial raid* is first recorded in 1915, but it does not appear to have survived very long.

> 1914 *Whitaker's Almanack*: British air raids on Cologne and Dusseldorf.

allergy *n* (1911) hypersensitivity to the action of some particular foreign material, for example certain foods, pollens, micro-organisms, etc. The term was an adaptation of German *Allergie*, which was coined by C. E. von Pirquet in 1906 from Greek *allos* 'other' and *ergon* 'activity', the underlying meaning being 'changed reaction'. English acquired the adjective *allergic* in the same year.

Alzheimer's disease *n* (1912) a serious disorder of the brain which manifests itself in premature senility. The term, first published in the *Journal of Nervous and Mental Diseases* in 1912, commemorates the German neurologist Alois Alzheimer (1864–1915). It remained largely in the vocabulary of medical specialists until the 1970s, when the higher profile of the disease brought it forcibly to public notice. The abbreviated name *Alzheimer's* is first recorded in 1954.

> 1912 S. C. Fuller (title): Alzheimer's Disease (*senium præcox*): the report of a case and review of published cases.

appeasement *n* (1919) pacification of an enemy. The extension of the original general sense 'appeasing' into the geo-political sphere began after World War I with positive connotations of bringing peace and lessening the likelihood of a renewed outbreak of conflict. It was not until the late 1930s, when British prime minister Neville Chamberlain applied the term to his policy towards Germany, which was reviled in many quarters as conciliation by the offering of excessive concessions, that the word took on the negative aspect which it has retained ever since. The verb *appease* in this sense is first recorded in 1939.

1919 *General Smuts' Messages to the Empire*: In our policy of European settlement the appeasement of Germany... becomes one of cardinal importance.

1920 Winston Churchill: Here again I counsel prudence and appeasement. Try to secure a really representative Turkish governing authority, and come to terms with it.

1939 *Annual Register*: One of the new Foreign Minister's first steps was to extend to Germany the methods of appeasement—as the Prime Minister was fond of calling them—which were now being tried with Italy... So far were they from trying to 'appease' the Dictators that they might rather be described as 'facing up' to them.

1939 *New Statesman*: First, provided that there is a Russian pact, proposals that now smell of appeasement in the most dangerous sense at once become proper and, indeed, the only possible policy.

assembly line *n* (1914) a group of machines and workers concerned with the progressive assembly of some product. The key concept of 20th-century mass production made its original impact in the US motor industry.

1926 *Scientific American*: The illustration shows the chassis on the assembly line.

atomic bomb *n* (1914) a bomb whose explosive power derives from the fission of heavy atomic nuclei (see **fission (1939)**). At the beginning of the 21st century it can still cause a frisson to recall that although such weapons were not built in reality until the mid 1940s, they were being discussed while World War I was in progress. The alternative **atom bomb** is not recorded before 1945.

1914 H. G. Wells: The three atomic bombs, the new bombs that would continue to explode indefinitely.

1917 Simeon Strunsky: When you can drop just one atomic bomb and wipe out Paris or Berlin, war will have become monstrous and impossible.

atomic power *n* (1914) the power released by the fission of heavy atomic nuclei (see **fission (1939)**). The term was originally virtually a synonym of the slightly earlier **atomic energy (1906)**, but in time it came to be applied more specifically to the power of nuclear weapons and to the electricity produced by nuclear power stations.

audio *adj, n, prefix* (1913) Coined (from Latin *audire* 'to hear', and perhaps partly on the model of *audiometer* (1879)) to denote sound, especially recorded or transmitted sound. At first the term was largely restricted to the combination *audio-frequency*, but in the 1930s its use began to broaden out. Compare **video (1935)**.

1919 E. W. Stone: Frequencies from 25 to 10,000 cycles per second are termed *audio frequencies*.

1934 *Wireless World*: The division between radio and audio at 10 kilocycles is quite arbitrary.

avant-garde *n* (1910) the pioneers or innovators in any art in a particular period. The term was borrowed from French, where it means literally 'vanguard'.

1910 *Daily Telegraph*: The new men of mark in the avant-garde.

birth control *n* (1914) contraception. Compare **family planning (1931)**. *Contraception* itself dates from the 1880s.

1914 *The Woman Rebel* (heading): The Birth Control League.

1936 D. V. Glass: Condoms are listed as preventatives of disease and not as birth-control appliances, and are thus easily available.

black out *v* (1919) to extinguish or conceal all lights in (a place) as an air-raid precaution. The associated noun is first recorded in the 1930s (see **black-out (1935)**).

> 1919 *Illustrated London News*: No longer 'blacked out': London herself again.

Blighty *n* (1915) one's home country. The word was used by British soldiers serving abroad, especially during World War I, to refer to Britain. It was originally picked up by British servicemen in India from Hindi *bilāyatī*. 'foreign', hence 'British'.

> 1915 *Times*: The only thing they looked forward to was getting back to 'Blighty' again.

blues *n* (1912) a style of jazz which developed from black southern American secular songs and is usually characterized by a slow tempo and flattened thirds and sevenths. The name comes from *the blues* 'sadness', reflecting the generally melancholic aspect of the music.

> 1912 W. C. Handy (tune-title): Memphis Blues.
>
> 1923 *Daily Mail*: Noisy 'jazz' music ... is being driven out ... by the soft pulsing of muffled melody in new tunes known as 'Blues'.

Bolshevik *adj, n* (1917) (a member) of that part of the Russian Social Democratic Party which took Lenin's side in the split that followed the second congress of the party in 1903, seized power in the 'October' Revolution of 1917, and was subsequently renamed the (Russian) Communist Party. The term is derived ultimately from Russian *bolshoi* 'big'; they were in fact in a minority after the split, but they adopted the name on account of a majority they achieved on a particular vote at the 1903 congress. Non-anglicized versions of the word are recorded in English texts before 1917, but this appears to be the year in which it was naturalized, along with the derivatives *Bolshevism* and *Bolshevist.*

bomber *n* (1915) originally, someone who throws or places a bomb. The use of the word to mean 'a military aircraft designed to carry and drop bombs', first recorded two years later, dominated the early and middle years of the 20th century, but thereafter the activities of terrorists brought the original sense back to the fore. In the first example below, it means specifically 'one of a bombing party'.

> 1915 John Buchan: The bombers ... seizing one of these rocket-like bombs from their belts ... hurl them high above the parapet.
>
> 1917 *'Contact'*: The fighters guard the bombers until the eggs are dropped.

camouflage *n, v* (1917) (to conceal from the enemy with) methods or materials such as paint, smoke-screens, shrubbery, etc. The word is a borrowing from French, which in turn got it from Italian *camuffare* 'to disguise', but its ultimate origins are unknown.

> 1917 *Daily Mail*: The act of hiding anything from your enemy is termed 'camouflage' ... The King paid a visit to what is called a camouflage factory ... The King saw all the latest Protean tricks for concealing or, as we all say now, for 'camouflaging' guns, snipers, observers.

chain store *n* (1910) one of a series of stores belonging to one firm and dealing in the same type of goods. The term originated in the US.

chemical warfare *n* (1917) warfare using asphyxiating or nerve gases, poisons, defoliants, etc.

> 1917 Winston Churchill: Chemical warfare must be one of the ... leading features of our campaign of 1918.

cinema *n* (1913) a building where films are shown. English originally acquired the word *cinema* around 1909 in the sense 'cinematograph', and this extended meaning probably represents a shortening of such terms as *cinema hall* and *cinema theatre* (although our record of these is either contemporary with or later than *cinema* on its own).

> 1913 *Punch*: Our Village Cinema.

climax *n* an orgasm. This was apparently a coinage by the birth-control pioneer Marie Stopes to avoid mystifying her readers with *orgasm*, which in the course of the 19th century had become the technical term for what the *OED*, with stately definition, calls 'the height of venereal excitement in coition', but which was likely still to be unfamiliar to the layperson. The word was subsequently also used as a verb.

> 1918 Marie Stopes: In many cases the man's climax comes so swiftly that the woman's reactions are not nearly ready.

> 1982 Shirley Conran: After he climaxed, he kissed her gently on the lips.

colour-bar *n* (1913) racial discrimination, especially by whites against blacks.

> 1914 W. G. Lawrence: Relations between English and Hindu professors are bad, and there is a distinct colour bar except in the Mission colleges.

Commonwealth *n* (1917) an association of states comprising Britain and most of its former colonies and dominions. The expression 'commonwealth of nations' had been used with reference to the British Empire by Lord Rosebery in 1884 ('The British Empire is a commonwealth of nations'), but it was the South African statesman Jan Smuts who formulated the modern concept of the Commonwealth and suggested its name. The 'British Commonwealth of Nations' was established by the Statute of Westminster in 1931. After World War II the name was modified to simply 'British Commonwealth', and the 'British' was frequently dropped.

> 1917 J. C. Smuts: The British Empire is much more than a State... We are a system...of nations and states...who govern themselves, who have been evolved on the principles of your constitutional system, now almost independent states, and who belong to this group, to this community of nations, which I prefer to call the British Commonwealth of nations.

> 1940 Winston Churchill: So bear ourselves that if the British Commonwealth and Empire lasts for a thousand years men will still say, 'This was their finest hour.'

> 1958 *Times*: It is proposed to change the name of Empire Day forthwith to Commonwealth Day.

conscientious objector *n* (1916) someone who refuses on grounds of conscience to do military service. The term was actually coined at the end of the 19th century for 'someone who objects on principle to being inoculated', but came into its own during World War I, when people who refused to fight were the subject of widespread public scorn.

> 1916 Aldous Huxley: Conscientious objectors were not so disgustingly hectored as they seem to have been in London.

coupon *n* (1918) any of a series of tickets entitling the holder to a share of rationed food, clothing, etc. (The term also became more ephemerally familiar in Britain at this time as a result of the so-called 'Coupon' Election of 1918, in which Lloyd George distributed slips of paper ('coupons') containing recommendations of particular parliamentary candidates.)

> 1918 *Times*: A whole coupon [at the Express Dairy] entitled one to have stewed steak and carrots, two sausages, or cold ham and tongue.

> 1948 Nevil Shute: I ought to get another suit, but there never seem to be any coupons.

crash *v* (1910) of an aircraft or its pilot: to fall or come down violently with the machine out of control. The derived noun is first recorded in 1917. The application to motor vehicles comes from this aeronautical usage; it is not recorded until the 1920s.

> 1910 R. Loraine: The machine leapt higher, . . . then—paff!—I came to earth, having stalled and crashed.

> 1917 *Sphere*: This particular victim of a 'crash' had been compelled to lie abed...for several weeks.

Cubism *n* (1911) a movement in painting and sculpture, initiated by Pablo Picasso and Georges Braque, which emphasized the structure of objects by combining geometric shapes to give several simultaneous viewpoints. The word is an anglicization of French *cubisme*, which dates from 1908 and was allegedly coined by a member of the Hanging Committee of the Salon des Indépendants. As a canvas by Braque was being carried by, this person is supposed to have exclaimed, 'Encore des Cubes! Assez de cubisme!' ('Still more cubes! That's enough cubism!'). The derived *cubist* entered English in the same year.

> 1911 *Illustrated London News*: Paris is perturbed by the Cubism and the Cubists of the Salon d'Automne.

D-Day *n* (1918) the military code name for a particular day fixed for the beginning of an operation. It is particularly associated with the day (6 June 1944) of the invasion of the Atlantic coast of German-occupied France by Allied forces, but its origin long predates that. The 'D' simply represents the first letter of *day*.

> 1918 *Field Order No. 8, First Army, Allied Expeditionary Force*: The First Army will attack at H-Hour on D-Day with the object of forcing the evacuation of St. Mihiel salient.

> 1944 *Times*: The Canadians landed on D Day at Bernières-sur-Mer.

death ray *n* (1919) a ray that causes death. It was a staple of pulp science fiction in the middle years of the 20th century.

> 1919 Bertram Munn: Had the man once used his death rays he was watched carefully enough to have been caught... red-handed.

denial *n* (1914) the usually unconscious suppression of painful or embarrassing feelings, reactions, or desires. The usage was introduced into English as a technical term in psychoanalysis by A. A. Brill's translation of Sigmund Freud's *Psychopathology of Everyday Life*. It became known to a wider public in American English in the 1980s, in the phrase *in denial*.

> 1992 *Village Voice* (New York): 'You're living in denial. Abortion is killing your baby.' He sounds the prolifers' warning of never-ending guilt, as if morality were mere avoidance of pain.

director *n* (1911) someone who directs a film. This meaning of the verb *direct* is itself not recorded before 1913, but the two words probably emerged hand in hand.

> 1911 *Moving Picture World*: The director explains to the players the action of a... scene.

> 1913 F. W. Sargent: Director, one who produces photoplays, directing the preparation and action.

donor *n* (1910) a person or animal from whom something is removed to be introduced into another organism. The earliest application of the term is to someone who gives blood for use in a transfusion (the term *blood-donor* is not recorded before 1921). By 1918 there is evidence of its use for an animal, alive or dead, from which an organ or tissue is removed for surgical transplantation (this usage does not seem to have been extended to human beings until the 1950s).

> 1910 *Johns Hopkins Hospital Bulletin*: The serum of both donor and donee is capable of agglutinating the corpuscles of the other.

> 1921 *Lancet*: In a recent number of the *Guy's Hospital Gazette* the editor protests against the too free use of students as blood-donors.

> 1971 *Daily Telegraph*: Doctors should only be allowed to remove an organ if the donor has given his consent in writing or if the nearest relative that it is practicable to contact, has given consent.

extrovert *n* (1918) a person whose behaviour is characterized by an interest in interacting with other people and the external world. Originally a technical term in psychology, it was subsequently used more generally for 'an outgoing person'. It first appeared in 1915 in the form *extravert*, which actually makes more etymological sense (from Latin *extra* 'outwards'), but the spelling *extrovert*, which was modelled on **introvert (1918)**, has swept the board.

1918 P. Blanchard: Jung's hypothesis of the two psychological types, the introvert and extrovert,—the thinking type and the feeling type.

family values *n* (1916) values supposedly learnt or reinforced within a traditional, close family unit, especially high moral standards and discipline (viewed as being in decline). The phrase was used as a slogan by the political right in the 1990s.

1996 *Times*: A highly disciplined election-year drive to present himself as the champion of conservative 'family values'... He has urged a return to school uniforms to encourage discipline and announced moves denying welfare benefits to teenage mothers who leave school or refuse to live at home.

film star *n* (1914) a popular film actor or actress. The synonymous *cinema star* is first recorded a year before, but soon lost out to *film star. Movie star*, the preferred American term, is first recorded in 1919.

1913 Valentia Steer: To become a cinema 'star' is not an easy matter.

1914 Robert Grau: The greatest film stars in the world.

1919 H. L. Wilson: [They saw] how much they were paying their president... quoted beside some movie star's salary.

Freudian *adj* (1910) of Sigmund Freud (1856–1939), the Austrian psychiatrist who developed psychoanalysis. The term quickly picked up connotations of repressed sexuality (see the first quote below), but there is no evidence of its use in the sense 'unwittingly revealing one's true (sexual) feelings' (as in *Freudian slip*) until the late 1950s.

1915 E. B. Holt: The idea has gone abroad that the term 'Freudian' is somehow synonymous with 'sexual'.

1963 Nicholas Blake: It was an odd little slip of the tongue... They call them Freudian slips nowadays.

front line *n* (1915) the most forward line of a military combat force. The term was originally used in the context of the trench warfare in France in World War I.

1915 Ian Hay: That sudden disturbance in the front-line trench.

1917 Ford Madox Ford: I hope to get to Mesopotamia as I am not fit for the front line.

gas mask *n* (1915) a mask used as a protection against poisonous gas.

1915 *War Illustrated*: French soldiers wearing anti-poison gas masks and respirators.

gene *n* (1911) a hereditary unit located on a chromosome which determines a specific characteristic or function in the organism. The term is an adaptation of German *Gen*, coined in 1909 by Wilhelm Johannsen (see the quote below) from the Greek base *gen-* 'be born'.

1911 Wilhelm Johannsen: I have proposed the terms 'gene' and 'genotype'... to be used in the science of genetics. The 'gene' is nothing but a very applicable little word, easily combined with others, and hence it may be useful as an expression for the 'unit-factors', 'elements' or 'allelomorphs' in the gametes, demonstrated by modern Mendelian researches.

grass roots *n* (1912) the rank-and-file of the electorate or of a political party. This is a specific political use (of US origin) of a more general metaphor, first recorded in 1901: 'the fundamental level'. By the end of the century it was firmly ensconced as a political cliché.

1912 *McClure's Magazine*: From the Roosevelt standpoint, especially, it was a campaign from the 'grass roots up'. The voter was the thing.

1966 *New Statesman*: The grassroot Tory still prefers to touch his forelock and reverence his 'betters'.

Great War *n* (1914) World War I. The name had previously been used of the Napoleonic wars. It continued to be the main term (alongside the colloquial *Kaiser's War*) for the conflict of 1914–18 among the generation that had lived through it, but once *World War I* (1939) and *World War II* (1939) had been coined it gradually went out of general use.

1914 *Maclean's Magazine*: Some wars name themselves... This is the Great War.

homosexual *n* (1912) a homosexual person. The earliest recorded instance of the noun in English is in a text translated from German, as is the earliest record of the adjective *homosexual* (1892).

> 1912 Eden Paul: An adult homosexual who as a child once did some needlework for a joke.

Hun *n* (1914) a derogatory name during World War I and afterwards for a German (soldier) or for Germans collectively. The term originally denoted a nomadic Asiatic people who invaded Europe in the Dark Ages, and had actually been applied dismissively to Germans in English since the late 18th century. This rather more specific usage was inspired by a speech delivered by Wilhelm II to the German troops about to sail for China on 27 July 1900, in which he enjoined them to fight like Huns (*The Times* reported (30 July 1900): 'According to the Bremen Weser Zeitung the Emperor said:–"... No quarter will be given, no prisoners will be taken. Let all who fall into your hands be at your mercy. Just as the Huns a thousand years ago, under the leadership of Etzel (Attila) gained a reputation in virtue of which they still live in historical tradition, so may the name of Germany become known in such a manner in China that no Chinaman will ever again even dare to look askance at a German"').

> 1914 Rudyard Kipling: Stand up and meet the war. The Hun is at the gate!
>
> 1915 *Daily Mail*: She [*sc.* a Norfolk girl] told me how the eldest [brother 'at the front'] had held up three 'Huns' in a mill... She used the word 'Hun' quite naturally, with no hint of contempt or bitterness.

imperialism *n* (1918) (in Communist usage) the imperial system or policy of the Western powers. The term became a Cold War mantra. The derived *imperialist* is first recorded in 1963.

> 1918 *Manchester Guardian*: The Menshevik and the small bourgeois parties have published a declaration calling on workers all over the world to rally to the support of the Russian Revolution against the Imperialism attacking it.
>
> 1959 *Daily Telegraph*: Hence, perhaps, the decision to revert to 'Western imperialism' as target of a fresh hate-campaign in Iraq.
>
> 1963 *New Statesman*: The reported Chinese memorandum... [refers to] Krushchev's 'capitulationist' attitudes towards the 'imperialists'.

instant *adj* (1912) of a processed food: that can be prepared for use immediately. The usage originated in the US.

> 1915 E. B. Holt: I wish I had... drunk less of that hot-wash that my wife calls instant coffee.

intelligence test *n* (1914) a test to measure someone's mental skills.

> 1914 *Eugenics Review*: General ability, estimated by intelligence tests, is largely hereditary.

introvert *n* (1918) a person whose behaviour is characterized by a lack of interest in interacting with other people and the external world. Originally a technical term in psychology, it subsequently came to be used more generally for 'a shy self-absorbed person'. Compare **extrovert (1918)**.

> 1918 P. Blanchard: Jung's hypothesis of the two psychological types, the introvert and extrovert,—the thinking type and the feeling type.

isotope *n* (1913) one of two or more atoms with the same atomic number that have different numbers of neutrons. The term was coined from Greek *isos* 'equal, same' and *topos* 'place'.

> 1913 Frederick Soddy: The same algebraic sum of the positive and negative charges in the nucleus, when the arithmetical sum is different, gives what I call 'isotopes' or 'isotopic elements', because they occupy the same place in the periodic table. They are chemically identical, and save only as regards the relatively few physical properties which depend upon atomic mass directly, physically identical also.

jazz *n* (1913) a type of improvised syncopated popular music, originally as played by black bands in the southern US to accompany a type of ragtime dance. It was after World War I that jazz spread from New Orleans and the Deep South to New York, Chicago, and other big US cities, and began to establish itself as one of the main musical art-forms of the 20th century. The ultimate origins of the word *jazz* remain controversial. The earliest trace of it is in crap-shooters' slang in the Los Angeles/San Francisco area around 1912, where it seems to have denoted some sort of desirable 'fluence' on the dice, to bring luck. It soon spread to the language of baseball players, where it was used to mean 'pep' or 'verve', and that seems to have been the conduit by which it seeped into music. Where the crap-shooters originally got it from, though, we do not know, despite many ingenious suggestions (e.g. that it came from the nickname of one Jasbo Brown, an itinerant black musician along the Mississippi (*Jasbo* perhaps being an alteration of *Jasper*), or that it crossed the Atlantic with West African slaves). Probably the least unlikely candidate is slang *jasm*, a variant of *jism* 'semen, sperm', which was used metaphorically for 'energy, spirit'.

> 1913 *Bulletin* (San Francisco): The team which speeded into town this morning comes pretty close to representing the pick of the army. Its members have trained on ragtime and 'jazz'.

> 1916 *Ragtime Review*: The 'Jaz' bands that are so popular at the present time.

> 1922 Carl Engel: Jazz is rag-time, plus 'blues', plus orchestral polyphony; it is the combination, in the popular music current, of melody, rhythm, harmony, and counterpoint.

join up *v* (1916) to enlist in the armed forces.

> 1916 'Boyd Cable': Just joined up to get a finger in the fighting?

ladies' *n* (1918) a women's public lavatory. The parallel sense of *gentlemen's* is not recorded until the late 1920s.

> 1918 Katherine Mansfield: Also, when she goes to the 'Ladies', for some obscure reason she wears a little shawl.

land *v* (1916) to bring (an aircraft) to the ground. The usage is first recorded in print in 1916, although no doubt it was in existence well before then: its intransitive counterpart, 'to come to ground from the air', dates from the late 18th century (initially in the context of balloons).

> 1916 Horatio Barber: I'll guarantee to safely land the fastest machine in a five-acre field.

legend in one's lifetime *n* (1918) someone so famous that they are the subject of popularly repeated stories even in their own lifetime. Lytton Strachey's phrase prophetically set the tone for the celebrity culture of the late 20th century.

> 1918 Lytton Strachey: She [i.e. Florence Nightingale] was a legend in her lifetime, and she knew it.

Leninist *adj, n* (1917) (a follower or supporter) of the Russian revolutionary leader V. I. Lenin (1870–1924) or of his doctrine. The term was coined contemporaneously with *Leninite*, which however barely survived a couple of years. The derivative *Leninism* is first recorded in 1918. Leninists believe in *Marxism-Leninism* (the term is first recorded in English in 1932), a version of Marxism adopted by Lenin to reflect contemporary developments in Russia and in capitalist societies.

> 1917 *Times*: General Korniloff has been placed under the same ban as M. Kerensky, and renewed instructions for the arrest of both have been issued by the Leninist committee... Trotsky, on behalf of the Leninite 'Government', has telegraphed to all the representatives of Russia abroad.

mass murder *n* (1917) the murder of very large numbers of people, either serially or (more usually) simultaneously. It was a term for which the 20th century found ample use as it ground on. See also **genocide (1944)**.

> 1931 Scott Nearing (title): War: organized destruction and mass murder by civilized nations.

> 1967 Hannah Arendt: The bulk of the armed SS served at the Eastern front where they were used for 'special assignments'—usually mass murder.

mini- *prefix* (1919) very small of its kind. A prefix formed from the first two syllables of *miniature* (probably also with some input from *minimum*). The earliest example we have of it, in the word *minimeter*, is actually atypical, because this denoted an instrument for measuring very small distances. The *mini-* we are familiar with today, referring to a scaled-down version of something else, began to come into its own in the 1930s, largely as an element in proprietary names, such as *minipiano* and *minicamera* (the latter was subsequently abbreviated to *minicam*). It was the 1960s that saw the real explosion in the use of *mini-*, possibly initiated by the popularity of the *Mini-Minor* (1959), a small car manufactured originally by the British Motor Corporation, and reinforced by the fashionability of high hemlines, which encouraged coinages like **miniskirt (1965)** and *minidress* (1965).

> 1934 *Trade Marks Journal*: Minipiano... Pianos. Brasted Bros. Ltd.,... London,... piano manufacturers; and C.A.V. Lundholm Aktiebolag (a Joint Stock Company organised under the laws of Sweden),... Sweden; merchants.

> 1936 *Miniature Camera Magazine*: It is perhaps to be expected that all sorts and conditions of industries and businesses should have sprung up around the successful Minicamera.

> 1954 *Life*: The new 'mini-pig'... is ideal for medical research, which is what he was bred for.

> 1966 *Times Review of Industry*: With the 'mini-budget' having withdrawn another £500m. from internal demand.

> 1970 *New Scientist*: The minipill was developed for one reason alone: because it was believed to provide safe contraception.

> 1999 *BBC Music Magazine*: Then there's the... free brochure, full of informative mini-reviews of the best of all the new releases.

> 2005 *Radio Times*: Most of Mr Madeley's cracks are fed to him as a result of the insane ideas of the general public—genetically modified mini pet elephants being one, for example.

ministry *n* (1916) The name given to certain departments of the British government. Hitherto they had gone under such designations as *office* and *board. Ministry* had been used since at least the 1840s for government departments in foreign countries, notably Russia, but during World War I it became the favoured term for any newly founded government department in Britain, and remained so until the 1960s, when it began to be overtaken by *department*.

> 1916 *Whitaker's Almanack*: Munitions, Ministry of, Minister, Rt. Hon. D. Lloyd George, M.P.

moron *n* (1910) an adult with a mental age of between eight and twelve. The term (based ultimately on Greek *mōros* 'stupid') was first adopted and given this meaning by the American Association for the Study of the Feeble-minded in 1910. Already by the 1920s it was being used (as is commonly the fate of new technical terminology attached to the mentally subnormal) as an insult, and it is no longer in technical use.

> 1910 H. H. Goddard: The other (suggestion) is to call [feeble-minded children] by the Greek word 'moron'. It is defined as one who is lacking in intelligence, one who is deficient in judgement or sense.

motorcade *n* (1913) a procession of motor vehicles. This blend of *motor* and *cavalcade* originated in the USA. It was not the first of such formations based on *cavalcade* (*camelcade* dates from the 1880s), but it has proved the most durable.

> 1913 *Arizona Republican*: The motorcade can make its music self supporting and donate large and salubrious gobs of melody to the natives at all points along the line... This 'motorcade' came from a suggestion thrown out by the sporting editor of the *Republican*. It was immediately accepted by several local automobile owners, whereupon, the sporting editor [Lyle Abbott] became the busiest man in Phoenix and hammered away at the 'motorcade' a term which, by the way, he had invented sometime before in order that newspapers might keep pace with the developments of vehicular transportation.

movie *n* (1912) a motion picture, a film. The word is an abbreviation of *moving picture* (1896). It originated in the USA, and is still the main term there. It is often used in the plural to denote the motion-picture industry, or a film show.

1913 *Home Chat*: The comparatively small towns [in America] have installed 'movies'—as they call them over there—in their schools.

mushroom *n* (1916) a cloud (of smoke, dust, etc.) that spreads upwards and outwards, in the shape of a mushroom. This was a metaphor that found its natural home in 1945, when the first atom bomb was detonated.

1916 John Buchan: There was the dull shock of an explosion and a mushroom of red earth.

1945 *New York Times*: At first it was a giant column that soon took the shape of a supramundane mushroom.

mustard gas *n* (1917) a colourless oily liquid which is a powerful poison and blistering agent, and which was first used in warfare by the Germans in 1917, at Ypres.

1917 *Nation* (New York): The Germans have just invented a new and particularly powerful weapon in their so-called 'mustard gas'.

napoo, napooh *interj, adj, v* (1915) originally an exclamation meaning 'done, finished, no more', but subsequently used adjectivally in the sense 'finished', and also 'dead', and as a verb, 'to finish or kill'. It represents a British soldiers' version of French *(il n'y e)n a plus* 'there's no more', picked up during war service in France. It proved to be one of the more durable pieces of World War I slang.

1915 Ian Hay: You say 'Na pooh!' when you push your plate away after dinner . . . 'Poor Bill got na-poohed by a rifle-grenade yesterday.'

1943 J. B. Priestley: You're as good as dead—just waitin' to stiffen. Fini-napoo!

National Service *n* (1916) see **national serviceman (1949)**.

newsreel *n* (1914) a short cinema film dealing with news and current affairs. It was the staple form of in-motion news reporting until television news came of age in the late 1950s.

1916 *Wells Fargo Messenger*: Some companies issue their news reels twice a week.

1928 *Manchester Guardian Weekly*: There are four motion picture newsreel cameramen, and four 'still' photographers.

new town *n* (1918) (in Britain) a planned urban area designed to ease the congestion of a nearby large city, usually one with special provision for housing, employment, and amenities for a delimited population. The term is first recorded in the title of a pamphlet in 1918, but it did not come into general use until such towns started being built after World War II.

1948 Josephine Tey: The little house on the outer rim of the 'new' town.

nuclear *adj* (1914) of atomic nuclei (see **nucleus (1912)**).

1914 *Engineering*: A point raised by Professor Rutherford concerning the effective nuclear charge.

1945 H. D. Smyth: The pile was first operated . . . on December 2, 1942 . . . This was the first time that human beings ever initiated a self-maintaining nuclear chain reaction.

nucleus *n* (1912) the positively charged central constituent of the atom, comprising nearly all its mass but occupying only a very small part of its volume and now known to be composed of protons and neutrons. Physicists as far back as Michael Faraday in the 1840s had used the term *nucleus* (from Latin, literally a 'kernel') for the hypothetical central point of an atom, so the way was prepared for Ernest Rutherford to employ it when the real nature of atomic structure had been elucidated. In his original 1911 paper (see the quote below) he referred to it simply as a 'central charge'; *nucleus* followed in 1912.

1912 Ernest Rutherford: In a previous paper [1911] I have given reasons for believing that the atom consists of a positively charged nucleus of very small dimensions, surrounded by a distribution of electrons in rapid motion, possibly of rings of electrons rotating in one plane.

Oedipus complex *n* (1910) the name given by Sigmund Freud to the complex of emotions which he found were aroused in a child by its subconscious sexual desire for the parent of the opposite sex, which, if not resolved naturally, may lead to repression, guilt feelings, and an inability to form normal emotional or sexual relationships. It was based on the plot of Sophocles' play *Oedipus Tyrannus*, in which Oedipus unknowingly kills his father and marries his mother.

> 1910 Ernest Jones: The Œdipus-complex as an explanation of Hamlet's mystery.

park *n* (1916) an open space where cars and other vehicles can be left. The word is usually preceded by the name of the type of vehicle—but the compound **car park** is not recorded until 1926.

> 1916 Arnold Bennett: Audrey's motor-car... was waiting in the automobile park outside the principal gates.

peace offensive *n* (1917) a sustained campaign or effort to bring about peace. The word often implies a cynical attempt to further one's own warlike aims by appearing to promote peace.

> 1918 Siegfried Sassoon: There are indications that the enemies' peace offensive is creating the danger which is its object.
>
> 1939 *War Illustrated*: Mr. Chamberlain stated in the House of Commons that nothing in the German 'peace offensive' could modify the attitude which Great Britain had felt it right to take.

people's republic *n* (1918) a title assumed by a number of left-wing or Communist states (e.g. People's Republic of China).

> 1949 *Times*: Mr. Rákosi... said... that 'the Hungarian Republic must be developed into a People's Republic'.
>
> 1975 *Bangladesh Times*: The Magura Journalists Association in a meeting held recently at Magura hailed the Government of the People's Republic of Bangladesh for creating the new district of Magura.
>
> 1978 Lord Hailsham: Probably our own monarch would not survive the institution in Britain of... a people's republic.

persona *n* (1917) the set of attitudes adopted by individuals to fit themselves for the social roles which they see as theirs. This originated as a technical term in Jungian psychology, but subsequently it came to be used more generally for 'the personality an individual presents to the world'.

> 1917 C. E. Long: The persona is always identical with a typical attitude, in which one psychological function dominates, e.g. feeling, or thought, or intuition.

Photostat *n* (1911) the proprietary name of a kind of photocopying machine, later also applied to a copy made on such a machine, and used also as a verb (first recorded in 1914). The term was registered as a trademark in the US in 1911. It means literally 'making light stationary'.

poison gas *n* (1915) a lethal gas (e.g. phosgene) used in warfare.

> 1915 H. W. Wilson: After the great chemical experiment with poison gas in April, the Germans had been able to advance to the manor-house... The Duke of Würtemberg... had apparently become convinced, after his poison-gas victory in April, that chemical methods of making war were the most successful.

posh *adj* (1918) At first in the meaning 'smart, stylish, first-rate', but the connotations of snobbish exclusivity or refinement which mark its present-day use soon crept in. The origins of the word have been much discussed but remain mysterious. The suggestion that it is derived from the initials of 'port outward, starboard home', referring to the more expensive side for accommodation on ships formerly travelling between Britain and India, is often put forward but lacks foundation. There may be some connection with obsolete 19th-century slang *posh* 'a dandy'.

1918 *Punch*: Oh, yes, Mater, we had a posh time of it down there.

1923 P. G. Wodehouse: Practically every posh family in the country has called him in at one time or another.

1957 John Osborne: *Jimmy*: Haven't you read the other posh paper yet? *Cliff*: Which? *Jimmy*: Well, there are only two posh papers on a Sunday.

post-impressionism *n* (1910) a school of painting, exemplified especially by Cézanne, Gauguin, and Van Gogh, which rejected the more strictly representational aspects of impressionism and emphasized personal vision. The term (and the derived adjective and noun *post-impressionist*) were introduced to Britain via an exhibition of such paintings organized by Roger Fry in 1910.

1910 *Poster*: Grafton Gallery. Manet and the Post-Impressionists.

P.O.W. (1919) an abbreviation of *prisoner-of-war* which seems not to have come into widespread use until World War II.

1941 *War Illustrated*: P.O.W. camps in Germany and Poland are shown in this map.

prestigious *adj* (1913) having high status or glamour; conferring prestige. The usage has found disfavour in some purist quarters, on the grounds that the etymological (hence, 'true') meaning of the word is 'involving trickery, illusory'. However, the use of *prestige* for 'high status, glamour' goes back to the early 19th century, and it is somewhat bizarre to take exception to the employment of the derived adjective in the same sense. Objections to it seem to have surfaced after World War II: there is no reference to it in early editions of *Fowler's Modern English Usage*, and the awkward *prestigeful*, recommended by some usage writers for those who could not stomach *prestigious*, is not recorded before 1956. The controversy has now largely faded away.

1913 Joseph Conrad: 'You have had all these immense sums . . . What have I had out of them?' It was perfectly true. He had had nothing out of them—nothing of the prestigious or the desirable things of the earth.

profiteer *n* (1912) someone who seeks to make excessive gain (e.g. by the extortionate sale of necessary goods). This and the associated noun *profiteering* came into their own during World War I as terms of opprobrium for those who made a profit out of manufacturing or supplying material for the Allied war effort. A law was passed against the practice in Britain in 1919, called the Profiteering Act.

1914 *Englishwoman*: The tricks of the armament profiteers are fresh in the public mind.

1914 *New Age*: England is at war upon profiteering.

psyche *n* (1910) the conscious and unconscious mind and emotions, especially as influencing and affecting the whole person. This was an adoption into psychiatric terminology of a word previously denoting more vaguely the soul or spirit (as distinguished from the body). It is ultimately from Greek *psukhē* 'breath, life, soul'.

1910 C. G. Jung: Disease is an imperfect adaptation; hence in this case we are dealing with something morbid in the psyche.

psychoanalyse *v* (1911) to subject to or treat by psychoanalysis. The verb is a back-formation from *psychoanalysis* (1906), on the model of *analysis, analyse* (*analyse* itself is first recorded in the sense 'to psychoanalyse' in 1909). *Psychoanalyst* 'someone who practises or has training in psychoanalysis' is first recorded in the same year.

1911 *American Journal of Psychology*: It is . . . hoped that Freud will . . . psychoanalyze Goethe . . . The business of the psychoanalyst is to provide a means by which the emotion attached to a repressed complex may find expression, by being transformed.

public relations *n* (1913) activities to promote a favourable relationship and good image with the public. A prophetic example of the term is recorded over a hundred years before in the writings of American statesman Thomas Jefferson ('Questions calling for the notice of Congress, unless indeed they shall be superseded by a change in our public relations now awaiting the determination of others' (1807)), but it did not establish itself until the 20th century. The abbreviation *PR* is first recorded in 1942.

> 1913 *Electric Railway Journal*: Effective publicity to deal with questions of public relations and to consider the molding of public opinion by the presentation of real facts.

quantum *n* (1910) a discrete quantity of electromagnetic energy proportional in magnitude to the frequency of the radiation it represents. The word is from Latin, the neuter of *quantus* 'how great'. The concept was introduced by the German physicist Max Planck in 1900. He called it an *Energieelement* 'energy element', not a *quantum*, but he did use *quantum* in a passing reference to the electronic charge ('das Elementarquantum der Elektricität'). The first to use it in its current sense was Albert Einstein (1905) in a paper in German discussing the nature of light.

> 1910 *Science Abstracts*: The absorption of the corresponding light-quantum.
>
> 1913 *Report of the British Association for the Advancement of Science*: Assuming that an oscillator can only emit definite, discontinuous quantums of energy, Planck showed that their magnitude is proportional to the frequency.

quantum theory *n* (1912) a theory of matter and energy based on the concept of *quanta*, developed from ideas of Max Planck and Albert Einstein, and forming the basis of *quantum mechanics*. It was originally (in 1911) called *quanta theory*, but the singular form prevailed.

> 1912 *Monthly Notices of the Royal Astronomical Society*: The constant of nature in terms of which these spectra can be expressed appears to be that of Planck in his recent quantum theory of energy.

race relations *n* (1911) interaction between people of different races. First recorded in the title of a paper, 'Race relations in the Eastern Piedmont region of Georgia', in the *Political Science Quarterly*, it has been a key socio-political term of the century, particularly in the contexts of the US and South Africa, and also of post-colonial Britain.

> 1977 *Whitaker's Almanack*: A Lords amendment to the Race Relations Bill . . . was reversed in the Commons on Oct. 27.

racialist *n* (1917) an advocate or practitioner of **racialism (1907)**.

> 1917 *Debates in the Canadian House of Commons*: We all become nationalists in the true sense of the word, as distinguished from provincialists and racialists.

rationing *n* (1917) the distribution of food, fuel, etc. in restricted allocations. See also **coupon (1918)**.

> 1917 *Times*: The German Government now knows all about rationing, but while it has been learning the German people has eaten up its supplies.

red *adj, n* (1917) (a) Bolshevik or Communist. The use of *red* as a (generally negative) synonym for socialist or anarchist, both adjective and noun, goes back to the middle of the 19th century ('I dreamt that I stood in the Crystal Halls, With Chartists and Reds at my side', *Punch* (1851)). It referred to the colour of a party badge. It was therefore ready and waiting after the revolution of 1917 to be applied to Russian Communists, who themselves adopted the symbolism of the colour (e.g. in their flag).

> 1919 *Times*: That I was prepared to create a Red Revolution in England . . . is something which I have never said.
>
> 1922 Sinclair Lewis: Say, juh notice in the paper the way the New York Assembly stood up to the Reds?

refugee *n* (1914) someone driven from their home by war or the fear of attack or persecution; a displaced person. English originally adapted the word from French *refugié* at the end of the 17th century as a term for the French Huguenots who came to

England after the revocation of the Edict of Nantes in 1685. For the next 250 years it denoted an asylum-seeker, but this new meaning, with its accent on flight from home rather than seeking refuge, was made familiar by the wars of the 20th century.

> 1914 E. A. Powell: The road from Antwerp to Ghent . . . was a solid mass of refugees.

rocket *n* (1919) an engine that provides thrust by the ejection of burnt fuel; also, any elongated device or craft (such as a flying bomb, a missile, or a spacecraft) in which such an engine is the means of propulsion. Hitherto, the word's application had been restricted to the firework.

> 1919 R. H. Goddard: It is possible to convert the rocket from a very inefficient heat engine into the most efficient heat engine that ever has been devised.

> 1920 *Photo Play*: The theory of a Professor Goddard that a rocket could be sent to the moon.

role *n* (1913) the behaviour that an individual feels it appropriate to assume in adapting to any form of social interaction. It has become a key term in the jargon of social psychology. See also **role model (1957)**.

> 1913 G. H. Mead: This response to the social conduct of the self may be in the rôle of another—we present his arguments in imagination and do it with his intonations and gestures . . . In this way we play the rôles of all our group; indeed, it is only in so far as we do this that they become part of our social environment.

sabotage *n* (1910) deliberate destruction of property or disruption of systems in order to obstruct normal functioning. This borrowing from French was at first treated as a foreignism, but quickly became naturalized. Its use as a verb is first recorded in 1918. The French word itself is a derivative of *sabot* 'wooden shoe', and the underlying connotations are of clattering about noisily in such shoes, and hence of working clumsily and wrecking things.

> 1910 *Church Times*: We have lately been busy in deploring the sabotage of the French railway strikers.

> 1918 *New Appeal*: Testimony . . . that the companies are sabotaging the government.

sacred cow *n* (1910) someone or something that must not be criticized. It was originally US journalists' slang, based on the veneration of cows as sacred by the Hindus.

> 1910 *Atlantic Monthly*: In the office these corporations were jocularly referred to as 'sacred cows'.

sanctions *n* (1919) action taken by one state or alliance of states against another as a coercive measure, often to enforce a violated law or treaty. It became a key tool of 20th-century power-diplomacy (if ultimately discredited in favour of more direct action).

> 1919 George Bernard Shaw: Such widely advocated and little thought-out 'sanctions' as the outlawry and economic boycott of a recalcitrant nation.

schizophrenia *n* (1912) a psychotic disorder involving withdrawal from reality, hallucinations, delusions, etc. The term was originally coined in German by Eugen Bleuler in 1910 as *Schizophrenie*, from Greek *skhizein* 'to split' and *phrēn* 'mind'.

> 1912 *Lancet*: This little volume is a translation of a series of articles by Professor Bleuler which appeared . . . during 1910 and 1911, in which he advances a theory of the negativism so frequently met with in dementia praecox or schizophrenia.

scooter *n* (1917) a child's foot-powered vehicle consisting of a footboard with a wheel at each end and an upright steering handle; also (in full *motor-scooter*), a motor-powered vehicle based on this. As the quotes below show, the toy scooter was in use before World War I, but written records of it are lacking. The first motor-powered scooter, made in New York in 1915, was called the 'Auto-Ped'.

> 1917 *Autocar*: For some months past it has been known in this country that the 'scooter' in America has developed into something rather beyond the child's plaything so popular in the

British Isles. Until quite recently, however, the American motor-driven 'scooter' has not been seen in London.

1919 *Times*: The 'scooter' we knew before the war was a new terror to the pavement.

1919 *Isis*: The Proctor . . . on a motor-scooter, accompanied by a couple of attendant 'bullers' on a push-bike.

self-determination *n* (1911) freedom to decide one's own form of government. Originally a translation of German *Selbstbestimmung*, a coinage of the philosopher Johann Gottlieb Fichte, it was given currency in English initially by US President Woodrow Wilson's frequent use of it in the aftermath of World War I, and latterly by the worldwide decolonizations of the second half of the century.

1911 *Encyclopedia Britannica*: The more enlightened of the emperors . . . made a genuine endeavour to give a due share in the work of government to the various subject races. But nothing could compensate for the lack of self-determination.

self-service *adj, n* (1919) (operating) a system by which customers in a shop, restaurant, etc. serve themselves instead of being attended to or waited on by the staff. A later synonym was *serve-yourself* (1937).

1919 *Ladies' Home Journal*: The Duffy-Powers Company, operating a full-fledged department store in Rochester, New York, inaugurated self-service—that is, the customers, not the store, provide the service—in its grocery department . . . After several months . . . , not only are all the self-service departments reported on a self-supporting basis, but with sales increasing.

serial *n* (1914) a film shown in a number of episodes; hence, a radio or, later, a television play broadcast in usually weekly episodes. The usage was an adaptation of the earlier application to a novel published in serial form, which dates from the mid 19th century.

1939 *B.B.C. Handbook*: An interesting aspect of the year's radio-dramatic work was the development of serial plays. The serial feature, which is the backbone of American radio, had made comparatively few appearances here before 1938 . . . Publishers . . . found that the 'Monte Cristo' serial caused a great demand for the novel.

sex discrimination *n* (1916) unfavourable treatment motivated by prejudice against members of a particular sex. The term, which originated in the US, was not in widespread use until the 1960s (when it was joined by *sexual discrimination*).

1916 *Campaign Text-Book* (National Woman's Party): Enfranchised women in the United States regard the removal of sex discrimination from our national constitution as a political need of primary importance.

sex drive *n* (1918) the impulse which motivates satisfaction of sexual needs. A roughly contemporary synonym is *sex urge* (1920).

1918 R. S. Woodworth: The association is not entirely a spreading of the sex drive into the esthetic sphere.

1920 Margaret Sanger: This man is not concerned with his wife's sex urge, save as it responds to his own at times of his choosing.

sex object *n* (1911) a person towards whom, or thing towards which, the sexual impulse is directed. This was originally a technical term in psychology, but latterly, under the influence of feminist writing, it has come to be applied (with negative connotations) to a person regarded only as the object of sexual desire.

1911 *American Journal of Psychology*: Instead of sublimating the sex impulse, [Leonardo da Vinci] directed it towards the physical Jesus in toto. It was simply the substitution of one sex object for another.

1980 Graham Greene: Deane is not an actor: he is a sex object. Teenage girls worship him.

sex symbol *n* (1911) a person who is the epitome of sexual attraction and glamour.

1976 Botham & Donnelly: The olive skin of the man [i.e. Rudolph Valentino] who would . . . become the world's first and most enduring sex symbol.

shell shock *n* (1915) a severe neurosis originating in trauma suffered under fire. The term is particularly associated with World War I, in which soldiers on the Western Front were subjected to a seemingly incessant barrage of shell-fire. A colloquial World War II synonym was *bomb-happy* (1943).

> 1918 E. A. Mackintosh: The Corporal . . . collapsed suddenly with twitching hands and staring, frightened eyes, proclaiming the shell-shock he had held off while the work was to be done.

silent *adj* (1914) of a cinema film: unaccompanied by sound recording. The term came into use only after the possibility of talking pictures had been contemplated (see **talkie (1913)**).

> 1914 *Writer's Bulletin*: Even in filmdom . . . there are a dozen who hold the art of the silent drama in reverence.

> 1918 *New York Times* (heading): Two opera stars in silent films.

S.O.S. *n* (1910) The international radio code-signal of extreme distress, used especially by ships at sea. The letters were chosen because they are easy to transmit in Morse, but they are conventionally interpreted as 'Save Our Souls'. Their most famous early use was in the fruitless distress signals put out by the sinking *Titanic* in 1912. Their use was discontinued in 1998.

> 1910 J. A. Fleming: This signal, S,O,S, has superseded the Marconi Company's original high sea cry for help, which was C,Q,D.

soviet *n* (1917) any of a range of elected legislative and executive councils operating at all levels of government in the USSR. The word is a borrowing of Russian *sovet* 'council', which was also applied to various revolutionary councils set up prior to the establishment of socialist rule in 1917. See also **Soviet (1920)**.

> 1917 *Times*: A meeting of the Central Committee of the Soviet was held . . . at which the situation on the front was considered.

space-time *n* (1915) time and three-dimensional space regarded as fused in a four-dimensional continuum containing all events—a key concept in the evolution of the idea of relativity. The term is a direct translation of German *Raumzeit*.

split personality *n* (1919) a condition in which a person manifests two or more distinct personalities. The term is often used loosely by laypeople to mean 'schizophrenia'.

> 1919 M. K. Bradby: The split personalities of hysterics and mediums . . . have a subjective meaning.

storm troops *n* (1917) originally a general term (translated from German *Sturmtruppen*) for 'shock troops'—high-calibre soldiers specially trained to lead an attack. From the 1920s it was also applied specifically to the troops of the Nazi *Sturmabteilung*. The derivative *storm-trooper* is first recorded in 1933.

> 1923 *Times*: Bands of 'storm troops' paraded the streets, singing the Fascist war songs.

> 1933 *Palestine Post*: The Nazi storm-troopers at noon on Friday, cleared the Berlin law courts of Jewish judges.

streamlined *adj* (1913) having a streamline form (see **streamline (1907)**). After World War I, the sort of flowing lines and slender elongated rounded forms demanded by streamlining became a distinguishing feature of contemporary design in general.

> 1913 *Aeroplane*: [The aeroplane's] small span and carefully streamlined body.

> 1934 Herbert Read: 'Streamlined' is popularly, if inaccurately, used as a term of approval for the design of any object in daily use.

studio *n* (1911) a room in which films are shot. The usage evolved from the earlier sense, 'a room in which a photographer works' (1881).

> 1911 C. N. Bennett: Covered-in studios provided with expansive glass roofs for daylight work . . . are hardly among the first flights of commercial Kinematographic enterprise.

sub *n* (1917) a colloquial abbreviation of *submarine* (1899).

> 1917 J. M. Grider: We were supposed to look out for gulls which they say usually follow in the wake of a sub.

summer time *n* (1916) a standard time (in advance of ordinary time) adopted in some countries during the summer months. The English term arose from the introduction of such a standard in the British Isles in 1916, and was enshrined in the Summer Time Act. The period affected was from 21 May to 30 September. It was also known as *British Summer Time* (first recorded in 1930).

> 1916 *Times*: Of the changes which have already proved themselves to be changes for the better, that which immediately affects the greatest number of people is the introduction of 'summer time'.

tabloid *n* (1918) a popular newspaper which presents its news and features in a concentrated, easily assimilable, and often sensational form, especially one with smaller pages than those of a regular newspaper. This is a noun use of a word which had first appeared with journalistic connotations in the expression *tabloid journalism* (1901). As the quotes below make clear, the credit for the *tabloid* goes to Lord Northcliffe (Alfred Harmsworth), founder of the *Daily Mail* and of the modern concept of popular journalism.

> 1918 W. E. Carson: Since 1908 Alfred Harmsworth, like his famous 'tabloid', has disappeared from view.

> 1926 *Encyclopedia Britannica*: The introduction of tabloids may be explained . . . by the passing remark of Lord Northcliffe, 'If some American does not start one I shall have to come over to do it.'

talkie *n* (1913) a picture with audible dialogue (as opposed to a silent film). Formed from *talking picture*, on the model of **movie (1912)**, it was most often used in the phrase *the talkies*. The term preceded the commercial introduction of such films by about fifteen years, and went out of active use towards the end of the 1930s, once the novelty of such things had worn off. Nowadays it is applied only to early sound films.

> 1913 *Writer's Bulletin*: The silent 'Movies', so popular to-day, will become tame in comparison with the 'Talkies'.

> 1921 *Daily Colonist* (Victoria, British Columbia): All have seen the movies, now people are to have the opportunity of seeing and hearing the 'Talkies' . . . The author . . . of the remarkable speaking photoplay, 'Shell Shocked' is in the city.

tank *n* (1916) an armoured military vehicle moving on a tracked carriage and mounted with a gun, designed for use in rough terrain. The word was originally officially adopted in December 1915 as a secret code name for use during development work. It was supposedly chosen because the vehicle was thought to look like a benzene tank. Tanks were first put into commission on the Western Front on 15 September 1916.

> 1916 *Times*: 'Tanks' is what these new machines are generally called, and the name has the evident official advantage of being quite undescriptive.

tear gas *n* (1917) a tear-causing gas used in warfare and crowd-control.

> 1917 Wilfred Owen: It was only tear-gas from a shell, and I got safely back (to the party) in my helmet.

Technicolor *n* (1917) a proprietary name (originally registered in the US in 1917) for various processes of colour cinematography, especially ones employing dye transfer and separation negatives. The *Techni-* element of the term is supposedly a tribute to the Massachusetts Institute of Technology, the alma mater of Technicolor pioneer Herbert T. Kalmus. It is often spelled *Technicolour* in British English, despite its trademark status.

> 1930 *Punch*: Show of Shows at the Tivoli, the latest and greatest of technicolour talkie reviews.

traffic jam *n* (1917) (a stoppage caused by) a condition in which road traffic cannot proceed freely and comes to a standstill. The term is American in origin. (A previous near-synonym was *traffic block* (1896), which survived well into the 20th century: 'Soon they were embedded in a traffic block in the Strand,' Evelyn Waugh, *Vile Bodies* (1930).)

1926 *Sunset*: Traffic jams: how Western cities are trying to reduce congestion on down-town streets.

unconscious *n* (1912) that part of the psyche not subject to direct conscious observation but inferable from its effects on conscious behaviour. In his psychoanalytic theory, Freud applied the term specifically to processes activated by desires, fears, or memories which are unacceptable to the conscious mind and so repressed.

1912 Sigmund Freud: The term *unconscious*, which was used in the purely descriptive sense before, now comes to imply something more. It designates not only latent ideas in general, but especially ideas with a certain dynamic character, ideas keeping apart from consciousness in spite of their intensity and activity.

undercarriage *n* (1911) the landing-gear of an aircraft. In modern usage the term generally denotes the aircraft's wheels and their struts, but originally it covered any of a range of skids, floats, etc. It is an aeronautical adaptation of a word which originally referred to the framework that supports the body of a carriage, wagon, etc.

1911 *Harper & Ferguson*: The under-carriage was formed of wheels alone.

vitamin *n* (1912) any of a range of naturally occurring substances essential for the control of the body's metabolic processes. The original form of the word was *vitamine*. It was coined by Casimir Funk from Latin *vita* 'life' and *amine* (because he thought vitamins contained amino acids). The main modern spelling *vitamin* was introduced to avoid any erroneous connection with amines (see the 1920 quote below).

1912 Casimir Funk: It is now known that all these diseases, with the exception of pellagra, can be prevented and cured by the addition of certain preventive substances; the deficient substances, which are of the nature of organic bases, we will call 'vitamines'; and we will speak of a beri-beri or scurvy vitamine, which means a substance preventing the special disease.

1920 J. C. Drummond: The criticism usually raised against Funk's word Vitamine is that the termination '-ine' is one strictly employed in chemical nomenclature to denote substances of a basic character, whereas there is no evidence which supports his original idea that these indispensable dietary constituents are amines... The suggestion is now advanced that the final '-e' be dropped, so that the resulting word *Vitamin* is acceptable under the standard scheme of nomenclature... which permits a neutral substance of undefined composition to bear a name ending in '-in'. If this suggestion is adopted, it is recommended that the somewhat cumbrous nomenclature introduced by McCollum (Fat-soluble A, Water-soluble B), be dropped, and that the substances be spoken of as Vitamin A, B, C, etc.

western *n* (1912) a film portraying life in the American West in the 19th century, usually through idealized stock situations and characters, especially cowboys and gun-fights. The adjective *western* in this sense is first recorded a couple of years earlier ('It is almost impossible to criticize these Wild Western films, because cowboys are likely to do almost anything', *Moving Picture World* (1910)).

1912 *Moving Picture World* (advert): 'The Fight at The Mill'... A powerful Western, distinctly unusual among typical 'Westerns' containing a beautiful story and a dashing Indian battle that will interest and instruct.

white collar *adj, n* (1919) (wearing) the white collar regarded as characteristic of someone who does non-manual work. The term originated in the US. (The manual worker's blue overalls were later to inspire the companion term *blue-collar* (1950).)

1919 Upton Sinclair: It is a fact with which every union workingman is familiar, that his most bitter despisers are the petty underlings of the business world, the poor office-clerks... who, because they are allowed to wear a white collar..., regard themselves as members of the capitalist class.

1921 *Ladies' Home Journal*: Urban chain restaurants have accustomed white-collar boys and girls to tasty viands, albeit in limited amounts.

woman's magazine *n* (1912) a magazine devoted to women's interests. The alternative form *women's magazine* is first recorded in 1920, and has gradually become the preferred variant.

1912 *Magazine Maker* (title): Making a woman's magazine.

1920 P. G. Wodehouse: Heaven knows what a women's magazine wants with my sort of stuff, but they are giving me fifteen thousand of the best for it.

X chromosome, Y chromosome *n* (1911) the two types of sex chromosome, one of which (X) is associated with femaleness and the other (Y) with maleness. The symbol *X* had first been applied to this chromosome (in German) by Hermann Henking in 1891, in the *Zeitschrift für wissenschaftliche Zoologie.* The earliest example of its use in English is in a paper by T. H. Montgomery in the *Transactions of the American Philosophical Society* in 1902: 'One of these three [chromosomes of *Protenor belfragei*], that designated *x* in Figs. 119–123, imposes by its relatively very large volume... We shall call this the "chromosome x".' The parallel use of *Y* is first recorded in a paper by E. B. Wilson in *Science* in 1909: 'The X-element... appears as a "large idiochromosome" which has a synaptic mate... The latter chromosome, or its homologue, I shall designate as the "Y-element".' But the actual formulations *X chromosome* and *Y chromosome* are not found before 1911.

1911 *Biological Bulletin*: We have associated the X and Y chromosomes of the male with sex-determination, but possibly they have some other meaning.

THE 1920S

The twenties, if the old cliché is to be believed, roared (the expression *roaring twenties* is not actually recorded until 1930: 'The giants of the roaring 'twenties ought to be able to achieve glory of some sort in half as many years', *Saturday Review*). After the horrors and traumas of the Great War, the world was hungry for gaiety. A generation of youth had been 'lost', and those who stepped into its shoes were determined to enjoy themselves. So for the leisured and the moneyed this was the decade of the *flapper* and the *bright young thing* and the *hearty*, and also of the *good time girl* and the *gold-digger.* They danced their flippant dances—the *black bottom*, the *Charleston*, the *camel walk*, the *heebie-jeebie*, the *shimmy* (1918)—with fierce determination. They visited the *flicks* (the cinema), and went to *cocktail bars*, where they drank *delish* 'delicious' *gimlets* and *sidecars* (types of cocktail). All too too *sickmaking* (1930) if you didn't have the *lettuce* 'cash'.

The trivialities of personal appearance could once more be paid serious attention: the 20s saw the first *beauticians* and *beauty salons*, and also the first *beauty queens* and *bathing beauties*; and *face-lifting* was now possible. The hair could be *shingled* or *bingled* (varieties of short style for women), or disciplined into a severe *Eton crop*; and (fittingly) more permanently, the *perm* put in its first appearance. *Oxford bags* and *plus-fours* proved to be a passing fad, but *Levi's* survived the century, as did the *sweatshirt* and the *T-shirt.* Women for the first time wore *scanties* and *teddies* (types of undergarment), and *girdles* and suchlike *foundation garments* presaged the demise of 19th-century whalebone and laces. But perhaps the greatest sartorial advance of the 1920s was the *zipper* (or, as the British called it, the *zip*), which so neatly encapsulates the 20th century: instead of wasting five or six precious seconds of your life laboriously buttoning or unbuttoning your fly, you can do it in one with the zip (whose very name promises efficient speed).

On the subject of unbuttoning, in the 1920s people were beginning to find it easier to talk about sex. *Sex* itself as a term for sexual intercourse dates from then, as do *sexy, sex appeal, sexpert*, and sexationalism. The words *heterosexual* and *lesbian* are first recorded as nouns in the 20s (but homophobia was still the orthodoxy: *fag, pansy*, and *queer* are 20s words too). In the cinemas, girls could swoon over the *sheik* (played by Rudolph Valentino, the first truly mass-appeal idol), while round the corner in the burlesque theatre, men were getting their first eyeful of *stripping*.

All this in the world of the haves. But what of the have-nots? As the world turned to peaceful pursuits after the conflagration of 1914–18 (*demob* and *deration* are both words of the 20s), survivors came home with hopes for a better society and jobs for all. But *recession*, *redundant*, and *deflation* are 20s words too. For the many, there was not harmony and plenty, but want. It was the era, too, that saw the beginning of *organized crime*, and of *racketeering*.

On the international scene, the consequences of the war started to fester. In the 20s, the world first heard of *Fascism*, *National Socialists*, *blackshirts*, *goose-steppers*, *putsches*, and the *Duce*. The terms *totalitarian* and *liquidate* came ominously on the scene, as did *bacteriological warfare* and *chemical weapon*. Against all this, new concepts such as *peaceful coexistence* (a Soviet invention), *non-violence*, and *security* can have inspired little confidence in the future.

Science and technology still offered a way forward, however, and the 1920s saw additions to the lexicon such as *proton* and *photon*, *insulin*, *oestrogen*, and *penicillin*, *Geiger counter* and *cosmic rays*. The last perhaps smacks more of *science fiction* than of science fact, and the 20s was a fruitful period for the crystal-ball school of word-creation, particularly in the area of space-travel. Among its contributions to the future were *astronaut*, *colour television*, *rocket ship*, and *spacesuit*. But perhaps the most famous coinage of this sort was *robot*, originally a Czech word, which came to be seen as the vehicle by which 20th-century humanity would realize its aspiration to leave behind the mundane physical tasks of everyday life and devote itself to leisure and contemplation.

For in many ways the 20s were the first decade of the modern age. Many aspects of the 19th century survived into the first fifteen years of the new century, but World War I blew a lot of them away. Many of the key features of later 20th-century life, along with their terminology, began to be put in place during the 20s. Take transport. On the roads, the products of the automakers' tireless assembly lines were becoming widely available, and a whole new vocabulary of mass car culture was called into being: A *road* and *by-pass*, *hit-and-run* and *hitch-hike*, *ring road* and *roundabout*, *road sense* and *road safety*, *speed cop*, *traffic lights*, and *white lines*, *car parks* and *petrol stations* (or, in the US, *parking lots*, *filling stations*, and *gas stations* (1932)). If you could not afford a car of your own, you could take a *trolleybus* or a *chara* (a coach). *Airgirls* like Amy Johnson and Amelia Earheart were pioneering new airline routes, and *air terminals* were being constructed for the comfort of passengers.

The technology of radio transmission had developed to a stage at which, early in the decade, public broadcasting could begin. A whole new lexicon had to evolve in a very short period to accommodate it, and *listeners-in* soon became familiar with terms like *crystal set* and *valve set*, *news bulletin* and *news reader, outside broadcast* and *on the air, commentary* and *commentate*, and even such basic items as *broadcast* and *programme*. Although the word *television* dates from the first decade of the century, the 20s saw the first practical demonstration of television, and the words *televise* and *look in* were born (as also, less successfully, were *televisor* 'television', and *watch in*). In the cinema, the films began to talk in earnest. The development had already been anticipated in the term *talkie* (1913), but again the actuality entailed a mushroom growth of new vocabulary (*soundtrack, phonofilm, Movietone, Vitaphone*).

Nearly every decade has its fads and crazes that give it a certain quirky individuality. In the 1920s, people suddenly went mad for the *pogo stick*. *Pelmanism* (a system of memory training, and a card game based on it) was all the rage; and in genteel drawing rooms where previously bridge had been the rule, they could not get enough of *mah-jongg* (a Chinese game played with small tiles rather than cards). Could these be the same people who now embraced the German passion for going around with no clothes on? Certainly English found room for two words for this (*naturist* and *nudism*) in the 20s.

This post-war decade saw the coming of age of the blend—a type of word which is formed by merging two existing words together. Some still familiar ones had emerged before 1900 (*brunch*, for instance, a blend of *breakfast* and *lunch*), but it was the 1920s that really started taking a liking to them. Perhaps the best-known of all dates from then—*motel*. *Chunnel* was coined long before the Channel tunnel itself was constructed (after which its rate of usage seems to have nosedived), and *mirthquake* and *sexationalism* have belied their apparent ephemerality. Such items are meat and drink to journalists and headline writers, and if you can combine them with (more or less) cuddly animals, you have neologisms to die for—hence the extensive press coverage given to *swooses* (a swan crossed with a goose), *tigons* (the offspring of a tiger and a lion), and (later) *ligers* (1938).

abominable snowman *n* (1921) a creature alleged to exist in the Himalayas, but sighted more regularly in the pages of the English-speaking press during the rest of the century. The name is a literal translation of the Tibetan term (see the quote below). In the 1930s the alternative *yeti* (from Tibetan *yeh-teh*, literally 'little manlike animal') arrived in English.

> 1921 *Times*: The men were never seen... but footprints were found which were suspected of being those made by these men, who are apparently known to the Tibetans as *Meetoh Kangmi*, or 'Abominable Snowmen', and small colonies of these people are believed to exist on the slopes of Everest, Chumalhari, and Karola.

absenteeism *n* (1922) the persistent absence of employees from their place of work or of pupils from school. The word originated in the early 19th century, denoting landlords who lived far away from their estates.

> 1941 *Punch*: Committee on National Production... we shall do our best to decrease absenteeism during the coming winter.

aerosol *n* (1923) a system of colloidal particles dispersed in the air or in a gas. The term was coined from *aero-* + *solution*. The meaning '(the substance in) a dispenser packed under pressure', more familiar to laypeople, is not recorded before the 1940s.

> 1923 Robert Whytlaw-Gray: Aerosol is a convenient term to denote a system of particles of ultra-microscopic size dispersed in a gas, suggested to us by Prof. Donnan.

air *n* (1927) the air considered as a medium for the transmission of radio waves. It was used mainly in the expressions *on the air* and *off the air* (later *on air* and *off air*) 'being/not being broadcast' and *over the air*.

> 1928 *Daily Express*: They will speak into the microphone as usual, but before being put 'on the air' their voice modulations will be turned upside down.

astronaut *n* (1929) a traveller in space. Coined when the concept was mere ambition, it survived to become the accepted term when such people actually existed. The adjective *astronautical* is first recorded in the same year. Compare **cosmonaut (1959), spaceman (1942)**.

> 1929 *Journal of the British Astronomical Association*: That first obstacle encountered by the would-be 'Astronaut', viz., terrestrial gravitation... Prof. Oberth... has just been awarded the £80 prize offered for the most successful solution of the 'astronautical' question.

> 1957 Patrick Moore: The astronauts taking off for the planet Hesikos remain standing upright.

> 1961 *Times*: President Kennedy spoke to Commander Alan Shepard by radiotelephone a few minutes after the astronaut was delivered by helicopter to the deck of the aircraft carrier Lake Champlain.

atonal *adj* (1922) applied to a style of musical composition in which there is no conscious reference to any scale or tonic—an important feature of 20th-century avant-garde serious music. The related noun *atonality* is also first recorded in 1922.

> 1922 A. E. Hull: I have been working for two years at a system of non-tonal harmony, which I had long been unable to christen. Now, after visiting no less than seven foreign countries I not only find that the thing is widely known as Atonality, but [etc.]... Keyboard chord-writing as well as linear, tonal as well as Atonal.

bacteriological warfare *n* (1924) the use, as a means of war, of bacteria to spread disease in the enemy. A later and less specific term was *biological warfare* (1946). The practice also came to be known more colloquially *germ warfare* (1938).

bathing beauty *n* (1920) an attractive young woman in a bathing suit, especially one taking part in a beauty contest. An alternative term was *bathing belle*. By the 1960s both were sounding distinctly passé.

> 1955 *Times*: Tell the miners what Yarmouth has to offer—Tommy Trinder, Charlie Chester, Ronnie Ronalde, 'hot-dogs', bathing beauties, and all.

beautician *n* (1924) someone who runs a beauty salon; a beauty specialist. The term originated in the US.

> 1926 *Glasgow Herald*: The immense growth of 'beauty parlors' in the United States has added to the American language the word 'beautician'.

beauty queen *n* (1922) the winner of a beauty contest. The term originated in the US (*beauty contest*, incidentally, is first recorded in 1899).

> 1922 *New York Times*: The winning beauty will be heralded as America's 'Beauty Queen'.

beauty salon *n* (1922) an establishment where cosmetic and other treatments are given to improve personal beauty. The term was coined in the US as a slightly more upmarket name for what was originally called a **beauty shop (1901)**.

> 1922 *American Hairdresser*: A. Simonson on September 5 opened new beauty salons at 54 West 57th street.

blackshirt *n* (1922) a member of the *Fasci di Combattimento*, paramilitary units founded by Mussolini in 1919 and forming the backbone of the Fascist party of Italy. They were named after the black shirts (in Italian *camicia nera*) they wore. In the 1930s the term was also applied to British Fascists.

> 1934 H. G. Wells: It was a gathering of Mosley's black-shirts.

> 1934 *Daily Mail* (headline): Hurrah for the Blackshirts.

broadcast *v* (1921) to transmit by radio or television. The verb originally denoted scattering seed by hand, so the underlying idea is of disseminating widely. The corresponding noun, and the derivative *broadcaster*, are first recorded in 1922. All were in place for the imminent start of public broadcasting.

> 1921 *Discovery*: The [wireless] station at Poldhu is used partly for broadcasting Press and other messages to ships, that is, sending out messages without receiving replies.

> 1922 *Daily Mail*: The Prince of Wales ... made a great hit as a 'broadcaster' ... when he delivered a message by wireless to the Boy Scouts.

business lunch *n* (1926) a midday meal at which business deals are discussed or done. American in origin, they became a key feature of 20th-century commercial life (although proverbially they consist more of lunch than of business).

by-pass *n* (1922) a road built around a town, congested area, etc. so as to relieve traffic.

> 1922 *Daily Mail*: New roads and by-passes, which should remove some of these danger spots.

car park *n* (1926) an open space, a building, etc. for the parking of motor vehicles. A slightly earlier American term was *parking lot* (1924).

> 1926 *Daily Mail*: Glastonbury Car Park. Indignation has been aroused ... by a proposal ... to purchase part of the land ... as an extra parking space for motor cars.

cat *n* (1920) a fellow, guy; also, in later use, a person of either sex. The term originated in African-American slang; it was later strongly reinforced by **cat** 'jazz enthusiast' **(1931)**.

> 1959 Alston Anderson: 'At-dam, man, youre the selfishest kat I seen yet.

cocktail party *n* (1928) a drinks party, usually in the early evening. Concoctions called 'cocktails' had been drunk in the US since at least the early 19th century, but it was not until the mid 1920s that the modern cocktail, with its whole associated culture of parties and bars and its veneer of sharp modern sophistication, impinged significantly on the rest of the Western world. (The novelist Alec Waugh claimed that he invented the cocktail party by serving a rum swizzle to astonished friends who thought they had come for tea at his flat in the spring of 1924.) The cocktail names *Gibson* (1930), *gimlet* (1928), and *sidecar* (1928) date from around this time.

> 1928 D. H. Lawrence: She almost wished she had ... made her life one long cocktail party and jazz evening.

cold turkey *n* (1921) a method of treating drug addicts by sudden and complete withdrawal of the drug, instead of by a gradual process. The term is first recorded in North America, and presumably came from the earlier adverbial usage 'suddenly, without preparation or warning' ('I'd lost five thousand dollars... "cold turkey"', Robert Service (1910)), but the origins of that are unknown.

> 1921 *Daily Colonist* (Victoria, British Columbia): Perhaps the most pitiful figures who have appeared before Dr. Carleton Simon... are those who voluntarily surrender themselves. When they go before him, [drug addicts] are given what is called the 'cold turkey' treatment.

collective farm *n* (1925) a farm, especially in the USSR, consisting of the holdings of several farmers, run by a group of people in cooperation, usually under state control. The term was slightly preceded into English by *collective farming*, in a translation of a text by Lenin: 'The local and central Soviet authority aims... to foster collective farming' (1919).

> 1958 *New Statesman*: From a visit to two collective farms... he concludes that Israeli Left-wingers are doctrinaire and spartan.

colour television *n* (1929) television in which the pictures are transmitted and displayed in colour rather than black and white. John Logie Baird gave a demonstration of colour television in London in 1928, but it was not until 1953 that the first successful system was adopted for broadcasting, in the US.

columnist *n* (1920) someone who writes a newspaper column. This particular application of *column* to a regular newspaper article by a particular writer (in which sense it was, to begin with, often facetiously spelled *colyum*) seems to have emerged in the US around the turn of the century: 'The most important development on America's editorial pages during the past quarter of a century has been the evolution of the "colyum",' H. W. Davis (1926).

> 1926 *Spectator*: One of the best known 'columnists' of the American press.

combine harvester, combine *n* (1926) a harvesting machine that cuts, threshes, and cleans grain. The term originated in the US. The machine was probably the biggest single technological development in arable farming in the 20th century, which transformed much of the British landscape from a pattern of small medieval fields into a mini-prairie. *Combined* had been used in the designations of multi-purpose agricultural machines since the middle of the 19th century ('In the afternoon the combined mower and the Illinois mower were put upon trial, in a beautiful field of timothy', *Illinois State Register* (1857)), and the variant *combined harvester* is also on record.

> 1926 Kansas City Star: Hundreds of combines will be in the fields in southern, central, and western Kansas by Wednesday.

commentary *n* (1927) a description of some public event broadcast or televised as it happens. Originally the term was always used in the expression *running commentary*, to distinguish it from comment on previous happenings. The derivative *commentator* is first recorded in 1928.

> 1929 *B.B.C. Year-Book 1930*: Tennis... provides excellent material for a running commentary, although the commentators find the strain of following the strokes... with an instantaneous spoken description very great.

conservation *n* (1922) the preservation of the environment, and especially of natural resources. To begin with, it was an ecologists' term; it did not start to become a buzzword until the late 1950s. *Conservationist* is first recorded in the same year.

> 1922 *Encyclopedia Britannica*: A very important by-product of the conservation-movement was the development at Washington of a mania for the establishment of reservations in Alaska... The most ardent of the conservationists failed to recognize the urgent importance of conserving the salmon and halibut fisheries.
>
> 1958 *New Biology*: Conservation as a world problem.

cosmetic *adj* (1926) of surgery: improving or modifying the appearance. The term *plastic surgery* is first recorded in 1839.

> 1926 *Encyclopedia Britannica*: Cosmetic and plastic surgery, especially of the face, has undergone considerable improvement following our large experience in the war.

cosmic rays *n* (1925) high-energy radiations from outer space with great penetrative power which reach the surface of the earth. They were discovered by the American physicist R. A. Millikan.

> 1925 R. A. Millikan: Our experiments brought to light . . . a cosmic radiation of . . . extraordinary penetrating power . . . We obtained good evidence that these cosmic rays shoot through space in all directions.

crisp *n* (1929) a thin sliver of potato fried until crisp and eaten cold. As a commercial product they achieved great popularity in the 1930s, particularly, in Britain, the Smith's brand, sold in paper packets with a little blue-paper twist of salt inside. Initially they were usually called in full *potato crisps*, but by the second half of the century the abbreviated form was the norm. Neither term is very familiar in the US, where these delicacies are usually called *potato chips*.

> 1950 T. S. Eliot: Potato crisps? No I can't endure them.

deadline *n* (1920) a time by which material has to be ready for inclusion in a particular issue of a publication. The usage, originally US, appears to have come from the earlier printers' sense 'a guide-line marked on the bed of a printing-press', which in turn was based on the US military sense 'a line drawn round a military prison, beyond which a prisoner is liable to be shot down', which dates from the mid 19th century.

> 1920 *Chicago Herald & Examiner*: Corinne Griffith . . . is working on 'Deadline at Eleven', the newspaper play.

demob *v* (1920) a colloquial abbreviation of *demobilize* (1882)—i.e., 'to release from military service'. It was an 'end-of-the-war' word. The parallel noun, short for *demobilization*, seems not to have come into widespread use until the conclusion of World War II (see **demob (1934)**).

> 1920 *Glasgow Herald*: Some young soldiers . . . who had been recently demobbed.

equal opportunity *n* (1925) equal chance and right to seek success in one's chosen sphere regardless of social factors such as class, wealth, race, religion, and sex. As a general phrase, or slogan, this has probably always taken second place to the synonymous *equality of opportunity*, first recorded in 1891 ('It will possibly, however, be contended that here the ideal is equality of Opportunity', *Economic Review*), but it has acquired a niche for itself in adjectival use since the 1960s in the specific context of anti-discriminatory legislation, especially in the area of employment.

> 1925 D. H. Lawrence: They talk about 'equal opportunity': but it is bunk, ridiculous bunk. It is the old fable of the fox asking the stork to dinner.
>
> 1963 *New York Times*: Mr. Screvane proposed to the Board of Estimate that $3,400,000,000 in city pension funds be invested only in securities of equal-opportunity employers.

establishment *n* (1923) a social group exercising power generally, or within a given field or institution, by virtue of its traditional superiority, and by the use especially of tacit understandings and often a common mode of speech, and having as a general interest the maintenance of the status quo. The English journalist Henry Fairlie, in the *Spectator* article quoted below, is generally credited with bringing the term into wide currency, although, as the other quotations show, it had been around for some time before 1955, and the historian A. J. P. Taylor used it in exactly Fairlie's sense in a *New Statesman* article in 1953.

> 1923 Rose Macaulay: The moderns of one day become the safe establishments of the next.

> 1945 Douglas Goldring: It was a head-on collision between two acknowledged leaders of the literary avant-garde and the powerful forces of what Ford Madox Ford used to call the Establishment.

> 1955 Henry Fairlie: By the 'Establishment' I do not mean only the centres of official power—though they are certainly part of it—but rather the whole matrix of official and social relations within which power is exercised.

estrogen *n* (1927) see **oestrogen (1927)**.

face-lifting *n* (1922) cosmetic plastic surgery to improve the appearance of facial skin. Early terminology was in a state of flux, as the quote below shows; the long-term winner, *face-lift*, is not recorded until 1934.

> 1922 Florence Courtenay: The 'face-raising' or 'face-lifting' process which does away with wrinkles, mouth and eyelines and sagging cheeks by literally 'lifting' off part of the old face and replacing it.

> 1934 Rose Macaulay: What I needed . . . was a face-lift . . . I should have a new, young, tight face.

Fascism *n* (1922) the principles and organization of a body of Italian nationalists, which was organized in 1919 to oppose Communism in Italy, and, as the *partito nazionale fascista*, under the leadership of Benito Mussolini (1883–1945), controlled that country from 1922 to 1943. The term first appeared in English texts in 1921 in the original Italian form *fascismo*, but the anglicized version dates from 1922, as does *Fascist*, which itself had been used in English in the Italian plural form *fascisti* in 1921. The word is based on Italian *fascio* 'bundle, group' (the Fascists used the ancient Roman 'fasces', a magistrates' emblem of authority consisting of a bundle of rods bound round an axe, as their symbol). The term was being applied to a similar right-wing movement in Germany as early as 1923.

> 1922 *Daily Mail*: Signor Mussolini, the Fascist leader, to-day made his first speech in the Chamber.

> 1923 *Contemporary Review*: Fascism in Germany will never be more than one of several factors.

fat cat *n* (1928) an inordinately wealthy person. In original US slang use the term was applied specifically to a rich backer of a political party, but since then it has broadened out into a general term of opprobrium for people who have more money than others think they should and have acquired it without hard work.

> 1928 F. R. Kent: These capitalists have what the organization needs—money to finance the campaign. Such men are known in political circles as 'Fat Cats'.

> 1998 *Private Eye*: It's hard to see how his campaign to charge British Library readers fees, while giving fat cat bosses handouts, fits with Demos' concern for 'information have-nots'.

flapper *n* (1921) a pleasure-seeking young woman who flouted the conventions of the time, and was looked upon by those who disapproved of such things as flighty and indecorous. The antecedents of the word are not easy to disentangle. In the foregoing sense it is one of the defining words of the 'Roaring Twenties', but this may well be a compound of two separate sources. From the 1880s onward a *flapper* was both a 'prostitute' (there may be some connection with Northumberland and Durham dialect *flap* 'flighty young woman') and a 'teenage girl' (apparently so called because her hair had not yet been 'put up', and so it still 'flapped' around—either unrestrained or in a pigtail). There are strong traces of these uses (particularly the latter) in *flapper* (and derivatives like *flapperish* and *flapperdom*) during the 1920s, and it is not always clear whether the previous or the newer meaning is intended. The introduction of full female suffrage in Britain in 1928 gave rise to the so-called 'flapper vote' (previously only women of 30 and above could vote).

foreplay *n* (1929) sexual stimulation that precedes intercourse. It became a key term in the clinical vocabulary of 20th-century sexology.

> 1953 Alfred Kinsey: Many persons . . . feel that the intensity of the ultimate orgasm is heightened by extended foreplay.

fridge, frig *n* (1926) a colloquial abbreviation of *refrigerator*, probably at least partly modelled on the trade name *Frigidaire*. The earlier spelling was *frig* (or *'frig*), and this survived well into the second half of the century.

> 1926 E. F. Spanner: Best part of our stuff here is chilled, and with no 'frig plant working, the mercury will climb like a rocket.
>
> 1935 C. Brooks: Do you mean that you keep a dead body in a fridge waiting for the right moment to bring her out?
>
> 1939 Monica Dickens: Your frig is out of order and the trifle hasn't got cold.

friendly *adj* (1925) belonging to or allied with one's own armed forces. The usage was originally a World War I expression, applied for example to shells fired by one's own artillery as they whizzed over the trenches on their way to the enemy's lines. Later it became associated particularly with the phrase *friendly fire*, used in the Vietnam War and the Gulf War as a euphemism for bombardments which hit one's own troops or installations.

> 1941 *Civil Engineering* (US): The range of friendly bombing aircraft permits assembly of tactical operating units.
>
> 1991 *Independent*: Since the war began, more American troops are thought to have been killed by 'friendly fire' than by the Iraqis, most by air-launched missiles.

fuck off *v* (1929) to go away. *Fuck* in its literal sense has been around since at least the 13th century, but written references to its various extended uses are extremely thin on the ground before the end of the 19th century. No doubt *fuck* as an expletive, *fucking* as an intensifier, *fuck off*, and so on had been in widespread use for a long time, but they existed under a taboo which denied them access to print. Post-World War I writers such as James Joyce, Henry Miller, and (as in the quote below) Frederic Manning broke the taboo, but only at the cost, initially, of having their work banned. It was not until 1965 that *fuck* and its companion 'four-letter word' *cunt* found their way into a mainstream English dictionary—the *Penguin English Dictionary*. See also **four-letter word (1934)**.

> 1929 Frederic Manning [the time-frame is World War I]: As soon as a bit o' shrapnel comes their way, [they] fuck off 'ome jildy, toot sweet.

fundamentalism *n* (1923) a religious movement, which originally became active among various Protestant bodies in the US after World War I, based on strict adherence to certain tenets (e.g. the literal truth of Scripture) held to be fundamental to the Christian faith. The corresponding noun *fundamentalist* is first recorded in 1922. The application of the term to other religions (e.g. Islam) is first recorded in the 1950s.

> 1923 *Daily Mail*: Mr. William Jennings Bryan... has been exerting the full force of his great eloquence in a campaign on behalf of what is termed 'Fundamentalism'.
>
> 1981 *Observer*: The new, or rather very old, Islam, the dangerous fundamentalism revived by the ayatollahs and their admirers.

goose-stepper *n* (1923) someone who does the goose-step. The expression is often used with the implication of a zombie-like soldier serving a tyrannical dictatorship. The term *goose-step*, denoting a ceremonial march performed without bending the knees, dates from the early 19th century, but in the 20th century it became particularly associated with militaristic German regimes ('Doing the Prussianist goose-step by way of pas de triomphe', C. E. Montague (1922)).

> 1923 H. L. Mencken: The first made them almost incapable of soldierly thought and conduct; the second converted them into cringing goose-steppers.

greenhouse effect *n* (1929) the phenomenon whereby the surface and the lower atmosphere of a planet are maintained at a relatively high temperature owing to the greater transparency of the atmosphere to visible radiation from the sun than to infra-red radiation from the planet (in other words, the atmosphere traps heat). Although the term was coined in the 1920s, the phenomenon did not begin to give public concern until the 1980s, when the resultant warming of the atmosphere was seen as posing a long-term threat to the environment.

> 1929 W. J. Humphreys: Their joint effect on earth radiation is far greater, so much so, indeed, that they produce a very marked greenhouse effect.

> 1989 *Which?*: The destruction of the tropical rain-forest is also contributing to the greenhouse effect, since forests help to regulate the amount of carbon dioxide in the atmosphere.

guinea-pig *n* (1920) a person or thing used like a guinea-pig as the subject of an experiment.

> 1923 H. G. Wells: And may I ask . . . the nature of this treatment of yours, these experiments of which we are to be the—guinea pigs, so to speak? Is it to be anything in the nature of a vaccination?

health farm *n* (1927) a residential centre to which people go to improve their health or fitness (e.g. by exercise or dieting). The term, which originated in the US, is early evidence of the Western middle classes' increasing obsession with their bodies as the century progressed.

> 1927 Ernest Hemingway: Jack started training at Danny Hogan's health farm over in Jersey.

heterosexual *n* (1920) a heterosexual person. It is a noun use of the adjective *heterosexual*, which dates from the early 1890s. This early example is in a translation of a text of Sigmund Freud's, and it did not come into widespread use until the 1960s.

> 1920 Joan Riviere: To convert a fully developed homosexual into a heterosexual.

hijack *v* (1923) originally a Prohibition-era slang term, denoting the theft of contraband in transit, or robbing a bootlegger of his illicit goods. The main modern connotation, of commandeering a vehicle, and especially an aircraft, in transit, did not develop until the 1960s. The word is perhaps a back-formation from *hijacker* (also first recorded in 1923), which may have been coined from *highway* + *jacker* 'one who holds up'. See also **skyjack (1961)**.

> 1925 *Times*: A shooting affray between bootleggers and 'hijackers' (men who prey on bootleggers) took place . . . in a lodging-house on the west side of New York.

hitch-hike *v* (1923) to travel by means of lifts in vehicles. The verb originated in the US. By 1927 it had been joined by the nouns *hitch-hike* and *hitch-hiker*.

> 1927 *Glasgow Herald*: There are apparently hitchhikers in the United States who boast they can travel 500 miles free of charge without walking more than 10.

holism *n* (1926) a term coined from Greek *holos* 'whole' by the South African soldier and statesman Jan Smuts (1870–1950) to designate the tendency in nature to produce wholes (i.e. bodies or organisms) from the ordered grouping of unit structures. With it came the adjective *holistic*, which became something of a buzzword in the latter part of the century (especially in the expression *holistic medicine* (1960), denoting an approach to medical treatment that seeks to deal with the whole person).

> 1926 J. C. Smuts: The whole-making, holistic tendency, or Holism, operating in and through particular wholes, is seen at all stages of existence.

Hollywood *n* (1926) the world of American film-making, as typified by Hollywood, an area near Los Angeles in California, the chief production centre of the US cinema industry. The 1920s also saw the first of a range of Hollywood derivatives, such as *Hollywoodesque* and *Hollywoodish*.

> 1927 *Daily Express*: The cottage is so picturesque and Hollywoodesque that . . . it is more like a 'set' than a real house.

> 1929 Edgar Wallace: A high-class school at Brighton, where girls are taught to . . . use lipstick and adore the heroes of Hollywood.

Hoover *n, v* (1926) (to clean with) a vacuum cleaner, originally one of a type with the proprietary name 'Hoover' (registered in 1927). The US Hoover company, named after its founder W. H. Hoover (1849–1932), began manufacturing vacuum cleaners in the first decade of the 20th century. As a generic term, *Hoover* is almost exclusively British.

> 1926 *Army & Navy Stores Catalogue*: A Hoovered room . . . is . . . free from dust.

> 1934 *Punch*: Her bodywork's smart and strikes the eye. Clean-swept as though with a Hoover.

ice cube *n* (1929) a small artificially made piece of ice, used especially for cooling drinks. It became one of the cornerstones of 20th-century American/Western civilization.

> 1929 Max Lief: She dashed into the kitchen and came back with a bowl of ice-cubes and some more bottles.

id *n* (1924) the part of the psyche associated with instinctive impulses and demands for immediate satisfaction. The term is a use of Latin *id* 'it', as a rendering of German *es* 'it', that was adopted by Sigmund Freud (*Das Ich und das Es* 'The I and the It' (1923)) following its use in a similar sense by Georg Groddeck (*Das Buch vom Es* 'The Book of the It' (1923)). In the quote below, Freud's first English translator explains how the appropriate English equivalent was decided on.

> 1924 Joan Riviere: The essay . . . describes the various allegiances the ego owes, its mediate position between the outer world and the id, and its struggles to serve all its masters at one and the same time. [Translator's note.] To translate the German 'es', which means 'it' and thus implies the impersonality of the mind apart from its ego, the Latin 'id' has been selected . . . Keep in mind this dissection of the mental apparatus that I have proposed, namely, into ego, super-ego and id.

inferiority complex *n* (1922) a neurotic condition resulting from a persistent unrealistic sense of inadequacy, often compensated for by aggressive behaviour.

> 1924 Compton Mackenzie: I could psycho-analyse all Bloomsbury now. They all suffer from an inferiority complex. Either they feel themselves intellectually inferior to Newton or physically inferior to Sandow or morally inferior to Christ.

infrastructure *n* (1927) all the elements that together make up the basic supporting structure of an undertaking. The term was borrowed from French, where it is first recorded in 1875. As the second quote below shows, by the middle of the century it had already acquired its bad reputation as a jargon word.

> 1927 *Chambers's Journal*: The tunnels, bridges, culverts, and 'infrastructure' work generally of the Ax to Bourg-Madame line have been completed.

> 1950 Winston Churchill: In this Debate we have had the usual jargon about 'the infrastructure of a supra-national authority'.

insulin *n* (1922) a hormone produced in the islets of Langerhans (in the pancreas) which controls blood glucose levels. The word originated in French. Based on Latin *insula* 'island' (from its place of secretion), it was coined in 1909 by Jean de Meyer as *insuline.* This was introduced into English by E. A. Schäfer in 1914 (see the 1926 quote below), but it did not make much impact. It was not until the team of Canadian scientists led by Banting, Best, and Macleod, who discovered the use of the hormone for treating diabetes, reintroduced it in the anglicized form *insulin* in 1922 that it became widely known.

> 1922 F. G. Banting, C. H. Best, etc.: Purified alcoholic extracts of pancreas, for which we suggest the name insulin, when injected subcutaneously into normal rabbits cause the percentage of sugar in the blood to fall within a few hours.

> 1926 E. A. Schäfer: To this autacoid the name insulin is applied. [Note] The term was introduced by de Meyer (Arch. di fisiol., vii., 1909). In ignorance of this it was employed as a convenient term to denote the autacoid of the islet tissue in the first edition of this work, published in 1916. It was independently adopted by the Toronto workers [i.e. Banting and Best] in 1922.

intelligence quotient *n* (1921) a number arrived at by means of intelligence tests and intended to express the degree of intelligence of an individual in relation to the average for the age-group, which is fixed at 100. The term is a translation of German *Intelligenz-quotient*, which was coined in 1912 by W. L. Stern. The abbreviated form *I.Q.*, first recorded in 1922, has become much better known than the full version.

> 1921 C. L. Burt: If a child's mental age be divided by his chronological age, the quotient will state what fraction of ability the child actually possesses . . . This fraction may be termed . . . the child's 'intelligence quotient'.

> 1922 R. S. Woodworth: Brightness or dullness can also be measured by the intelligence quotient, which is employed so frequently that it is customarily abbreviated to 'I.Q.'

I.R.A. *n* (1921) the Irish Republican Army.

> 1921 George Bernard Shaw: The I.R.A. is flushed with success.

iron curtain *n* (1920) the hypothetical barrier between the Soviet bloc and the West, especially during the Cold War. It was Winston Churchill who, in his speech at Westminster College, Fulton, Missouri on 5 March 1946, effectively established the term *iron curtain* in the English language, where it was to outlast the bloc which it circumscribed. But he did not invent it. The first person on record as using it was Ethel Snowden (the wife of Philip Snowden, the British Labour politician), in a book called *Through Bolshevik Russia*, although it is unclear whether she actually coined it herself. It caught on to some extent, but more as a general term for an inviolable barrier than as a specific East-West divider. The impetus for this, towards the end of World War II, appears to have come from Germany: Josef Goebbels, the German propaganda minister, wrote of 'ein eiserner Vorhang', which means 'an iron curtain', but was translated in *The Times* on 23 February 1945 as 'an iron screen', and on 3 May of the same year *The Times* reported the German foreign minister Schwerin von Krosigk as speaking of 'the iron curtain'. It was soon taken up in the English-speaking world: in an article in the *Sunday Empire News* entitled 'A Curtain Across Europe', Sir St Vincent Troubridge wrote of 'an iron curtain of silence' separating East from West.

> 1920 Mrs. Philip Snowden: We were behind the 'iron curtain' at last!

> 1945 *Times*: In the East the iron curtain behind which, unseen by the eyes of the world, the work of destruction goes on is moving steadily forward.

> 1945 Sir St Vincent Troubridge: Yet at present an iron curtain of silence has descended, cutting off the Russian zone from the Western Allies.

> 1946 Winston Churchill: From Stettin, in the Baltic, to Trieste, in the Adriatic, an iron curtain has descended across the Continent.

> 1953 *Encounter*: If they live behind the Iron Curtain they can do none of these things—for, while the Communists agree that knowledge is power, they are persuaded that they are already in essential possession of both.

isolationism *n* (1922) a national policy of not engaging in economic or political relations with other countries. The term is often applied specifically to the policy of the US in the first part of the 20th century. The related *isolationist* is first recorded in 1899.

> 1930 *Headway*: Add to this the fact that half the people . . . who have emigrated to America in the last generation or so are Europeans who have left Europe because they wanted to get away from Europe, and the secret of America's 'isolationism' is very largely explained.

Kleenex *n* (1925) the proprietary name (originally American) of an absorbent disposable cleansing paper tissue. (The generic *paper handkerchief* is first recorded in 1907.)

> 1925 *Picture-Play Magazine* (advert): This secret of famous stage beauties . . . is simply the use of Kleenex in removing cold cream and cosmetics . . . This soft velvety absorbent is made of Cellucotton . . . Use it once, throw it away.

lesbian *n* (1925) a female homosexual. The adjective *lesbian*, commemorating the alleged homosexuality of the Greek female poet Sappho who lived on the island of

Lesbos, was in use at the end of the 19th century, but this is the first known instance on record of the noun. (The similarly inspired *Sapphism* 'female homosexuality' also dates from the late 19th century, but has not survived so well.)

> 1925 Aldous Huxley: After a third-rate provincial town, colonized by English sodomites and middle-aged Lesbians, which is, after all, what Florence is, a genuine metropolis will be lively.

Levi's, Levis *n* (1926) a type of (originally blue) denim jeans or bibless overalls, with rivets to reinforce stress-points, patented and produced as working clothes in the 1860s, and adopted as a fashion garment in the 20th century. The form *Levi's* is a proprietary term in the US. The name comes from the original American manufacturer, Levi Strauss, and by the second half of the 20th century had become the cool World English alternative to *jeans* as the name for the garment the youth and would-be youth of the world were wearing.

> 1957 Jack Kerouac: Dean was wearing washed-out tight levis and a T-shirt.

liquidate *v* (1924) to put an end to, abolish; to wipe out; to kill. The verb is an adaptation of Russian *likvidírovat'* 'to liquidate, wind up' which became a key element in the 20th-century euphemization of oppression.

> 1939 V. A. Demant: The Trotskyists... are 'liquidated' as being insufficiently dialectical to see that the policy of the Russian State at any moment has absolute finality.

listener-in *n* (1922), **listener** *n* (1923) someone listening to the radio. The verb *listen in* had its beginnings in the wireless telegraphy of the first decade of the century, and it embraced domestic listeners when public broadcasting came on the scene in the early 1920s ('Radio today is a continuous performance. You... listen in... to the music of today... the news of the minute, stock quotations, and so on', *Scientific American* (1922)). It was also turned into a noun ('A listen-in. The Queen... listened to a recitation sent out from Marconi House', *Daily Mail* (1922)). *Listener-in* was born at the same time, but all began to go out of use around the middle of the century: *listen in* completely, as watching television replaced listening to the radio as the chief source of domestic entertainment, and *listener-in* replaced by the more-or-less contemporary *listener.*

> 1922 *Daily Mail*: The limited service has already established itself in high favour with 'listeners-in'.
>
> 1923 *Radio Times*: It seems to me that the B.B.C. are mainly catering for the 'listeners' who own expensive sets.

long-playing *adj* (1929) designating a gramophone record that plays for longer than the standard time, specifically a microgroove record designed to be played at 33⅓ revolutions per minute. The specific application dates from the late 1940s, when the new type of microgroove record was introduced; the abbreviation **LP (1948)** came on the scene then too.

> 1929 *Wireless Magazine*: Long-playing dance records.
>
> 1948 *Electronic Engineer*: A new library of recorded music has been announced... which consists of a series of long-playing 10 and 12 in. records run at 33⅓ r.p.m

macho *adj* (1928) male, and especially manly or virile. The earliest example may be an isolated one; the word does not seem to have come into common use (originally in the US), with all its connotations of overweening masculinity, until the 1950s. It was borrowed from Mexican-Spanish. See also **machismo (1948)**.

> 1928 *Nation*: Here was I in their midst, a Macho Yankee Gringo, yet treated with consideration.
>
> 1959 Norman Mailer: Every American writer who takes himself to be both major and macho must sooner or later give a *faena* which borrows from the self-love of a Hemingway style.

market *v* (1922) to place or establish (a product) on the market, especially by means of promotion strategies. The verb is a back-formation from *marketing*, first recorded in this sense in the 1880s.

means test *n* (1929) an official investigation into someone's financial circumstances to determine whether they are eligible for a welfare payment. The practice became a notable 20th-century political football, reviled by the left as demeaning and intrusive, supported by the right as discouraging scroungers. The term is first recorded as a verb in 1963.

> 1930 *Economist*: We should not cavil greatly at the principle of granting, on the basis of a means test, maintenance allowances for children compelled to attend school.

> 1963 *Economist*: All university awards are means-tested now.

media *n* (1923) newspapers, radio, television, etc. collectively, as vehicles of mass communication. The term was originally a shorthand form for *mass media* (in which collocation it is first recorded). It did not become widespread outside advertising-industry jargon until the 1950s, when its increasingly frequent use as a mass noun, with a singular verb, began to enrage purists wedded to its status as a Latin plural. The heavily ironic respelling *meeja*, intended partly to poke fun at the media's perceived self-importance, is first recorded in 1983.

> 1923 S. M. Fechheimer (title): Class appeal in mass media.

> 1929 E. O. Hughes: The advertising media to which reference will be made . . . are newspapers, journals, magazines and such-like printed publications.

> 1958 *Times Literary Supplement*: The media which appeal to our visually conscious age call for organizing ability as well as individual talent.

> 1966 Kingsley Amis: The treatment of media as a singular noun . . . is spreading into the upper cultural strata.

> 1971 *Radio Times*: The media have an ambiguous relationship with the radical left.

> 1972 *Times*: Miss Allen seems to be under the impression that the media is confined to newspapers.

> 1983 *Guardian Weekly*: Part of the reason Mailer is such fun is his self-appointed mission to smash the consensual tea party held by the cultural bureaucrats and 'meeja' liberals.

mercy *adj* (1927) intended to alleviate suffering. The usage was probably based ultimately on French *coup de grâce*, which had been translated into English as long ago as 1702 as *mercy-stroke*. Over the decades it has become most firmly established, especially in newspaper language, in the euphemistic role of denoting as uncontroversially as possible the taking of life in order to bring an end to pain or suffering, notably in the phrase *mercy killing*.

> 1927 *Daily Express*: The 'mercy bullet' . . . contains a chemical which is released on striking the animal. The fluid in the blood will cause temporary unconsciousness.

> 1952 Joyce Cary: Think of Oates' suicide in the Antarctic, or thousands of 'mercy killings', which are technically murder.

motel *n* (1925) a hotel catering primarily for motorists, especially one comprising self-contained accommodation with adjacent parking space. The word, which originated in the US, was an early and classic example of the 20th century's passion for blends.

> 1925 *Hotel Monthly*: The Milestone Interstate Corporation . . . proposes to build and operate a chain of motor hotels between San Diego and Seattle, the hotels to have the name 'Motel'.

National Socialist *adj, n* (1923) (a member) of the German National Socialist Workers' Party led by Adolf Hitler after 1920. The pronunciation of the first two syllables of the original German, *Nationalsozialist*, is the source of **Nazi (1930)**. The term *National Socialism*, denoting the ideology and practice of the Nazis, including particularly racist nationalism and state control of the economy, is not recorded in English until 1931.

> 1923 *Times*: At the conclusion of a National Socialist meeting last night Herr Hitler's storm troops . . . attempted to march through Munich.

naturist *n, adj* (1929) (an advocate or practitioner) of communal nudity in private grounds. The term is first recorded a few years before *naturism* (1933), and seems from the beginning to have had rather wider currency. Its attractions as a euphemism are obvious (see the 1963 quote below), but it is also intended to convey attention to environmental concerns, healthy living, etc. and a return to 'nature', as the quote from Parmelee's *Nudity in Modern Life* suggests. See also **nudism (1929)**.

> 1929 Maurice Parmelee: We have all heard of so-called 'naturists', who insist that man . . . should discard everything artificial such as . . . clothing, books, cooked food, etc.

> 1961 *Daily Telegraph*: Delegates . . . at the annual conference of the British Sun Bathing Association . . . agreed . . . to substitute 'naturism' for 'nudism'.

> 1963 *Daily Telegraph*: The description 'a nudist camp', according to the naturist terminology, is defunct . . . Instead club members are asked to use the expression 'sun club' or 'naturist club'.

neutron *n* (1921) an electrically uncharged sub-atomic particle whose mass is very slightly greater than that of the proton. Before its discovery in 1932 it was conceived as a close association of a proton and an electron. Rutherford (who communicated Glasson's 1921 paper to the Royal Society) discusses this concept in a paper of 1920 cited by Glasson, but without using the word *neutron*. Harkins (of Chicago) seems to have coined the term independently.

> 1921 W. D. Harkins: Any complex atom has a mass and weight 0·76 per cent less than the hydrogen atoms (neutrons) from which it may be assumed to be built . . . The term neutron represents one proton plus one electron.

> 1921 J. L. Glasson: In the ordinary atom of hydrogen we have a single electron separated from the nucleus by a distance of the order of 10–8 cm. It is here contemplated that a more intimate union of the two is possible . . . Such a particle, to which the name *neutron* has been given by Prof. Rutherford, would have novel and important properties. It would, for instance, greatly simplify our ideas as to how the nuclei of the heavy elements are built up.

> 1930 Ernest Rutherford et al.: The existence of a neutron, i.e. a close combination of a proton and electron, has been suggested.

never-never *n* (1926) a system of paying for purchases by periodic instalments over an extended period. The expression is a British colloquialism; the more sober *hire-purchase* dates from the 1890s.

> 1926 Edgar Wallace: Her uncle . . . drove a taxi which he . . . had purchased on the 'never never' system. You pay £80 down and more than you can afford for the rest of your life.

news bulletin *n* (1923) a brief television or radio programme in which the news is announced. The abbreviated *bulletin* is first recorded in this sense in 1925.

> 1923 *Radio Times*: 10.0.—Time signal, general news bulletin. Broadcast to all stations, followed by London News and Weather Report.

> 1925 *Times*: The news given out as a bulletin on a very recent Sunday from the London Station must have made many listeners pause.

nudism *n* (1929) the doctrine or practice of living in the nude. The cult began in Germany after World War I, and has since spread to other parts of the Western world, to the bemusement of those who do not follow it. The name is apt to provoke sniggers, and from the beginning *naturism* has often been preferred by practitioners (see **naturist (1929)**). The noun and adjective *nudist* is also first recorded in 1929.

> 1929 *Time*: Made in Germany, imported to France, is the cult of Nudism, a mulligan stew of vegetarianism, physical culture and pagan worship . . . Much publicity has been given the Nudist colony on an island in the Seine near Paris . . . A U.S. parallel would be if elegant Editor Frank Crowninshield of *Vanity Fair* should suddenly appear as a vegetable-eating, hairy-chested Nudist.

> 1935 *Punch*: 'A real tent . . . Think of the saving. Hotel bills, nothing. Meals, practically nothing. Clothes, nothing whatever.' 'Pamela,' I said imploringly, 'not Nudism.'

oestrogen *n* (1927) a hormone produced mainly by the ovary and responsible for the development and maintenance of female secondary sex characteristics. The term is first recorded in the US form *estrogen*, which was registered as a proprietary name in 1927 (see the quote below). It was coined from *oestrus/estrus* 'period of ovulation'.

> 1936 *Journal of the American Medical Association*: 'Estrogen' is a registered trademark belonging to Parke, Davis and Company... This firm has commendably agreed to relinquish its proprietary rights in the name on its adoption by the Council as a generic term.

peaceful coexistence *n* (1920) in the foreign policy of the Soviet Union, peaceful relations with other countries. The early quotation from Lenin has never been thoroughly verified, and certainly the term did not come into widespread use in English until the time of the Cold War, when it had the additional connotation of avoidance of nuclear confrontation.

> 1920 *New York Evening Journal* [Interview with Lenin]: Our plans in Asia? The same as in Europe: peaceful coexistence with the peoples, with the workers and peasants of all nations.

> 1961 *Times*: Mr. Khrushchev, ... at a New Year banquet... in the Kremlin, ... raised his glass and bade the whole company drink to peaceful coexistence.

pecking order *n* (1927) a pattern of behaviour first observed in hens and later recognized in other groups of social animals, in which those of high rank within the group are able to attack those of lower rank without provoking an attack in return. The term is a translation of German *Hackliste*, coined by T. J. Schjelderup-Ebbe in the early 1920s. The now familiar metaphorical usage, applied to human beings, is not recorded before the 1950s, but the potential for it is evident in the first quote below.

> 1928 Aldous Huxley: Observing the habitual and almost sacred 'pecking order' which prevails among the hens in his poultry yard... the politician will meditate on the Catholic hierarchy and Fascism.

> 1955 Harold Nicolson: In a perfect classless society... similar pecking orders must exist.

penicillin *n* (1929) an antibiotic obtained from penicillium moulds. The original agent named by Alexander Fleming was obtained from a culture of *Penicillium notatum*, but in its fully realized form, as isolated and purified by Howard Florey and E. B. Chain at Oxford, it can be produced from a variety of species. It revolutionized the treatment of infection, and saved many lives on the battlefield in World War II.

> 1929 Alexander Fleming: In the rest of this article allusion will constantly be made to experiments with filtrates of a broth culture of this mould, so for convenience and to avoid the repetition of the rather cumbersome phrase 'Mould broth filtrate', the name 'penicillin' will be used. This will denote the filtrate of a broth culture of the particular penicillium with which we are concerned.

> 1941 H. W. Florey, etc.: Enough evidence has now been assembled to show that penicillin is a new and effective type of chemotherapeutic agent, and possesses some properties unknown in any antibacterial substance hitherto described.

photocopy *n, v* (1924) (to make) a photographic reproduction of something. The history of the term is not entirely clear. In the first quote below, the combination could well be *photo + copying machine*, not *photo copying + machine*. The first unequivocal reference to *photocopy* comes in the second edition of *Webster's New International Dictionary of the English Language* (1934), but its use does not appear to have become widespread until the 1940s, with the advent of modern methods of xerography. See also **Xerox (1952)**.

> 1924 C. W. Hackleman: Photo copying machines. In Fig. 2015 is shown a machine for making copies of records, drawings, ... flat merchandise, etc., by a simplified method of photography, the copies being made in enlarged, reduced or natural size directly upon sensitized paper.

> 1948 *Library Association Record*: There are private photocopying firms in most cities.

photogenic *adj* (1928) making a good subject for photography; that shows to good advantage in a photograph or film. The usage originated in the US. It may have been a borrowing from French *photogénique* (which was occasionally adopted unchanged in early use), but the word *photogenic* had been in the language since the early 19th century in various technical senses (including as a synonym for *photographic*). It spawned several similar adjectives, including *radiogenic* (1928) and *telegenic* (1939).

> 1931 Sam Goldwyn: An actor may be 'photogenic' and have personality and appearance, but that is not enough.

polyester *n* (1929) a polymer in which the units are joined by the ester linkage -COO-. It was to be a word that stayed largely in the laboratory until the 1950s. Polyester resins are widely used in plastics, paints, etc. but it was the discovery of polyester fibre in the early 1940s (see the first quote below) that paved the way for its widespread use as a clothing fabric in the second half of the 20th century.

> 1958 *Manchester Guardian*: Polyester fibre was discovered in 1941 by Mr. J. R. Whinfield and Dr. J. T. Dickson in the laboratories of the Calico Printers' Association.

> 1977 *R.A.F. News* (advert): 'Tootal' Polyester/Cotton Wedgwood Blue Shirts.

pop *adj, n* (1926) denoting music of wide popular appeal, especially to young people. As a noun, *pop* originally denoted an individual popular song or other piece of music, a usage which gradually died out except in certain fixed phrases, such as *top of the pops*. The current application to popular music in general is first recorded in 1954. At first the term designated merely popularity, and covered a wide range of styles (e.g. varieties of jazz). The sense of a specific genre (featuring, for example, strong rhythms and electronic amplification) did not begin to emerge until the 1950s.

> 1926 *American Mercury*: She coos a pop song.

> 1945 S. Hughes: Cole Porter's 'Begin the Beguine'... has twice the regulation number of bars that a good 'pop' should have.

> 1954 *Unicorn Book 1953*: A magazine... each December publishes a list of the year's top pop music and musicians.

> 1970 *Observer*: In the world of pop, the death of Jimi Hendrix on Friday from a suspected overdose of drugs will seem as if Tchaikovsky or Mozart had also been struck down at only 24.

prison-camp *n* (1925) a camp in which prisoners, especially political prisoners or prisoners-of-war, are confined.

> 1925 *Scribner's Magazine*: The scene is a Turkish prison-camp during the recent war.

programme *n* (1923) a radio (or, later, television) show.

> 1923 *Radio Times*: From November 14th last year... we have... transmitted roughly 1,700 distinct evening programmes.

Prohibition *n* (1922) (the period (1920–33) of) the banning of the manufacture, sale, and transportation of alcoholic drink in the US. The term *prohibition* had been used in the US for the banning of alcohol since the 19th century ('The State of Vermont has struggled arduously to arrive at the summit level of entire prohibition', *Annual Report of the Executive Committee of the American Temperance Union* (1851)), and it is not always possible to distinguish this usage from early references to the period during which the ban was in force. (Incidentally, the term *bootlegger* 'a smuggler of illicit alcohol', which came into prominence during Prohibition, dates from the late 1880s; it probably originally referred to someone who concealed contraband in his boot.)

> 1922 *Daily News*: So far as the movement against Prohibition is concerned, the victory of Mr. Edwards, Governor of New Jersey, is only a gesture. As Governor he promised to make the State as wet as the Atlantic.

promotion *n* (1925) the furtherance of the sale of something by advertisement or other modes of publicity. Originating in the US, it is a specialized 20th-century application of the more general sense 'furtherance, advancement', which dates from the 15th century. The related usage of the verb *promote* is not recorded before 1930.

> 1928 *Publishers' Weekly*: Promotion cannot be done without waste... But the idea back of the new mergers is the idea of outlets, of promotion, of selling more goods.

> 1930 *Publishers' Weekly*: The books all to be individualized in appearance and fully promoted.

property-owning democracy *n* (1923) a democratic society characterized by private home ownership. The phrase is often associated with Sir Anthony Eden, British Conservative prime minister in the mid 1950s, and it became a mantra of the Thatcher administration of the 1980s, but in fact it dates from a time when owner-occupation had begun to increase significantly in Britain (in 1900 over 90 per cent of the population lived in rented or tied accommodation).

> 1923 *Spectator*: It remains to state as clearly as may be what means lie ready to develop a property-owning democracy.

> 2001 *Observer*: To the Right, it offered the camphorous odour of Thatcher's mothballed property-owning democracy.

publicize *v* (1928) to bring to the notice of the public; to give publicity to; to advertise.

> 1928 *Weekly Dispatch*: Nowadays the potential star has to be managed and publicised.

queer *adj* (1922) homosexual. The usage, which originated in the US, does not seem to have become widespread until the 1930s, when it is first recorded as a noun, meaning 'a homosexual person'. One of the main insult-words for homosexuals in the middle part of the century, changing social attitudes from the 1960s onwards gradually placed it under a taboo.

> 1922 *The Practical Value of the Scientific Study of Juvenile Delinquents* (Children's Bureau, US Department of Labor): A young man, easily ascertainable to be unusually fine in other characteristics, is probably 'queer' in sex tendency.

> 1936 Lee Duncan: There was even a little room . . . where the 'fairies', 'pansies', and 'queers' conducted their lewd practices.

rationalize *v* (1922) to give plausible reasons for (one's behaviour) that ignore, conceal, or gloss its real motive. The verb is used both transitively and intransitively.

> 1922 Henry Somerville: It is clear that the patient is rationalising, and that as a matter of fact he is eaten up with jealousy.

> 1925 Joan Riviere: The patient's consciousness naturally misunderstands them and puts forward a set of secondary motives to account for them—rationalizes them, in short.

rationalize *v* (1926) to organize (economic production or the like) according to rational or scientific principles so as to achieve a desired or predictable result. The word has often subsequently been used as a euphemistic camouflage for reducing the size of an operation, firing employees, etc.

> 1926 Eugene Grossmann: International cartels will be able to rationalise production in a way impossible in the present state of affairs.

> 1962 *Listener*: Their numbers go down: they are 'rationalized'. In 1920 there were nine evening newspapers in London; now there are two.

recession *n* (1929) a temporary decline or setback in economic activity or prosperity. There was more than a hint of euphemism in the coining of this term, traces of which remained even at the end of the 20th century.

> 1929 *Economist*: The material prosperity of the United States is too firmly based, in our opinion, for a revival in industrial activity—even if we have to face an immediate recession of some magnitude—to be long delayed.

> 1938 Eric Ambler: 'Trade recession' they called it . . . As far as I could see there wasn't a great deal of difference between a trade recession and a good old-fashioned slump.

recycle *v* (1926) to reuse (a material) in an industrial process. Originally this was a technical term used mainly in the oil-refining industry and, later, in the nuclear industry. The more widespread application to the processing of waste to make it usable is not recorded until 1960.

> 1960 *Aeroplane*: It has systems which reduce all organic waste to a small amount of ash and recycle urine and waste water into drinkable water.

request *n* (1928) a letter etc. asking for a particular record, song, etc. to be played on a radio programme; hence, a record, song, etc. played or sung in response to such a request.

1928 *Radio Times*: The B.B.C. can never promise to comply with requests, for . . . suitable opportunities may not arise for weeks or even months . . . Children's Hour request week.

1949 *Radio Times*: Listeners' requests played by Sandy Macpherson at the B.B.C. theatre organ.

robot *n* (1923) originally denoting one of the mechanical men and women in Karel Čapek's play *R.U.R.* ('Rossum's Universal Robots') (1920), and subsequently applied to a machine (sometimes resembling a human being in appearance) designed to function in place of a living agent, especially one which carries out a variety of tasks automatically. Čapek (1890–1938) coined the word from Czech *robota* 'forced labour', which is related to German *Arbeit* 'work'. Its first recorded occurrence in English is in Selver's translation of Čapek's play.

1923 Paul Selver: You see . . . the Robots have no interest in life. They have no enjoyments.

1945 *Sun* (Baltimore): A robot, which never forgets, will do the job.

1998 *Sunday Times*: Scientists in Albuquerque have already made robots the size of sugar cubes.

runway *n* (1923) a specially prepared surface on an airfield for the taking off and landing of aircraft. The term originated in the US.

1923 *Aviation*: A wonderful landmark—Boston Airport with its T type runways.

science fiction *n* (1929) imaginative fiction based on postulated scientific discoveries or spectacular environmental changes, often set in the future or on other planets and involving space or time travel. The term is actually first recorded in 1851 in the work of one William Wilson, but it did not have quite the same connotations as the modern word, and there is no evidence of any continuity of usage between then and the late 1920s. The abbreviation *S.F.* is also first recorded in 1929; *sci-fi* not until 1955. In the 21st century it became fashionable to refer to the genre as *speculative fiction* (*science fiction* having perhaps acquired too many wacky connotations).

1929 *Science Wonder Stories*: The editor of this publication [Hugo Gernsback] addressed a number of letters to science fiction lovers. The editor promised to pay $50.00 for the best letter each month on the subject of 'What Science Fiction Means to Me.' . . . The S.F. Magazine. (Science-Fiction).

service charge *n* (1929) a charge (usually a percentage of the total bill) made for services rendered. It is a method of extracting more money from customers, especially in restaurants, with which the 20th century was to become increasingly familiar.

1955 Raymond Chandler: I paid a service charge on the bill . . . This service charge is supposed to take the place of tipping.

sex *n* (1929) sexual intercourse. The usage commonly occurs in the phrase *have sex* (*with*).

1929 D. H. Lawrence: If you want to have sex, you've got to trust At the core of your heart, the other creature.

1962 *Listener*: Why wasn't Bond 'more tender' in his love-making? Why did he just 'have sex' and disappear?

1962 *Woman's Own*: Those trends in our society that make sex before marriage so easy.

sex appeal *n* (1924) attractiveness that arouses sexual desire. The daring new term was initially often abbreviated defensively to *S.A.*

1924 *American Mercury*: An actress with sex appeal is four times out of five a more effective actress.

1926 *American Mercury*: The girl is a looker with an armful of S.A. (sex appeal).

sexy *adj* (1925) concerned with sexual activity; sexually attractive. The first known record of the word is actually in a French text, in the sense 'about or full of sex' ('Depuis que Joyce a publié un livre qu'ils croient 'sexy'—cet état d'esprit n'a pas d'équivalent français—on s'en empare... que sa méthode sert de modèle à des gens qui... se disent surréalistes', *La Nouvelle Revue Française* (1925)), but this is backed up by an instance of the derived noun *sexiness* from the same year.

> 1925 *Glasgow Herald*: The stallion seems to vanish altogether near the end of the story, and the Welsh groom is put into prominence, with mere 'sexiness' thus supplanting magnificent vitality.

> 1928 *Sunday Dispatch*: Australian audiences... like sex plays, but they mustn't be too sexy.

social mobility *n* (1925) the possibility of movement between different social levels that exists in a society, or to different fields of employment or interest, or to new areas, within the same social level. The term was coined by the sociologist P. A. Sorokin, and used by him as the title of a book in 1927. It remains more academically respectable than the contemporaneous *social climbing*.

> 1925 P. A. Sorokin: We used to think that in the United States 'social mobility' was greatest.

soundtrack *n* (1929) the narrow strip at one side of a cine film that carries the sound recording. The term soon became familiar to devotees of the new talking pictures.

Soviet *n, adj* (1920) (a citizen) of the Soviet Union. See also **soviet (1917)**.

> 1920 *Commercial & Financial Chronicle*: [Clemenceau] insisted upon writing the final paragraph, 'affirming that the Allies had not changed their attitude towards the Soviets'.

> 1920 *Russian Economist*: This is the secret of 'bourgeois' diplomacy, and this riddle is being solved by Soviet diplomacy and with it by all the Russian-speaking people.

spacesuit *n* (1929) a protective pressurized garment worn by someone going into space. The term provides yet another instance of science fiction anticipating real life.

> 1929 *Science Wonder Stories*: Normal communication by speech would be impossible. Of course, this is not true of enclosed, air-filled rooms... But it is true when one is out 'in the open' (in the space suit).

> 1962 John Glenn: G-suits are not to be confused with pressure suits (or, now, spacesuits) which the Astronaut wears during space flight to maintain atmospheric pressure at high altitudes.

spin-dry *v* (1927) to remove excess water from (washing) by spinning it rapidly in a rotating perforated drum. The term *spin-drier* is not recorded before 1939.

> 1927 *Saturday Evening Post*: It takes the Savage [Washer & Dryer] just one-tenth the time to spin-dry the entire load in its own tub.

> 1939 *Architectural Review*: The laundry is all electric, and is equipped with a Rotary Washer and Spin Dryer, and Rotary Ironer, in which all the laundry of the house can be done without resort to clothes lines.

Stalinism *n* (1927) the policies pursued by Josef Stalin (1879–1953), leader of the Soviet Communist Party and head of state of the Soviet Union, based on but later deviating from Leninism, especially the formation of a centralized, totalitarian, objectivist government. The derivative *Stalinite* is also first recorded in 1927, the longer-lived *Stalinist* in 1928.

> 1927 *Daily Telegraph*: A violent denunciation of 'Stalinism' and its 'terrorising of the party'... The struggle between the Trotskists and the Stalinites.

> 1928 *Observer*: Open calculations measured in advance by the Stalinists.

stereophonic *adj* (1927) giving the impression of a spatial distribution in reproduced sound; especially, employing two or more channels of transmission and reproduction so that the sound may seem to reach the listener from any of a range of directions. The shortened form *stereo* is first recorded in 1954, and by the early 1960s was being used as a noun to denote a piece of stereophonic equipment (in those days, usually a record player).

> 1964 *House & Garden*: The wall unit houses the stereo.

sun-bather *n* (1929) someone who sits or lies in the sun (e.g. to get a tan). *Sun-bathing* is first recorded as long ago as 1600, and the now almost disused *sun bath* was quite common in the 19th century, but it was the 1920s that saw the beginnings of the 20th century's love affair with the sun ('If preparing for a sun-bath, a swim, or both, slip into the Jantzen Sun-suit!', advert, *Punch* (1929)). The verb *sun-bathe* (probably a back-formation) is first recorded in 1941.

> 1929 *Daily Express*: The groups of Lido sun-bathers.

> 1941 Agatha Christie: I oiled myself and sunbathed.

surrealist *adj, n* (1925) (a practitioner) of a movement in art and literature seeking to express the subconscious mind by any of a number of different techniques, including the irrational juxtaposition of realistic images and the creation of mysterious symbols. The French term *surréalisme*, coined by Guillaume Apollinaire around 1917, was taken over by the poet André Breton as the name of the movement, which he launched with his *Manifeste du Surréalisme* in 1924. At first it and its derivative *surréaliste* were taken over in their French form into English, and it was not really until the 1930s that the anglicized versions we are familiar with today became established (*surrealism* is first recorded in 1931).

> 1925 Roger Fry: That beastly young Surrealist Masson.

> 1931 *French Review*: Since the opening of the twentieth century, only three schools have counted [in French literature], unanimism, between 1908 and 1911, surrealism, about 1924, and populism in 1929.

teenage *adj* (1921) denoting someone in their teens. The term originated in North America. See also **teenager (1941)**.

> 1921 *Daily Colonist* (Victoria, British Columbia): All 'teen age' girls of the city are cordially invited to attend the mass meeting to be held this evening.

televise *v* (1927) to transmit or broadcast by television. The word was a back-formation from **television (1907)**, based on other verbs ending in *-ise*, such as *revise*.

> 1928 *Television*: The subject who is being 'televised' had to face a powerful battery of blinding lights.

throw-away *adj* (1928) designed to be thrown away after use. The adjective provided a convenient if glib metaphor for 20th-century civilization. See also **disposable (1943)**.

> 1928 *Weekly Dispatch*: You can . . . clean your face at intervals with those throwaway hankies you buy from any chemist.

toiletries *n* (1927) preparations for use in washing or grooming. Note the pseudo-French form in the first quote below.

> 1927 *Glasgow Herald*: One really up-to-date shop coins a new and compact name for these indispensable odds and ends and calls them 'toiletteries'.

> 1927 *Hollis Street Theatre Programme* (US): Her keen individuality finds in the inimitable *Djer-Kiss odeur* a refreshing complement; she fastidiously insists upon it in all her toiletries!

totalitarian *adj* (1926) denoting a regime or system of government which imposes a monolithic unity by authoritarian methods. The word was an adaptation of Italian *totalitario* 'complete, absolute; totalitarian'. The noun *totalitarianism*, also presaging the era of European dictators, is first recorded in this year too.

> 1926 B. B. Carter: Anti-Fascism . . . has, however, a positive sense if it is taken to represent an element antagonistic to the 'totalitarian' and absolute position of Fascism . . . This would mark the end of Fascist 'totalitarianism' and the renewal of political dualism.

traffic light *n* (1929) one of a set of changing coloured lights for the regulation of traffic; usually used in the plural. The term *traffic light* seems actually to have been coined by Rudyard Kipling. He used it in a futuristic story called 'As Easy as A.B.C.' (1912), and applied it to a light used for the guidance of aircraft ('They began turning out traffic-lights and locking up landing-towers'). This never caught on in real life, however. When the sort of traffic lights we are familiar with today were introduced after World War I, they were initially known as *traffic regulation lights* (1920), but the shorter form soon became established in general usage.

> 1929 *Saturday Evening Post*: T is for Traffic Light, bane of all motorists.

transvestite *n* (1922) a person with an abnormal desire to wear the clothes of the opposite sex. The term was an adaptation of German *Transvestit*, which was coined from Latin *trans-* 'across' and *vestire* 'to dress'. It is first recorded as an adjective in 1925. The related noun *transvestism* is first recorded in 1928 (the alternative *Eonism*, which was suggested by the sexologist Havelock Ellis—see the quote below—but never really caught on, was based on the name of the Chevalier Charles d'Éon (1728–1810), a French adventurer who wore women's clothes).

> 1922 James van Teslaar: Among the transvestites (personifiers) we find the most pronounced examples of marked homosexuality and stressed bi-sexuality.

> 1928 Havelock Ellis: It was clearly a typical case of what Hirschfeld later termed 'transvestism' and what I would call 'sexo-aesthetic inversion', or more simply, 'Eonism'.

T-shirt *n* (1920) a simple short-sleeved collarless garment for the upper body. The term originated in the US. The first T-shirts were men's undershirts of this design, and they were so called because they formed the shape of a letter T when laid out flat.

> 1920 F. Scott Fitzgerald: Amory, provided with 'six suits summer underwear . . . one sweater or T shirt . . . ' set out for New England, the land of schools.

unilateral disarmament *n* (1929) disarmament by one state, irrespective of whether others take similar action. Since the 1950s the term has come to imply specifically 'nuclear disarmament' (it is from around that time that the derivative *unilateral disarmer* begins to appear in the record).

> 1929 *Times*: Lord Salisbury agreed that unilateral disarmament had probably reached its limits.

> 1935 Clement Attlee: I want to recall to the House what our position is as a party on the question of defence . . . We do not stand for unilateral disarmament.

> 1960 *Guardian*: One can be a pacifist and a unilateral disarmer, prepared to accept the consequences for oneself and one's country.

> 1984 Sue Townsend: Went back to Pandora's and watched the Labour Party Conference vote for unilateral disarmament . . . If elected the Labour Party would chuck all their nuclear weapons away.

V.D. (1920) an abbreviation of *venereal disease*. This term had its origins in the 17th century, but then and for some time afterwards it applied specifically to syphilis. Its institutionalization as a general word for all sexually transmitted diseases may be signalled by the appearance of this euphemistic abbreviation. Towards the end of the 20th century it was replaced by *sexually transmitted disease* (*STD*).

> 1920 *Annual Report of the Chief Medical Officer, Ministry of Health*: V.D. clinic. Suggested plan of arrangement of a . . . hut.

voyeurism *n* (1924) gratification gained from observing the sex organs or sexual activities of others. The term is a derivative of **voyeur (1900)**.

> 1924 James van Teslaar: Voyeurism, erotic gratification experienced at looking at another's sexual organs; morbid desire to peep into secrets.

war to end war(s) *n* (1921) a war which is intended to make (or assumed to have made) subsequent wars impossible. It was a term usually applied, with a naive optimism, to World War I, probably on the model of H. G. Wells's *The War that Will End War* (1914).

> 1921 George Bernard Shaw: There was a war called the War to End War. In the war which followed it about ten years later, none of the soldiers were killed; but seven of the capital cities of Europe were wiped out of existence.
>
> 1949 Ernest Benn: If . . . war debts between nations had been wiped off the slate, and reparations in money never attempted, the 'war to end war' might have achieved its high purpose.
>
> 1967 Walter Lippman: Each of the wars to end wars has set the stage for the next war.

wimp *n* (1920) a feeble, spineless, or ineffectual person. The origins and development of the word remain something of a mystery. There is one isolated example of it from 1920 (see below), but then it disappears from view in print until the 1960s. This fleeting early appearance is, however, supported by a sighting of the derived adjective *wimpish* in 1925. It would seem that *wimp* lay relatively dormant for about forty years, before undergoing a sudden surge of popularity in the US in the early to mid 1960s, which sustained it in widespread use until the end of the century. It infiltrated British English in the 1970s. Its source has never been definitely established, but the likeliest explanation is that it is a back-formation from *whimper*; there appears to be no connection with the slang *wimp* 'woman' (1923), which was exclusively British.

> 1920 George Ade: Next day he sought out the dejected Wimp.
>
> 1925 Sinclair Lewis: They looked like lunching grocers: brisk featureless young men; . . . wimpish little men with spectacles, men whose collars did not meet.
>
> 1984 *Sunday Telegraph*: In daily life Ronnie Lee is a wimp. Put him in a balaclava and he thinks he's a he-man.

zipper *n* (1925), **zip fastener, zip fastening** *n* (1927), **zip** *n* (1928) a form of fastener for clothes, luggage, etc., consisting of two flexible strips with interlocking projections closed or opened by a sliding clip pulled along them. *Zipper* was registered in the US as a trademark in April 1925 (with use of the term claimed since June 1923), but in the sense 'boots made of rubber and fabric'. It is no longer a proprietary term in any of its uses. British English has always preferred *zip fastener* and plain *zip*.

> 1925 *Scribner's Magazine* (advert): No fastening is so quick, secure, or popular as the 'zipper'.
>
> 1927 *Daily Express*: Many of the new sports suits have zip-fasteners.
>
> 1928 E. M. Forster: He felt the shirt . . . and he gave the zip at the throat a downward pull.

The 1930s

After the febrile gaiety of the 1920s, the gloom—the hangover, almost—of the 1930s. It was a decade constantly in waiting, it seemed, for the fate which seemed certain to befall it: a renewed conflagration in Europe, which would perhaps consume the whole world. From the *Depression* at its beginning to *World War II* at its end it was a dark and fearful time, and this is reflected in the vocabulary of the era.

1930 found the world in the depths of an economic slump. Jolted by the spasm of the 1929 Wall Street crash, which stifled economic activity in the US, the world's industry and trade slowed down to danger levels, and millions were thrown out of work. It was the era of *skid row* and of *Hoovervilles* (temporary shanty towns in the US), and also of the remembered danger of *hyperinflation*. Steps were taken—there was *reflation*, and in the US Roosevelt's *New Deal*—but far-reaching damage had been done: in Germany, the Depression contributed to the rise of Hitler's Nazi movement.

English-speakers became familiar in the 1930s with a large amount of new terminology emanating from Germany, which by the end of the decade would send a chill down their spines. They read of *brownshirts* (members of the *Sturmabteilung*, a Nazi militia) and *swastikas*, of the *Gestapo* and the *Third Reich*. They were introduced to the concept of the *Aryan*, and the cult of the *Führer* and his *Hitlerite* followers. Above all they learned the word *Nazi*, which came to stand as the symbol of the evil which overtook Europe and the rest of the world.

On the other side of the scales were *appeasement* (a term first used at the end of World War I) and diplomacy. Internationalism was refining itself and producing ambitious new terminology: this was the age of *coexistence*, of *collective security*, of *defence*, of *power politics*—of a *brave new world*, even. But it all came to nothing at *Munich*. As the world prepared for war in 1939, it could look back on a shoddy decade of *fellow-travellers* and *fifth columnists*, of *show trials* and *stateless persons*.

By the time hostilities actually started, the 1930s had a mere four months left to run. But so well anticipated was the event that a good deal of later familiar wartime vocabulary was already in place. Various aspects of *civil defence* had been dinned into people. They knew all about *air-raid precautions* (for instance, the *black-out*). They were prepared to be chivvied into their *Anderson shelters* (small prefabricated air-raid shelters) by *air-raid wardens* if the threat of German *dive-bombing* became reality. They realized they might be *evacuated*, or have *evacuees billeted* on them. Perhaps they had heard the new term *Blitzkrieg* too, although they could scarcely have realized what significance it would hold for many of them by the end of 1940.

Some of the hardware of war had introduced itself, too—*Bren guns* and *Asdic* (an anti-submarine echo-sounding device), *ack-ack* and *flak*, the new *interceptor* fighters, and the mysterious and ominous *secret weapon* (product of the 1930s *arms race*). Chillingly, *germ warfare* announced its presence as well. The concept of the *partisan* and of *resistance* were in place by 1939, as was *scorched earth*.

Against this background of menace and fear, what did people do to cheer themselves up? New forms of mass entertainment were coming of age in the 1930s. There were talking pictures and the wireless, and by the end of the decade public television broadcasting had begun. For the first time in Britain, filmgoers were visiting *Odeons* to see all the *Oscar*-winners from Hollywood. They also had the chance to drop in casually to a *news theatre* to catch the latest newsreel or cartoon, or even a *documentary*. On the wireless, *soap operas* were in the US starting their extraordinary march towards the centre of people's lives, and *newscasters* and *sportscasters* were bringing the most up-to-date world developments into their homes. The *crooners'* latest offerings could be heard, as could *commercials*, with their catchy *jingles*. If you wanted to make your own musical selection, you could use the new *record players* and *radiograms*, *jukeboxes* and *nickelodeons*, and the *tape recorder* was making its debut. Those fortunate enough to have television sets could *view* the novel *telecasts*, and rejoice in being the first *televiewers*.

If live entertainment was what you wanted, you could go and see a *musical*, or a *revusical* (a cross between a revue and a musical). And for more active involvement still, there was no shortage of new dances in the 1930s, from the *jitterbug* and the *jive*, the *Lindy hop* and the *Susie Q*, to the more homely *conga*, *palais glide*, *Lambeth Walk*, and *Knees up, Mother Brown*. For those whose inclination was more voyeuristic than participative, there were the new *fan dancers* (female dancers who titillatingly manipulated fans to conceal their (nearly) naked bodies) and the even more daring *striptease* dancers. Or you could simply stay at home and play *Monopoly*—or manipulate your *yo-yo*.

Key elements of later 20th-century underwear terminology fell into place in the 1930s: *bras*, *briefs*, and *underpants* all put in their first appearance, not to mention the *negligee*. The concept of *casual* clothes was born, and that powerful icon the *twin set* came on the scene. The *trouser suit* and *platform soles* were heard of briefly, before disappearing until the 1970s—a resurrection not to be achieved by the *co-respondent shoe* (a two-tone shoe). Cosmetic innovations included *eye shadow* and *lip gloss*. But undoubtedly the major newcomer in the fashion field was *nylon*, the first of the man-made fibres which were to transform the clothes we wore in the second half of the 20th century.

Fashions in food were not ripe for change yet. A trickle of adventurous new items was maintained—*courgettes, pasta, pizzas*—but the *burger* is probably the most influential gastronomic contribution of the 1930s. *Scampi* were exotic novelties, and *muesli* was still on the wilder shores of vegetarianism. There were *fruit gums* and *Mars bars* for the kiddies, *Gibsons* (a gin-and-vermouth cocktail) and *gin-and-its* for the grown-ups; *Rice Krispies* for breakfast and *rock salmon* (a euphemism for various commercially unpopular fish) for supper. *Lounge bars, milk bars,* and *snack bars* catered for every taste. And before the decade was over, the first of the wartime make-do foodstuffs had appeared—*macon* (bacon made from mutton) and *Spam*. But the most telling pointers to humanity's eating habits in the second half of the 20th century were *quick-frozen* food and *supermarkets*.

The internal-combustion engine was tightening its stranglehold on Western society. To placate it, we built *dual carriageways* and *clover leaves, lay-bys* and *traffic islands, car ports* and *drive-ins*. *Parking meters* made their debut in the US, while in Britain *Belisha beacons* sprouted on city streets. The concept of the *learner* (*driver*) emerged, and the *drunkometer* was tried out as a solution to *drunk driving*.

Science uncovered *mesons, neutrinos,* and *positrons,* and put a name to *deoxyribonucleic acid*. In the field of *nuclear physics, fission, heavy water,* and *deuterium* anticipated the exploding of the first atomic bomb, while the *Turing machine* (named after the English mathematician Alan Turing) gave a theoretical foretaste of the computer. The terms *electron microscope, polythene, satellite, semiconductor,* and *test-tube baby* all made their first appearances, and a new planet was named—*Pluto*.

The 1930s were the decade of the masses, of unified populaces. There were *social services* for the *underprivileged, marriage guidance* for unhappy couples, and lessons in *parentcraft* for anxious mothers- and fathers-to-be. The appearance of *dailies* and *baby-sitters* reflected the post-World War I servant problem, and hinted at further *embourgeoisement* 'adoption of middle-class lifestyles' to come. Whether you lived in an *open-plan* house, a *studio flat*, or a *Tudorbethan* 'mock-Tudor' villa, *mod cons* such as *washing-up machines, sink units,* and *electric blankets* made up for the absence of domestic help.

The 1930s were also the decade that produced perhaps the most notorious of the century's euphemisms, *senior citizen*. It signalled the growing difficulty the 20th century experienced in referring to old age, just as *underprivileged, slow learner,* and *defence* indicated that we were becoming squeamish about poverty, lack of intelligence, and the use of military power. Other circumlocutions, though, like *smallest room* 'lavatory', looked back to Victorian embarrassments.

The slang of the 1930s looked in two directions too. The likes of *feeding* 'boring, annoying', *oojah-cum-spiff* 'all right', and *shy-making* 'embarrassing' conjure up a passing British era, but in the jazz clubs of the US, African-American English was brewing up *cool*, *groovy*, *hep-cat*, and *send*, which in the 1940s and 50s would be on the lips of the young all round the English-speaking world.

ack-ack *n* (1939) anti-aircraft gunfire, or an anti-aircraft gun. The term was originally an abbreviation of *anti-aircraft*, using the then current military signalling code *ack* for the letter *a*. The civilian populations of British cities became all too familiar with it during World War II.

affirmative action *n* (1935) positive action by employers to ensure that minority groups are not discriminated against during recruitment or employment. Originally and mainly a US term, it was not in widespread use until the 1960s, after which it slotted comfortably into the euphemistic language of political correctness.

air-conditioning *n* (1930) the process of cleaning air and controlling its temperature and humidity before it enters a room, building, etc. The term had been in use since the first decade of the 20th century with reference to various industrial processes, but it was not until the 1930s that it (and derivatives such as *air-conditioned* and *air-conditioner*) became familiar in the context of controlling (and particularly cooling) indoor human environments.

> 1937 *Times*: The trustees of the National Gallery will discuss a scheme to air-condition the gallery.

air hostess *n* (1934) a female flight attendant on a passenger aircraft. The term gradually superseded the earlier *stewardess* (1931). The abbreviated *hostess* is first recorded in 1936, the sexless *flight attendant* not until 1947.

air-raid precautions *n* (1935) measures (especially legally enforceable ones) taken to minimize casualties and damage in the event of an air raid (e.g. extinguishing lights—see **black-out (1935)**). These were more generally known in Britain during World War II by the abbreviation *A.R.P.*

algorithm *n* (1938) a process, or set of rules, usually one expressed in algebraic notation. At first, the word was used almost exclusively by mathematicians; contemporary usage in the fields of machine translation, linguistics, and particularly computing (where it is a key term) dates from around 1960. In origin the term is a variant of *algorism*, a word of Arabic ancestry denoting the Arabic system of numbers.

American dream *n* (1931) the ideal of a democratic and prosperous society which is the traditional aim of the American people; a catchphrase used to symbolize US social or material values in general, especially as proselytized around the world in the latter part of the 20th century.

> 1931 J. T. Adams: If the American dream is to come true and to abide with us, it will, at bottom, depend on the people themselves.

appease *v* (1939) see **appeasement (1919)**.

arms race *n* (1936) competition between unfriendly nations or other groups in the accumulation and development of weapons. The phenomenon, in its modern form, probably dates from the years preceding World War I, but it was first called the *arms race* in the 1930s, when the world was again arming itself for coming conflict. The term persisted into the Cold War, in the context of nuclear weapons.

> 1936 *Hansard Commons*: This House cannot agree to a policy which in fact seeks security in national armaments alone and intensifies the ruinous arms race between the nations, inevitably leading to war.

Aryan, Arian *adj, n* (1932) in Nazi ideology, (a member) of a Caucasian Gentile race, especially of a Nordic type. The term originally denoted the precursor of the languages spoken in most of modern Europe and parts of southwest Asia and India, which would now be called *Proto-Indo-European*. It came to be applied to the speakers of this language, and in the 19th century it was taken up by various nationalistic historical and romantic writers. It was given especial currency by M. A. de Gobineau, who linked it with the theory of the essential inferiority of certain races. The Nazis revived and distorted it in the 1920s.

> 1933 *Times* (translation of Hitler's *Mein Kampf*): The exact opposite of the Aryan is the Jew.

autopilot *n* (1935) a concertinaed version of *automatic pilot* (1916). Modern air travel would be unthinkable without it.

> 1935 *Flight*: No information is available concerning the degree of accuracy which the 'Autopilot' will give in bumpy weather.

baby-sitter *n* (1937) someone who looks after a child while its parents are out, especially in the evening. The term originated in the US. The derived verb *baby-sit* is first recorded in 1947. By the 1960s *sit* was being used on its own with the same meaning, and later in the 20th century it began to attach itself to other objects of guardianship (mainly in *house-sit*).

> 1937 C. R. Walker: There are two high-school girls in the neighborhood who hire out for twenty-five cents an evening as 'baby sitters' when the family wants to go to the movies.

> 1966 John Gloag: He wondered if Willy would be able to get Mrs Hillman in to sit. Friday was a bad night.

banana republic *n* (1935) a small state, especially in Central America, whose economy is almost entirely dependent on its fruit-exporting trade. The colloquial term's usual connotations are of capricious and unstable government, with frequent revolutionary punctuations.

battery *n* (1931) a series of hutches, cages, or nesting-boxes in which laying hens are confined for intensive laying or poultry are reared and fattened. In the second half of the 20th century the term absorbed all the negative connotations of modern industrialized agriculture (see **factory farming (1964)**).

> 1953 Arthur Watkyn: It ain't right to ask 'uman beings to live like Battery Hens.

Belisha beacon *n* (1934) a post about seven feet high surmounted by a flashing amber-coloured globe and erected on the pavement in Britain at officially recognized pedestrian crossings of the highway. It was named after Leslie Hore-Belisha, Minister of Transport 1931–7, and has remained a familiar feature of the British urban landscape.

benzedrine *n* (1933) a type of amphetamine drug. The word was registered in 1935 as a proprietary name, based on *benzoic* and *-edrine* (as in *ephedrine*). The original application of the drug was as a treatment for colds, but its stimulant effect soon made it popular in recreational use (in which role a tablet is often called a *benny* (1955)).

billet *v* (1936) to assign quarters to (civilian evacuees). The verb was used especially with reference to children evacuated from British cities during World War II, and at that time *billetees* figured largely in life on the home front.

> 1939 *Punch*: It was when you first heard that little Sidney and the others were to be billeted on you.

> 1939 *Times*: Mrs. Miniver . . . will cope in a wonderful manner with refractory billetees.

bingo *n* (1936) a game (often played in public halls etc. for prizes) in which numbers are called out at random and the winner is the first person to cross off all the corresponding pre-numbered squares on his or her card. The name, which presumably came from *bingo* the exclamation of pleasurable surprise, originated in the US; it was not until the 1950s that it began seriously to spread to British English, where hitherto the game had usually been called **housey-housey (1936)**. The game itself, a slightly modified version of what had previously been known as *lotto* or *tombola*, became immensely popular in Britain from the 1960s onwards, with hundreds of underused cinemas being converted into *bingo halls* (1964).

black market *n* (1931) unauthorized dealing in commodities that are rationed or of which the supply is otherwise restricted. After a slow start in the 1930s, mainly in the area of currency dealing, the term really took off in the disrupted economic circumstances of World War II and its aftermath, when items notionally rationed or unobtainable could often be bought if you knew the right person and had the right money. It was at this point that a range of derivative terms appeared, such as *black marketer, black marketeer,* and *black marketeering,* as well as the concertinaed form *blacketeer* (1942). See also **spiv (1934)**.

> 1931 *Economist*: The growth of an unofficial or 'black' market in sterling exchange.
>
> 1942 *New Statesman*: If Jewish black-marketeers flourish in England, it is an indication of the inefficiency of the Government in checking this pursuit.

black-out *n* (1935) the extinguishing, covering, or obscuring of lights as a precaution against air raids etc.; also, the resulting darkness. A derivative of the verb **black out (1919)** in the same sense, the word came into its own during World War II, when British civilians became used to dark streets and windows heavily muffled against the escape of even a chink of light.

> 1942 Evelyn Waugh: It's like walking in the blackout with a shaded torch. You can see just as far as the step you're taking.

Blimp *n* (1934) a character (in full *Colonel Blimp*) invented by the cartoonist and caricaturist David Low (1891–1963), pictured as a rotund pompous ex-officer voicing a rooted hatred of new ideas. He was a reactionary militaristic figure who struck a chord in 1930s Britain, to the extent of inspiring adjectives such as *blimpish* and *blimpian* and nouns like *blimpery* and *blimpism.* The ultimate inspiration for the term was the tubby airship called a *blimp* (1916), the name of which may have come from its original official designation as of the type 'B (limp)' (as opposed to 'A (rigid)').

> 1937 George Orwell: Easy to laugh at . . . the Old School Tie and Colonel Blimp.
>
> 1938 *New Statesman*: The modern clothes *Hamlet* at the Old Vic has excited a lot of Blimpish indignation.

Blitzkrieg *n* (1939) an attack or offensive launched suddenly with great violence with the object of overwhelming the defences immediately—a tactic (supported by dive-bombing and rapid armoured advances) successfully deployed by Germany in invading its neighbours in the early years of World War II. In German the word means literally 'lightning war'. See also **blitz (1940)**.

> 1939 *War Illustrated*: In the opening stage of the war all eyes were turned on Poland, where the German military machine was engaged in Blitz-Krieg—lightning war—with a view to ending as soon as possible . . . Everything was ready for the opening of the 'Blitzkrieg' on the West.

B.O. *n* (1933) see **body odour (1933)**.

bodyline *adj, n* (1933) denoting intimidatory short-pitched fast bowling directed at the batsman's head or upper body. The term had its genesis in the threat posed by Donald Bradman, the most prolific batsman of all time. Desperate for a way to get the Australian out cheaply, Douglas Jardine, appointed captain of the M.C.C. team to tour Australia in 1932–33, fixed on this idea of fast leg-theory, with several fielders close in on the leg side to catch the ball as the batsman fended it off. It was to be carried out by Harold Larwood, one of the fastest bowlers ever, and Bill Voce. Predictably, several Australian batsmen were hit (although not Bradman), and the Australian board of control protested strongly (see the quote below), using the new and graphic term *bodyline.* Even in the next century the affair and the word still have resonances in the world of cricket.

> 1933 *Times*: The Australian Cricket Board of Control has sent the following telegram to the M.C.C.: 'Body-line bowling has assumed such proportions as to menace the best interests of the game, making the protection of his body by a batsman his main consideration [etc.].'

body odour *n* (1933) the smell of the human body, especially the unpleasant odour of stale sweat. The term is essentially a 20th-century advertisers' euphemism, used originally in the promotion of soap, deodorants, etc. (the earliest recorded example (see the first quote below) is from *Murder Must Advertise* by Dorothy Sayers, who had herself been an advertising copywriter). It is best known in the abbreviated form *B.O.*, first recorded in the same year.

> 1933 Dorothy Sayers: Do you ever ask yourself about Body-Odour?
>
> 1933 *Saturday Evening Post*: Those 'B.O.' ads. I laughed at—is the joke on me?

bra *n* (1936) a brassière (see **brassière (1909)**). This was originally a colloquial abbreviation, but it quickly became established as the standard term. At first, *bra* vied with *bras* (pronounced /bræz/), as in the first quote below, but it was not a prolonged contest.

> 1936 W. B. M. Ferguson: She wore nothing but a 'bras', the briefest of French knickers, and the sheerest of white silk hose.
>
> 1937 *Night & Day* (advert): The Bra is one of the famous 'Alphabet' Bra's.

brave new world *n* (1933) a society in which 'progress' has produced a nightmarish 'utopia'. Ultimately the expression comes from Shakespeare's *Tempest* 5:1 ('How beauteous mankind is! O brave new world, that hath such people in't'), but it was Aldous Huxley's use of it as the title of a novel (1932), a fable about a future scientifically trouble-free but stultifying and alienating society, that propelled it into the language, where it continues to be powerfully evocative.

Bren gun *n* (1937) a type of light quick-firing machine-gun. The name was coined from Brno, the town in Czechoslovakia where the gun was first produced, plus the first syllable of Enfield, the north London borough (then in Middlesex) housing the British Royal Small Arms Factory.

bubble-gum *n* (1937) chewing-gum which can be blown into large bubbles. It was originally a US word. (The term *chewing-gum*, incidentally, is first recorded in 1850.)

burger *n* (1939) a hamburger. The term *hamburger* (or in full *hamburger steak*) is first recorded in 1889. By the 1930s its last two syllables were being used as a suffix in the names of various similar products with different ingredients (e.g. *nutburger* (1934), *chickenburger* (1936), *cheeseburger* (1938), *porkburger* (1939), *beefburger* (1940), *Vegeburger* (1972)), and by the end of the decade it had become a word in its own right. The syllable *ham-* no doubt encouraged this proliferation, although of course there is no ham in a hamburger; its name comes from the German city of Hamburg. In the 21st century *burger* is commoner than the full form *hamburger.*

cat *n* (1931) a jazz enthusiast or performer. The term was originally US jazz slang, and presumably a specialization of the earlier **cat** 'fellow, guy' **(1920)**. It subsequently spread into general youth slang, with musical connotations wider than just jazz, and in the 1950s became familiar in British English. Unlike *cool*, with which it was often paired, it has not made a subsequent comeback, so its resonances now are exclusively of the middle years of the 20th century. See also **hep-cat (1938)**.

> 1932 *Melody Maker* [quoting Louis Armstrong]: All the cats were there.
>
> 1958 *Observer*: On one side was the frenetic . . . bumptiousness of the rock-'n'-rollers, on the other the calculated indifference of the cool cats.

cheesecake *n* (1934) photographs of sexually attractive young women scantily clothed. A slang expression, it originated in the US.

> 1942 *Time*: The supreme Empress of Cheesecake, the very Marlene Dietrich, . . . was fittingly crowned by the Treasury as the champion bond seller.

civil defence *n* (1939) the organization and training of civilians for the preservation of lives and property during and after air raids or other enemy action. The term arose among preparations for World War II, and continued in use when the threat later became a nuclear one.

> 1939 *Times Weekly*: It is impossible now to say where air raid precautions end and where civil defence begins.

clip-joint *n* (1932) a club, bar, etc. charging exorbitant prices. A slang expression, it originated in the US. The underlying idea is probably that customers have their money 'clipped' off them, as if with a pair of scissors.

> 1933 Stanley Walker: The worst creature, of all the army of parasites who carried on their trade along Broadway during the speakeasy period, was the proprietor of the 'clip joint'... The clip joint preys on the New Yorker and the out of town sport alike.

cocktail cabinet *n* (1933) a cupboard, often of vulgar design, in which alcoholic drinks are kept. The term hijacks the 1920s sophistication of *cocktail* (see **cocktail party (1928)**) for an article of furniture which may contain anything from a decanter of whisky to a half-empty bottle of faded sherry. It encapsulates social-mountaineering aspirations of the middle years of the 20th century.

> 1958 *Times*: He can afford to buy, on hire purchase, telly, cocktail cabinet, and washing machine.

coloured *n* (1938) a dark-skinned person, especially a black. In South Africa the term was applied specifically to a person of mixed race, constituting a distinct grouping under the apartheid laws.

> 1965 *Listener*: In his own country [he] will put on his 'to let' signs 'no coloureds please'.

colour supplement *n* (1939) a supplement in a newspaper etc. containing coloured illustrations. By the 1960s the term had acquired the connotation 'sophisticated lifestyle'.

> 1966 *Listener*: The young Poles long for western luxuries like cars and clothes and the other bonuses of colour-supplement living.

commercial *n* (1935) an advertisement broadcast on radio or television. The term originated in the US.

> 1935 *Fortune*: We used no media other than radio to feature this soup... using one-third of our commercials on Campbell's Chicken Soup.

conga (1935) a Latin-American dance of African origin, usually performed by several people in single file and consisting of three steps forward followed by a kick. It was very popular in the middle years of the 20th century when a party reached a particular level of conviviality. The word comes from American Spanish *danza Conga* 'dance from the Congo'.

cool *adj* (1933) used as a term of approval. The history of *cool* in the 20th century is somewhat complex. It first emerged recognizably with the meaning 'excellent, wonderful' in African-American English in the interwar years, but it is not entirely clear where this came from. Perhaps it was a development of an earlier US slang sense 'shrewd, clever', which itself probably evolved from general English 'impudent'. It reached a wider audience via jazz musicians after World War II, by which time it was being overlaid with connotations of 'laid-backness' (this was probably a jazz contribution) and of 'fashionableness' or 'stylishness' (harking back to an earlier sense 'suave, sophisticated', which itself grew out of 'shrewd, clever'). It was a core item of youth slang in the 1940s and 50s (e.g. in expressions like *cool cat*). As is usually the case with such items, the next generation found it laughably passé, but it made a comeback towards the end of the 20th century.

> 1933 *American Negro Stories*: Sho wisht [his wealth] wuz mine. And whut make it so cool, he got money 'cumulated. And womens give it all to 'im.

> 1953 *Time*: The latest Tin Pan Alley argot, where 'cool' means good, 'crazy' means wonderful.

> 1958 *Observer*: On one side was the frenetic... bumptiousness of the rock-'n'-rollers, on the other the calculated indifference of the cool cats.

> 2005 *Observer*: If Rooney could be persuaded not to tell the referee to 'Fuck off' on television... the would-be Rooney in the park might not think it was a cool thing to do either.

crooner *n* (1930) a male vocalist who sings popular sentimental songs in a low, smooth voice, especially into a closely held microphone. They were the musical heart-throbs of the 1930s and 40s.

> 1933 *Punch*: Bing Crosby the crooner . . . croons to his feminine class and is crooned to in reply.

crumpet *n* (1936) women regarded as (potential) sexual partners. A British slang term, its origin is unclear, but it probably comes from a male equation of sexually available women with toothsome delicacies (as with *tart*). Towards the end of the 20th century it came to be applied even-handedly to men.

> 1936 James Curtis: Fancy staying up as late as this and not having no crumpet.

> 1987 *Observer*: His performance as a trendy and hung-up LA painter in 'Heartbreakers' made him the thinking woman's West Coast crumpet.

curvaceous *adj* (1936) having a voluptuous figure; shapely. The originally American colloquialism is characteristic of an era (1930s to 1950s) when large breasts and wide hips were the thing.

> 1936 *Screen Book Magazine*: The curvaceous lady [i.e. Mae West] receives from Paramount just as many dollars per week for her scenario work as she receives for her acting.

defence *n* (1935) the military resources of a country. Mainly applied to equipment, personnel, etc. which is just as likely to be used for attack as for defence, but by the end of the 20th century the usage had so successfully insinuated itself into the language that its euphemistic origins are no longer immediately obvious.

> 1935 Clement Attlee: I am glad to hear that the Government are thinking of the question of having a Defence Minister.

demo *n* (1936) a colloquial abbreviation of *demonstration*, originally in the sense 'a public display of group opinion'. From the standpoint of the 21st century it tends to be associated with the bolshie 1960s and 70s, but it was well established by World War II.

> 1936 James Curtis: The anti-war demo last week.

> 1949 Angus Wilson: Norman's out at the demo. At Trafalgar Square.

demob *n* (1934) a colloquial abbreviation of *demobilization* 'release from military service at the end of hostilities'. The term was on many lips in 1945 and '46, often preceding another noun (as in *demob suit*, a suit issued to a soldier on demobilization). See also **demob (1920)**.

> 1945 *Daily Mirror*: It's 'total' demob. now—Many home by year's end.

> 1949 Geoffrey Cotterell: The mockery of the black Homburgs and umbrellas, the demob suits, whose patterns one often recognised [etc.].

deoxyribonucleic acid *n* (1931) any of the nucleic acids which yield deoxyribose on hydrolysis, which are generally found in and confined to the chromosomes of higher organisms, and which store genetic information. The original form of the term, as first recorded in Levene and Bass's book *Nucleic Acids*, was *desoxyribonucleic acid*, but *deoxyribonucleic*, which also dates from the 1930s, has largely replaced it. The more manageable and familiar abbreviation *DNA* is first recorded in 1944. After DNA's doubly helical molecular structure was expounded by James Watson and Francis Crick in 1953, the term became widely known outside the scientific community.

Depression *n* (1934) the financial and industrial slump of 1929 and subsequent years. The usage is a specific application of a term which had been in general use, in expressions like *depression in commerce* and *depression of trade*, since the late 18th century. It remains iconic of the 1930s.

> 1935 John Guthrie: 'I thought you had a baby.' 'No, darling,' said Carol. 'None of us are having them now. It's the depression.'

dig *v* (1934) to understand. The term originally appeared in jazz slang, and is found mainly in African-American English. The origins of the usage, which certainly was not widespread before the mid 1930s, are obscure. It has been claimed that it was introduced into the vocabulary of jazz by Louis Armstrong in the mid 1920s, but this has never been substantiated. Nor have suggestions that it came from an African language (such as Wolof *deg* or *dega* 'to understand') or from Romany *dik* 'to look, see'. Probably it is just an unexplained metaphorical extension of *dig* 'to excavate'. See also **dig (1939)**.

> 1941 *Life*: Dig me?

dig *v* (1939) to appreciate, like, admire. The term appeared originally in jazz slang, and is found mainly in African-American English. It evolved from *dig* 'to understand' (see above) and, like it, remains powerfully evocative of the 'hip' talk of the middle years of the 20th century.

> 1949 Leonard Feather: Dizzy didn't dig the band's kind of music and the band didn't dig Dizzy.

dive-bomb *v* (1935) to attack with bombs at a low level after diving. The technique was pioneered and perfected by the German Luftwaffe, particularly using the Junkers Ju 87 'Stuka'. Its principal object was to terrorize civilians. The noun *dive-bomber* (probably a direct adaptation of German *Sturzkampfflugzeug*, of which *Stuka* is an abbreviation) is first recorded in 1937.

> 1935 *Evening News*: In dive-bombing, which is the most accurate form of aerial attack on surface targets yet devised, the aircraft is aimed bodily at the target in the course of an almost vertical dive, which is maintained for several thousands of feet.

documentary *n* (1932) a film based on real events or circumstances, and intended primarily for instruction or record purposes. The noun usage arose out of a slightly earlier adjectival one: 'The Documentary or Interest Film, including the Scientific, Cultural and Sociological Film', P. Rotha (1930). The genre was pioneered in Britain by John Grierson, who is often credited with introducing the term into English.

> 1932 *Cinema Quarterly*: Documentary is a clumsy description, but let it stand. The French who first used the term only meant travelogue.

drop-out *n* (1930) someone who withdraws from participation, especially in a course of study or in society in general. An originally American colloquialism, it is first recorded in 1930, but the 1960s and 70s were its heyday.

> 1967 *New Statesman*: An international gathering of misfits and drop-outs, smoking pot and meditating in the Buddhist temples.

dumb down *v* (1933) to simplify or reduce the intellectual content of (especially published or broadcast material) so as to make it appealing or intelligible to a large number of people. It was originally a US expression; British speakers became belatedly familiar with it in the 1990s.

> 1980 James Michener: Education has taken very backward steps in the last 20 years—for example, the so-called dumbing down of the textbooks.

Durex *n* (1932) the British proprietary name of a type of contraceptive sheath, often used generically for a condom. It is said to have been coined in 1929 by the chairman of the London Rubber Company, A. R. Reid, when he was travelling home by train one evening. For several decades it enjoyed virtually generic status in Britain, until Aids began to make *condom* more familiar in the 1980s.

dysfunctional *adj* (1936) not functioning properly. The noun *dysfunction* (first recorded in 1916) originated as a medical term, but its derived adjective has become a treasured piece of 20th-century socio-speak.

1978 *Times Literary Supplement*: The eighty-six men assigned to the 'dysfunctional' group also lacked any quasi-marital partnership and often expressed regret about their homosexuality, but they were sexually more active and promiscuous.

ecosystem *n* (1935) a community of organisms and its environment which function as an ecological unit. The word had become common currency by the end of the 20th century, with the spread of eco-awareness, but it took some time to establish itself even as a technical term after its coinage by A. G. Tansley in the 1930s.

electric blanket *n* (1930) an electrically warmed blanket. The early 20th century's love affair with the wonders of electricity extended into the 1930s, throwing up ever more ingenious subjects for electrification.

1930 *Punch*: Had a rotten night. My electric blanket fused and I had to get up to mend it.

electron microscope *n* (1932) a microscope in which the resolution and magnification of minute objects is obtained by passing a stream of electrons through a system of electron lenses. The word was an adaptation of the German term *Elektronenmikroskop*, coined in 1932 by Ernst Brüche.

eleven plus *n* (1937) the age (between 11 and 12) at which pupils in Britain leave primary schools. The term became better known in the 1950s as the name of an exam taken at this age before entering one of the various types of secondary school, and it came to symbolize the principle of educational selection which did battle with comprehensive schooling in Britain in the latter part of the 20th century.

end *n* ***the end*** (1938) the limit of what can be endured; the worst imaginable. A British middle-class colloquialism characteristic of the middle decades of the 20th century.

1938 Ngaio Marsh: The sort of people who go there are just simply The End . . . the most unspeakable curiosities.

1959 Gillian Freeman: Donald, you really are the absolute end.

escalation *n* (1938) incremental succession. The term was originally applied (in the US) to the arms race, then to increases in prices and wages, and, during the Cold War, to the development of 'conventional' warfare into nuclear warfare, or the use of successively more powerful types of weapons in war. The related verb *escalate* is a back-formation, not recorded before 1959. Both usages have attracted the hostility of those who appear to think that a higher authority has decreed that *escalat-* words should only refer to moving staircases.

1938 *Kansas City Star*: Escalation means the building of bigger battleships when other nations do so.

1959 *Guardian*: The possibility of local wars 'escalating into all-out atomic wars'.

evacuate *v* (1938) to remove (inhabitants of an area liable to aerial bombing or other hazards) to safer surroundings. The word powerfully evokes the social disruption of the World War II years.

1938 *Times*: Authorities of our large towns will wonder whether or not to evacuate more than children.

evacuee *n* (1934) an evacuated person. First recorded in 1934 in the second edition of *Webster's New International Dictionary* as a French borrowing in the form *évacué*, with *évacuée* for females, actual usage shows it quickly assimilated to English in a decade of insecure domicile (see **evacuate** above).

existential *adj* (1937) concerned with human existence as seen from the point of view of existentialism. *Existential philosophy* was a slightly earlier term for what is more usually termed **existentialism (1941)**, the fashionable philosophy of the middle years of the 20th century.

*a*1937 Moritz Geiger: 'Existential Philosophy' is a collective term for many problems, many methods of thinking, many points of view . . . The distinguishing feature of all existential philosophy is the fact that its basic category is existential significance.

face-lift *n* (1934) see **face-lifting (1922)**.

family planning *n* (1931) the planning and controlling of the number of children in a family and the intervals between them. The term is often used as a euphemistic cover for *contraception*. See also **birth control (1914)**.

> 1945 *Lancet*: Growing numbers of women attending 'family planning' centres.

fantastic *adj* (1938) wonderful, marvellous. This colloquial usage rapidly took over from earlier senses of the word, such as 'bizarre' and 'illusory', much to the alarm of some purists ('This abuse of a once-useful word is beyond cure. All that you can do is to keep to a minimum the childish informal use of *fantastic*', *The Right Word at the Right Time* (1985)), and at the beginning of the 21st century is its main meaning.

> 1938 Margery Allingham: Oh, Val, isn't it fantastic?... It's amazing, isn't it?

fellow-traveller *n* (1936) someone who sympathizes with the Communist movement without actually being a party member. The expression is a direct translation of Russian *poputchik*, which was used of non-Communist writers sympathizing with the Revolution. It became a vogue term in the Communist witch-hunting era of the Cold War.

> 1942 Evelyn Waugh: 'I was never a party member.' 'Party?' 'Communist party. I was what they call in their horrible jargon, a fellow traveller.'

fifth column *n* (1936) originally the column of supporters which General Mola declared himself to have in Madrid, when he was besieging it in the Spanish Civil War, in addition to the four columns of his army outside the city (in Spanish, *quinta columna*); hence, the term was applied during World War II to a body of one's supporters in an attacked or occupied foreign country, or to the enemy's supporters in one's own country. The derived *fifth columnist* is first recorded in 1940.

> 1939 *War Illustrated*: This looks to me like the Nazis' 'fifth column' in Belgium ready for the invasion.

> 1940 George Bernard Shaw: If you call Stalin a bloodstained monster you must be shot as the most dangerous of Fifth Columnists.

Filofax *n* (1931) a proprietary name, registered in 1931 and based on a colloquial pronunciation of *file of facts*, for a portable filing system for personal or office use, consisting of a loose-leaf notebook with separate sections for appointments, notes, addresses, etc., usually in a wallet with spaces for pens, credit cards, and other personal items. It was a notable sleeper of a word: it subsisted in obscurity for many decades before leaping to sudden fame, even notoriety, in the 1980s as the quintessential yuppie accessory. See also **personal organizer (1985)**.

fission *n* (1939) the splitting, either spontaneously or under the impact of another particle, of a heavy nucleus into two approximately equal parts, with resulting release of large amounts of energy—a process which forms the basis of nuclear reactors and atomic bombs. The technical term was long preceded by the colloquial **split the atom (1909)**. See also **fusion (1947)**.

flak *n* (1938) anti-aircraft fire. The word was borrowed from German, where it was formed from the initial elements of the compound *Fliegerabwehrkanone*, literally 'pilot-defence-gun'; this denoted an anti-aircraft gun. The metaphorical sense 'adverse criticism' is first recorded in 1968.

> 1941 *Times*: Blenheim and Beaufort aircraft of Coastal Command flew through intense flak.

> 1972 *New Yorker*: Getting much flak from Women's Lib?

four-letter word *n* (1934) a word considered obscene, especially any of several monosyllabic English words referring to the sexual or excretory functions or organs of the human body. It has been argued that the emergence of this euphemism reflects a proliferation in the use of such words during World War I (see **fuck off (1929)**).

> 1960 *Times*: Having regard to the state of current writing, it seems that the prosecution against *Lady Chatterley* can only have been launched on the ground that the book contained so-called four-letter words.

fruit machine *n* (1933) a coin- or token-operated gambling machine which pays out according to the combination of symbols (often representations of fruit) appearing on the edges of wheels spun by the operation of a lever. Originally the expression was something of a colloquialism, but it has long since been the standard term. The blackly humorous synonym *one-arm(ed) bandit* is first recorded in 1938.

führer, fuehrer *n* (1934) part of the title (*Führer und Reichskanzler* 'Leader and Imperial Chancellor') assumed by Adolf Hitler in 1934 as head of the German Reich, on the model of *Duce* 'leader', the title assumed by Mussolini. Originally in English it denoted Hitler himself, but it was later also applied ironically to any authoritarian leader.

gay *adj* (1933) homosexual. The adjective has been used to mean 'sexually dissolute' since the 17th century, and by the early 19th century it was being applied to people earning a living by prostitution. It is possible that male prostitutes catering to homosexual men provided the conduit through which it passed from 'living by prostitution' to 'homosexual'. Another element in the equation may be *gaycat*, US hobos' slang for a tramp's companion, usually a young boy, and often his sexual partner; this is first recorded about the turn of the 20th century, but its origins are unknown. An earlier clue still is a reported 1868 song called 'The Gay Young Clerk in the Dry Goods Store' by the US female impersonator Will S. Hays, but the precise semantic status of *gay* here remains speculative. Whatever its antecedents, the earliest reliable printed record of it comes from 1933, in the US; it was largely restricted to the private argot of homosexuals until the mid 1960s, but from then on it started to 'come out', and by the 1980s had become a standard English term. It is first recorded as a noun, meaning 'homosexual person', in 1953. In 21st-century British youth slang it made an abrupt change of direction, being used to denote something of poor quality.

> 1933 Ford & Tyler: Gayest thing on two feet.

> 1974 Kate Millett: I talked at DOB in August, candid, one gay to another.

> 2006 *Radio Times*: I was appalled to see the BBC's board of governors rule that the word 'gay' can be used to mean 'lame' or 'rubbish' without causing offence. In defending its use by Radio 1's Chris Moyles, the governors argued that such talk was widespread among young people.

Gestapo *n* (1934) the secret police of the Nazi regime in Germany, notorious for their brutal methods. The term originated as a German acronym based on *Geheime Staatspolizei* 'Secret State Police', the name of an organization set up by Hermann Göring in Prussia, 1933, and extended to the whole of Germany in January 1934.

G.I. *n* (1939) an enlisted man in the US Army. The term appears to have originated as an abbreviation of *galvanized iron*. It was in use as early as 1907 in the US Army in semi-official designations such as *G.I. can*. This came to be misinterpreted as *government-issue*, and was applied to words such as *shoe* and *soap*. It also went with *soldier*, and in due course this combination was shortened to simply *G.I.* The term became familiar in Britain in the latter years of World War II, when thousands of US troops were stationed there.

glamour boy *n* (1939) a young man who possesses glamour; in World War II British slang often applied specifically (and, by other services, with a tinge of envy) to members of the RAF, particularly fighter pilots, whose exploits in the Battle of Britain and well-cultivated reputation for swashbuckling had made them contemporary heroes.

goon *n* (1938) a stupid person; a fool; also, someone hired, especially by racketeers, to terrorize workers; a thug. A slang term, originating in the US. The immediate inspiration seems to have been 'Alice the Goon', a slow-witted, muscular character in the comic strip 'Thimble Theater, featuring Popeye' by E. C. Segar, which first appeared in 1933. It remains unclear whether Segar knew, and was prompted by, the earlier *goon* 'stolid person' (1921). The usage led on during World War II to *goon* in the sense 'guard in a prisoner-of-war camp' and perhaps also to the *Goon* of *The Goon Show* (see **Goon (1951)**).

> 1938 Raymond Chandler: Some goon here plays chess. You?
>
> 1971 *Blitz* (Bombay): Attempts on his life by goons allegedly employed by the Calcutta police authorities.

grass *n* (1932) a police informer. An item of British criminals' slang, it is probably short for *grasshopper*, rhyming slang for *copper* 'policeman' (also said to be rhyming slang for *shopper* 'one who "shops" or betrays', which would be slightly more appropriate but lacks supporting evidence). The verb, meaning 'to betray (someone) to the police', soon followed.

> 1938 Graham Greene: I wouldn't grass, Spicer said, unless I had to.

green belt *n* (1932) an officially designated belt of open countryside in which all development is severely restricted, usually enclosing a built-up area and designed to check its further growth. The term is redolent of mid 20th-century urban planning.

groove *n* ***in the groove*** (1932) performing exceptionally fluently or well; hence more generally, doing well. The expression originated in US jazz slang.

> 1933 *Fortune*: The jazz musicians gave no grandstand performances; they simply got a great burn from playing in the groove.

groovy *adj* (1937) in the groove; hence, used as a term of general commendation: wonderful, excellent. Originally US jazz slang, it reached its high watermark in the 1950s and 60s, and subsequent usage has been mainly in ironic quotation marks.

guesstimate *n* (1936) an estimate which is based on both guesswork and reasoning. An originally American conflation of *guess* and *estimate*, it has been one of the most vigorous survivors of the craze for blends which first struck the 1920s (see p. 59).

> 1936 *New York Times*: 'Guesstimates' is the word frequently used by the statisticians and population experts.

heavy water *n* (1933) a type of water, especially deuterium oxide, consisting (almost) exclusively of molecules containing hydrogen with a mass number of 2, used in some types of nuclear reactor. The term was held in some awe by non-scientists in the early days of nuclear energy, and there was much head-shaking during World War II over reported attempts by Germany to get its hands on supplies of the substance for its own nefarious purposes.

hep-cat *n* (1938) a devotee of jazz, swing music, etc.; someone who is up to date or stylish. Originally a US slang word; see **hip (1904)**.

> 1955 *Science News Letter*: This is not cool chatter between some young hep-cats in a smoke-filled jazz joint.

hobbit *n* (1937) in the stories of J. R. R. Tolkien (1892–1973), any of a race of diminutive people, resembling human beings but with furry feet. Tolkien, who originated the word, claimed in a piece of post-hoc etymologizing that its underlying meaning was 'hole-builder'. When the Tolkien cult began to grow in the 1960s, a number *hobbit*-derivatives sprang up, such as *hobbitomane* and *hobbitry*.

> 1937 J. R. R. Tolkien: In a hole in the ground there lived a hobbit.

hood *n* (1930) a thug or violent criminal. A slang term, mainly US, it is associated particularly with the gang warfare in American organized crime from the 1920s onwards. It is an abbreviated form of *hoodlum*.

> 1930 *American Mercury*: None of those St. Louie hoods are going to cut in here, see?

hopefully *adv* (1932) it is to be hoped (that). Originally US, it may have been modelled on German *hoffentlich* in the same sense. It is a usage which latterly has excited a good deal of hostility, for no very good reason. It was little used in British English before the 1970s, and its arrival set off a spate of ill-informed anti-Americanism (in fact US purists tend to get just as steamed up about it as British ones do).

> 1932 *New York Times Book Review*: He would create an expert commission . . . to consist of ex-Presidents and a selected list of ex-Governors, hopefully not including Pa and Ma Ferguson.

> 1971 *Guardian*: Prototype wooden rocking horses . . . Hopefully they will be available in the autumn at prices from £120.

hostess *n* (1936) see **air hostess (1934)**.

house arrest *n* (1936) detention in one's own home. This was a popular way of dealing with political dissidents in the 20th century, particularly as the term can give a euphemistic gloss to the proceedings.

housey-housey *n* (1936) the British term in the middle decades of the 20th century for the game latterly known mainly as **bingo (1936)**. It is an elaboration of the earlier name *house*, which apparently originated in the army and presumably refers to the winner getting a full 'house' of numbers on his or her card.

include someone **out** *v* (1937) to exclude someone. The expression was one of the first and best-known 'Goldwynisms'—surreally paradoxical twistings of the English language supposedly perpetrated by the American film producer Sam Goldwyn (1882–1974) (once the legend was established, most of them were no doubt actually dreamed up by his publicity team to keep it going). Others include 'In two words—impossible' and 'Verbal contracts aren't worth the paper they're written on'. (The word *Goldwynism* is first recorded in 1937.)

insecure *adj* (1935) lacking in self-confidence; chronically apprehensive. The word has been in use with very general application since at least the 17th century, but its adoption as a term in psychology—originally mainly child psychology—dates from the 1930s, and 20th-century anxiety ensured there was always plenty of call for it.

> 1935 F. B. Holmes: Karl is very insecure and clings to adults . . . The fearful children were more frequently described as being dependent upon adults for help . . . and as appearing generally insecure.

interceptor *n* (1930) a fast aircraft which is designed specifically to intercept and shoot down hostile aircraft. The term reflects a change in the concept of the fighter aircraft from one which fought 'dogfights' with other similar aircraft (as in World War I) to one whose main role was to shoot down enemy bombers.

> 1934 *Times*: The modern interceptor was evoked by the fast day bomber.

interdisciplinary *adj* (1937) relating two or more disciplines or branches of learning; contributing to or benefiting from two or more disciplines. It was an educational buzzword of the latter part of the 20th century.

> 1972 *Language*: Child language acquisition has proved to be one of the more important interdisciplinary areas of the past decade.

iron lung *n* (1932) a kind of respirator for giving prolonged artificial respiration mechanically, consisting of a metal case that fits over the patient's chest or trunk with an airtight aperture for the neck, so that air can be forced into and out of the lungs by producing rhythmic variations in the air pressure in the case. This grim apparatus became familiar as a polio counter-measure in the middle decades of the 20th century. See also **polio (1931)**.

jingle *n* (1930) a short verse or song in a radio or television commercial or in general advertising. The word in its very sound seems to encapsulate the perceived annoyingness and triviality of 20th-century advertising. It is a specific usage of the more general sense 'a simple, repetitive, catchy rhyme or tune', which dates back to the 17th century.

> 1930 Abraham Flexner: Let the psychologists study advertising . . . in order to understand what takes place when a jingle like 'not a cough in a carload' persuades a nation to buy a new brand of cigarettes.

jive *v* (1939) to dance to fast lively music, originally a form of jazz and later, in the 1950s and 60s, rock and roll. The word, which originated in the US, can also be used as a noun, to denote this sort of dancing. Its earliest meaning, dating from the 1920s, is 'misleading or empty talk', but it is not known where it came from.

> 1957 *Observer*: Young people from the East End and the West End came there [the Humphrey Lyttelton Club] to jive or listen.

jukebox *n* (1939) a machine that automatically plays selected gramophone records when a coin is inserted. It was an essential adjunct to the youth-music revolution of the 1940s and 50s, when one stood in the corner of every coffee bar. An earlier synonym was *juke organ* (1937), but it did not survive long. The word *juke* itself originated in the 1930s as an African-American slang term for a roadhouse or brothel. It probably came from *juke* or *joog*, a word meaning 'wicked' or 'disorderly' in the Gullah language, a creolized English of South Carolina, Georgia, and northern Florida.

L (1936) an abbreviation of *learner*. Its main use is in *L-plate*, denoting a sign with a capital *L* on it which in Britain must be displayed on a car driven by a learner. We now take them for granted, and the thought of unidentified novices driving around is somewhat alarming.

> 1936 *Motor Manual*: 'L' plates must be carried at the front and rear of the car.

live *adj* (1934) (of a performance) heard or watched at the time of its occurrence, as distinguished from one recorded on film, tape, etc. Modern recording technology has broken the bond between time and events, posing a challenge to the concept 'alive': dead performers can speak on the radio and move on the screen, and need to be distinguished from those who are actually breathing at the moment of transmission. *Live* does the job (later in the century the waters were muddied with such usages as 'recorded live').

> 1934 *B.B.C. Year-Book*: Listeners have . . . complained of the fact that recorded material was too liberally used . . . but . . . transmitting hours to the Canadian and Australasian zones are inconvenient for broadcasting 'live' material.

Loch Ness monster *n* (1933) a large unidentified aquatic creature alleged to live in Loch Ness, a long deep lake in northern Scotland. Periodic claimed sightings of it from the 1930s onwards have provided much-needed relief to news editors on slow days. The pet-name *Nessie* is first recorded in 1945.

> 1933 *Inverness Courier*: The Loch Ness 'monster' was seen near the west end of the Loch.

logo *n* (1937) the identifying symbol of an organization, publication, or product. An abbreviation of *logotype*, which was originally a printers' term for a piece of type with two or more separate elements. Any self-respecting company would now feel naked without its own logo.

luxury *adj* (1930) of high quality, and usually expensive; also, providing sumptuous comfort. It became a key adjective in 20th-century advertisers' hyperbole.

> 1934 George Bernard Shaw: The rich tourists in the palace hotels and luxury liners.

male chauvinism *n* (1936) an attitude attributed to men of excessive loyalty to members of the male sex and of prejudice against women. The term originated in the US. The noun *male chauvinist* is first recorded in 1940, but it was not until the late 1960s, when the women's movement hit its stride, that both usages became really widespread. Plain *chauvinism*, with the implication 'male chauvinism', is first recorded in 1968 ('The chauvinism... they met came from individuals and was not built into the institution itself', *Voice of the Women's Liberation Movement*), and *male chauvinist pig*, a term of contempt and abuse for a male chauvinist, in 1970.

> 1936 Clifford Odets: You and your male chauvenism.

> 1940 Joseph Mitchell: She called Bill a male chauvenist, yelled something about the equality of the sexes, and ran out.

> 1970 *Time*: European women have accepted their lot much more readily than their American counterparts. Recently, however, growing numbers... have launched their attack on male chauvinism.

> 1970 *New Yorker*: Hello, you male-chauvinist racist pig... Repent Male Chauvinists.

marriage guidance *n* (1935) the giving of advice on problems connected with marriage, usually as a form of social service. It is a relatively early example of the vocabulary of counselling, which over the succeeding decades impinged more and more on the stiff-upper-lip self-reliance of the British.

> 1970 Germaine Greer: Women are not happy even when they do follow the blue-print set out by... marriage guidance counsellors and the system that they represent.

mod con *n* (1934) short for *modern convenience* 'an amenity, device, fitting, etc. of the sort that is usual in a modern house', a piece of estate agents' jargon first recorded in 1926. The abbreviation itself started out amongst the house agents, but has since established itself (often tongue in cheek) in the general language. It is usually used in the plural.

> 1934 *Punch*: An advertisement... describing just such a house as we wanted. Just the right number of rooms, 'five minutes from the station, h. & c. in all bedrooms, all mod. cons.'

muesli *n* (1939) a dish, originating in Switzerland, consisting of a cereal (usually oats) and fruit to which milk is added, often eaten as a breakfast dish. It had first been introduced into Britain in the 1920s under the name *Birchermuesli*, after its proponent Dr Bircher-Benner, who served it to patients in his 'natural health' clinic in Zürich. Originally restricted largely to the health-food fringe, it leapt to fame in the high-fibre boom of the 1970s, becoming the trendy breakfast dish. Its consumption is now closely associated with the *Guardian*-reading classes.

> 1998 *Private Eye*: Bring a spoonful of Heritage® Muesli up to your mouth and enjoy an opportunity to preserve our agricultural genetic heritage.

Munich (1938) the English name of *München*, the capital of Bavaria, used allusively with reference to a meeting of representatives of Germany, Britain, France, and Italy on 29 September 1938, when (by the 'Munich Agreement') the Sudetenland of northern and western Czechoslovakia was ceded to Germany. Its connotations were usually of naive and dishonourable appeasement, particularly on the part of the British prime minister who concluded the agreement, Neville Chamberlain. In the succeeding years a small range of opprobrious derivatives were formed from it, including *Municheer*, *Munichism*, and *Munichite*.

> 1938 Harold Nicolson: Go up to Leicester. Bertie Jarvis says that I have put the women's vote against me by abusing Munich.
>
> 1962 Michael Foot: At Bridgwater, Vernon Bartlett, ... won a spectacular victory in the teeth of all the 'peace' propaganda of the Munichites.

Muzak *n* (1935) the proprietary name (registered in Britain in 1938) of a system of piped music for factories, restaurants, supermarkets, etc.; it is also used loosely, and generally disparagingly, to designate recorded light background music generally. The coining of the word is generally attributed to the US soldier and electrical engineer George Owen Squier (1865–1934). It appears to have been a blend of *music* and *Kodak* (at that time *Kodak* was one of the best known trade names in the world, so it would have been a natural choice).

> 1960 *Guardian*: Canned music, or Muzak ... will to-day ooze into yet another corner of the world.

National Socialism *n* (1931) see **National Socialist (1923)**.

Nazi *adj, n* (1930) (a member) of the National Socialist Workers' Party in Germany, led by Adolf Hitler from 1920 and in power from 1933 to 1945. The form of the word is a German representation of the pronunciation of the first two syllables of German *Nationalsozialist*. Before the end of the 1930s *Nazi* was being applied to similar fascist parties and organizations elsewhere, and in due course it became a general term of condemnation for any sort of right-wing oppression. See also **National Socialist (1923)**.

> 1930 *Times*: Herr Hitler, the leader of the victorious National-Socialists (Nazis), has very carefully refrained from saying anything ... Herr Hitler, the leader of the National Socialists, speaking at the last big Nazi election meeting.
>
> 1973 *Guardian*: 'Nazi' has become an indiscriminate political cliché applied to insensitive bureaucrats, Americans in Vietnam, IRA Provos, British paras in Ulster, Black September, Zionists, et al.

New Deal *n* (1932) the programme of social and economic reform in the US planned by the Roosevelt administration of 1932 onwards.

> 1932 F. D. Roosevelt: I pledge you—I pledge myself—to a new deal for the American people.

newscaster *n* (1930) someone who reads the news on radio or television. The term originated in the US, and did not spread significantly to British English until the mid 1950s, when it was consciously introduced by the newly formed Independent Television (see the quote below). Based, of course, on *broadcaster*; similar later US formations include *sportscaster* and *racecaster*, both first recorded in 1938.

> 1956 *Annual Register 1955*: I.T.A. news was planned, intentionally, as something different from the traditional, wholly dignified, and impartial B.B.C. news, and was given instead from a personal angle, from less orthodox sources, by a skilful team of 'newscasters'.

nylon *n* (1938) a type of high-strength synthetic material. It was one of the earliest and best-known of the man-made fibres which had such a transforming effect on 20th-century life. Amongst the first products was the nylon stocking, which almost attained the status of an unofficial currency when brought to war-deprived Europe by US service personnel (*nylons* in this sense is first recorded in 1940).

The origin of the name *nylon* has excited speculation, particularly in the light of its resemblance to the initial elements of *New York* and *London*. The matter was clarified in the following letter to *Women's Wear Daily* by John W. Eckelberry of the du Pont Co. in 1940: 'The word is a generic word coined by the du Pont Co. It is not a registered name or trademark ... We wish to emphasize the following additional points: First, that the letters n-y-l-o-n have absolutely no significance, etymologically or otherwise ... Because the names of two textile fibers in common use—namely "cotton" and "rayon", end with letters "on" ... it was felt that a word ending in "on" might be desirable. A number of words ... were rejected because it was found they were not sufficiently distinct from words found in the dictionary, or in lists of classified trademarks. After much deliberation, the term "nylon" was finally adopted.'

Odeon *n* (1930) any of numerous cinemas in a chain built in Britain by Oscar Deutsch or his company in the 1930s. The word is an adaptation of Greek *odeion*, which denoted a building for musical performance (the coincidental identity of the word's first two letters with Oscar Deutsch's initials inspired a post-hoc acronymization of *Odeon* as 'Oscar Deutsch entertains our nation'). It became almost synonymous with *cinema* in British English in the middle decades of the century, and continues to convey many of the connotations of the lavish architectural style in which the originals were built.

Oscar *n* (1934) one of the statuettes awarded by the Academy of Motion Picture Arts and Sciences, Hollywood, USA, for excellence in film acting, directing, etc. These awards have been made annually since 1928. Margaret Herrick, a former secretary of the Academy of Motion Picture Arts and Sciences, is said to have remarked in 1931 that the Art Deco-style statuette reminded her of her 'Uncle Oscar', namely Oscar Pierce, an American wheat and fruit grower; the name stuck.

paramilitary *adj, n* (1935) of or being a force or unit whose function and organization are similar or ancillary to those of a professional or regular military force, but which has no official status. The coinage of the term may have been inspired by French *paramilitaire*, which dates from around 1920. Its profile was decisively raised in the 1970s, when it came to be applied, in the sense 'quasi-military' and with virtually euphemistic force, to armed terrorist organizations run on military lines. The noun, denoting a member of such an organization (especially in Northern Ireland), is first recorded in 1975.

> 1936 *Punch*: Let us at once impale the new and unnecessary mongrel 'paramilitary'—'paramilitary forces (S.A., S.S., Labour Corps and other organisations)'.

> 1975 *Economist*: The co-ordinating committee of the Loyalist paramilitaries . . . also supports Mr Craig.

> 2000 John Simpson: We drive for hours . . . looking at the torched houses and the paramilitary thugs lounging at the roadblocks.

parking meter *n* (1936) a coin-operated meter which registers the time a vehicle has been parked. The term, which originated in America, is often abbreviated to simply *meter*. The devices were not introduced in Britain until the end of the 1950s, but within a decade they had become an accepted (though unloved) part of city streetscapes.

> 1936 *American City*: In July . . . there came to the attention of the officials in Dallas a device known as the parking meter.

> 1960 *Daily Telegraph*: What promises to be the most important experiment in traffic control starts next Monday, when car parking over the whole of Mayfair becomes subject to meters.

pizza *n* (1935) an Italian foodstuff consisting of a breadlike base with various savoury toppings. In Italian the word means literally just 'tart' or 'pie', but its ultimate origins are unknown. Earliest references to it in English are as an exotic foreign dish; not until the 1950s did its career as a fast-food star begin. Italian *pizzeria*, denoting a restaurant specializing in pizzas, is first recorded in English in 1943.

> 1957 *Sunday Times*: The Pizza Napoletana has travelled the world. In Paris restaurants, in Shaftesbury Avenue milk bars, in South Kensington coffee shops the pizza has become acclimatised.

platinum blonde *adj, n* (1931) (a woman) with hair of a silvery-blonde colour: in the middle years of the 20th century, and often with chemical assistance, the height of sophisticated sexiness. The term was in its early years particularly associated with the American film actress Jean Harlow (1911–37), who starred in a film called *Platinum Blonde* (1931).

1931 *Daily Express*: Miss Binnie Barnes, who appears as a platinum blonde in 'Cavalcade', is seen here as a brunette. Nature gave her auburn-red hair.

polio *n* (1931) poliomyelitis, especially the paralytic form. The term *poliomyelitis*, of which this is an abbreviated form, is first recorded in 1878; it gradually replaced the previous *infantile paralysis*. The abbreviation followed mid-century epidemics, which made *polio* a word to fear. They were brought to an end in the 1950s by the administration of an effective vaccine, the *Salk vaccine* (named after the US virologist Jonas Salk (1914–95), who developed it; the term is first recorded in 1954). See also **iron lung (1932)**.

1931 *Survey* (heading): Panic and polio.

1940 *Time* (heading): Polio scare.

polythene *n* (1939) a tough, light, translucent thermoplastic made by polymerizing ethylene and used especially for moulded and extruded articles, as film for packaging, and as a coating. It was one of the range of new plastics that transformed everyday life in the 20th century. The word is a contraction of *polyethylene*, also first recorded in this sense in 1939, and the preferred form in US English.

prefab *adj, n* (1937) (a house or other building) that is prefabricated. In Britain the term was applied specifically to a light, often single-storey house of the kind built in large numbers during and after World War II when it was necessary to rehouse many people in a short time. They remained a familiar part of the urban scene for many decades—a good deal longer than originally envisaged.

1947 Nevil Shute: Any young couple might live in a prefab when they start off first.

production line *n* (1935) (a method of mass-producing goods using) an assembly line (see **assembly line (1914)**). Latterly the term has often been used with connotations of sterile uniformity.

1958 *Listener*: I suggest one of those 'production-line' chickens, which is big enough for four.

quick-frozen *adj* (1930) frozen rapidly to facilitate long storage at a low temperature. Preservative freezing (and the adjective *frozen*) had been applied to foodstuffs since the middle of the 19th century, but it was the technique of subjecting them to a sudden low-temperature blast, eliminating the formation of ice crystals, that paved the way for the late 20th century's freezer food culture. *Quick-frozen* remained the vogue term in the middle years of the century, but it gradually gave way to the simpler *frozen*.

1930 *Popular Science*: Clarence B. Birdseye . . . succeeded in placing quick-frozen fish on the market.

racist *n, adj* (1932) (an advocate) of belief in the superiority of a particular race, leading to prejudice and antagonism towards people of other races. The associated noun *racism* is first recorded in 1936. In the 1930s, the words were usually used with reference to the Nazis' theories of racial superiority, but in the latter part of the century their context is usually prejudiced treatment of blacks and Asians. They were latecomers in a field already occupied by **racialism (1907)** and **racialist (1917)**, but over the decades they have gradually become the main forms.

1934 H. G. Wells: So much for the Hitlerite stage of my development, when I was a sentimentalist, a moralist, a patriot, a racist.

1977 Martin Walker: A strike of the Asian workers against racism in the factory.

rat-race *n* (1939) a fiercely competitive struggle or contest. The term originated in America. Its main modern connotation, characterizing 20th-century human existence as a soul-destroying competitive struggle to maintain one's position in work or life, does not seem to have crystallized until the 1950s.

1958 *Spectator*: Modern economic life is more like a rat-race than a rational way of life.

raygun *n* (1931) a weapon that can emit harmful or lethal rays. The word is redolent of earlier and (as they seem at the beginning of the 21st century) simpler and less sophisticated days of science fiction.

> 1958 *Spectator*: But as a space-veteran who once triggered a ray-gun with Flash Gordon, let me advise you to read on.

reflation *n* (1932) a deliberate increase in the supply of money, so as to revive economic activity. The term (modelled on *inflation* and *deflation*) arose out of efforts to bring to an end the economic depression of the early 1930s, and it established a permanent and prominent place for itself in economists' jargon in the financially up-and-down decades that followed. The derivative *reflationary* is contemporary.

> 1932 *Times Literary Supplement*: The 'reflationary' policy of the American Government will in the end, he thinks, set prices rising again.

resistance *n* (1939) organized covert opposition to an occupying or ruling power, especially (usually with a capital *R*), in World War II, the underground movement formed in France in June 1940 with the object of resisting the authority of the German occupying forces and the Vichy government.

> 1940 *Times*: General de Gaulle . . . broadcast from London a message to the French nation last night. The text of his speech . . . is as follows: . . . Whatever happens the flame of French resistance must not and shall not be extinguished.

> 1946 Aldous Huxley: I was sent a number of French books recently . . . Novels about the Resistance—half heroism, half unutterable moral squalor.

satellite *n* (1936) a man-made object placed in orbit round an astronomical body, typically the Earth. An English translation of Jules Verne's *Begum's Fortune* in 1880 spoke of a space projectile 'endowing the Earth with a second satellite', but the terminology did not really meet the concept in its modern sense until the 1930s. The science-fiction writer Arthur C. Clarke is often credited as being the first to set out the real possibilities for such an object, in the 1945 article in *Wireless World* quoted below. Theory became practice in 1957 (see **sputnik (1957)**).

> 1936 *Discovery*: The scheme for building a metal outpost satellite and propelling it in a fixed orbit 600 miles above the earth's surface.

> 1945 Arthur C. Clarke: This 'orbital' velocity is 8 km per sec. (5 miles per sec), and a rocket which attained it would become an artificial satellite, circling the world for ever with no expenditure of power.

> 1957 *Times*: The Russian satellite soaring over the United States seven times a day has made an enormous impression on American minds.

secret weapon *n* (1936) a weapon (often of potentially decisive force) classified as secret. The somewhat paranoid term arose out of the long build-up to war in the 1930s, when potential enemies were suspected of developing nameless horrors in their weapons research establishments.

> 1939 Winston Churchill: The magnetic mine . . . may perhaps be Herr Hitler's much vaunted secret weapon.

> 1945 *Science News Letter*: The proximity fuze, a tiny radio set device in the nose of the projectile, is rated as the U.S.A. No. 2 secret weapon.

send *v* (1932) to transport with delight; to carry away. The verb originated in jazz slang, and in the 1950s came to typify for older generations the outlandish vocabulary of pop- and fashion-obsessed youth.

> 1958 *Spectator*: The girls wore thick eye-makeup and 'sent' expressions.

senior citizen *n* (1938) an old person, especially one who is past the age of retirement. American in origin, it is one of the 20th century's classic euphemisms, and an early sign of its uneasiness with the concept of old age.

> 1938 *Time*: Mr. Downey had an inspiration to do something on behalf of what he calls, for campaign purposes, 'our senior citizens'.

sit-in *n* (1937) a strike, demonstration, etc. in which people occupy a workplace, public building, etc., especially in protest against alleged activities there. The term originated in America, and really came into its own in the protest-chic of the 1960s.

> 1965 Mrs. L. B. Johnson: Some of the Civil Rights marchers had walked into the White House . . . and refused to budge. A sit-in in the White House!

skid row *n* (1931) a run-down area of a town where the unemployed, vagrants, alcoholics, etc. tend to congregate. The term originated in US slang as an alteration of the earlier *skid road* in the same sense. This originally denoted literally 'a track formed by skids along which logs are rolled'; it then came to be applied to any part of town inhabited by loggers, and from there moved inexorably downhill. There was no shortage of such places to apply it to in the depression-haunted 1930s.

slim *v* (1930) to attempt to become thinner by dieting. The word had been preceded by the synonymous and equally euphemistic *slenderize* (1923), but it has been *slim* that has come out on top.

> 1930 *Punch*: The hostess ate hardly any. She is slimming.

soap opera *n* (1939) a radio or television serial dealing especially with domestic situations and often characterized by melodrama and sentimentality. The 'soap' part of the name comes from the fact that some of the early sponsors of the programmes (in America) were soap manufacturers. It is foreshadowed in 'These fifteen-minute tragedies . . . I call the 'soap tragedies' . . . because it is by the grace of soap I am allowed to shed tears for these characters who suffer so much from life', *Christian Century* (1938). The 'opera' element is an echo of the earlier *horse opera* 'a Western' (1927). The abbreviated form *soap* is first recorded in 1943.

social services *n* (1933) services supplied for the benefit of the community, especially any of those provided by the central or local government, such as education, medical treatment, social welfare, etc. In Britain, the term became a familiar element in the political scenery in the second half of the 20th century.

> 1976 *Times*: There is more demand to cut taxes than to expand social services.

sound barrier *n* (1939) the obstacle to supersonic flight posed by such factors as increased drag and reduced controllability, which occur when aircraft not specially designed for such flight approach the speed of sound. 'Breaking' the sound barrier was something of a holy grail for aeronautical engineers around the middle of the 20th century, and spoken of in hushed terms. The deed was done for the first time by the US Bell X1 rocket aircraft in 1947. The obstacle was also called the *sonic barrier* (1946).

> 1955 *Times*: The bang that shook London early on Tuesday morning was caused . . . by a Gloster Javelin breaking the sound barrier.

spacecraft *n* (1930) a vehicle designed to travel in space. The word was destined (along with **space vehicle (1946)**) to become the 'serious' term for such vehicles when they were actually built, with the earlier *spaceship* (1894) being relegated to the sci-fi annexe.

> 1932 David Lasser: Our experience with cosmic speeds and distances is not equal to the task of guiding a space-craft on its perilous journey.

Spam *n* (1937) the proprietary name (registered in the US in 1937) of a type of tinned cooked meat consisting chiefly of pork. The word has also (with lower-case initial) been applied loosely to other types of tinned luncheon meat. It is probably a conflation of *spiced ham*, although the quote below tells a different story. In Britain Spam became synonymous with the dull and meagre diet of World War II, and eventually turned into something of a laughing stock. On the word's transformation into Web jargon, see **spam (1994)**.

> 1937 *Squeal*: In the last month Geo. A. Hormel & Co... launched the product Spam... The 'think-up' of the name [is] credited to Kenneth Daigneau, New York actor... Seems as if he had considered the word a good memorable trade-name for some time, had only waited for a product to attach it to.

spiv *n* (1934) a man who lives by his wits and has no regular employment, especially one engaging in petty black-market dealings and often characterized by flashy dress. It is a British slang word, probably dating back to the underworld argot of the 19th century but first recorded in 1934. It is very likely related to obsolete slang *spiff* 'a well-dressed man', but the origins of that are obscure. The spiv reached his apotheosis during World War II and the succeeding years, when the disrupted economic conditions allowed ample scope for unofficial trading (a pair of nylons here, a few packets of cigarettes there) and other petty crime. He became a stock figure in the English social comedy, represented on screen by such stereotypes as 'Flash Harry' (played by George Cole) in the St Trinian's films and Private Walker in *Dad's Army*.

> 1952 Joan Henry: In appearance, he resembled the typical spiv; with coat-hanger shoulders, and pointed shoes, and a smile that would have been an asset to any confidence man.

striptease *n* (1936) a kind of entertainment in which a female (or sometimes a male) performer undresses gradually in a tantalizingly erotic way in front of an audience, usually to music. The elements of the term can be traced back to late 1920s America, when both *strip*, as a noun (1928) and a verb (1929), and *tease* (1927) first appeared. The combination *strip-teaser* is first recorded in 1930, and *striptease* is apparently a back-formation from that. The synonymous *stripper* also dates from 1930.

> 1929 *Variety*: She has the unadornment stuff to herself, since the other gals never strip beyond regulation soub garb.

> 1930 *Variety*: Detroit censor pinches four stock strippers.

> 1937 *Daily Telegraph*: Can anything be said in defence of the present public interest in 'strip-tease' and nudist or semi-nudist displays on stage?

supermarket *n* (1933) a large self-service shop selling a wide range of groceries and household goods, and often one of a chain of stores. The term originated in America. The idea of such a shop was not new (the earliest example had been the chain named 'Piggly-Wiggly', founded in 1916 by Clarence Saunders in Memphis, Tennessee, which had many of the familiar features, such as customers picking their choice of goods from open shelves and paying for them as they left), but the term *supermarket* was.

> 1933 *New York Times*: In a move interpreted by the trade as an effort to help both corporate chains and independent wholesale grocers fight the competition of 'super-markets' which have sprung up in the last two years, the Associated Grocery Manufacturers of America, Inc., yesterday drew up a proposed model law for States which may seek to prevent the sale of standard grocery products at or below purchase price... For three months now a large supermarket in New Jersey has been doing a business reputed to average $100,000 a week.

> 1933 *Chain Store Age*: The 'One-stop-drive-in super market' provides free parking, and every kind of food under one roof.

supersonic *adj* (1934) involving, pertaining to, capable of, or designating speeds greater than the speed of sound. *Supersonic* originally denoted sound waves or vibrations with frequencies greater than those audible to the human ear (it is first recorded in that sense in 1919), but the need to talk about faster-than-sound flight overtook it, and that original meaning has now been largely taken over by *ultrasonic* (1923).

> 1936 *Aircraft Engineering*: The wing shows what the Germans call a 'supersonic profile', because the aeroplane is supposed to fly the greater part of its route at supersonic speeds.

swastika *n* (1932) a cross with a right-angled projection at the end of each arm, used as the symbol of Nazism. The word, which comes from Sanskrit *svastika*, a derivative of *svastí* 'well-being, luck', originally denoted an ancient cosmic or religious symbol of this form. English adopted it as the equivalent of German *Hakenkreuz*, literally 'hook-cross', ensuring the speedy obliteration of any former connotations.

tape recorder *n* (1932) an apparatus for recording sounds on magnetic tape and afterwards reproducing them. The original machines, also called *wire recorders*, used steel tape, which did not make for easy portability (the name of one, called the *Blattnerphone* after its inventor, L. Blattner (1881–1935), is first recorded in 1931). The present-day type, using plastic tape covered with iron oxide, came in after World War II. See also **tape record (1905)**.

test-tube baby *n* (1935) applied originally to a baby conceived by artificial insemination, and latterly to a baby that has developed from an ovum fertilized outside the mother's body. With its powerful connotations of unnaturalness, the term began as and has remained a stick with which to beat the idea of scientifically aided procreation.

> 1935 Emil Novak: There has been . . . a good deal of unfortunate newspaper discussion on the subject of artificial insemination and 'test-tube babies'.

> 1978 *Times*: The world's first test-tube baby, a girl, was born by caesarian section just before midnight at Oldham and District General Hospital, Greater Manchester . . . The embryo was implanted in Mrs Brown's womb after being fertilized in Mr Steptoe's laboratories.

Third Reich *n* (1930) the German state under the rule of Adolf Hitler and the Nazi party, 1933–45; the regime of Hitler. The term is a partial anglicization of German *Dritte Reich* 'Third Empire', which is first recorded as the title of a 1923 book by A. Moeller van den Bruck. (The 'First' Empire in this context was the Holy Roman Empire (up to 1806) and the 'Second' the Imperial German state 1871–1918).

> 1930 *Times*: Asked to give some idea of the 'Third Reich', Herr Hitler said the old Germany was a State of great honour and of glorious events, but the conception of 'the people' was not the central pillar of its structure. The second State had placed democracy and pacificism in the centre. They hoped for the Third Reich, which would have as its keystone the conception of the people and the national idea.

twit *n* (1934) a fool; a stupid or ineffectual person. A slang expression, originally British, which came into widespread use in the 1950s and 60s, although it had been around since before World War II; in the 1970s it gained some currency in US English, largely through British television sitcoms. Thereafter it began to go out of fashion. It may be connected with the ancient verb *twit* 'to reproach', but there is probably also some influence of *nitwit* 'fool' (1922), a word of dialectal origin.

> 1970 Nicholas Fleming: No one but a prize twit or Captain Oates would have ventured out in this weather.

underpants *n* (1931) an under-garment covering the lower part of the body (and in some cases part of the legs). The term is generally applied to a man's garment. So firmly established is the whole family of *pants* words for 'underwear' in British English at the beginning of the 21st century that it seems hard to imagine a pre-*pants* era, but hitherto such items had largely (and the word is used advisedly) been known as *drawers* or, in the case of women, *knickers*. **Panties** is first recorded in 1908, but in reference to dolls' clothing, and it does not seem to have come into general use until the late 1920s; early references to *pants* in this sense can be difficult to disentangle from those meaning 'trousers', but again the usage was current by the late 1920s. *Briefs* (1934) soon joined the party. Not until the latter part of the 20th century did alternatives, such as *boxers*, begin to challenge the pre-eminence of *pants* and *underpants* for men's wear—a development perhaps assisted, or reflected, by the use of *pants* as an adjective denoting something despised or condemned.

underprivileged *n* (1935) people without the advantages and opportunities enjoyed by most members of the community. The word is actually recorded as an adjective towards the end of the 19th century, but it did not begin to take off as a key 20th-century euphemism for 'poor people' until the 1930s.

> 1935 A. P. Herbert: She had spent a long time persuading one of the 'underprivileged' to go to hospital to have an operation.

unquote (1935) used in speaking (usually paired with *quote*) to indicate the end of a quotation. It began (in America) as a device used in giving dictation, but soon spread into ordinary speech, and thence into writing imitating speech.

> 1935 e. e. cummings: But he said that if I'd hold up publication of *No Thanks* for 15 days he'd kill unquote a page of Aiken . . . The Isful ubiquitous wasless&-shallbeless quote scrotumtightening unquote omnivorously eternal thalassa pelagas or Ocean.

up-tight *adj* (1934) in a state of nervous tension or anxiety; worried, on edge. The word originated in US slang. There is a large gap in the record between the first recorded example and the mid 1960s, when this usage really took off, but it seems likely that it was simmering in the spoken language in the interim.

> 1934 J. M. Cain: I'm getting up tight now, and I've been thinking about Cora. Do you think she knows I didn't do it?

> 1969 Collier Young: He looked worried. Really worried. As the kids say, he was up-tight.

video *adj, n, prefix* (1935) coined (from Latin *videre* 'to see') as a visual equivalent of **audio (1913)**, and applied specifically to that which is displayed on a television or other similar screen. In later US noun use the word also denoted television as a broadcasting medium. As a prefix it took part in a relatively modest number of formations through the 1940s, 50s, and 60s, but the trickle became a flood in the 70s and 80s (see **videotape (1953)**). See also **video (1958)**.

> 1935 *Discovery*: They are providing ever better products and service to enable the listening public to get more enjoyment from the 'audio' programmes . . . and will be ready to cater for those who wish . . . to see such 'video' items as may become available.

viewer *n* (1935) someone who watches or is watching television. When public television broadcasting became actual rather than potential, the term gradually took over from the earlier *looker-in* (1927) and the contemporary but short-lived *televiewer* (1935).

> 1936 *Times*: At Alexandra Palace yesterday, when the new television service of the B.B.C. was officially opened, the Postmaster-General and others had to address themselves not only to listeners, but to 'viewers'. Within a radius of some 25 miles, 'viewers' saw and heard a ceremony which the speakers rightly described as historic . . . There was a speech by Mr. R. C. Norman, chairman of the B.B.C. who was the first to use the word 'viewers' in its new meaning.

V.I.P. *n* (1933) an abbreviation of *very important person* (or, in the earliest recorded instance, *personage*). The usage proliferated during and after World War II. It has been occasionally treated as an acronym, and pronounced /vip/. Amateur psychologists may see in the term an early symptom of the late 20th century's obsession with celebrity.

> 1946 Evelyn Waugh: I found I had been categorized VIP–Very Important Person. It seemed odd to be asked 'Are you a VIP?'

weapon of mass destruction *n* (1937) a weapon intended to cause widespread destruction and loss of life. The usage enjoyed a low profile until the 1990s, when it was widely taken up as a cover-term (generally used in the plural) for chemical, biological, and nuclear weapons. Its length made it an obvious candidate for abbreviation, as **WMD (1991)**. It figured largely in the controversy over the armaments possessed by the Saddam Hussein regime in Iraq in the early 21st century.

> 1937 *Times*: Who can think without horror of what another widespread war would mean, waged as it would be with all the new weapons of mass destruction.

1991 *Congress Record*: The permanent five members of the U.N. Security Council met in Paris . . . where they declared their intent to seek the elimination of the transfer of weapons of mass destruction (WMD) and missiles.

2003 *Morning Star*: He asks if the international community could prevent the unthinkable—the use of a weapon of mass destruction by a terrorist organisation.

witch-hunt *n* (1938) a single-minded and uncompromising campaign against a group of people with unacceptable views or behaviour (in early use, mainly Communists), especially one regarded as unfair or malicious persecution.

1938 George Orwell: Rank-and-file Communists everywhere are led away on a senseless witch-hunt after 'Trotskyists'.

1977 *Gay News*: During the operation—labelled a 'witch-hunt' by the local gay community—28 men were arrested.

The 1940s

The 1940s were the pivotal decade of the century. World War II, which began in the last months of 1939, occupied the energies of most nations on the planet for the best part of six years. The two atom bomb explosions at Hiroshima and Nagasaki in 1945, which marked its effective end, were also the hinge of the century. The second half of the 1940s saw the putting in place of the elements that would shape the world's events for the following forty years: the ideological contest between East and West, decolonization, international cooperation, the development of nuclear weapons, and of the computer.

From the *phoney war* (or *sitzkrieg*) at its beginning to the *war trials* at its end, from the *acronyms* of its military bureaucrats to the slang of its ordinary soldiers, World War II contributed an enormous amount of new vocabulary to the English language—much of it necessarily ephemeral (few now remember *Coventrate*—see below), but much, too, that still resonated at the end of the century (*final solution, collaboration*).

It was the war, above all, that first stretched out its tentacles towards civilian populations. In Britain, this took the form, in 1940, of the *blitz*: *bombed-out* families surveyed the smoking ruins of their homes; the *bomb-sites* began to appear that would disfigure British cities for decades to come; Coventry was *Coventrated* ('intensively bombed'—a usage inspired by German air raids on the city in 1940), and later there came the *Baedeker raids* (German air-raids in 1942 on places of historical and cultural importance in Britain, named after the 'Baedeker' guide books). Towards the end of the war it would be the *V-1s* (or *buzz-bombs*, or *doodlebugs*, or *flying bombs*) and the *V-2s*. To meet the threat of invasion, Britons joined the *Home Guard*; to produce precious fuel, some became *Bevin boys* (named after Ernest Bevin, the wartime Minister of Labour) down the mines; *clippies* (female conductors) 'manned' the buses. It was a time of *cannibalizing* and *make do and mend*. For eating out there were *British restaurants*, while at home there were (if you had the points) such delicacies as *luncheon meat* (notably **Spam (1937)**), *national* milk, butter, etc., *Woolton pie* (an unappetizing vegetable pie), and, later, *snoek* (a type of fish). To supplement this meagre fare, there were always the *blacketeers* 'black-marketeers'. The Americans (providers of *lend-lease*) arrived, bringing their *Kilroy* to join the British Mr Chad, with his graffiti'd *wot no?* slogan (a complaint against shortages). When they left, they took many *G.I. brides* with them.

Others, answering the *call-up*, carried the war to the enemy, with *bazookas* and *Sten guns* and *napalm* and *saturation* bombing. They fought in *jeeps*, *dukws* (amphibious vehicles), and *landing craft*; as *commandos*, *paratroops*, and *pathfinders*, as *Desert Rats* and as *Chindits* (Allied troops in Burma); against *E-boats* and *panzers* (German torpedo-boats and tanks). They used *psychological warfare* (but not *biological warfare*). In the Far East they encountered *banzai* and *kamikaze*. Then came *D-Day*, and there were *mulberry harbours* and *Bailey bridges* (rapid-assembly harbours and bridges) to be built as the *second front* advanced. Then the enormities of Nazi *genocide*, the *final solution*, the **Holocaust (1957)**, came to be revealed: the **concentration camps (1901)**, the *extermination camps*, the *gas chambers*. Meanwhile, in occupied countries, the *Resistance* had been active (in France, the *Maquis*); but there was also *collaboration*, and the *Quisling*.

The unprecedented levels of organization and bureaucratization stemming from the mobilization of most of the adult population, the governmental control of most aspects of economic (and other) activity, and multi-level cooperation between the Allied powers led to a mushroom growth of official bodies, committees, military groups, plans, and projects. Most of them seemed to have lengthy, multi-word titles which the urgency of war demanded should be abbreviated. Hence the rash of acronyms and other initialisms produced in the 1940s (e.g. *BABS* 'blind approach beacon system', *BAOR* 'British Army of the Rhine', *PLUTO* 'pipeline under the ocean', *SHAEF* 'Supreme Headquarters, Allied Expeditionary Force'; see **acronym (1943)**), which set a seemingly irresistible pattern followed by the rest of the 20th century.

At the other end of the lexical spectrum, the stress and comradeship of war produced a wealth of slang, much of it of the 'whistling in the face of adversity' type (a dangerous military operation, for instance, became a *party*). To take one small part of the whole as an example, the Royal Air Force (whose aircrew suffered the highest death rates of all British service personnel) was a rich source: *angels* 'height in thousands of feet' and *bandits* 'enemy aircraft', *stooging* 'flying aimlessly', *getting weaving* 'getting going quickly', and *going for a burton* 'being killed', *gremlins* 'technical problems' and *shaky dos* 'close shaves', *prangs* 'crashes' and *tail-end Charlies* 'rear gunners', all became familiar to a public following the pilots' exploits.

In 1945–46, **demob (1934)**, and the problems of peace. On the continent of Europe there were still *displaced persons* in *transit camps*, while in Germany there was still *denazification* work to be done (and *fraternization* to be discouraged). At home there was austerity, and simple pleasures (*holiday camps*, and the *baby boom*), but also a promise of a fresh start and a brighter future in the *welfare state* (in Britain exemplified by the *National Health* and *National Assistance*, and also the prospect of *comprehensive* education).

In Europe, the *Marshall Plan* (a US financial-assistance scheme) and other forms of *aid* set war-ravaged economies on their feet. Pessimists feared *Big Brother*, but the *teenagers* had other things to worry about.

At the end of the war, the Western powers and the Soviet Union were somewhat uneasy allies, but it soon turned sour. The *Cold War* got under way, which was to separate the world into capitalist and communist power blocks (*West* and **East (1951)**, dominated respectively by the two *superpowers*, the US and the USSR) for the next four decades. The **iron curtain (1920)** and (around China) the *bamboo curtain* descended. The *terrorist* appeared on the international scene (in Palestine), and English obtained the word *apartheid*. The *card-carrying crypto-communist*, that bogey figure of the 1950s, popped up for the first time.

To set against these depressing developments, international cooperation was producing institutions such as the *United Nations* and the *Security Council*, while in Europe, *Benelux* (a customs union of Belgium, the Netherlands, and Luxembourg) gave a foretaste of future integration.

The fear which fuelled the Cold War was, of course, largely caused by the *atom bomb* (*A-bomb* for short, *fusion bomb* for the technically minded, *super-bomb* or simply *the bomb* for the apocalyptically minded, but all anticipated by many decades by **atomic bomb (1914)**), which the US possessed and the Soviet Union acquired in 1949. The world was having to get used quickly to the possibility of being *atomized* by *nuclear* weapons. And as if this were not enough, there was now talk of a *hydrogen bomb*, exploded by nuclear *fusion* and perhaps delivered by a *guided missile*. *Ground zero* was not the place to be. But peaceful uses of nuclear energy were being discussed too, and *fuel rod* and *pile* entered the language.

Another newcomer of far-reaching import was *computer* (*electronic brain* was a contemporary synonym, but it failed to last the course). The development of such machines was only in its embryonic phase, but already many now-familiar elements of computational terminology were falling into place: *analogue* and *digital*; *bit*, *data*, and *memory*; *language* and *program*; *hardware*, *punchcard*, and *input*. This was not the only area in which the *boffins* and *backroom boys* had been working during and after the war, though. Other new developments and discoveries of the decade included *radar* and *sonar*, *radio telescopes* and *transistors*, *holograms* and *biotechnology*, *bosons* and *plutonium*, *antibiotics* and *DDT*. And then there was the *jet engine*, or *turbojet*, which was to revolutionize aviation in the second half of the century; the *delta wing* was the new shape in the sky.

The *space age* was, if not completely in the realms of science fiction, still in the planning stage; *space vehicles*, *boosters*, and *re-entry* were being discussed, but *spaceman* turned out not to have long-term credibility—its fate lay with *flying saucers* and *aliens*.

As post-war consumerism began to get into its stride, new goodies appeared on the market (many available on *H.P.*). You could have *double glazing* for your house, a *blender* for the kitchen, *Formica* work surfaces, and write the cheque with a *biro* or *ball-point pen*. You could take a *bubble bath*, and wrap up your sandwiches in *foil*. If you had despaired of dowdy *utility* clothes, the shops now had the *New Look* (the style introduced by Christian Dior in 1947). The young in the 1940s were wearing *pedal pushers* (knee-length trousers), *bobby sox* (ankle socks), and *zoot suits* (men's suits with a long draped jacket), and sported *crew cuts* and *peek-a-boo* hairstyles (covering one eye). Women could cultivate their shape with the new lightweight *pantie-girdles* and *roll-ons* (the successors to corsets), or show it off to sensational effect with the *bikini*.

You could go out and dance to *boogie* and *bop*, or listen to the offerings of *disc jockeys* on the radio. And if you preferred not to, you were probably *square*.

A-bomb *n* (1945) an abbreviation, current during the 1940s and 50s, of **atom bomb (1945)**.

1945 *Daily Mirror*: Jap Radio says Evacuate—'Ware A-Bombs.

acronym *n* (1943) a word formed from the initial letters of other words. The term originated in the US; it was coined from the prefix *acr-* 'outer end, tip' (from Greek *akros*) plus *-onym*, as in *homonym*. Its precise application varies, but strictly speaking it denotes a combination pronounced as a word (e.g. *NATO* from *North Atlantic Treaty Organization*, *SHAEF* from *Supreme Headquarters Allied Expeditionary Force*) rather than as just a sequence of letters. It is often taken too to include words formed from initial syllables (e.g. *sitrep* from *situation report*), and hybrids of letters and syllables (e.g. *radar* from *radio detection and ranging*). It is a quintessentially 20th-century way of creating new words—there is little or no evidence of it before 1900. No doubt the proliferation of polynomial governmental agencies, international organizations, and military units as the century has progressed (the last particularly during World War II) has contributed significantly to its growth. Most remain as simple initialisms ('alphabet soup agencies' they were called in the US during F. D. Roosevelt's presidency), but as soon as the letter-sequence takes on (by accident or design) the lineaments of a pronounceable English word, it seems we cannot resist the temptation to turn it into an acronym.

1943 *American Notes & Queries*: Words made up of the initial letters or syllables of other words . . . I have seen . . . called by the name acronym.

aid *n* (1940) material help given by one country to another, especially economic assistance or material help given by a rich to a poor or underdeveloped country.

1940 *Economist*: The United States' aid to Britain would be rendered ineffective.

1974 M. B. Brown: The underdeveloped countries complain also of the overpricing of goods and shipping in their manufactured imports from developed lands, particularly in the case of aid-supported supplies.

air-lift *n* (1945) transportation of supplies or troops by air, especially during a state of emergency. The term was mainly familiarized by the 'Berlin air-lift' of 1948, when Allied aircraft flew thousands of tons of essential supplies into the city over a period of nearly a year after it had been blockaded by the Russians.

1948 *News Chronicle*: This is the first British plane to crash on the air lift, which began in June.

alien *adj, n* (1944) (a being) from another planet, especially one visiting the Earth. It is a usage largely restricted to science fiction; its negative connotations (hostility, creepiness, etc.) would make it impolitic to use in the presence of a real alien. It was popularized in particular by the Ridley Scott film *Alien* (1979). The noun is first recorded in 1953.

1944 *Astounding Science Fiction*: An alien ship, all right . . . He looked at the thing. It was alien . . . , horribly different from anything on Earth.

1953 William Tenn: The first of the aliens stepped out in the complex tripodal gait that all humans were shortly to know . . . so well.

antibiotic *n* (1944) any of a class of substances produced by living organisms and capable of destroying or inhibiting the growth of micro-organisms, especially one of these substances used for therapeutic purposes. The term *antibiotique* (literally 'injurious to life') was coined in French around 1889. English had adapted it as *antibiotic* before the end of the 19th century, but it was not until the 1940s, with the development of bactericides like penicillin, that it really took off (including conversion into a noun).

1944 *Lancet* (title): The Mould Antibiotics.

1949 H. W. Florey et al: The antibiotics comprise substances with diverse chemical structures and biological activities. They range in their action from those which inhibit the growth of certain strains of bacteria in a highly selective manner to those which are relatively toxic to all living cells.

apartheid *n* (1947) the name given in South Africa to the segregation of the inhabitants of European descent from the non-European (coloured or mixed, Bantu, Indian, etc.), a policy introduced in 1948. It comes from Afrikaans *apartheid*, literally 'separateness', which is first recorded in 1929. Within a decade it had been joined by the synonymous (and equally euphemistic) English *separate development* (1955).

> 1948 *Cape Times*: Mr. P. O. Sauer . . . will explain the application of the apartheid policy on the railways.

atom bomb *n* (1945) a bomb whose explosive power derives from the fission of heavy atomic nuclei. The alternative **atomic bomb** was in use as long before as 1914, but *atom bomb* had to wait until theory became reality with the dropping of two such bombs by the US on the Japanese cities of Hiroshima and Nagasaki in August 1945. The term was often abbreviated to **A-bomb (1945)** in the 1940s and 50s.

> 1945 *Times*: An impenetrable cloud of dust and smoke had covered the target area after the atom bomb had been dropped at Hiroshima.

automation *n* (1948) automatic control of the manufacture of a product through a number of successive stages. The term is also applied more broadly to the application of automatic control to any branch of industry or science, and by extension, to the use of electronic or mechanical devices to replace human labour. The coinage of the word is usually attributed to Delmar S. Harder of the US. The back-formation *automate* is first recorded (in the form *automated*) in 1952.

> 1952 *Cleveland* (Ohio) *Plain Dealer*: Another 'automated' line, less spectacular than the block line, machines the cylinder head.

> 1953 *Manchester Guardian Weekly*: Many factories are spending large sums on 'automation', that is, the adoption of automatic machines working together with little labour.

backroom boy *n* (1941) someone engaged in essential but unpublicized work, especially (secret) research. The germ of the term appears in the first quote below, from Lord Beaverbrook, then Minister of Aircraft Production, although it is not recorded in its finished form until 1943.

> 1941 Lord Beaverbrook: Now who is responsible for this work of development on which so much depends? To whom must the praise be given? To the boys in the back rooms. They do not sit in the limelight. But they are the men who do the work. Many of them are Civil Servants.

> 1944 *Times*: The man most responsible for the development of the rocket projectile . . . is Group Captain John D'Arcy Bakercarr, . . . whose 'backroom boys' at the Ministry of Aircraft Production have worked unremittingly with him.

Big Brother *n* (1949) the head of state in George Orwell's novel *1984*; hence, an apparently benevolent, but ruthlessly omnipotent, state authority.

> 1949 George Orwell: On each landing . . . the poster with the enormous face gazed from the wall . . . Big Brother is watching you, the caption beneath it ran.

> 1953 *Economist*: The distrust of the concierge who is also a police spy, of the admirable focusing device which the big block provides for the watchful eye of Big Brother.

bikini *n* (1948) a brief two-piece swimsuit for women. The term was coined in French in 1947 ('Bikini, ce mot cinglant comme l'explosion même . . . correspondait au niveau du vêtement de plage à un anéantissement de la surface vêtue; à une minimisation extrême de la pudeur', *Le Monde Illustré*), apparently drawing a parallel between the explosive effect of the swimsuit on French males and the US atom bomb test on Bikini Atoll in the Marshall Islands in July 1946.

> 1948 *Newsweek*: This . . . French beauty . . . shows the 1948 countertrend against the skimpy 'Bikini' style . . . which swept French beaches and beauty contests last year.

biotechnology *n* (1947) the branch of technology concerned with the development and exploitation of machines in relation to the various needs of human beings. The usage largely gave way to the later 'use of living organisms in production processes' (see **biotechnology (1972)**).

> 1947 *Science*: Hours of work, on-the-job feeding, rest periods, etc. are also phases of the physiology of work which form an important part of a comprehensive biotechnology.

bit *n* (1948) a unit of information derived from a choice between two equally probable alternatives or 'events'. The word, a blend of *binary digit*, is usually applied to such a unit stored electronically in a computer. See also **byte (1964)**.

> 1948 C. E. Shannon: The choice of a logarithmic base corresponds to the choice of a unit for measuring information. If the base 2 is used the resulting units may be called binary digits, or more briefly bits, a word suggested by J. W. Tukey.

blitz *n* (1940) an air raid or a series of air raids conducted with great intensity and ferocity, specifically the series of air raids made on London and other British cities by the German Luftwaffe in 1940–41. The word is a shortening of **Blitzkrieg (1939)**. It is also used as a verb, meaning 'to bomb intensively' or 'to destroy, drive out, etc. by aerial bombing'.

> 1940 *Daily Express*: Blitz bombing of London goes on all night . . . In his three-day blitz on London Goering has now lost 140 planes.
>
> 1940 *Daily Sketch*: Neighbourhood Theatre braved the blitz and yesterday presented a new play.
>
> 1942 *Annual Register 1941*: 70,000 meals had to be provided by the Emergency kitchens for people 'blitzed' out of their homes.

boffin *n* (1945) someone engaged in 'backroom' scientific or technical research. The colloquial term's origins have never been satisfactorily explained. It seems to have been first applied by members of the Royal Air Force to scientists working on radar. They may have got it from Royal Navy slang *boffin* 'elderly officer' (1941), but as it is not known where that came from, it fails to advance the investigation much further.

> 1945 *Times*: A band of scientific men who performed their wartime wonders at Malvern and apparently called themselves 'the boffins'.
>
> 1948 Lord Tedder: I was fortunate in having considerable dealings in 1938–40 with the 'Boffins' (as the Royal Air Force affectionately dubbed the scientists).

bomb *n* ***the bomb*** (1945) the atomic or hydrogen bomb, as (threatened to be) used by any country as a weapon of war, and regarded as unique because of its utterly destructive effects. 'Ban the bomb' (1960) became the slogan of advocates of nuclear disarmament in the 1960s.

> 1945 *Times* (headline): Victory and the Bomb.
>
> 1959 *Sunday Times*: Twenty years ago, I mean: before the war, the Bomb, the satellites, the space-travellers and the nudist paradises.

classified *adj* (1944) classified as secret for reasons of national security and forbidden to be disclosed except to specified persons. The term originated in the US.

> 1949 *New York Herald Tribune*: The B-47 will combine characteristics which are still classified, with range equivalent to the B-29 range.

cold war *n* (1945) hostilities short of armed conflict, consisting of threats, violent propaganda, subversive political activities, etc. It is first recorded as a general term, but the specific application to the state of affairs existing between the USSR and the western powers after World War II was soon in place. It lasted, with periodic changes in temperature, until the Communist regimes in eastern Europe collapsed in the late 1980s. The West declared itself the winner.

> 1945 George Orwell: A State which was . . . in a permanent state of 'cold war' with its neighbours.
>
> 1947 Walter Lippmann (title) The cold war. A study in U.S. foreign policy.
>
> 1948 *Hansard Commons*: The British Government . . . should recognize that the 'cold war', as the Americans call it, is on in earnest, that the third world war has, in fact, begun.

collaboration *n* (1940) traitorous cooperation with the enemy. The word was initially used with reference to local cooperation with the Germans in France and other occupied countries (and as such probably borrowed directly from French). The related verb *collaborate* is first recorded in 1941, its derivative *collaborator* in 1943. See also **Quisling (1940)**.

> 1940 *Economist*: Pétain may be outvoted on the question of mitigating the peace terms by some sort of shameful collaboration.

> 1941 *Annual Register 1940*: The futility of attempts to 'collaborate' with their German conquerors.

> 1946 George Orwell: At this moment, with France newly liberated and the witch-hunt for collaborators in full swing.

commando *n* (1940) a member of a body of picked men trained originally (in 1940) as shock troops for repelling the threatened German invasion of England, later for carrying out raids on the Continent and elsewhere. The word was subsequently applied to similar troops of other countries. It was originally used in South Africa for a 'raiding party of Boers' (it is first recorded in that sense in 1809), and became more widely known in English during the South African War (Boer War).

> 1940 Winston Churchill: Plans should be studied to land secretly by night on the islands and kill or capture the invaders. This is exactly one of the exploits for which the Commandos would be suited.

commitment *n* (1948) the state of being involved in political or social questions, or in furthering a particular doctrine or cause, especially in one's literary or artistic expression; moral seriousness or social responsibility in artistic productions. The word is a translation of French *engagement*, a key term in existential politico-aesthetics, introduced by Jean-Paul Sartre. The adjective *committed* emerged around the same time, and the corresponding reflexive verb *commit oneself* is first recorded in 1950. Alongside this little nest of *commit* words, English also freely used more literal translations of the French originals (see **engaged (1947)**).

> 1948 Philip Mairet: [An] important Sartrean concept—engagement—is here translated as 'commitment'... At the very heart... of existentialism, is the absolute character of the free commitment, by which every man realises himself... What counts is the total commitment, and it is not by a particular case or particular action that you are committed altogether.

> 1956 Colin Wilson: Sartre, whose theory of commitment or 'engagement'... led him to embrace a modified communism.

> 1959 *Books of the Month*: Christopher Logue... has become 'engaged', or 'committed', which means that he is striving to write poetry touching the everyday life of ordinary people.

comprehensive *adj* (1947) designating a secondary school or a system of education which provides for children of all levels of intellectual and other ability. These levels were characterized, under the reforms introduced in Britain under the 1944 Education Act, as 'grammar', 'modern', and 'technical'. The companion terms *bilateral* (denoting schools offering two such levels) and *multilateral* (two or more levels; see the first quote below) soon faded away, but *comprehensive* (all levels) remained as a touchstone of equal-opportunity education, or a threat to the excellence of traditional grammar schools, depending on your point of view, into and beyond the 1960s, when (almost) universal comprehensive education was introduced in Britain. The word is first recorded as a noun, denoting a school of this kind, in 1958.

> 1947 *Ministry of Education Circular*: Combinations of two or more types of secondary education are often referred to as bilateral, multilateral or comprehensive... A comprehensive school means one which is intended to cater for all the secondary education of all the children in a given area without an organisation in three sides.

> 1959 *Punch*: His son is at a Public School... His younger daughters both attend The local Comprehensive.

computer *n* (1945) an automatic electronic device for performing high-speed mathematical or logical operations. The term *computer* had been in use for 'a calculating machine' since the late 19th century; and forerunners of the computer as we would recognize it at the beginning of the 21st century had been in (theoretical) development for some time too: so it is not particularly easy to tell when the concept and the term met. Several recorded examples of the word come fairly close, but the consummation of the marriage cannot be dated to before 1945, when the name 'electronic numerical integrator and computer' (usually abbreviated to *ENIAC*) was given to such a device being developed in the US (the first quote below shows that the alternative term *computing machine* was then current). See also **electronic brain (1946)**.

> 1945 J. Eckert et al. (title): Description of the ENIAC and comments on electronic digital computing machines.
>
> 1946 *Electronics*: The servomechanism is part of the computer, and . . . computers of this type have become known as electronic computers.
>
> 1947 *Mathematical Tables and Other Aids to Computation*: We are engaged at the RCA Laboratories in the development of a storage tube for the inner memory of electronic digital computers.

consumerism *n* (1944) protection of the consumer's interests. The usage originated in the US, and the derivative consumerist followed in the mid 1960s. Compare **consumerism (1960)** for a radically different take on the meaning of the word.

> 1944 *New Republic*: Some of the oldest and most successful consumer enterprises grew independently of the rural impulse that in recent years has been most active in spreading the idea of consumerism.
>
> 1972 *Times*: Ralph Nader and his consumerists appear to have scored a minor victory.

counselling *n* (1940) the giving of professional advice or help on social or psychological problems; a notable growth industry of the latter half of the 20th century. At first probably mainly familiar to laypeople in the context of marriage guidance (see **marriage guidance (1935)**), by the 1960s it had extended its influence to many areas that had previously been the province of the amateur shoulder to cry on (or, in British culture, of the stoical stiff upper lip). *Counsellor* with the same connotations is also first recorded in 1940.

> 1940 C. R. Rogers: The finest touches of artistry will not make counselling contacts helpful if they are basically unsound in principle . . . There must be a warmth of relationship between counsellor and counselee.
>
> 1959 *Listener*: There is no doubt that some students need counselling or even psychological treatment in these testing years.
>
> 1987 *Money*: If you are earning $20,000 a year or less, debt counselors say your net income may leave only enough for essentials.
>
> 1988 *Daily Telegraph*: Schools and parents . . . received an offer yesterday of free stress counselling for teachers and children plucked from the wreck.

crew cut *n* (1942) a closely cropped style of haircut for men (apparently first adopted by boat crews at Harvard and Yale Universities). In the 1940s and 50s it became almost a symbol of stereotypical virile American youth. The term is foreshadowed by *crew-cropped* (1938), which never caught on to the same extent. It is first recorded (in 1940) in the form *crew haircut*; *crew cut* itself is not known to have put in an appearance before 1942.

cybernetics *n* (1948) the theory or study of communication and control in living organisms or machines. Its implications of automated decision-making made it a hot concept in the 1940s and 50s. The term was coined by the US mathematician Norbert Wiener (1894–1964) from Greek *kubernētēs* 'steersman' (which also lies behind English *govern*). A similar coinage had actually been made in French (*cybernétique*) over a century before by A.-M. Ampère, with the meaning 'the art of governing'.

> 1948 Norbert Wiener: We have decided to call the entire field of control and communication theory, whether in the machine or in the animal, by the name Cybernetics.
>
> 1958 *Listener*: The claim of cybernetics is that we can treat organisms as if they were machines, in the sense that the same methods of synthesis and analysis can be applied to both.

data *n* (1946) the quantities, characters, or symbols on which operations are performed by computers and other automatic equipment, and which can be stored or transmitted in the form of electrical signals, records on magnetic tape or punched cards, etc. See also **data processing (1954)**.

> 1946 *Mathematical Tables & Other Aids to Computation*: The [IBM card] reader scans standard punched cards . . . and causes data from them to be stored in relays located in the constant transmitter.

disc jockey *n* (1941) someone who introduces and plays recordings of popular music, especially on radio. The term, which is of US origin, was marginally preceded by *record jockey* (1940), but that never really caught on. The abbreviation **DJ** is first recorded in 1961, its orthographic realization *dee-jay* in 1955.

> 1941 *Variety*: Gilbert is a disc-jockey who sings with his records.

disposable *adj* (1943) designed to be thrown away after one use. Early usage (in the US) mostly relates to nappies, but the word soon spread to other (mainly paper-based) products, perhaps lending the concept more gravity than the earlier **throw-away (1928)**.

> 1943 L. E. Holt: The disposable paper diapers are a great convenience and involve relatively little expense.

> 1965 *Sunday Times (Colour Supplement)*: A lot of ward equipment is disposable now—things like catheters or blood drips . . . Bed pans and bottles are made of papier maché, to be disposable.

dissident *n* (1940) someone who openly opposes the policies of the government or ruling party, especially in a totalitarian system.

> 1940 Edmund Wilson: He took the position that the voters . . . had the right to confer power on whom they chose; that for a dissident like himself to refuse to submit to their choice would constitute an act of insurrection.

DNA *n* (1944) see **deoxyribonucleic acid (1931)**.

electronic brain *n* (1946) an early and fairly colloquial term for a computer (see **computer (1945)**). It started out as a rather general word for any electronic apparatus able to perform calculations or other vaguely cerebral functions ('An "electronic brain", which helps pilots test-fly new airplanes, has been invented by flight research engineers of Consolidated Vultee Aircraft Corporation. Technically, the device is known as a "flight recorder" ', *Aero Products* (1945)), but soon attached itself fairly firmly to the electronic computer.

> 1946 *Lancet*: Another war secret now disclosed is an electrical calculating machine which has been built in the United States and has been called an 'electronic brain', or more accurately an Electronic Numerical Integrator and Computer—ENIAC.

engaged *adj* (1947) of an artist: completely involved in political, moral, or social questions. It is a translation of the term *engagé* used by French existential philosophers (itself imported into English *au naturel* in the mid 1950s). The more usual English equivalent is *committed* (see **commitment (1948)**).

> 1947 John Hayward: This is not to say that literature must become 'engaged', as one school of continental writers now insists; that it must . . . 'take sides' in the social revolution.

> 1955 Graham Greene: I don't know what I'm talking politics for. They don't interest me and I'm a reporter. I'm not engagé.

espresso *n* (1945) strong coffee made by forcing steam or hot water at high pressure through powdered coffee beans. The term was an adaptation of Italian *caffè espresso*, which means literally 'pressed-out coffee'. At first treated as an exotic foreignism, it did not get its feet under the English table until the rise of the coffee-bar culture in the 1950s (see **coffee bar (1956)**), by which time it was often being further anglicized to *expresso*.

1945 A. Boucher: I was drinking a caffé espresso, a strong, bitter, steamed coffee.

1955 *New York Times*: Also new are the numerous small Coffee Expresso Snack Restaurants off Dublin's Grafton Street.

ethnic *n* (1945) a member of an ethnic group or 'ethnic minority' (itself also a term that dates from the mid 1940s). The adjective *ethnic* had been used as a technical term in anthropology since the middle of the 19th century, denoting social grouping based on a range of physical and cultural characteristics, but it was not until the 1930s, with the increasing compromising of the term *race* (see **racist (1932)**), that it came to be widely used, originally in the US, with specific connotations of racial difference (usually in the context of a minority grouping within a larger whole). The noun usage evolved from this, and came to serve a euphemistic function, as also did the adjective.

1963 Terence & Pauline Morris: It is the general view of the prison staff that the majority of 'coloureds' and 'ethnics' are West Indians.

existentialism *n* (1941) a doctrine that concentrates on the existence of individuals, who, being free and responsible, are held to be what they make themselves by the self-development of their essence through acts of the will (which, in the Christian form of the theory, leads to God).The existentialist movement was mainly originated by the Danish writer Søren Kierkegaard (1813–55), who frequently used the term *Existents-forhold* 'condition of existence, existential relation'. It was developed in the 20th century chiefly in continental Europe by Jaspers, Sartre, and others. Its emphasis on the individual alone in an indifferent or hostile universe caught the mood of the middle decades of the century, and it was the fashionable philosophy of the 1940s and 50s. The English word *existentialism* was adapted from German *Existentialismus*, which is first recorded in 1919. The derivative *existentialist* is first recorded in English in 1945, and the related *existential* before 1937.

1941 Julius Kraft: Kierkegaard, Nietzsche, and pragmatism are examples of real or possible starting points of existentialism, capable of being multiplied by further examples.

1945 A. J. Ayer: Philosophically, [Sartre] is usually described as an Existentialist.

1957 *Observer*: We asked Miss Greco what Existentialism implied. Apparently its essence is summed up by 'whatever you do, you become'.

fax *n, v* (1948) (a copy of a document obtained by) facsimile telegraphy, in which the document is scanned and the resulting signal is transmitted by wire or radio. Originally US, the term is a respelling of the *facs-* of *facsimile*. The technology had been around for a long while, but the word did not start to become really well known until the 1970s (which is when the verb is first recorded).

1948 *Time*: The big news about 'fax' was that, technically, the bugs were pretty well worked out of it.

1979 *Datamation*: Who will fax the mail?

final solution *n* (1947) a literal translation of German *Endlösung*, the name given to the Nazi policy, from 1941, of exterminating Jewish people in Europe.

1947 *Trial of German Major War Criminal* (H.M.S.O.): Final solution of the Jewish question.

1949 Dorothy Macardle: As the 'final solution', camps fitted with gas-chambers, electrocution plants and huge crematoria were erected in Poland.

flying bomb *n* (1944) a pilotless jet-propelled aeroplane with an explosive warhead, originally and specifically one of a type first used by the Germans against England in June 1944 (see **V-1 (1944)**).

1944 *Times*: Strong measures to counter the flying bombs have been continued throughout the week-end.

flying saucer *n* (1947) a disc- or saucer-shaped object reported as appearing in the sky and alleged to come from outer space. The immediate post-World War II period appears to have been chosen by aliens as the right time to pay the Earth (or more usually the US) a visit, a circumstance linked by amateur psychologists with American fears of nuclear attack by the Soviet Union and by conspiracy theorists with secret US weapons tests. However, the comparison of unidentified objects seen in the sky to 'saucers' can be traced back to the 19th century ('When directly over him it [i.e. a flying object] was about the size of a large saucer and was evidently at a great height', *Denison* (Texas) *Daily News* (1878)). Compare **UFO (1953)**.

> 1947 *Times*: During the past fortnight reports that dish-like objects, nicknamed 'flying saucers', have been seen travelling through the air at great speed . . . have come from the United States and Canada.

> 1965 *New Society*: When Kenneth Arnold saw something from his airplane near Mount Rainier in June 1947, he gave them the happy name of flying saucers.

fraternization *n* (1944) contacts between occupying troops and local inhabitants that contravene military discipline. The term was applied specifically to sexual relations between Allied troops and German women after World War II. It was a specialization of the general sense 'friendly relations between occupiers and occupied', which dates from the mid 19th century.

> 1945 *New Statesman*: At present it is not clear whether rape [by occupying troops] is a crime to be punished by death, or whether it should be classified as fraternisation, for which the penalty is a fine, or non-fraternisation, which is a laudable act.

freedom-fighter *n* (1942) someone who takes part in a resistance movement against the established political system of a country. The word was a frequent actor in the post-colonial struggles of the second half of the century. It is notoriously paired and contrasted with **terrorist (1947)**.

> 1964 *Annual Register 1963*: Mr. Obote had played a prominent part in the Addis Ababa conference . . . offering training grounds for 'freedom fighters' against South Africa.

fusion *n* (1947) the formation of a heavier, more complex nucleus by the coming together of two or more lighter ones, usually accompanied by the release of relatively large amounts of energy. The reaction is the basis on which the hydrogen bomb is designed (as opposed to the **atomic bomb (1914)**, which works by **fission (1939)**). The aim of harnessing it to produce cheap energy remains one of the holy grails of science at the beginning of the 21st century.

> 1947 *Science News Letter* (heading): Atom fusion gives energy.

> 1952 *Economist*: This may have been a hybrid bomb, part atom, part hydrogen, but enough to prove that the scientists have solved the problem of releasing energy by nuclear fusion.

Gallup poll *n* (1940) a public-opinion poll conducted along the lines established by the US journalist and statistician George Horace Gallup (1901–84). In 1935 he set up the American Institute of Public Opinion, and in 1936 successfully predicted the result of the presidential election.

gamesmanship *n* (1947) skill in winning games, especially by means that barely qualify as legitimate. Coined by the British humorist Stephen Potter, on the model of (and in deliberate contrast to) *sportsmanship*, the term was used by him in the title of a book on the subject (see the first quote below). He exploited the suffix *-manship* liberally himself to make other creations, and it became a minor word-formation craze for a while (see below, and see also **brinkmanship (1956)**).

> 1947 Stephen Potter (title): The theory & practice of gamesmanship or the art of winning games without actually cheating.

> 1952 Edward Grierson: This was so like Laura, with whom a hand she could not play was a hand wasted, but Mr. Clarke, a practitioner of 'gamesmanship' himself, would not be rushed.

> 1973 *Nature*: He has some useful and pointed things to say on 'grantsmanship'.

gas chamber *n* (1945) a sealed enclosure in which people are killed by means of poison gas, specifically one of those used by the Germans for their extermination programme during World War II. This was a grisly new use for a term that had started life innocuously enough in the late 19th century, denoting an apparatus used in microscopy for studying the action of different gases on structures or organisms. A contemporary synonym was *gas oven*, but this gradually went out of use, perhaps because it was seen as robbing the victims of their dignity.

> 1945 *Daily Mirror*: The Germans knew what to do with women with white hair, or too exhausted to work. For them was the gas-chamber.
>
> 1945 George Orwell: Was it true about the German gas ovens in Poland?

genocide *n* (1944) the deliberate and systematic extermination of an ethnic or national group. The term was coined specifically in response to the Nazis' slaughter of six million Jews (about two-thirds of European Jewry) in concentration camps during World War II. See also **Holocaust (1957)**.

> 1944 R. Lemkin: By 'genocide' we mean the destruction of a nation or of an ethnic group.
>
> 1945 *Sunday Times*: The United Nations' indictment of the 24 Nazi leaders has brought a new word into the language—genocide. It occurs in Count 3, where it is stated that all the defendants 'conducted deliberate and systematic genocide—namely, the extermination of racial and national groups . . .'

gobbledygook *n* (1944) official, professional, or pretentious verbiage or jargon. The term was introduced by Maury Maverick, chairman of the US Smaller War Plants Corporation (and a descendant of the cattle-owner Samuel A. Maverick, begetter of the word *maverick*). He did not invent it out of thin air, though: it is a variation on the earlier US slang *gobbledygook*, which originally denoted a prostitute specializing in fellatio; this in turn was based on the phrase *gobble the goo* 'to perform fellatio'. Presumably it was the sound of the word (suggestive of a fatuous turkey) that drew Maverick to it, rather than its meaning.

> 1944 *American Notes & Queries*: Gobbledygook talk: Maury Maverick's name for the long high-sounding words of Washington's red-tape language.
>
> 1945 *Tuscaloosa* (Alabama) *News*: The explanations sound like gobbledegook to me.

ground zero *n* (1946) that part of the ground situated immediately under an exploding bomb, especially a nuclear one (for maximum effect, nuclear bombs are detonated before they actually hit the ground). The term achieved a high profile early in the 21st century when it was adopted to designate the site of the ruins of the World Trade Center in Lower Manhattan, New York City, destroyed by terrorist attacks on 11 September 2001.

> 1955 *Bulletin of Atomic Science*: There was no noticeable contamination even at ground zero at Hiroshima.

group therapy *n* (1943) psychotherapy involving more than one patient at a time, in which the changing interaction between the patients is part of the therapeutic process. The technique was pioneered in the early part of the 20th century (see the second quote below), but the term is not recorded before 1943.

> 1943 S. R. Slavson (title): An introduction to group therapy.
>
> 1948 *Science News*: The first recorded use of group therapy was the experiment of Dr. J. H. Pratt in Boston [in 1905].

guided missile *n* (1945) a missile operating by remote control or as directed by equipment carried in the weapon. This was one of the key 'fear' words of the 1950s, when such weapons, armed with nuclear warheads, were at the cutting edge of Cold War deterrence.

hardware *n* (1947) the physical components of a system or device (originally and mainly a computer) as opposed to the procedures required for its operation. Compare **software (1960)**.

> 1947 D. R. Hartree: The ENIAC [an early type of computer]... I shall give a brief account of it, since it will make the later discussion more realistic if you have an idea of some 'hardware' and how it is used, and this is the equipment with which I am best acquainted.

> 1960 *Times*: Both punched card and computer 'hardware' will continue to develop very rapidly.

holiday camp *n* (1940) a complex of chalets, places of entertainment, etc., designed for family holidays. The term was not new—it had been applied before World War II to camps for children (not unlike the US *summer camp*) on the continent of Europe. The institution in the modern sense began before the war too (Billy Butlin opened his first holiday centre at Skegness, Lincolnshire, in 1936), but had its heyday in the 1940s and 50s, catering to those whom the war had deprived of holidays but accustomed to regimentation.

> 1940 *Manchester Guardian Weekly*: Then there were the Holiday Camps, cheap, social, with every modern convenience and all the modern pleasures. Their official hosts and hostesses mapped out the day with a colossal time-table of delights.

> 1949 Monica Dickens: I've got to go to a holiday camp to do some sketches of happy campers for publicity.

H.P. *n* (1945) an abbreviation of *hire purchase* (1895). The concept (as that date suggests) was well established, but (bypassing the slightly bizarre first quote below) it was the consumer boom of the 1950s that produced the heyday of hire purchase, and encouraged the abbreviation.

> 1945 *Daily Mirror*: 'Stop H.P. babies'... Mothers...have to pay for their babies on the hire-purchase system because of the high charges of maternity homes.

> 1959 *New Statesman*: The artisan class lives in new houses and pays off the telly and the car on HP.

hydrogen bomb *n* (1947) an immensely powerful bomb in which the energy released is derived from the fusion of hydrogen nuclei in an uncontrolled self-sustaining reaction initiated by a fission bomb. When it was actually made (by the US in 1952, later by the Soviet Union and others) this successor to the atom bomb sent the temperature of the Cold War plunging still further. The abbreviation *H-bomb* is first recorded in 1950.

> 1947 *New York Times*: Hydrogen bomb. New and improved atomic bombs were discussed at the recently held forum of the Northern California Association of Scientists.

> 1954 Winston Churchill: The development of the hydrogen bomb raises strategic and political issues.

integration *n* (1940) the bringing into equal membership of a common society of those groups or people previously discriminated against on racial or cultural grounds. The usage appears to have begun (ironically) in South Africa. The back-formed verb *integrate* is first recorded in 1948.

> 1940 T. J. Haarhoff: For the great task that awaits us in South Africa is a task of integration, of making the Union into a unity.

> 1948 *Richmond* (Virginia) *Times-Dispatch*: Democrats 'integrate' Negroes for campaign.

jeep *n* (1941) a small, sturdy four-wheel-drive US army vehicle, used chiefly for reconnaissance. The name is a spelling of the initials *GP* 'general purpose', probably influenced by the name 'Eugene the Jeep', a creature of amazing resource and power, first introduced into the cartoon strip 'Popeye' on 16 March 1936 by his creator E. C. Segar. It is recorded as being previously applied in 1937 to a type of commercial motor vehicle.

jet engine *n* (1943) an engine utilizing jet propulsion to provide forward thrust, especially an aircraft engine that takes in air and ejects hot compressed air and exhaust gases. The term *jet propulsion* is first recorded in 1867, and the concept of powering aircraft and spacecraft with a high-speed jet of gas had long been toyed with, but the first practicable jet engine was not developed until the 1930s, by Frank Whittle (who had patented the idea in 1930). It was a type of gas turbine, and that is how it was generally referred to by those concerned with it. The first flight by an aircraft powered by Whittle's engine took place in 1941. *Jet engine* was soon shortened to *jet*, both in isolation and in combination with other nouns (*jet plane, jet fighter*, etc.). The first such aircraft to enter military service was the Messerschmitt Me 262, a two-engined fighter which was deployed by the German Luftwaffe in 1944, and that is also the year in which *jet* is first recorded in English as meaning 'an aircraft powered by a jet engine'.

> 1943 *Journal of the Royal Aeronautical Society*: In general, the jet engine performance is given not in h.p. but in kg. of thrust.
>
> 1944 *War Illustrated*: The first enemy jet-plane to fall in Allied lines was shot down over Nijmegen on October 5 by six R.A.F. Spitfires; it was a Me 262.
>
> 1944 *Saturday Evening Post*: The British had flown a jet plane successfully, and now the USAAF proposed to develop a twin-engined jet fighter of its own.
>
> 1944 *Collier's*: The jet . . . is capable of faster flight at low altitudes than any airplane with conventional engines and propeller.

lone *adj* (1949) designating a parent who does not live with a partner and thus has most or all of the responsibility for bringing up a child or children. Latterly it has been preferred to *single*, as it avoids suggesting 'unmarried' (and hence excluding the divorced, widowed, etc.).

> 1976 *Economist*: In 1956, only 56,000 lone mothers were living on supplementary benefit . . . ; in 1974, the figure was 245,000.
>
> 1997 *Glasgow Herald*: The proportion of children living in lone-parent families has almost tripled since 1972 and there were 12 lone mothers to every lone father.

loo *n* (1940) the lavatory. A British word of much discussed but still undetermined etymology. Amongst the most widely touted conjectures are some connection with *Waterloo* ('Waterloo' was the trade name of a type of iron water cistern in the early 20th century) and *gardyloo*, a cod-French warning ('Watch out for the water!') supposedly shouted to unwary passers-by by 18th-century Edinburgh householders about to empty the contents of a chamber-pot from an upstairs window (untenable chronologically). Perhaps the likeliest explanation is that it comes from French *lieu*, literally 'place', short for *lieux d'aisance* 'places of easement', a euphemism for 'lavatory', brought back from France by British soldiers who served there in World War I. As for when it appeared, there is a probable earlier reference to it in another book by Nancy Mitford, champion of 'U' and 'non-U' (see **U (1954)**): 'The absence in his speech of such expressions as "O.K. loo"... "we'll call it a day" ' (1932). It has rearranged the landscape in that British social minefield, the vocabulary of places of excretion: it initially invaded mainly the territory of *lavatory*, but during the 1970s it started to become more and more frequent among *toilet*-users.

> 1940 Nancy Mitford: In the night when you want to go to the loo.
>
> 1943 Cecil Beaton: They had dressed, teeth brushed, breakfasted, had visited the loo, and were on their precarious journey all in a question of fifteen minutes.

LP *n* (1948) an abbreviation of *long-playing* (*record*) 'a microgroove gramophone record designed to be played at 33⅓ revolutions per minute' (see **long-playing (1929)**).

> 1948 *Musical American*: The new disc, called LP (long playing) Microgroove, requires a new pickup.
>
> 1958 *Times*: Stereo records will give almost as much playing time as present LPs.

machismo *n* (1948) the quality of being macho; male virility, masculine pride. Like its parent adjective **macho (1928)**, this acquisition from Mexican Spanish does not seem to have made much headway in English at first, but in the 1960s it found a niche as a put-down of exaggerated masculinity.

marriage bureau *n* (1942) an agency which arranges introductions with a view to marriage. In the latter decades of the 20th century the term gave way to alternatives such as *dating agency*, as such a frank admission of seeking a spouse became less socially acceptable.

> 1942 Oliver & Benedetta: How much better it would be if there were an organization that could arrange the actual match-making and see that suitable people met each other. And this was my idea for the Marriage Bureau.

miniaturize *v* (1946) to produce in a smaller version; to make very small. Early usage was largely restricted to technical contexts; the verb really came into its own in the last three decades of the 20th century, particularly in the area of electronics.

> 1951 *Electronic Engineer*: Miniaturized components generally are becoming more and more readily available.

mobile phone *n* (1945) a telephone that can operate without being physically linked to a telephone line. In early usage the term was applied to radio-telephones installed in cars. It was not until the late 1970s, when it started to be used for the new cellular telephones (for which *cellular* (1977) remains the preferred term in American English), that it really began to take off. In the 1980s the *mobile* (the shortened form is first recorded in 1986) became a symbol of success, a yuppie accessory. By the 1990s it was ubiquitous, and a severe source of irritation in trains, restaurants, and other public places subjected to its warble and the one-sided conversation of its user. At the end of the 20th century there were over 10 million mobile phones in Britain alone.

> 1965 *Newsweek*: There is a pocket of mobile phone owners in New York . . . but the fad hasn't yet caught on in other cities, where car phones are generally for professional purposes.

> 1992 Iain Banks: Rather than phone from the airport, Lewis had hired a mobile along with the car but then when they'd tried to use it, it hadn't worked.

Ms (1949) a title prefixed to the surname of a woman, regardless of her marital status. It originated in the US as an orthographic and phonetic compromise between *Miss* and *Mrs.* Although not recorded in its present form until the late 1940s, something of the sort had, as the first quotation below makes clear, been in the wind for some time (an early approximation to it can be seen in: 'In addressing by letter a woman whose status is in doubt, should I write "M's" or "Miss"?', *New York Times* (1932)). *Ms* did not begin to make real headway, though, until the 1970s, when it was vigorously championed by the burgeoning feminist movement. Despite a strong rearguard action by diehard opponents (whose arguments have included its alleged unpronounceability and its confusability with the abbreviation for *manuscript*), by the end of the 20th century it had firmly established its place in the language. It is sometimes written as *miz*, especially when used other than as a title.

> 1949 Mario Pei: Feminists . . . have often proposed that the two present-day titles be merged into . . . 'Miss' (to be written 'Ms.').

> 1952 *The Simplified Letter* (US): Use abbreviation Ms. for all women addressees. This modern style solves an age-old problem.

> 1952 *The Simplified Letter* (revised edition): Use abbreviation Ms. if not sure whether to use Mrs. or Miss.

> 1971 *Publishers' Weekly*: A crowded New York press conference heard this morning that a new magazine, called Ms. (pronounced 'Miz'), will begin publication in January.

> 1972 *Village Voice* (New York): Cavett addressed her as Mrs. Morgan and asked her if she would rather be called a miz and she said she didn't care.

> 1974 *Daily Telegraph*: The Passport Office yesterday conceded the right to women to call themselves Ms (pronounced Miz) on their passports instead of Mrs or Miss. This followed a month's campaign by Women's Lib.

napalm *n* (1942) a jelly made from petrol and a type of aluminium soap, used in flame-throwers and incendiary bombs. The name is a conflation of *naphthenic* and *palmitic acid*. Its use as a verb, meaning 'to attack or destroy with napalm', dates from the time of the Korean War.

> 1950 *New York Times*: Troops were napalmed when they were found hiding in caves at the dead end of a canyon.
>
> 1952 René Cutforth: He was no longer covered with a skin, but with a crust like crackling which broke easily. 'That's napalm,' said the doctor.

national serviceman *n* (1949) a conscript in the British armed forces. The term *National Service* is first recorded in 1916, when compulsory military recruitment was introduced in Britain ('It is proposed to appoint at once a director of National Service, to be in charge of both the military and civil side of universal national service', *Hansard Commons* (1916)), and it was used again when conscription was reintroduced in 1939, but it was not until 1947, when the National Service Act provided for peacetime conscription, that the term found a secure place in the language. Under the system, up to 150,000 civilians were called up for military service every year; it was abolished in 1962.

> 1949 *Times*: The Secretary of State for War gave an assurance that no national service man would be posted to the Far East with less than 18 weeks' service.

Newspeak *n* (1949) the name of the artificial language used for official communications in George Orwell's novel *1984*, often applied to any corrupt form of English, especially the propagandist and ambiguous language of some politicians, broadcasters, etc. It became the inspiration for a range of neologisms ending in *-speak* (see **-speak (1957)**).

> 1949 George Orwell: Syme was a philologist, a specialist in Newspeak. Indeed, he was one of the enormous team of experts now engaged in compiling the Eleventh Edition of the Newspeak Dictionary... Do you know the Newspeak word *goodthinkful*?... Newspeak was the official language of Oceania and had been devised to meet the ideological needs of Ingsoc, or English Socialism. In the year 1984 there was not as yet anyone who used Newspeak as his sole means of communication, either in speech or writing.
>
> 1966 *Punch*: Accusing the Prime Minister of 'the same old excuses', [the *Daily Telegraph*] labelled 'redeployment' as 'new-speak', which would be 'victimisation of the workers' in any but a Labour Government.

nuclear *adj* (1945) using nuclear energy as a source of explosive power, or as a source of electricity. See also **nuclear (1954)**.

> 1945 *Engineering Journal*: In view of the source of the energy, the current terms 'atomic bomb' and 'atomic power' might well be replaced by the more exact terms 'nuclear bomb' and 'nuclear power'... A large stationary power installation might be used for heat and motive power in the Arctic or Antarctic regions... where the difficulty of transporting other fuels... outweigh[s] the disadvantages and difficulties of operating and maintaining a nuclear power plant.
>
> 1948 *Nuclear Science Abstracts*: Fourth, nuclear weapons have not reached their maximum size in the present type bomb.
>
> 1955 *Tribune*: Nuclear power stations are designed to be safe.
>
> 1957 *Observer*: To keep the British nuclear deterrent up to date on its present scale in relation to the Soviet defence will cost more and more each year.

organic *adj* (1942) of farming or gardening: growing plants without the use of chemical fertilizers, pesticides, etc., adding only organic (i.e. chemical-free) fertilizers to the soil. This application of *organic* to fertilizers is first recorded in the 1860s, but it remained rare until the 1940s. In the 1970s the usage was extended to foods grown by such methods.

> 1942 J. I. Rodale: What is claimed roughly for these organic methods of farming is that they increase the fertility of the soil, produce much better tasting crops, ... reduce weeds, do away with the necessity of using poisonous sprays, improve the mechanical structure of the soil.
>
> 1972 *Daily Telegraph*: The organic food market is booming.

outsider *n* (1946) in literary criticism: the archetypal artist or intellectual seen as a person isolated from the rest of society. It is a specific use of the earlier 'someone who does not "fit in" ' (first recorded in 1907), instigated by its adoption as the English title of Albert Camus's novel *L'Étranger*, and later cemented by Colin Wilson's *The Outsider*, a study of alienated heroes in modern fiction.

> 1956 Colin Wilson: Many great artists have none of the characteristics of the Outsider. Shakespeare, Dante, Keats were all apparently normal and socially well-adjusted.

> 1957 *Times Literary Supplement*: [Colin Wilson's] original contribution was simply the Outsider gimmick.

paedophile, pedophile *n* (1949) someone who is sexually attracted to young children. The term is a derivative of **paedophilia (1906)**. At first largely restricted to specialist psychology texts, it began to emerge into the public domain in the 1970s, and by the end of the 20th century was everyday tabloid fare.

> 1951 *Group Psychotherapy* (heading): Psycho-dramatic treatment of a pedophile.

> 1976 *Publishers Weekly*: Hilary is nine... She's at the mercy of the old man she calls the Devil, actually a pathetic pedophile.

paratroops *n* (1940) a body of soldiers (to be) dropped by parachute from aircraft flying over enemy territory. The singular *paratrooper* is first recorded in 1941.

> 1940 *Notes & Queries*: Parachutists dropped as troops, or to establish themselves in the enemy's country... have now been shortened to 'paratroops'.

> 1941 *Time*: The paratroopers... had never been in an airplane when it was landed.

personnel department *n* (1943) the department within an organization concerned with the recruitment and well-being of its personnel. The term was later often shortened to *personnel* (first recorded in 1960).

> 1943 J. B. Priestley: Mr. Cheviot... was very keen on the personnel department and welfare generally.

> 1960 Muriel Spark: I'm just mentioning a factor that Personnel keep stressing.

pin-up *adj, n* (1941) (denoting) a favourite or sexually attractive young person, the typical subject of a photograph fixed to a wall etc. The term originated in the US.

> 1941 *Life*: Dorothy Lamour is No. 1 pin-up girl of the U.S. Army.

> 1943 *Sun* (Baltimore): Bob Hope, radio and film comedian, today emerged victorious as the official pin-up boy of the WAC contingents here.

plutonium *n* (1942) a transuranic metallic element which is formed indirectly from uranium in nuclear reactors and occurs naturally in trace amounts, is chemically similar to uranium, and is very reactive; the longest-lived isotope (plutonium 244) is produced for use in nuclear weapons and as fuel. The name was given to it because it is the next element after neptunium in the periodic table, as Pluto is the planet next beyond Neptune. It was previously applied to barium in the early 19th century, but that usage did not survive long.

> 1942 Seaborg & Wahl: Since such formulae are confusing when the symbols '93' and '94' are used, we have decided to use symbols of the conventional chemical type to designate these elements. Following McMillan, who has suggested the name neptunium... for element 93, we are using plutonium... for element 94. The corresponding chemical symbols would be Np and Pu.

postmodern *adj* (1949) subsequent to, or later than, what is 'modern'. Early uses of the term are all fairly general in application, but in the 1960s it began to be employed specifically in the arts to denote a movement in reaction against that designated 'modern' (the derivatives *postmodernism* and *postmodernist* date from that period). It became best known in the late 1970s in its application to a school of architecture that reverted to more traditional, formal, even classical styles.

> 1949 Joseph Hudnut (heading): Post-modern house... He shall be a modern owner, a post-modern owner, if such a thing is conceivable. Free from all sentimentality or fantasy or caprice.

1979 *Time*: The nearest man Post-Modernism has to a senior partner is, in fact, the leading American architect of his generation: Philip Cortelyou Johnson.

PR *n* (1942) an abbreviation of *public relations* '(the maintenance of) a good relationship between an organization, firm, etc., and the general public, by means of advertising, positive communication, etc.' This latter term is first recorded as long ago as 1807, in the writings of Thomas Jefferson ('Questions calling for the notice of Congress, unless indeed they shall be superseded by a change in our public relations now awaiting the determination of others'), but it did not become institutionalized in its full modern meaning until the second decade of the 20th century ('Effective publicity to deal with questions of public relations and to consider the molding of public opinion by the presentation of real facts', *Electric Railway Journal* (1913)), since when it has inserted its soft focus into most aspects of our lives.

1944 Alaric Jacob: The remains of the P.R. unit set off down the desert road.

1963 Herbert Kubly: Your students are giving you an excellent PR.

program *n, v* (1945) a set of instructions that are fed into a computer to enable it to perform operations on data. The verb senses 'to supply (a computer) with a program' and 'to organize or convert (data) into a program' are first recorded in the same year. The usage is of American origin, so it was eventually the US spelling *program* that became the World English form (although at first *programme* was preferred in British English).

1945 J. P. Eckert et al. Description of ENIAC (University of Pennsylvania): The problem of programming the ENIAC... In this fashion, problems involving numbers of multiplications far in excess of 24 can be programmed.

1946 *Nature*: Control of the programme of the operation of the machine [i.e. ENIAC, an early form of computer] is also through electrical circuits.

psychological warfare *n* (1940) the use of hostile or subversive propaganda to undermine morale and cause confusion and uncertainty.

1940 *Current History*: Psychological warfare and how to wage it... Psychological warfare is the fight conducted by the state with psychological weapons to strengthen its own prestige... and to weaken that of the enemy.

quiche *n* (1949) an open flan or tart with a savoury filling, a speciality of the Lorraine region of France. Originally in Britain largely confined to cookbooks and cookery columns as an alien strangeness, the quiche was suddenly fashionable and then omnipresent in the 1970s. The predictable reaction set in, and it soon became a sad derided thing in some quarters, with a reputation for vegetarian wimpishness. The word itself comes ultimately, via French, from German *Kuchen* 'cake'.

1979 Posy Simmonds: Quiches are marvellous! They're all out of my freezer. Now, the vegetarian ones are at the front.

Quisling *n* (1940) a traitor to one's country; someone who collaborates with occupying forces, especially during World War II. The term is a generic use of the name of Major Vidkun Quisling (1887–1945), Norwegian officer and diplomat, who collaborated with the Germans during their occupation of Norway from 1940 to 1945. It was taken up with some enthusiasm during World War II (perhaps partly because it has a sound suggestive of mean-spiritedness and untrustworthiness), and was even transformed into a verb, *quisle* 'to betray one's country'.

1940 *Times*: Comment in the Press urges that there should be unremitting vigilance also against possible 'Quislings' inside the country [i.e. Sweden]... There seem to have been no Quislings, partly because it was unnecessary to 'quisle' in a country which, as the Nazis have always said 'could be taken by telephone'.

radar *n* (1941) a system for detecting the presence of objects at a distance, or ascertaining their position or motion, by transmitting short radio waves and detecting or measuring their return after being reflected. The acronym was formed (in the US) from the initial letters of *radio detection and ranging*, which eventually supplanted the synonymous *radiolocation* (1941) in British English.

> 1941 *New York Times*: The Navy undertook a special enlistment campaign today to recruit men for training in maintenance of the radio device known as 'Radar', which is used to locate ships and aircraft that are hidden by fog or darkness.

> 1943 *News Chronicle*: He described Radar as 'probably the most dramatic new weapon to come out of this war'.

redbrick *adj* (1943) used, often condescendingly, to denote a British university founded in the late 19th or early 20th century in a large industrial city, with buildings of red brick, as distinct from the older universities (especially Oxford, Cambridge, the ancient universities of Scotland, and some of the London colleges) built predominantly in stone, and also as distinct from the new universities founded after World War II. The term is first recorded in a book called *Redbrick University* by 'Bruce Truscot' (the pseudonym of E. Allison Peers, Gilmour Professor of Spanish at Liverpool University 1922–52).

> 1943 Bruce Truscot: The range of interests represented in a Redbrick staff common-room . . . It may be natural enough for him to go on to Red-brick, but to . . . enter Oxbridge is something infinitely more exciting.

Resistance *n* (1944) the underground movement formed in France in June 1940 with the object of resisting the authority of the German occupying forces and the Vichy government. The term was subsequently applied to similar movements in other countries. References to the underlying concept of 'resistance' are on record in English before 1944 ('General de Gaulle . . . broadcast from London a message to the French nation last night. The text of his speech . . . is as follows: . . . Whatever happens the flame of French resistance must not and shall not be extinguished', *Times* (1940)), but not to the capitalized form of the word as the name of the organization.

> 1944 *Daily Telegraph*: Mr. Wareing reveals . . . the existence of a Resistance plan to seize power.

rock *v* (1948) to perform, or dance vigorously and in an improvised way to, popular music with a strong beat. In early use, the term often had sexual connotations. In the early 1950s it gradually shaded into the more specific 'to play or dance to rock and roll music' (see **rock and roll (1954)**).

> 1948 Moore & Reig (song-title): We're gonna rock.

> 1953 Freedman & De Knight (song-title): We're gonna rock around the clock.

scramble *v* (1940) to make a rapid take-off; to become airborne quickly. This was originally RAF usage (see the second quote below), applied to Battle of Britain fighter squadrons' swift response when German raiders were spotted. It is also used as a transitive verb, meaning 'to order a squadron to scramble', and as a noun.

> 1940 George Barclay: The squadron scrambled and intercepted some Do215s and Me110s . . . The squadron was off the ground which was the main thing, but they were scrambled too late to intercept . . . I came on the stage after this scrap and we had three scrambles.

> 1962 R. W. Clark: Another great time-saver was the use of a code for passing instructions to the fighters, and such R.A.F. terms as 'scramble' (for take-off) . . . were invented during these experiments [on radar interception, 1936].

Sellotape *n* (1949) the proprietary name (registered in 1949) of a plastic self-adhesive tape. The element *Sell-* is based on the first syllable of *cellulose*, reflecting the material from which it was originally made. It is first recorded as a verb, 'to stick with Sellotape', in 1960.

sixty-four dollar question *n* (1942) originally, the question posed at the climax of a US radio quiz called *Take It or Leave It* (1941–48) for a prize of sixty-four dollars, used metaphorically to denote a difficult or crucial question. When the show transferred to

US television in 1955, its top prize inflated spectacularly to sixty-four thousand dollars, and this too has entered the language.

> 1942 J. R. Tunis: Here's the sixty-four dollar question. Will the team go to Miami?
>
> 1957 *Observer*: Mr. Macmillan said ... there was only one answer to the 64,000-dollar question—to increase production.

snog *v* (1945) to kiss and cuddle. The usage is a British colloquialism, also used as a noun. Its origins are obscure, although it may have something to do with dialectal *snug* 'to lie close together, cuddle'. It has maintained a remarkable consistency of usage among adolescents over the decades, and in the 1990s enjoyed a new lease of life as a transitive verb.

> 1960 Nina Epton: It is all right ... to cuddle. (The current term among teen-agers is 'snogging'.)
>
> 1995 *Private Eye*: A line of 'nutters' queuing for a turn to snog the Princess of Wales.

sophisticated *adj* (1945) of equipment, techniques, theories, etc.: employing advanced or refined methods or concepts; highly developed or complicated. The usage at first attracted the hostility of the linguistic diehards, particularly when, in the 1950s, it began to be widely applied to machinery, weapons, etc. Their objection, that *sophisticated* 'really' means 'refined, cultured', or even (its now moribund original sense) 'adulterated', has cut little ice in the long run.

> 1945 C. S. Lewis: The man was so very allusive and used gesture so extensively that Mark's less sophisticated modes of communication were almost useless.
>
> 1956 *New York Times*: Navy scientists are virtually exploring multidimensional space in a time machine in the search for what they call 'sophisticated' high-yield weapons.

soul *n* (1946) the emotional or spiritual quality of African-American life and culture, manifested especially in music. *Soul music* itself is often abbreviated to simply *soul* (both are first recorded in 1961).

> 1946 *Ebony*: He uses a bewildering, unorthodox technique and his playing is full of what jazzmen refer to as 'soul'.
>
> 1961 *Sunday Times*: The contemporary jazz cult of 'blues roots'—otherwise described as 'soul' or 'funk'.

space age *n* (1946) the period of human exploration and exploitation of space. The term is often used adjectivally to designate products supposed to be characteristic of this age.

> 1946 Harry Harper: We have had an age of steam-power, an age of electricity and of the petrol engine, and an age of the air, and now with the coming of atomic power the world should, in due course, find itself in the space age.
>
> 1980 *Times Literary Supplement*: Our space-age Palace of History—the new computerized Public Record Office at Kew.

spaceman *n* (1942) someone who travels in space. The sense 'someone who comes from another planet' is a later development. When space travel became a reality, **astronaut (1929)** was the largely preferred term, *spaceman* being somewhat tainted by its science-fiction origins.

> 1942 *Thrilling Wonder Stories*: Maybe Lambert was a spaceman. Maybe he wasn't, but if he knew anything at all about spaceman's lingo he'd have to give now.
>
> 1962 Alison Lurie: Amateur experts ... Visitors from another world ... They think they're space men.

space vehicle *n* (1946) a spacecraft, especially a large one (see **spacecraft (1930)**).

> 1946 *New York Times*: They are to serve as pioneers for the long-range guided missiles and 'space' vehicles.
>
> 1959 *Times*: In putting a space vehicle on to the moon the Russians have provided the most complete ... proof of the length of the lead that they now hold.

square *adj, n* (1944) (a person) holding conventional or old-fashioned views. The usage was originally US jazz slang, the opposite of *hep* or *hip* (see **hip (1904)**); later, especially in the **1950**s, it was used as a general term of teenage condemnation for anyone obviously over **21**. The adjective is first recorded in **1946**.

> 1944 *Sun* (Baltimore): *Square,* in musician's jargon, anyone who is not cognizant of the beauties of true jazz.

> 1944 Dan Burley: Are you going to be a square all your days?

> 1959 Norman Mailer: They wish this newspaper to be more conservative, more Square—I wish it to be more Hip.

superpower *n* (1944) a nation or state which has a dominant position in world politics, or has the power to act decisively in pursuit of interests which embrace the whole world; usually applied specifically in the post-World War II period to the United States of America and the Union of Soviet Socialist Republics.

> 1944 W. T. R. Fox: There will be 'world powers' and 'regional powers'. These world powers we shall call 'super-powers', in order to distinguish them from the other powers . . . whose interests are great in only a single theater of power conflict.

> 1957 *Foreign Affairs*: Britain is no longer a Super-Power.

supremo *n* (1944) someone holding the highest (military) authority. The word was acquired from Spanish (*generalissimo*) *supremo* 'supreme general', and used sporadically in English in the late 1930s in Spanish contexts. It attached itself as a nickname to Earl Mountbatten of Burma during his period as Supreme Allied Commander, South-East Asia (see the first quote below), and hence came to be applied to anyone holding the highest military command. By the 1960s it was being used colloquially for someone in overall charge in any sphere.

> 1944 *Daily Express*: Why the Supremo? . . . A handsome, romantic figure [i.e. Mountbatten]. Hence the Latin-sounding nickname.

> 1976 Harold Wilson: The successful attack by other ministers to prevent [Herbert Morrison] from becoming an economic supremo.

take-over *n* (1946) the assumption of control or ownership of a business concern by another company, especially by the acquisition of the majority of its shares, either by agreement or after a bid.

> 1946 *Sun* (Baltimore): I am giving this 'take-over' plan the pitiless publicity it deserves.

> 1953 *Times*: A certain type of financial operation described in general terms by Lord Hacking—the recent epidemic of 'take-over bids'.

> 1959 *Punch*: A surge of sentiment for Harrods has set in since the Fraser take-over.

teenager *n* (1941) someone in their teens. The word was formed (in the US) from **teenage (1921)**, and confirmed the status of the pre-twenties as a force to be reckoned with (and often patronized) in the second half of the 20th century.

> 1941 *Popular Science Monthly*: I never knew teen-agers could be so serious.

> 1952 Marguerite Steen: Do we have to behave like a couple of hysterical 'teen-agers?

terrorist *n* (1947) a member of a clandestine or expatriate organization aiming to coerce an established government by acts of violence against it or its subjects. It is a term, as is well known, used by those who do not share the organization's aims; if you think they are laudable, the members are **freedom-fighters (1942)**. The term actually has a long prehistory: it was originally applied (as an anglicization of French *terroriste*) to the Jacobins and their agents and partisans in the French Revolution, especially to those connected with the Revolutionary tribunals during the 'Reign of Terror'; and in the mid 19th century it was used to denote members of any of the extreme revolutionary societies in Russia.

> 1947 *Annual Register 1946*: The latest and worst of the outrages committed by the Jewish terrorists in Palestine—the blowing up of the King David Hotel in Jerusalem.

> 1956 Harold Nicolson: When people rise against foreign oppression, they are hailed as patriots and heroes; but the Greeks whom we are shooting and hanging in Cyprus are dismissed as terrorists. What cant!

Third World War *n* (1947) a hypothetical war, subsequent to World War II, involving most of the world's nations. The concept was in people's minds before World War II ended ('You will have to postpone your visit until the brief interlude between this war & world-war no 3', Duke of Bedford (1945)), and remained there throughout the Cold War. An alternative formulation is *World War III* (1959).

> 1947 *Civil & Military Gazette*: Sir John Boyd Orr... said in an interview... that a Third World War would be in the making unless some sort of world food plan was established.

> 1968 Kenneth Bird: Rattling their rifles as if they were fighting World War Three.

transistor *n* (1948) a semiconductor device in which the load current can be made proportional to a small input current, so that it acts like a valve but is much smaller and more robust, operates at lower voltages, and consumes less power and produces less heat. It was invented at Bell Labs in the eastern US in 1947. The word is a blend of *transfer* and *resistor* (a reference to the transfer of electrical signals across a resistor). Despite the lukewarm prediction in the second quote below, the transistor made possible the development of the computer and all the other electronic devices that so shaped the second half of the 20th century (including the *transistor radio* (1958), a term soon abbreviated to simply *transistor*).

> 1948 *New York Times*: A device called a transistor, which has several applications in radio where a vacuum tube ordinarily is employed, was demonstrated for the first time yesterday.

> 1952 *Electronic Engineer*: Although it is unlikely that the transistor will ultimately displace the electronic valve, there is no doubt that for many electronic applications the transistor... will be preferred because of its robust and compact form.

> 1966 John Betjeman: The endless anonymous croak of a cheap transistor Intensifies the loneliness I feel.

TV *n* (1948) an abbreviation of **television (1907)**. It originated in the US.

> 1948 *Fortune*: It is not where TV has gone, ... but the pace at which it is going that causes all the excitement... The average capital investment for a TV station is about $375,000.

underdeveloped *adj* (1949) designating a country or other region in which economic and social conditions fail to reach their potential level or an accepted standard. It was originally a kid-glove term, replacing the abrasively frank *backward*, but when in due course (as usually happens) it too began to sound patronizing, it was replaced by **developing (1961)**.

> 1949 Harry Truman: Fourth, we must embark on a bold new program for making the benefits of our scientific advances and industrial progress available for the improvement and growth of underdeveloped areas.

United Nations *n* (1942) originally, the Allied nations who united against the Axis powers in World War II; hence, used as the name (in full *United Nations Organization*) of an international peace-seeking organization of these and many other states, founded by charter in 1945. It is commonly abbreviated to *U.N.* (1946) or the acronym *U.N.O.* (1945).

> 1942 *Daily Telegraph*: But at any rate it will be long enough for Japan to inflict... losses upon all of the United Nations who have... possessions in the Far East.

> 1974 Paul Gore-Booth: Mrs Eleanor Roosevelt came to propose that the organization be called 'The United Nations'... I put forward a motion to the effect that we accept Mrs Roosevelt's proposal subject to a committee of jurists being satisfied that the term 'United Nations' presented no legal difficulty.

V-1 *n* (1944) a pilotless jet-propelled aeroplane with an explosive warhead used by the Germans against Britain between June 1944 and March 1945, killing over 5500 civilians. The *V* in its name was short for German *Vergeltungswaffe* 'reprisal weapon'.

It was powered by a pulse jet which made a characteristic and ominous buzzing noise (hence one of its nicknames, *buzz-bomb*). People on the ground quickly came to dread the silence after the engine cut out, which meant that the bomb was on its way down. Other current names for it, of varying degrees of officialness, were *flying bomb*, *doodlebug*, *robot bomb*, and *robomb*.

V-2 *n* (1944) a long-range liquid-fuelled rocket with an explosive warhead used by the Germans against Britain and the Low Countries in 1944 and 1945. It became the basis for both US and Soviet post-war rocket design. For the significance of its name, see **V-1 (1944)**.

V sign *n* (1941) originally applied to the letter *V* used as a written symbol of victory during World War II, or to the Morse Code representation of this, and subsequently to a two-fingered gesture representing *V* for *victory*, made palm outwards, which was made famous by the British prime minister Winston Churchill. The same name was later given to a gesture similar in form but made palm inwards, and with obscene intention.

> 1941 Winston Churchill: The V sign is the symbol of the unconquerable will of the occupied territories, and a portent of the fate awaiting the Nazi tyranny.
>
> 1973 *Daily Telegraph*: Two 'louts'... taunted him outside his home by shouting obscenities and making V-signs.

war trial *n* (1949) the trial of a person for a war crime or crimes. The term was used originally with reference to the series of trials of former Nazi leaders for alleged war crimes and crimes against humanity presided over by an International Military Tribunal formed from the victorious Allied Powers and held in Nuremberg in 1945–6. See also **war crime (1906)**.

> 1949 Raymond Chandler: There is an element of hypocrisy in these war trials.

welfare state *n* (1941) (a country with) a social system in which the welfare of members of the community is underwritten by means of state-run social services. The term is sometimes said to have been coined by Sir Alfred Zimmern in the 1930s, but it has not been traced in his published writings; the earliest known reference to it is in *Citizen and Churchman* by William Temple, Archbishop of Canterbury (see the first quote below). The theory was put into practice in Britain by the Labour government elected in 1945 (although many elements of a recognizable welfare state—such as state-funded old-age pensions—were in place long before the term was first thought of).

> 1941 William Temple: We have... seen that in place of the conception of the Power-State we are led to that of the Welfare-State.
>
> 1950 *Times*: This is one of the achievements for which the 'welfare State', with its vast apparatus of taxation, subsidies, family allowances, school meals, and other services, can claim credit.

West *n* (1946) the non-Communist states of the world in opposition to the Soviet bloc during the Cold War. It is more of a political than a geographical concept, so although most of its constituent states are to the west of the Soviet Union and its satellites—in Western Europe and North America—countries decidedly to the east, such as Australia, are admitted too. Compare **East (1951)**.

> 1946 Harold Nicolson: He is convinced that the Russians wish to dominate the world... The only way in which the West can counter this is to pool their philosophy of liberalism, put up a united front.

-wise *suffix* (1942) from the point of view of, as regards. The usage has its origins back in the Old English period, in expressions like *in cross wise* 'in the manner of a cross'. By the 14th century, the free noun *wise* had come to function as a suffix—thus, *crosswise*. This state of affairs continued undisturbed until the 20th century, when US English (perhaps under German influence) began using *-wise* to mean 'in respect of'. It has attracted a good deal of hostility from purists, but at the end of the century it was fairly well ensconced.

1942 E. R. Allen: It should be noted that there are two types of hydrogen atoms positionwise.

1958 *Spectator*: John Robert Russell, 13th Duke of Bedford . . . in twelve TV performances, was the greatest, successwise, among the aristocrats.

youth club *n* (1940) a social club provided for the spare-time activities of young people.

1940 *Times*: Youth clubs may be found in all districts of the city.

1957 John Osborne: I was teaching Art to a bunch of Youth Club kids.

The 1950s

In the 1950s, prosperity danced with anxiety. As the decade opened, the last of the post-war austerities were being shuffled off as, fuelled by the powerhouse of the US economy, Western nations began to feel affluent again. The 50s saw the start of the long consumer boom that reached a peak in the 60s, and did not receive a real check until the oil crisis of the 70s. Underpinning this economic *growth* were continuing scientific advances on all fronts, from medicine to computers—and towards the end of the decade came the greatest coup of all, as the holy grail of flight into space was grasped. But there was a worm in the bud. Science was not all peace and progress; it had also produced the nuclear bomb. The threat of human annihilation loomed over the 50s, like the very *mushroom cloud* of the bomb itself. The title of W. H. Auden's 1947 poem 'The Age of Anxiety' was appropriate to the coming decade.

To the 1940s, nuclear weapons were a novel terror. In the 50s they became part of the landscape, a background to daily lives. They even acquired a pet name: *nukes.* They progressed in destructive power (the *H-bomb*) and in the sophistication of their means of delivery (from *V bombers* (Britain's jet bombers) to *ICBMs* (intercontinental ballistic missiles)). The banal vocabulary of *thermonuclear* warfare had a shocking familiarity: *fall-out*, *overkill*, *megadeath* (the death of a million people). Everyone had heard of *kilotons* and *megatons*, of *strategic* and *tactical* nuclear weapons, and of comfortable old *conventional* weapons. There were many, though, who did not accept the official *deterrent* line. Towards the end of the decade the anti-nuclear protest movement began to grow. Groups such as *CND* were formed, and the term *unilateralist* 'advocating nuclear disarmament on the part of one's own country only' was added to the nuclear lexicon.

This was the background against which the Cold War ideological conflict between the *free world* and the *East* solidified. *NATO* and the *Warsaw Pact* forces peered suspiciously at each other over the Iron Curtain, while *Kremlinologists* tried to fathom Soviet intentions. *Summit* conferences were convened, at which differences between the two sides would hopefully be resolved, but all too often the outcome was a Russian *niet.* Meanwhile, in 1949, another Communist regime had established itself, in China, and the West had *Maoism* for a new enemy, berating it with a fresh set of insults (e.g. *paper tiger* 'a person, country, etc. that appears outwardly powerful or important but is actually weak or ineffective'). There were fears that the *domino* theory (suggesting that a political event or development in one country etc. would lead to its occurrence in others) was about to be proved. Back home in the US, anti-Communist paranoia manifested itself in *McCarthyism*. For nations that had decolonized and were unwilling to replace one dependency with another, *non-alignment* seemed the sanest alternative. As far as Europeans were concerned, the answer to war was unity; the 50s were the decade when the terms *common market* and *EEC* entered our vocabulary.

Among the most unsettling setbacks of the period for the West was the launch of the Soviet *sputnik* in 1957. Up till now, the US had assumed it was comfortably ahead in the *space race*, but suddenly there was a real prospect that the winners would be *cosmonauts* rather than astronauts. The result was an all-out US effort for a spectacular *moon-shot* in the next decade, culminating, hopefully, in a *soft landing*. Towards the end of the 50s the US public, and television viewers worldwide, watching the *count-down* to *blast-off*, started to become familiar with the *aerospace* jargon that would dominate the next two decades, as the *space programme* evolved. Meanwhile, on the lunatic fringe, the flying saucer had been respectabilized as the *UFO*.

Computers were starting to move out of university laboratories into commercial establishments, albeit still as very large whirring boxes with flashing lights. *Artificial intelligence*, *information technology*, and *data processing* had their beginnings, and terms like *bootstrap* and *modem*, *on-line* and *real time*, *print-out* and *RAM*, *Algol* and *FORTRAN* entered the language.

The *double helix* was discovered, and the *big bang* postulated. Surgeons operated on the *open heart*, performed *by-passes* and *transplants*, and fitted *pacemakers*. The *Salk vaccine* banished the mid-century scourge of polio, but, ominously, before the decade was out, *thalidomide* had appeared on the scene. Meanwhile, the world was going down with *Asian flu*.

Following the convulsions of wartime, Western society was establishing itself in new patterns that rejected the stratified deference of previous decades and the dirigisme of the 1940s. The 50s were the period of the *beat generation*, the *angry young man*, and the *crazy mixed-up kid*, of the *kitchen sink* and the *coffee bar*. It was the *teen* age: the decade in which young people thrust their way into the spotlight, whether they were *Teddy boys*, or *Hell's Angels*, or *beatniks*, or early *hippies*. It was the decade of *protest*, and sometimes of violence (the *flick knife* the weapon of choice), and to be old was to be a *cube* (a more extreme form of a 'square'). The slang of the period was US teenspeak, much of it inherited from the argot of jazz: *far out* and *way out*, *with it* and *swinging*, *a gas* and *the most* (all various forms of commendation), *split the scene* 'to leave', *see you later alligator*, anything ending in *-ville* ('squaresville', 'dullsville'). Not that the old order was entirely moribund, at least in Britain, where people still got very steamed up over the difference between *U* and *non-U*.

Music was a key element in the new youth culture—notably, of course, *rock and roll*, but there were other favourites, such as *country and western* and *skiffle*. The concept of the *group* was born, although it was not to achieve its apotheosis until the 1960s. *Deejays* played their records in *discotheques*, where the teenagers danced in their *jeans* and *ponytails*. But in the affluent 50s, the kids could also afford their own record players, and their money propelled songs into the *hit parade*, the *top ten*, *top of the pops*.

Other record buyers were playing their *albums* on the new *hi-fi* and *stereo* systems. But the biggest developments in electronic entertainment were going on in television, which in the course of the 1950s grew exponentially to become the world's leading medium of communication. From being an esoteric toy of the well-off at the start of the decade, it had by the end made the transition to being a taken-for-granted part of everyday life. In Britain, the turning point was the Coronation of Elizabeth II in 1953. New *Elizabethans* in their thousands bought televisions to watch the event, and millions of their neighbours huddled round their tiny screens to share the experience. The bug was caught, and the *goggle-box*—or simply *the box*—was there in the corner to stay, even though the audience had to make do with *panel games* rather than coronations. Meanwhile, in the US *pay television* and *breakfast-time television* were taking their first steps. In the cinema, directors experimented with *Cinerama* and *CinemaScope* (wide-screen techniques), and even with *Smell-o-Vision*, but a more significant long-term development was the appearance of *videotape*. The *transistor radio* also made its bow.

Our surroundings began to take on a spartan modernism. *High-rise* blocks (long familiar in the US but new to Britain) and *pedestrian precincts* dominated the new urban landscape, and architects embraced the *new brutalism's* deliberate harshness. In the visual arts it was the decade of *abstract expressionism* (the spontaneous creation of abstract forms) and *action painting* (created by random drippings and splashings), and of the beginnings of *pop art* (art deploying themes from popular culture).

In the world of fashion, the *A-line* (flaring from the waist) graced the middle of the decade, but by the time of the *sack dress* (an unwaisted dress) inspiration had run dry. We first wore *Bermuda shorts*, *Y-fronts*, and *stiletto heels* (though not as an ensemble), and *tracksuits* made their first appearance (initially confined to athletics tracks—very useful if you had just run a *four-minute mile*). Technology made its contribution with *Lycra* and the *drip-dry* shirt. The puffy *bouffant* hairstyle came in, reliant on *hair spray* and *back-combing*, while for men, if the *DA* (with the hair at the back of the head shaped like a duck's tail—short for *duck's arse*) was not for you, you could go for a *Tony Curtis* (combed backwards at the sides, forwards over the forehead).

Technology was beginning to dominate our diet, too. We could buy *sliced bread*; the first *fish finger* announced the arrival of frozen prepared dishes; and *fast food* appeared on the high street. But there were also signs of a growing penetration of foreign cuisines into the staid Anglo-Saxon gastronomic repertoire, exemplified by the likes of *doner kebabs*, *garlic bread*, *tandoori*, and *woks*.

On the roads, small and nippy were the watchwords. If you did not want a *bubble car* (a tiny car with a transparent domed top), or one of the new Minis, you could *scooter* around on a *moped* or a *Vespa* (an Italian make of motor scooter)—but watch out for the *traffic wardens* and *meter maids*. In the air, the helicopter came of age as a means of transport, and went into battle in the Korean War—hence *chopper* and *whirlybird*. And a completely new type of vehicle came on the scene: the *hovercraft*.

The *permissive* sixties were coming, ushered in by *the pill*. There were *sex kittens* on the screen and *kinky* sex in the Sunday papers. But the time was not yet ripe for *consenting adults* to come out of the *closet*. Meanwhile the teenagers of the next decade were still at home, playing with their *hula hoops*.

adult *adj* (1958) pornographic. The euphemism is based ostensibly on the notion of access restricted to adults, but it suggests the subtext 'likely to appeal to adults'—a rather seedy reflection on adulthood.

> 1958 *New Musical Express*: Unusual adult photo sets. S.a.e. Free exciting offer.

Afro-Caribbean *adj, n* (1958) of both Africa and the Caribbean. The term is applied especially to West Indians of African descent. It provided a further item in the late-20th-century litany of would-be politically correct terms for black people.

> 1958 *Oxford Mail*: Lessons in Afro-Caribbean dancing... for... members of the Oxford University Ballet Club.

angry young man *n* (1957) a young man who is dissatisfied with and outspoken against the prevailing state of affairs, current beliefs, etc. The expression had been in use since at least the late 1930s, and in 1951 the Irish writer Leslie Paul used it as the title of a book, but it first became commonly used, especially by journalists, after the production of John Osborne's play *Look Back in Anger* (first performed in 1956). The phrase did not occur in the play but was applied to Osborne by George Fearon, a reporter (see the first quotation below), and thence used particularly of young writers, usually of provincial and lower middle-class or working-class origin, who denounced or satirized the 'Establishment' and the abuses of the time; it was later applied by extension to any person, group, etc. in Britain and elsewhere who considered the times to be out of joint.

> 1957 George Fearon, *Daily Telegraph*: I had read John Osborne's play. When I met the author I ventured to prophesy that his generation would praise his play while mine would, in general, dislike it... 'If this happens,' I told him, 'you would become known as the Angry Young Man.' In fact, we decided then and there that henceforth he was to be known as that.

> 1958 *Times*: The angry young man who feels that life is short, and that he must make his mark early by carping at established ideas and institutions.

anti-matter *n* (1953) a hypothetical form of matter consisting of anti-particles. The existence of anti-particles, elementary particles of the same mass as a given particle but having an opposite electrical charge, was predicted in 1930 by the British physicist Paul Dirac ('We may call such a particle an anti-electron', Paul Dirac (1931)).

> 1963 *Daily Telegraph*: It is quite conceivable that there might exist a kind of looking-glass world, in which all matter is made up from anti-matter.

artificial intelligence *n* (1956) (the study of) the capacity of machines to simulate intelligent human behaviour. The term is commonly abbreviated to *AI* (first recorded in 1971—the 1970s was the decade when work in this field got seriously under way).

> 1971 *New Scientist*: The first major effort of the AI scientists was directed towards writing computer programs to translate automatically between languages.

asylum seeker *n* (1959) a person who seeks political asylum in another country. The term kept a low profile until the end of the 20th century, when controversy over the motivation of immigrants into the UK, and the apparent difficulty of distinguishing those who were really fleeing persecution from those who merely wanted to better themselves economically, set up a disputatious contrast between *economic migrant* (1962) and *asylum seeker*. The latter took over much of the terminological ground previously held by *refugee* (1685).

> 1959 *American Political Science Review*: Small and medium-sized countries most exposed geographically to the influx of asylum seekers must needs watch out for the slightest policy reaction of stronger powers.

> 2000 *Big Issue*: With regards to the debate around 'economic migrants' vs 'genuine' asylum seekers... a further aspect of British history should be acknowledged.

backlash *n* (1957) a sudden and adverse reaction, especially to a political or social development. The usage is a metaphorical extension of the earlier 'recoil produced by interacting parts of a mechanism', which dates from the early 19th century. It apparently originated in the context of racial tensions in the US in the 1950s.

> 1957 *Saturday Evening Post*: You're going to get a backlash—segregation's going to spread.

> 1964 *Listener*: The notorious white backlash (the voters, especially of immigrant origins, who fear the Negroes will move into their jobs and depress the value of their little houses).

beatnik *n* (1958) a member of the so-called 'beat generation'—an expression applied at first (around 1952) to a group of young people, predominantly writers, artists, and their adherents, in San Francisco, and later to similar groups elsewhere, who adopted unconventional dress, manners, habits, etc. as a means of self-expression and social protest. *Beatnik* was coined early in 1958 by the San Francisco columnist Herb Caen, no doubt under the influence of the contemporary buzzword **sputnik (1957)**. In due course the older generation took it up, often with obvious distaste, as a general word for a long-haired bohemian.

> 1958 *Daily Express*: [San Francisco] is the home and the haunt of America's Beat generation and these are the Beatniks—or new barbarians.

> 1959 *Guardian*: He calls a flat a 'pad' (Beatnik language).

> 1966 *English Studies*: In the mid-twentieth century the typical Bohemian has become the beatnik poet or pseudo-philosopher.

big bang *n* (1950) the explosion of a single compact mass, in which (according to one cosmological theory) the universe originated. For a decade or two the *steady state* (1948) theory, which viewed the universe as essentially unchanging in time and space, competed hotly with the explosion theory, but by the end of the 20th century it was generally agreed that the big-bangers had it.

> 1950 Fred Hoyle: One [idea] was that the Universe started its life a finite time ago in a single huge explosion . . . This big bang idea seemed to me to be unsatisfactory.

body bag *n* (1954) a strong bag in which a corpse is placed and transported (e.g. from the scene of an accident). The term originated in the US; the sight of body bags on television was said to have been a major factor in the American public's turning against the Vietnam War.

boutique *n* (1953) a small fashion-shop or department that sells ready-to-wear clothes designed by a couturier; a small shop selling trendy clothes or other articles, especially for young or fashionable people. The term is often used adjectivally, to denote the sort of articles bought in such a shop. It was a re-importation of a French word which had been used sporadically in English since the mid 18th century in the more prosaic sense 'small shop'. It enjoyed particular success in the 1960s, when, applied to a self-contained shop rather than an in-store department, it became almost synonymous with 'Swinging London', Carnaby Street, etc.

> 1957 *Observer*: The idea of 'Boutiques', those small shops set inside couture establishments to sell ready-to-wear.

> 1966 *Vanity Fair*: I . . . love the look of boutique clothes.

> 1966 Mary Quant: It was agreed that if we could find the right premises for a boutique . . . we would open a shop. It was to be a bouillabaisse of clothes and accessories . . . sweaters, scarves, shifts, hats, jewellery, and peculiar odds and ends.

brain-washing *n* (1950) the systematic and often forcible elimination from a person's mind of all established ideas, especially political ones, so that another set of ideas can take their place; this process regarded as the kind of coercive conversion practised by certain totalitarian states on political dissidents. The term is a literal translation of Chinese *xi nao*, and English acquired it via the Korean War. *Brain-washer* and the back-formed verb *brain-wash* soon followed.

> 1953 *Saturday Evening Post*: The anticommunist soldiers . . . may be blackmailed or brain-washed or third-degreed.

brinkmanship *n* (1956) the art of advancing to the very brink of war but not engaging in it. The term was coined by the US politician Adlai Stevenson (1900–65) in response to a remark by John Foster Dulles, the US Secretary of State: 'Says Dulles "...Of course we were brought to the verge of war... If you try to run away from it, if you are scared to go to the brink, you are lost... We walked to the brink and we looked it in the face"', *Time* (1956). His model was Stephen Potter's **gamesmanship (1947)** and similar formations.

> 1956 *New York Times*: [Adlai Stevenson] derided the Secretary [i.e. J. F. Dulles] for 'boasting of his brinkmanship—the art of bringing us to the edge of the nuclear abyss'.

> 1958 *Annual Register 1957*: Anglo-French 'brinkmanship' over Suez had failed to stop at the brink.

charisma *n* (1959) marked personal charm or magnetism which gives one the power to influence others. The word was originally brought into English around 1930 as a term used by the German social scientist Max Weber (1864–1920), denoting a gift or power of leadership or authority. The later 20th century made it at once more metaphysical and more mundane. Its ultimate source is Greek *kharisma* 'favour, divine gift'.

> 1967 *Spectator*: Like many of his generation, he succumbs to the Kennedy charisma, identifies himself with his hero.

closet *adj* (1952) secret, unacknowledged. The metaphor originated, in the US, from the notion of being hidden in a 'closet' or cupboard. The earliest recorded example relates to a secret drinker of alcohol, but it was with reference to homosexuality that the usage took off in the late 1950s, especially in *closet queen* (first recorded in 1959). The phrase *come out of the closet* 'to acknowledge publicly one's previously concealed homosexuality', first recorded in 1971, appears to derive from the adjectival usage rather than vice versa. See also **out (1990)**.

> 1961 *Social Problems* (US): 'Secret'...homosexuals...in the...'gay world'...are known as 'closet fags'.

> 1984 *Mail on Sunday*: His colleagues' retort is that Jimmy is a closet queen because he doesn't live with a woman.

> 1985 *Sunday Telegraph*: His defection [to Rome] is a blow because he was not a closet Papist intoxicated by bells and fancy vestments.

CND *n* (1958) An abbreviation of *Campaign for Nuclear Disarmament*, an organization formed in 1958 to campaign for Britain's nuclear disarmament.

coffee bar *n* (1956) an establishment where coffee and other non-alcoholic drinks are sold. The term is actually first recorded in 1905, but it was not until the 1950s that the concept (fuelled by newly fashionable Italian coffees—see **espresso (1945)**) took off: coffee bars became the centres of a now innocent-seeming youth culture, stimulated by nothing more intoxicating than rock and roll and talk.

> 1956 Louis McIntosh: This is Oxford's latest coffee-bar... The others are getting so tatty.

> 1957 *Times Literary Supplement*: The seedy group of coffee-bar philosophers...spouting their sad rehash of dated Fascist clichés.

common market *n* (1954) a group of countries imposing few or no duties on trade with one another and a common tariff on trade with outside countries. The term (with capital initials) later became the name of the trade association of France, the German Federal Republic, Italy, Belgium, the Netherlands, and Luxembourg instituted in 1958, and joined in 1973 by Britain, Denmark, and Ireland. It gradually gave way to *EEC* (1958) and thereafter to *EC* (1973) (see also **European Union (1991)**).

> 1954 *Annual Register 1953*: The provisions...for the gradual establishment of a European common market.

> 1957 *Economist*: The Common Market: a treaty to set up a European Economic Community signed at Rome in March by six countries.

conventional *adj* (1955) of bombs, weapons, warfare, etc.: not nuclear. The usage can be seen in embryo in 'We must decide whether the new fire package [i.e. the hydrogen bomb] will permit a reduction of our more conventional military weapons', *New York Herald Tribune* (1952).

> 1955 *Hansard*: This unique difference . . . between the hydrogen and the atomic weapon on the one hand and conventional weapons on the other.

cosmonaut *n* (1959) an astronaut, especially a Russian one. The word is an anglicization of Russian *kosmonavt*, on the model of **astronaut (1929)**. (The adjective *cosmonautic(al)* had previously been coined in English, apparently as a completely independent creation, with no particular reference to Russian space-travel. It is first recorded in 1947.)

> 1959 A. Shternfeld's *Soviet Space Science* (translation): Naturally, cosmonauts could leave an artificial satellite and move in outside space.

count-down *n* (1953) the action of counting in reverse, from a given number to zero, usually in seconds, to mark the lapse of time before an explosion, the launching of a missile, etc. The term originated in the US.

> 1953 *News* (Birmingham, Alabama): Observers on the mountain were able to hear the count-down on the drop from the control tower.

> 1958 *Observer*: The count-down began. At the count of 11 the very top of the rocket started spinning. Two . . . one . . . and then the firing command.

credit card *n* (1952) a card issued by an organization authorizing a named person to draw on its account or to make purchases on credit. The usage is a reapplication, originating in the US, of a term which in the late 19th century had been used for a 'traveller's cheque'. Compare **debit card (1975)**.

> 1952 *New York Times*: Anyone who can sign his name and pay his bills can charge his way through some of the better hotels, restaurants and night clubs of the country under a new credit card system known as the Diners Club.

> 1958 *Business Week*: American Express will present its new credit card to society Oct. 1.

cruise missile *n* (1959) a weapon in the form of a guided pilotless jet aircraft carrying a warhead and able to fly at low altitudes. It was often at the heart of controversy in the latter part of the 20th century, whether as the target of protests (as when US cruise missiles were stationed in Britain in 1983) or as a result of its use (for example, against Baghdad and other Iraqi targets). The term originated in the US.

data processing *n* (1954) the performance by automatic means of any operations on empirical data, such as classifying or analysing them or carrying out calculations on them. The term is usually applied specifically to such an operation carried out on a computer.

> 1954 *Instruments & Automation*: New 'Model CRC 102-A Electronic Computer' and its auxiliary . . . are designed for . . . data processing.

deterrent *n* (1954) the nuclear weapons of any one country or alliance, viewed as likely to deter potential aggressors. The term summed up the principle on which the long-running stand-off of the Cold War was founded: attack by atomic weapons is so appalling in its effect that no one in their right mind would provoke it.

> 1954 *Statement on Defence (Parliamentary Papers 1953–54)*: The primary deterrent, however, remains the atomic bomb and the ability of the highly organised and trained United States strategic air power to use it.

> 1959 *Observer*: Britain should also be prepared to give up her independent deterrent and stop the manufacture of nuclear weapons.

discotheque *n* (1954) a club etc. where recorded music is played for dancing. The word was borrowed from French, and in the 1950s mainly used still in the French form *discothèque*, referring to such establishments in France. It was not until dancing clubs playing pop records became fashionable in the early 1960s that it was fully naturalized (and abbreviated to **disco (1964)**, which soon became the usual form).

disinformation *n* (1955) (the dissemination of) deliberately false information, especially when supplied by a government or its agent to a foreign power or to the media, with the intention of influencing the policies or opinions of those who receive it. The word is perhaps an anglicization of Russian *dezinformatsiya*. This in turn may have been adapted from French *disinformation*, although the known chronology is not in favour of this sequence (the Russian word is first recorded in 1949, the French in 1954).

> 1955 *Times*: The elimination of every form of propaganda and disinformation, as well as of other forms of conduct which create distrust or in any other way impede the establishment of an atmosphere conducive to constructive international cooperation and to the peaceful coexistence of nations.

do-it-yourself *n* (1952) doing one's own household repairs and maintenance, usually as opposed to employing someone else to do it. The term arose in large part from the great increase in home ownership in the second half of the 20th century. In earlier times, when accommodation was much likelier to be rented, there was little incentive to save one's landlord money by doing repairs oneself. The phrase has been around in proverbial expressions for centuries ('If a man will haue his businesse well done, he must doe it himselfe', Thomas Drax (1616)), and Richard Barham endorsed its message of self-reliance in the *Ingoldsby Legends* ('If it's business of consequence, Do it yourself!' (*a*1845)). The derived *do-it-yourselfer* is first recorded in 1954, and the abbreviation *DIY* in 1955.

> 1952 *Time* Do-it-yourself has brought similar gains, and market shifts, to other industries.

> 1954 *New York Times*: To the do-it-yourselfer, plywood is as essential as paint, tools, plastics and ordinary lumber.

> 1955 *Practical Householder*: A central pool such as a 'D.I.Y. Club' from which . . . tools can be hired is the obvious advantage.

double helix *n* (1954) the structure of a DNA molecule, consisting of two spiral chains of polynucleotides coiled round the same axis. The term was introduced in a paper in the *Proceedings of the Royal Society* by Francis Crick and James Watson who, with the help of Maurice Wilkins and Rosalind Franklin, worked out the structure in the early 1950s. Watson used it as the title of a book in 1968.

> 1954 Crick & Watson (heading): Detailed configuration of the double helix.

> 1968 *New Scientist*: The symbol of the molecular biological age is without doubt the 'double helix' of DNA.

East *n* (1951) the states of eastern Europe during the Cold War; the Communist powers; the Soviet bloc. The term is almost always used in conjunction with *West* 'the non-Communist states' (see **West (1946)**).

> 1951 *Annual Register 1950*: There were more 'espionage' convictions . . . and the closing of the Czech Consulate-General in New York. These incidents, significant of the growing estrangement of East and West, were also . . . evidence that neither party wished to push its claims to the limit.

> 1959 *News Chronicle*: The harsh reality of the cold war, of East-West tension.

environment *n* (1956) the combination of external conditions that impinge on organisms living on the Earth—something that became increasingly an object of study and concern as the 20th century progressed (see also **environmentalism (1972)**). The usage is a specialized application of the more general 'the objects or the region surrounding something', which goes back to the early 19th century.

> 1956 P. S. Sears: The situation is clouded by a widespread confidence that this impact of man upon environment can continue indefinitely.

1967 Kenneth Mellanby: Perhaps the most obvious way in which man has contaminated his environment is by polluting the air with smoke.

fab *adj* (1957) in British slang, wonderful, marvellous. The word is a shortening of *fabulous* (which is not recorded in print in this sense until 1959). The usage really took off around 1963, when it became attached to the Beatles (sometimes called the 'Fab Four') and other Merseyside pop groups. After lying dormant for a while, it enjoyed a revival in the 1980s.

1963 *Times*: She stretched her stockinged toes towards the blazing logs. 'Daddy, this fire's simply fab.'

1963 *Meet the Beatles*: Most of the Merseyside groups produce sounds which are pretty fab.

1988 *National Lampoon*: And I just think it's fab!

fall-out *n* (1950) radioactive refuse of a nuclear bomb explosion; also, the process of deposition of such refuse. It was a substance about whose invisible perils its potential victims were much exercised during the Cold War.

1952 *New York Times*: Nevertheless, a good deal of radioactive stuff is picked up and carried by the wind and deposited all over the country... So far there have been no dangerous concentrations of radioactive 'fall-out', as it is called, that is outside of the proving grounds in Nevada.

1961 *John o' London's*: The make-it-yourself fallout shelter.

fast food *n* (1951) convenience food of a type which can be served quickly at a catering outlet or prepared quickly at home. The term, which originated in the US, is mainly used adjectivally with reference to eating places where foods are kept hot and ready to serve, or partially prepared so that they can be served quickly. See also **convenience (1961)**.

1951 *Fountain & Fast Food Service*: The partners have become old hands at spotting the type of conventioneer that will patronize their fast food service.

1977 *Times*: 'Fast food' requires no preparation by the customer. Traditional 'fast food outlets' like fish-and-chip shops are being superseded by Chinese, Indian, Kebab and fried chicken houses.

free world *n* (1955) the non-Communist countries of the world. A partisan usage, favoured by non- or especially anti-Communists.

1955 *Bulletin of Atomic Science*: The Soviet World and the Free World are running neck and neck in the training of scientists.

Goon *n* (1951) any of the members of the cast of a popular British radio comedy series, *The Goon Show* (originally called *Crazy People*), noted for its crazy and absurd brand of humour. The history of the word *goon* is remarkably complicated. In the 1930s it meant both 'a thug' and 'a fool' (see **goon (1938)**). The former (with perhaps a sprinkling of the latter) probably led to its use among Allied prisoners-of-war during World War II for 'a prison-camp guard', but Spike Milligan, creator of the Goons, denied that he got the name from that source (see the third quote below). He claims that it came from a cartoon character, presumably the same 'Alice the Goon' who inspired the original 1938 *goon*. No doubt the intervening years of use in the sense 'fool' had played a part too. Subsequent uses of *goon* to mean 'someone who behaves crazily' are not easy to distinguish from the earlier 'fool', but derivatives such as *goonery* and *goonish* were no doubt inspired by the radio Goons.

1951 *Radio Times*: Crazy people... Radio's Own Crazy Gang 'The Goons'... Spike Milligan... has compiled the 'Goon Show' material.

1951 *Picture Post*: Four young comics—Michael Bentine, Harry Secombe, Spike Milligan and Peter Sellers—have at last got together in a radio programme. In 'Crazy People' they put across their favoured kind of humour. This they call 'goonery'... General opinion was that if you like crazy, pun-dizzy, logic-smashing comedy that doesn't despise your intelligence, you'll like the Goons.

1971 Spike Milligan: Prisoners of war called their German guards *goons* but I got it from Popeye. There was a creature called the Goon which had nothing in the face at all except hair... I liked the word and we called it *The Goons*.

group *n* (1958) an ensemble of pop musicians, typically numbering between three and six. The term is first recorded in the compound *skiffle group*, but it did not really take off until the early 1960s, with the rise of groups such as the Beatles and the Rolling Stones. It commonly occurs in the compounds *pop group* and *rock group*. By the late 1960s *group* was becoming uncool, and was widely substituted by *band*.

> 1964 *Gramophone Popular Record Catalogue* (Artist Section): Barron-Knights, The... Call up the groups. Medley.
>
> 1967 *Listener*: Two of the Rolling Stones 'pop group' are sent for trial on drugs charges.
>
> 1967 *Melody Maker*: Groups who are going to give us action.

hallucinogenic *adj* (1952) of a drug: causing hallucinations. The related noun *hallucinogen*, denoting such a drug, is first recorded in 1954. At first familiar only to chemists and aficionados, in the LSD-taking 1960s both words became common currency.

> 1952 *Journal of Mental Science*: There are many other hallucinogenic drugs, but none has either such striking properties or such a simple chemical constitution as mescaline.
>
> 1954 Aldous Huxley: Lysergic acid, an extremely potent hallucinogen derived from ergot.

hi-fi *n, adj* (1950) that part of acoustics and electronics that deals with the design, construction, and use of equipment for the recording and reproduction of sound to a fairly high standard. In this original usage, *hi-fi* is simply an abbreviation of the noun *high fidelity* (first recorded in 1934), but it was soon being used adjectivally (see the first quote below), and in due course this became its main role. A new noun sense, 'a hi-fi record-player or other system', is first recorded in 1959.

> 1952 *Time*: Until last week, most 'hi-fi' sets, which reproduce music in the home with the clarity and realism of the concert hall, were custom-made from standard parts by small radio and phonograph shops at a cost of from $150 to $2,000.
>
> 1958 *Observer*: The choice of a loudspeaker system is quite the most important task confronting those in search of 'Hi-Fi'.
>
> 1959 Colin MacInnes: I put a disc on to his hi-fi.

hippie, hippy *n* (1953) originally a low-profile synonym of *hipster* (1941)—i.e. someone who is 'hip' or in touch with fashionable tastes—*hippie* suddenly made it into the big time in the mid 1960s as the name for a member of a culture, originally mainly on the West Coast of the US but eventually spreading throughout the youth of the Western (and indeed parts of the Eastern) world, characterized by an emphasis on non-violence and universal love and a general rejection of the mores of conventional society, especially regarding dress, personal appearance, and way of life. Numerous derivatives, such as *hippiedom* and *hippieness*, soon followed. Long after the original hippies themselves have wandered off into the sunset, the word remains current as a patronizing term for casualness or unconventionality of appearance or behaviour, especially in the young. See also **flower people, flower children (1967)**.

> 1953 Douglass Wallop: Man, I really get a bellyful of these would be hippies.
>
> 1967 *Sunday Truth* (Brisbane): A hippie is the LSD Age's equivalent of a beatnik, and they turn on with marihuana, LSD, benzedrine or merely with the idea of turning-on.
>
> 1968 *Blues Unlimited*: I guess California, and psychedelia, and hippieness have had the influence.
>
> 1998 *Food Illustrated*: The French seem impervious to the politics of food—while an organic movement exists, it is generally disdained as hippy.

hit parade *n* (1958) a list of the best-selling recorded songs over a given period. See also **top ten (1958), charts (1963)**.

> 1965 George Melly: His version of 'Rock Island Line'... was put out as a single and rose to be top of the Hit Parade.

Holocaust *n* (1957) the mass murder of the Jews by the Nazis in World War II. The specific application was introduced by historians during the 1950s, probably as an equivalent to Hebrew *hurban* and *shoah* 'catastrophe' (used in the same sense); but it had been foreshadowed by contemporary references to the Nazi atrocities as a *holocaust* (in the sense 'great slaughter', which dates from the early 19th century): 'The Nazis go on killing... If this rule could be relaxed, some hundreds, and possibly a few thousands, might be enabled to escape from this holocaust', *Hansard, Lords* (1943). At first the term was in common use mainly among Jews, but it gradually spread to a more general domain. See also **genocide (1944)**.

> 1957 *Yad Washem Bulletin*: Research on the Holocaust Period.
>
> 1962 Brian Glanville: The holocaust...was the inevitable end, the logical conclusion of the pogroms, the Mosley marches, the hatred.

image *n* (1958) a concept or impression, especially a favourable impression, created in the minds of the public, of a particular person, institution, product, etc. The usage came into the general domain from the advertising industry.

> 1958 J. K. Galbraith: The first task of the public relations man, on taking over a business client, is to 're-engineer' his image to include something besides the production of goods.
>
> 1958 Martin Mayer: David Ogilvy, of Ogilvy, Benson & Mather, apostle of the 'brand image'.
>
> 1962 *Listener*: Mr Gaitskell has improved his image by his determination at Scarborough and after.

information technology *n* (1958) the branch of technology concerned with the dissemination, processing, and storage of information, especially by means of computers. The term originated in the US; the abbreviation *IT* is not recorded before 1982.

> 1958 Leavitt & Whisler: The new technology does not yet have a single established name. We shall call it information technology.
>
> 1984 *National Westminster Bank Quarterly Review*: The development of cable television was made possible by the convergence of telecommunications and computing technology (...generally known in Britain as information technology).

jeans *n* (1956) close-fitting trousers made of denim, typically blue (*blue jeans*). The word had been used since the mid 19th century to denote a garment made of jean, a type of twilled cotton cloth, and blue trousers of this general sort had been manufactured in the US by Levi Strauss since the 1860s, but it was the mid 1950s that saw their adoption as a worldwide teenage uniform.

> 1957 *Times*: For miles and miles of suburban area you will rarely see a young woman out of blue jeans, shorts or slim-jim pants during the day.
>
> 1958 *Economist*: Girls in tight jeans and dazzle socks.

jet set *n* (1951) a smart set of wealthy people who conduct business by jet travel, or who make frequent journeys, e.g. to holiday resorts, by jet aircraft; also used more broadly to denote rich, sophisticated, fashionable people. The term originated in the US. Regular commercial jet travel actually began in 1952, when the De Havilland Comet entered service with B.O.A.C.

> 1951 *San Francisco Examiner*: You're strictly jet set... if you stake your claim in the dunes... never descend to ocean level except for a quick dunk.
>
> 1964 *Saturday Review*: The Jet Set... has rediscovered St. Tropez.

kitchen sink *adj, n* (1954) used initially to designate, dismissively, (the work of) a group of English realistic painters of the 1950s, and soon afterwards a group of English realistic playwrights and other authors of the same period. It is the latter usage, applied to the likes of Shelagh Delaney, John Osborne, and Arnold Wesker, that has become the most familiar. Their form of drama, portraying the lives of working-class or lower-middle-class people, invaded the fragrant drawing rooms portrayed by Noël Coward and Terence Rattigan and condemned them to several decades of oblivion. *Kitchen sink* has since come to be used more broadly as a metaphor for domestic squalor.

> 1954 David Sylvester (title): The kitchen sink . . . The post-war generation takes us back from the studio to the kitchen . . . The kitchen sink too . . . It is evident that neither objectivity nor abstraction is the aim of the young painters of the kitchen-sink school.
>
> 1960 *Times*: Mr. Ronald Duncan is reported as saying that the English Stage Company . . . presents only left wing 'kitchen sink' drama.

like *adv* (1950) used as an emphatic filler before either a single word (often an adjective or interjection) or even a whole clause. The slang usage, which originated in the US, is presumably a development of the filler *like* used after a phrase or clause, which is frequently condemned as characteristic of debased late-20th-century (youth) speech but in fact goes back at least to the late 18th century, and is widely evidenced in representations of 19th-century dialectal speech ('Might I be so bold as just to ax, by way of talk like, if [etc.]', Edward Peacock (1870)).

> 1950 *Neurotica*: Like how much can you lay on [i.e. give] me?
>
> 1970 *Time*: Afterward, a girl came up to me and said, 'You kinda look interested in this; did you know there are civil rights for women?' And I thought like wow, this is for me.
>
> 1971 *Black Scholar*: Man like the dude really flashed his hole card.

LSD *n* (1950) the drug lysergic acid diethylamide, used in experimental medicine and taken illegally as a hallucinogenic, especially in the 1960s. The term was probably borrowed from German, where it is first recorded in 1947 as an abbreviation of *Lysergsäure-diäthylamid.*

> 1950 *Diseases of the Nervous System*: We believe that L.S.D. 25 is a drug which induces a controllable toxic state within the nervous system, that re-activates anxiety and fear with apparently just enough euphoria to permit recall of the provoking experiences.
>
> 1964 *Daily Telegraph*: The tablets are believed to be a solid form of LSD, lysergic acid diethylamide. They can be obtained in certain clubs and public houses in London and other big cities.

mall *n* (1959) a shopping precinct. The usage originated in the US, and was slow to spread to British English. It was at first applied to an urban shopping precinct consisting of a central pedestrian area surrounded by shops; in this sense it is a development of the earlier *mall* 'a sheltered walkway serving as a promenade'. The application to a suburban shopping centre followed in the late 1960s.

megaton *n* (1952) a unit of explosive power equal to that of one million tons of TNT The coinage was called into being by the unparalleled power of the hydrogen bomb (throughout the whole of World War II only six megatons were used).

> 1952 *New York Herald-Tribune*: The first true super-bomb to be detonated is expected to have a power of two megatons.

meltdown *n* (1956) the melting of a nuclear reactor's fuel rods as a result of a defect in the cooling system, with the possible escape of radiation into the environment. The term has also been used metaphorically since the early 1980s for any disastrous collapse, especially a sudden rapid drop in the value of a particular currency or of assets, shares, etc.

> 1965 *New Scientist*: Overheated fuel may result in 'meltdown' and general contamination of the reactor system.
>
> 1992 *Financial Times*: Talk of a meltdown in Japan plunging Wall Street into crisis and the US economy back into recession.

meritocracy *n* (1958) government by people selected on the basis of merit in a competitive educational system; also, a society so governed, or a ruling or influential class of educated people. The term was introduced by Michael Young in his book *The Rise of the Meritocracy* (1958); derivatives such as *meritocrat* and *meritocratic* soon followed.

> 1958 Michael Young: Before the meritocracy was fully established, age-stratification as a substitute for the hereditary order may have been necessary for the sake of social stability.

1958 *Economist*: Mr Young's meritocratic Britain, though described with ostensible enthusiasm, is an odious place.

microwave oven *n* (1955) an oven in which food is cooked by passing microwaves through it, the resulting generation of heat inside the food making rapid and uniform cooking possible. The term was not widely used until the 1970s, when the vocabulary expanded (e.g. *microwave oven* was shortened to simply *microwave* (1972), which was also used as a verb, 'to cook with microwaves'). The synonymous *micro-oven* is recorded later ('A cooked meal that is quick-frozen and then re-heated in a matter of seconds in a micro-oven', *Punch* (1962)), but it never really caught on.

1965 *Economist*: Microwave ovens. A meal a minute.

1976 *Bon Appétit*: If you have a family that eats in relays, you'll find the microwave ideal.

1976 *National Observer* (US): I . . . microwaved them two at a time for one minute.

modem *n* (1958) a combined modulator and demodulator (such as is used in connecting a computer to a telephone line) for converting outgoing signals from one form to another and converting incoming signals back again. The term was coined from the initial elements of *modulator* and *demodulator*.

nerd *n* (1951) an ineffectual, unstylish, or socially inept person, usually male, especially one who is excessively or annoyingly studious. The slang usage arose in the US. It did not get up a head of steam until the late 1960s, on college campuses and among surfers and hot-rodders, and it spread from there to the general language. Its origins are unclear: a link has been suggested with *turd*, but it may simply come from the name of the character invented by the US children's author 'Dr. Seuss' (Theodore Geisel) ('And then, just to show them, I'll sail to Ka-Troo And Bring Back an It-Kutch, a Preep and a Proo, a Nerkle, a Nerd, and a Seersucker, too!', 'Dr. Seuss', *If I Ran the Zoo* (1950)). The derived adjective *nerdy* is first recorded in 1978.

1971 *Observer*: Nerds are people who don't live meaningful lives.

1978 *New York Times*: The nerdiest nerds on TV are really smart cookies.

1986 Maureen Howard: He feels . . . like a total nerd in his gentleman's coat with the velvet collar.

news management *n* (1958) manipulation of the news media, especially by public relations or press office—a black art further elaborated by politicians and their minions later in the 20th century (see **spin (1978)**).

1969 *New Yorker*: Mollentroff specialized in exposés of wrongdoing . . . he carried on a one-man crusade against government interference with the press, and pursued it with such zeal that, while he may not have coined the phrase 'news management', his name is associated with it in the minds of most people here.

1993 *Daily Telegraph*: It is less clear whether the Princess chose or was persuaded by friends and advisers to move from passive acquiescence in sympathetic media coverage to a strategy bordering on active news management of coverage of her marital collapse.

new technology *n* (1953) (a) technology that radically alters the way something is produced or performed, often involving computers.

1964 Marshall McLuhan: The ability of the artist to sidestep the bully blow of new technology . . . is age-old.

1970 Alvin Toffler: We frequently apply new technology stupidly and selfishly.

niet *n* (1957) a blunt refusal, especially on the part of a Soviet politician. As part of the Cold War shadow-play, the Soviet Union became notorious for its unwillingness to agree to anything suggested by the West, and its frequent pithy expression of this in the one Russian word *nyet* 'no' made for good newspaper headlines.

1957 *Time*: The Nyet Man . . . Gromyko's televised image became a symbol of the Cold War . . . As Russia's first U.N. representative, his *nyet*, uttered in the course of 26 Soviet vetoes, was a byword.

non-alignment *n* (1955) absence of political or ideological affiliations with other nations, especially with the most powerful nations. This was a geopolitical concept that emerged in response to the polarization of the two Cold War power blocks. The related adjective *non-aligned* is first recorded in 1960.

> 1955 *Times*: He extolled 'non-alignment' and co-existence.
>
> 1966 *Guardian*: The Canadians . . . believe that there is a real strategic danger of a nonaligned block composed of Austria, Switzerland, and France cutting Europe into two.

non-U *adj* (1954) see **U (1954)**.

nuclear *adj* (1954) of, possessing, or employing nuclear weapons. See also **nuclear (1945)**; compare **conventional (1955)**.

> 1954 *Commonweal* (heading): Nuclear war: a false dilemma.
>
> 1956 *Foreign Policy Bulletin* (heading): Nuclear tests: psychological defeat for West.
>
> 1958 *Annual Register 1957*: The resolution urged that the United Nations and the 'nuclear' Powers should immediately suspend all such tests.
>
> 1958 *New Statesman*: The response to last Monday's inaugural meetings of the Campaign for Nuclear Disarmament suggests that it is becoming a focus for a real movement of opinion on this issue.

on-line *adj* (1950) directly connected, so that a computer receives an input from or sends an output to a peripheral device, process, etc. as soon as it is produced; carried out while so connected or under direct computer control.

> 1965 *Mathematics in Biology and Medicine*: Without time-sharing, the 'on-line' use of a fast modern machine would be unthinkably costly.

oven-ready *adj* (1954) of poultry: having been plucked and had its neck, legs, and entrails removed before sale. This was a term born largely of the new mass market in poultry brought about by **factory farming (1964)**.

> 1960 *Farmer & Stockbreeder*: A new firm . . . has been formed with the aim of becoming one of the largest producers of oven-ready turkeys and ducklings in the country.

Parkinson's law *n* (1955) a principle enunciated by the British historian and journalist Cyril Northcote Parkinson (1909–93): work expands to fill the time available for its completion. He used the term as the title of a book, first published in 1957.

> 1955 *Economist*: Before the discovery of a new scientific law—herewith presented to the public for the first time, and to be called Parkinson's Law—there has . . . been insufficient recognition of the implications of this fact in the field of public administration.
>
> 1958 C. N. Parkinson: Parkinson's Law or the Rising Pyramid. Work expands so as to fill the time available for its completion.

permissive *adj* (1956) tolerant, liberal, allowing freedom. From the mid 1960s the adjective has mainly been used with the implication of freedom in sexual matters (see also **permissive society (1960)**).

> 1956 C. A. Tonsor: I realize that in the face of the permissive tendencies of the age, there is not much respect for rules.
>
> 1971 *Daily Telegraph*: Perhaps it is time . . . for Parliament to have another look at the whole subject of abortion, family planning and perhaps permissiveness in general.

pill *n* ***the pill*** (1957) the contraceptive pill. It was not a practical reality until the early 1960s.

> 1957 C. H. Rolph: He gives a modestly exciting account of the quest now going on . . . for what laymen like myself insist on calling 'the Pill'; and by this phrase . . . I mean the simple and completely reliable contraceptive taken by the mouth.
>
> 1969 *New Scientist*: As contraceptives, IUDs are not as effective as the pill.

population explosion *n* (1953) a rapid or sudden marked increase in the size of a population. The term originated in the US.

> 1953 *Time*: Latin America is in the midst of a 'population explosion'. Its people are multiplying 2½ times as fast as the populations in the rest of the world.

privatization *n* (1959) reversion from public to private ownership; denationalization. The related verb *privatize* is not recorded until 1970, and neither the noun nor the verb achieved a particularly high public profile in Britain until the Thatcher government of the 1980s started putting the idea into practice.

> 1959 *News Chronicle*: Erhard selected the rich Preussag mining concern for his first experiment in privatisation.

> 1970 *New Society*: Is the Office of Health Economics trying to hint that the best place to start totally privatising the National Health Service is at eye level?

protest *adj* (1953) composed, performed, or performing as a protest, especially against the prevailing establishment.

> 1953 John Greenway: Protest songs are unpleasant and disturbing.

> 1968 *Guardian*: Brave new causes for brave new protest singers.

> 1969 *Listener*: Can [Bob Dylan] have forgotten entirely the horrors that gave such a fine edge to his protest music?

psychedelic *adj, n* (1956) (a drug) producing an expansion of consciousness through greater awareness of the senses and emotional feelings and the revealing of unconscious motivations, often symbolically. The word, coined from Greek *psukhē* 'mind' and *dēloun* 'to make manifest, reveal', was originally suggested by the psychiatrist Humphry Osmond in a letter to Aldous Huxley early in 1956. He put it into the public domain in a scientific paper in 1957. It came into its own in the LSD-culture of the mid to late 1960s, when its application broadened out to denote the effect or sensation produced by a psychedelic drug, especially vivid colours, often in bold abstract designs or in motion. The derivative *psychedelia* is first recorded in 1967.

> 1956 Humphry Osmond: To fathom Hell or soar angelic, Just take a pinch of psychedelic (Delos to manifest).

> 1957 Humphry Osmond: I have tried to find an appropriate name for the agents under discussion: a name that will include the concepts of enriching the mind and enlarging the vision . . . My choice, because it is clear, euphonious, and uncontaminated by other associations, is psychedelic, mind-manifesting.

> 1967 *Wall Street Journal*: Psychedelic fabrics are becoming the rage.

> 1967 *Melody Maker*: Apparently today's hippie must be expanded and experienced in the whys and wherefores of psychedelia but it cannot be said that the products of this society are all 'junkie'.

> 1968 *Globe & Mail* (Toronto): 'Topless' dancers gyrating in the glow of psychedelic slides and lights.

> 1969 *Observer*: The very latest psychedelic colours, electric purples and greens.

ready meal *n* (1952) a complete dish (or sometimes two or more dishes packaged together) which needs only brief heating in a microwave or conventional oven to prepare it for eating.

recreational *adj* (1958) designating the taking of a drug on an occasional basis for pleasure, especially when socializing (as opposed to addictive consumption). The usage originated in the US, with more than a tinge of euphemism, or at least special pleading.

> 1972 *New York Times*: [The] percentage includes both drug abusers and recreational users, but does not include students who have merely experimented with drugs.

> 1994 *Independent on Sunday*: With youngsters now beginning to overdose on 'recreational' dance drugs like Ecstasy, they say, hardcore venues such as the Hangar should close.

rock and roll, rock 'n' roll *n* (1954) a type of popular dance-music characterized by a heavy beat and simple melodies, combining elements of rhythm and blues with country and western music. The expression, which in African-American English is a euphemism for sexual intercourse, had been used in the US in connection with popular dancing since at least the 1930s (there is a 1934 song by Sidney Clare called 'Rock and roll'), but this specific conjunction of music and name had to wait until the early 1950s. Among the music's earliest and now legendary exponents were Bill Haley and Elvis Presley. The spelling *rock 'n' roll* is first recorded in 1955, the derivative *rock 'n' roller* in 1956. The abbreviated *rock* is first recorded in 1957.

> 1954 *Billboard*: Alan Freed . . . will sponsor his first 'Rock and Roll Jubilee Ball' at the St. Nicolas Arena here on January 14 and 15.
>
> 1956 *Observer*: What else happened in 1956? Elvis Presley happened. So did Rock 'n' Roll.
>
> 1959 *Punch*: [Cliff] Richard, like most rock singers, dances from the knees in a style borrowed from African warriors.
>
> 1969 Nik Cohn: In 1951, a DJ called Alan Freed launched a series of rhythm reviews at the Cleveland Arena . . . These shows featured coloured acts but were aimed at predominantly white audiences and, to avoid what he called 'the racial stigma of the old classification', Freed dropped the term R&B and invented the phrase Rock'n'Roll instead.

role model *n* (1957) someone on whom others model their behaviour or actions.

> 1977 *New York Times Magazine*: If the teacher was a 'role model', parents were obviously unaware of it.

scene *n* (1951) a place where people of common interests meet or where a particular activity is carried on. Hence, more loosely, an activity or pursuit (especially a fashionable or superior one, or one which one favours); a situation, event, or experience; a way of life. This was originally a US jazz slang usage; it was taken up by the beatniks of the later 1950s (see **beatnik (1958)**), and retained a place in the 'cool' slang of succeeding decades.

> 1951 Elliot Paul: 'Nobody comes on this scene wearin' any green,' said another taller Negro.
>
> 1958 George Lea: Something on the scene you don't dig . . . It was a bad scene. It scared me, man.
>
> 1967 *Punch*: They come here to work because it's exciting and new and because it's the scene.
>
> 1975 David Lodge: Washing up was more his scene than body language.

silent majority *n* (1955) the mass of people whose views remain unexpressed, especially in political contexts; those who are usually overlooked because of their moderation. As a metaphor for 'those who have died (and gone to heaven)' the expression dates back to the 19th century, but its political status was established by Westley and Egstein's 1969 book *The Silent Majority.*

> 1955 C. V. Wedgwood: The King in his natural optimism still believed that a silent majority in Scotland were in his favour.
>
> 1970 *Time*: Who precisely are the Middle Americans? . . . They make up the core of the group that Richard Nixon now invokes as the 'forgotten Americans' or 'the Great Silent Majority'.

skiffle *n* (1957) a mainly British form of pop music in which the vocal part is supported by a rhythmic accompaniment of guitars or banjos and other more or less conventional instruments (e.g. a washboard). The name was borrowed from a much earlier US usage (first recorded in 1926), applied to a type of jazz played on improvised instruments. The word's ultimate origins are unknown.

> 1957 Christine Brooke-Rose: A skiffle group—consisting of two guitarists, a thimble-fingered drummer with a wooden washboard, and a man sweeping a carpet-brush rhythmically over three metal strings drawn taut across a saucepan.

sliced bread *n* (1958) bread sold already sliced (and wrapped). Such a boon was this article to late-20th-century men and women with no time to cut bread that it gave rise to the expression *the greatest thing since sliced bread* (first recorded in 1969) to denote anything or anyone particularly splendid, worthy to compare with the most stunning technological advances. Foodies, on the other hand, generally regard sliced bread with great distaste.

> 1958 John Mortimer: The trouble with living here, the butter gets as hard as the rock of Gibraltar. It blasts great holes in your sliced bread.

> 1972 P. G. Wodehouse: Bodkin regards you as the best thing that's happened since sliced bread.

sonic boom *n* (1952), **sonic bang** *n* (1953) the sudden loud noise heard when the shock wave from an aircraft travelling faster than sound reaches the ears. It was a familiar sound in the skies in the early 1950s, when aircraft developers were obsessed with breaking the **sound barrier (1939)**. By the time the supersonic airliner Concorde entered service in the mid 1970s the novelty had worn off; its sonic boom had it banned from many overland air-routes.

> 1952 *Times*: Aircraft travelling at about the speed of sound cause a loud bang, which has become known as the 'sonic boom'.

-speak *suffix* (1957) a particular variety of (spoken) language; a characteristic mode of discourse. The suffix is an element extracted from *Newspeak*, the name of the artificial language used for official communications in George Orwell's novel *1984* (see **Newspeak (1949)**). Since a leading characteristic of this is that it was put to corrupt purposes, not surprisingly most *-speak* formations tend to be negative in connotation.

> 1957 Myra Buttle: In the literary weeklies, the languages of criticism and theology have become one and book reviews all sound like sermons written in the most holy 'Double-Speak'.

> 1981 *Guardian*: 'I am very sorry that I cannot be with you today . . . I am most grateful and touched that you have decided to name a locomotive after me,' [the telegram] said in classic royalspeak.

sputnik *n* (1957) an unmanned artificial earth satellite, especially a Russian one. The term is applied specifically (usually with capital initial) to any of a series of such satellites launched by the Soviet Union between 1957 and 1961. The first Sputnik, launched on 4 October 1957, was the first artificial satellite. This Soviet space coup, which left the hitherto complacent Americans stunned, made *sputnik* one of the in-words of the late 1950s, and did much to promote the popularity of the ending *-nik* in English (see **beatnik (1958)**). *Sputnik* in Russian means literally 'travelling companion'; it is formed from *s* 'with' and *put'* 'way, journey', plus the agent suffix *-nik*.

> 1957 *Times*: Pride in the launching of the sputnik ('fellow-traveller'), as the satellite is called, as well as the guided missile, were reflected in a speech by Mr. Krushchev . . . last night . . . Mr. Khrushchev replied: 'To peace and to the sputnik as a symbol of peace!' . . . The régime which sends a second Sputnik girdling the earth has just emerged from another of its secretly contrived shifts of political power.

strategic *adj* (1957) of, delivering, or being nuclear weapons intended to destroy an enemy's capacity to make war. The contrast is usually with **tactical (1957)**, denoting nuclear weapons intended for short-range use.

> 1961 *Listener*: If it becomes unwise . . . to consider basing MRBMs or strategic bombers in Europe.

summit *n* (1950) the level of heads of state or heads of government, especially of the superpowers. Churchill's metaphor (see the first quote below) probably engendered the usage, but it did not really get under way until the middle of the decade, when characteristic compounds such as *summit conference* and *summit meeting* are first recorded. In due course *summit* came to be used elliptically for *summit conference*.

> 1950 Winston Churchill: It is not easy to see how things could be worsened by a parley at the summit, if such a thing were possible.

> 1955 *Times*: The senator's resolution demanding that the United States should refuse to attend the 'summit' conference.

1967 *Spectator*: The most certain result of the Glassboro summit, in fact, is no more than that Mr. Johnson's standing at home is now rather higher.

swinging *adj* (1958) uninhibited, ignoring conventions; lively and up to date: applied to people and places (notably, in the 1960s, *swinging London*) and to the decade of the 60s itself (*the Swinging Sixties*). Also used as a general term of approval: wonderful, marvellous, great. Colloquial. As the first quotation suggests, the usage arose out of US jazz parlance.

1958 *Publications of the American Dialect Society*: Swingin', the highest term of approval. May be applied to anything a jazzman likes, or any person.

1959 *Guardian*: [She] informed him that she wants a large place 'in a swinging part of town' . . . so he is looking around in Chelsea and Knightsbridge.

1964 Norman Vaughan: When people ask me how I feel about the months ahead, I tell them: 'Sometimes it's a bit dodgy, but most of the time it's swinging!'

1965 *Weekend Telegraph*: Diana Vreeland . . . editor of Vogue . . . has said simply 'London is the most swinging city in the world at the moment'.

1967 *Listener*: He does not fit into the Zeitgeist of the swinging 'sixties.

1971 Harold Wilson: The press publicized what they called the new swinging style of the Downing Street receptions.

tactical *adj* (1957) of, delivering, or being nuclear weapons intended for short-range use. The contrast is usually with **strategic (1957)**, denoting nuclear weapons intended to destroy the enemy's capacity to wage war. The usage arose out of the earlier application of *tactical* to bombing in support of one's ground forces, which evolved during World War I.

1976 Lord Home: The balance of argument through the years moved towards a substantial conventional force, but it was gradually rendered somewhat academic by the introduction of the tactical nuclear weapon.

Teddy boy *n* (1954) a youth affecting a style of dress and appearance held to be characteristic of Edward VII's reign, typically a long velvet-collared jacket, 'drainpipe' trousers, and sideburns. The style began in the late 1940s among a group of Guards officers calling themselves the 'Edwardians', who dressed in mock-Edwardian manner. It was taken up by the homosexual community and then, in the early 1950s, with an admixture of the 'spiv' look, by working-class youths. The Teddy boys' reputation for gang fighting soon led to the term being used more broadly for any youthful street rowdy. The abbreviated *Teddy* is first recorded in 1956, as is the still shorter *Ted*. The underlying allusion is, of course, to the familiar form of the name *Edward*.

1954 Anthony Heckstall-Smith: Craig was just such a fellow. Ronald Coleman, the leader of the 'Edwardians' or the 'Teddy Boys', the gang of young hooligans who ran amok on Clapham Common, was another.

1956 *Time*: The Ted's notion of sartorial splendor ranges from a caricature of Edwardian elegance to the zoot padding of a Harlem hepcat.

1959 *Times*: The growing tide of teddy-boyism, chiefly in the Athens-Piraeus area, forced the authorities to act.

thalidomide *n* (1958) a non-barbiturate sedative and hypnotic which was found to induce abnormalities when taken early in pregnancy, sometimes causing malformation or absence of limbs in the fetus. Babies born deformed to women who had taken the drug to relieve certain side-effects of pregnancy were dubbed in the press *thalidomide babies*. Over 500 such babies were born in Britain between 1959 and 1962. The drug was withdrawn in 1961. The name was extracted from its full name, *phthalimidoglutarimide*, which in turn was based ultimately on an abbreviated form of *naphthalene*.

1961 *Lancet*: We have just received reports from two overseas sources possibly associating thalidomide ('Distaval') with harmful effects on the fœtus in early pregnancy.

> 1962 *Guardian*: There is still no information about the number of 'thalidomide babies' in the country.

them and us (1957) people who are privileged or in authority contrasted with ordinary people. The implication is that the latter (the mass of the people) are exploited or oppressed by the former (a controlling élite). This use of *them* pre-dates its joining up with *us* ('The magic circle of "Them", the great ones. "They" were the élite, the prefects and the games captains', Winifred Holtby (1924)).

> 1957 Richard Hoggart: To the very poor, especially, they compose a shadowy but numerous and powerful group affecting their lives at almost every point: the world is divided into 'Them' and 'Us'.

thermonuclear *adj* (1953) denoting (the use of) weapons that utilize a nuclear reaction that occurs only at very high temperatures, namely fusion of hydrogen or other light nuclei—in other words, the hydrogen bomb. This was a military-political use of a word that had been a technical term in nuclear physics (designating such a reaction) since the 1930s.

> 1953 *Time*: Secretary of Defense Wilson, at his press conference, cast doubt on a suggestion that the Russians had a thermonuclear bomb 'in droppable form'.

top ten *n* (1958) the first ten tunes or records, CDs, etc. in the popularity charts (see **charts (1963)**) at a particular time. *Top twenty* is first recorded in 1959. See also **hit parade (1958)**.

> 1959 Francis Newton: Jazz has until recently simply not been big business in Britain, in the terms in which those who prepare records for the 'hit parade' of the 'top ten' or 'top twenty' think of it.

tranquillizer *n* (1956) any of a large class of drugs in widespread use since the 1950s for the reduction of tension or anxiety and the treatment of psychotic states. The alternative term *ataractic* (or *ataraxic*), proposed in 1955, never really caught on.

> 1957 *Times*: The rapidly increasing use of drugs described as 'tranquillizers' and 'ataraxics' . . . has become a cause of concern in many countries.

transplant *n* (1951) an operation in which an organ, tissue, etc. is transplanted from one person or animal to another. The verb *transplant* is first recorded in this sense in the late 18th century, but the organ concerned (as in the first record of the noun, quoted below) was a tooth. The earliest reference to internal organs comes at the start of the 20th century ('A . . . case in which a child . . . suffering from cretinism, had a portion of its mother's thyroid gland transplanted into its spleen', *Daily Chronicle* (1906)). The term did not become widely familiar until Christiaan Barnard performed the world's first successful heart transplant operation at the Groote Schuur Hospital in Cape Town in 1967.

> 1951 *Sun* (Baltimore): He decided to try a transplant [of a tooth].

> 1963 *Guardian*: Surgeons at St Bartholomew's Hospital, London, this week carried out the hospital's first kidney transplant operation.

> 1971 *Daily Telegraph*: Prof. Christiaan Barnard . . . is standing by to carry out his first transplant for two years.

trip *n* (1959) a slang term for a hallucinatory experience induced by a drug, especially LSD. The related verb, 'to experience drug-induced hallucinations', is first recorded in 1966.

> 1959 Norman Mailer: I took some mescaline . . . At the end of a long and private trip which no quick remark should try to describe, the book of *The Deer Park* floated into mind.

> 1966 *Time*: Such dangers do not deter the acid heads or 'psychedelics'—even though some users are willing to admit that they found no great 'show', or had a 'freak trip' (a bad one) or 'tripped out' (the worst kind).

U *adj* (1954) an abbreviation of *upper class*, used particularly in the context of vocabulary and other aspects of linguistic usage. It is contrasted specifically with *non-U* (1954), denoting that which is not (and by implication is not up to the standard of, less admirable or pleasing than) upper class. The two terms were introduced by Professor Alan Ross in a paper entitled 'U and non-U' in the journal *Neuphilologische Mitteilungen*, but it was not until 1956, when Nancy Mitford publicized them in a book called *Noblesse Oblige*, that they were taken up by non-linguists. For a time assigning synonyms to one camp or another became a popular dinner-party game, and sheep were divided from goats by whether they said *note paper* or *writing paper*.

1954 A. S. C. Ross (title): U and non-U . . . In this article I use the terms upper class (abbreviated: U), correct, proper, . . . to designate usages of the upper class; their antonyms (non-U, incorrect, not proper, . . .) to designate usages which are not upper class . . . As a boy I heard *not quite a gent* . . . used by non-U speakers.

1957 Ogden Nash: The Wicked Queen said 'Mirror, mirror on the wall' instead of 'Looking glass, looking glass on the wall' . . . So the Wicked Queen exposed herself as not only wicked but definitely non-U.

1962 Alison Lurie: 'I don't think he's really U, though, do you?' 'Oh no. Shabby genteel, maybe.'

UFO *n* (1953) an abbreviation of *unidentified flying object*, usually treated as an acronym and pronounced /'ju:fəʊ/. The full form, first recorded in 1950, had been introduced to lend an air of scientific respectability to what had hitherto been known mainly as **flying saucer (1947)**.

1950 *Chambers's Journal*: Project Saucer revealed that it had analysed 375 incidents of 'unidentified flying objects'.

1953 D. E. Keyhoe: The UFO was estimated to be between 12,000 and 20,000 feet above the jets.

1956 E. J. Ruppelt: UFO is the official term that I created to replace the words 'flying saucers'.

video *n* (1958) a video recorder, recording, or player (see **video (1935)**).

1958 *Observer*: The Video is like a combined tape-recorder and cinema camera. It records your television appearance complete with sound track and can be played back at the touch of a switch.

1968 *Observer*: The days of the disc, in the pop world at least, are numbered. For soon will come the video. We will have the top 20 videos which you plug into your home video-machine.

1984 Sue Townsend: We are the only family in our street who haven't got a video.

videotape *n* (1953) magnetic tape on which moving visual images, such as television programmes, can be recorded.

1953 *Wall Street Journal*: With further development of video tape techniques, numerous possibilities will open up. Small portable television cameras are already in wide use in industry, in stores, banks and schools.

1958 *Times*: The BBC's VERA which tape-records complete television shows, picture and sound combined, and the AMPEX and R.C.A. videotape machines which do the same job for the independent television contractors, will greatly facilitate the provision of such Press shows.

with it *adj* (1959) up to date, trendy. This slang expression proved a quickly worked-out seam among its original youthful users, but, as often happens with such items, the older generation then took it up and succeeded only in sounding past it.

1959 Richard Condon: They are with it, Raymond. Believe me, they are even away ahead of me.

1960 *Guardian*: The new Time and Tide, to borrow the language of the teen-ager, is 'with it'.

1962 *Listener*: Curtain designs for the really with-it 'contemporary home'.

1977 J. I. M. Stewart: The silly woman just thought it a with-it thing to say to a celebrated dramatist.

X (1950) used to denote films classified as suitable for adults only, or to which only those older than a certain age are to be admitted. In Britain the classification was replaced by *15* and *18* in 1983.

1950 *Times*: The X certificates . . . will cover films other than those of a 'horrific' character, which are 'wholly adult in conception and treatment'.

Xerox *n* (1952) a proprietary name (registered in 1952) for a make of photocopiers. It was based on the term *xerography* (1948), denoting a process of dry copying (from Greek *xēros* 'dry') using no liquid ink. It did not begin to make headway in the general language until the 1960s, when it became virtually a generic term, used both for 'a photocopy' and as a verb, meaning 'to photocopy'.

> 1966 *Economist*: In most American offices executives instruct subordinates to 'make me a Xerox of this report' rather than 'make me a copy of it'.

> 1972 Marcia Williams: The Rank Organization in Brighton installed a xerox copying machine in the office [at 10 Downing Street] and we also had an electric duplicating machine.

The 1960s

If ever a decade confidently announced that it had broken with the past and was setting off down heady new paths it was the 1960s. The children of the 1940s baby boom were making their presence felt, armed with ample spending power; the exploration of space was providing a spectacular swansong to the era of confidence in scientific progress (and doing it on small screens in the world's living rooms); the computer was beginning to send its invisible threads through all our lives. There were not just new inventions and new discoveries to talk about—in plenty—we sought new ways of looking at the world, and new modes of vocabulary to describe our experience of it.

The 1960s were the decade when the blend and the acronym entrenched themselves still further in the language, and prefixes and suffixes raised their profiles. Acronyms—words formed from the initial letters of other words—were essentially the children of World War II (see p. 110), but it was in the 1960s that they really established themselves in a big way outside the military field. Terms like *Cobol*, *laser*, *SALT*, *zip code*, *Lem*, *AWACS*, and *GIGO* slipped into the language, some so unobtrusively that their acronymic origins went largely unnoticed. Blending—the formation of compounds by partially merging two words—gained further ground, with the likes of *advertorial*, *docudrama*, *faction*, *identikit*, *medevac*, and *stagflation* entering the language; it was even responsible for the name of a new country: *Tanzania* (formed from *Tanganyika* and *Zanzibar*). The trend towards creating verbs out of nouns continued, with *access*, *action*, *format*, *keyboard*, and *nuke* joining the lexicon.

The encroachment of prefixes on to the territory of adjectives was a feature of 20th-century English, and in no decade was it more salient than the 1960s. *Mini-* led the way, and its enthusiastic reception in the fashion industry (*minidress*, *miniskirt*) opened the door to length variations in *midi-* and *maxi-*. *Eco-* and *Euro-* began highly successful careers in the 1960s, as, on a less exalted level, did *renta-* (as originally in *rentacrowd*). This was also the key decade for the suffix *-in* (as in *love-in*, *laugh-in*, and *teach-in*, as well as *sit-in*).

Our closer acquaintance with the wider universe was reflected in our vocabulary—not only as observed from the surface of the planet (*black hole*, *pulsar*, *quasar*, *singularity*), but experienced at first hand. From the moment

Yuri Gagarin's rocket blasted off in April 1961, space travel stepped from the wilder shores of science fiction to everyday reality, and the subsequent years of the decade familiarized us with such concepts as *re-entry, splash-down, launch windows*, and *moon walks*. We learnt to handle the jargon for all the hardware: *lander, module, moon buggy* (1971), *shuttle*. When astronauts reassured mission control that the situation was *nominal* 'within prescribed limits, normal', we nodded sagely.

But undoubtedly the area of technology that made the greatest lexical advances in the 1960s was computer science. As yet it was largely confined to specialists, but as *computeracy* spread and one by one various aspects of our lives became *computerized*, we would learn the significance of *bytes, chips, cursors, databases, mice, peripherals*, and *software*. We could *format* and *access* to our heart's content, fluent in *ASCII, BASIC*, and *Cobol*. We had the key to the computer's limitations—*GIGO* ('garbage in, garbage out'). And for our leisure moments there were *computer games*—and *computer dating*.

Out on the street in the 1960s, in the clubs and campuses, it was youth that was setting the agenda, and it is their vocabulary that in many ways carries the most telling resonances of the decade—60s' *vibes*. Their terms of commendation (*in, with it* (1959), *switched on, gear, fab* (1957), *knock-out, together*) and condemnation (*grotty, naff*) expressed the crucial judgements of the day. Their clans (*mods, rockers*) made the headlines, often with threats of *aggro* or *bovver*. But above all, it was the music. Picking up the impetus of 1950s rock and roll, the pop music scene exploded in the 1960s, and its sheer diversity contributed sackfuls of new vocabulary to the language. Each new music style or dance had a name more outlandish than the last (*the twist, bossa nova, frug, hully gully, Watusi, ska, acid rock*). In Britain, the *Merseybeat* reversed many years of American domination of the charts, and the *Beatlemania* that sent *popsters, groupies*, and *teeny-boppers* into a frenzy soon spread to the US. For those with ears not attuned to all this, the 1960s was also the decade in which the concept of *easy listening* first adorned our musical life.

In acknowledgment of the new commercial realities, the world of fashion shifted its beady eyes from haute couture to the lucrative youth market. Teenagers set the trends, and the hemlines—*minis, midis, maxis, kinky boots* and *Chelsea boots, flares* and *hipsters, thongs* and *caftans*. *Tights* (or *pantyhose*) saw off stockings and suspenders. As male hair lengthened, the *unisex* look came in.

As part of the same package came recreational drugs—comparatively innocent-sounding in retrospect, shocking though they were to authority's sensibilities at the time: *poppers* and *tabs, speed* and *acid, purple hearts* and *angel dust*. They opened the door in the latter part of the decade to the *alternative* (1970) world of the *flower children*, the *alternative society, psychedelia, be-ins* and *love-ins, Hare Krishna*, and the *Age of Aquarius*.

But hippies were not the only ones taking drugs in the 1960s. In an age of growing emphasis on the individual and their psyche, *uppers* and *downers* and *tranks* found a wide market, and there was no lack of customers for *Librium* and *Valium*, *Mandrax* and *diazepam*. A self-absorbed concern with health found lexical expression in items as diverse as *cellulite* and *holistic medicine*, *biorhythms* and *shiatsu*.

The 1960s were also the decade of the *permissive society*, when traditional four-letter words first appeared in respectable dictionaries. But in spite of the *swingers* hoping to *score* with *bunny girls* in *topless bars*, you still had a hard time if you deviated from the norm: *homophobia* was rife, and *kinks* kept a low profile.

The communications revolution was getting well under way, with *comsats*, *bleepers*, *pagers*, and *image makers*. We could watch (or listen to on our *trannies*) *chat shows*, *sitcoms*, *docudramas*, *phone-ins*, and *radiothons*. And, if we wanted to be independent of the network offerings, we had *cassettes* and *videos*. A less welcome sign of things to come was the first appearance of the *paparazzi*.

Other straws in the wind for future decades were civil rights legislation and moves towards racial desegregation in the US (where *bussing* provided a long-running controversy) and the beginnings of environmentalism (photos of the Earth taken from the Moon were a forceful argument for the *global village*: *biodegradable* and *unleaded* entered our vocabulary, species became *endangered* or *threatened*, and *eco-* was a strong contender for prefix of the decade) and of political correctness (the terms *sexism*, *ageism*, and *tokenism* were all coined in the 1960s).

In a world still frozen deeply in the Cold War, *doves* talked of *non-proliferation* and *SALT* (Strategic Arms Limitation Talks) while the minds of the *hawks* were more on *flexible response* and *surgical* strikes. Despite the *peaceniks*, it was the hawks who largely got their way over the Vietnam War—providing the US with a long-lasting scar on its national psyche, and ensuring that the English language now embraces such unlovely or ominous terms as *body count*, *dink* 'Vietnamese person', *frag* 'to kill with a fragmentation grenade' (1970), and *Agent Orange* (a defoliant; 1970).

abuse *n, v* (1969) applied to sexual or physical assault on a regular basis. The euphemism originated in the US, and in the last quarter of the 20th century largely replaced the previous circumlocutions *interfere with* (1948) and *molest* (1950).

> 1969 *New York Times*: The committee . . . made the charge in connection with the publication of 'A Series of Recommendations for the Protection of Abused Children Within New York City'.

> 1972 *Newsweek*: Other themes scheduled for prime-time dramatic treatment include impotency, castration, . . . and child abuse.

acid *n* (1966) the hallucinogenic drug LSD (lysergic acid diethylamide), the favourite pschedelia-inducer of the 1960s. The slang term, which originated in the US, is an extract of the drug's full scientific name. Devotees were widely known as *acidheads* (also first recorded in 1966).

> 1966 Hunter S. Thompson: Contrary to all expectations, most of the Angels became oddly peaceful on acid.

> 1968 Adam Diment: Acid heads are such nice people they want to be friends with the whole world.

> 1970 John Lennon: I was influenced by acid and got psychedelic, like the whole generation, but really, I like rock and roll and I express myself best in rock.

African-American *adj, n* (1969) designating American citizens of African descent; (a) black American. Although an isolated instance of the term is on record from as long ago as 1858, it did not begin to establish itself in a big way until the 1970s. By the second half of the 80s it had become the preferred term for US blacks.

> 1991 *New York Times Magazine*: Justice Marshall has long avoided using the term *black*, preferring *Negro* or, more recently, *Afro-American*. Jesse Jackson has been pressing the appellation *African-American*.

ageism, agism *n* (1969) prejudice or discrimination against people on the grounds of age, especially old age. The term originated in the US; it was one of the earliest of the spate of late-20th-century '-isms' inspired by *racism* (1936) and *sexism* (1968). The derivative *ageist* is first recorded in 1970.

alternative society *n* (1969) the aggregate of (predominantly young) people whose social organization (or lack of it) and cultural values purport to represent a preferable and cogent alternative to those of the established social order. See also **alternative (1970)**.

attitude *n* (1962) aggressive or uncooperative behaviour; a resentful or antagonistic manner. In the 1970s the usage, which originated in the US, started to take on a positive aspect, with implications of an independent or self-possessed outlook, and even of style or swagger. By the time it reached Britain in the 1990s it was even being applied to things, in the sense 'strong stylishness'.

> 1985 *Sunday Times*: I can't believe this restaurant. I ask the waiter for a clean fork and all I get is attitude.

> 1994 *Toronto Star*: In the early '70s, crepes were the foodstuff that ushered in the eating revolution—the pancake with attitude that took us from meat and potatoes into the modern world of gastrohype.

Beatlemania *n* (1963) addiction to the British pop group, the Beatles, and their characteristics; the frenzied behaviour of their admirers. The pattern was later followed to encapsulate the adulation of other pop groups (e.g. *Rollermania*, caused by the Bay City Rollers in the mid 1970s).

> 1963 *Times*: The social phenomenon of Beatlemania, which finds expression in handbags, balloons and other articles bearing the likeness of the loved ones, or in the hysterical screaming of young girls whenever the Beatle Quartet performs in public.

> 1964 *Daily Telegraph*: Outside, hundreds of squealing Beatlemaniacs carried such signs as 'We love you—never leave us'.

biodegradable *adj* (1961) susceptible to the decomposing action of living organisms, especially of bacteria. This was a key approval-term of the late-20th-century ecological movement, applied to things that can be thrown away or otherwise released into the environment without permanently damaging it.

> 1969 *Nature*: Biodegradable detergents are now a reality.

black hole *n* (1968) a region within which the gravitational field is so strong that no form of matter or radiation can escape from it except by quantum-mechanical tunnelling. It is thought to result from the collapse of a massive star. The name was no doubt partially inspired by the *Black Hole of Calcutta*, an incident in 1756 in which 146 people were incarcerated for a whole night in the punishment cell of the barracks in Fort William, Calcutta. By the 1980s its metaphorical possibilities (bottomlessness, threateningness, etc.) were being widely exploited.

> 1968 *American Scientist*: Light and particles incident from outside emerge and go down the black hole only to add to its mass and increase its gravitational attraction.

> 1980 *Time*: To the 1.7 million people added to the jobless rolls in April and May, the U.S. economy may well seem to have... been sucked into a black hole.

black power *n* (1966) power for black people; used as a slogan of varying implication by, or in support of, black civil rights workers and organizations. It originated in the US.

> 1966 *Times*: Young Negroes..., supporters of the 'black power' group led by Mr Stokely Carmichael.

blow *v* ***blow someone's mind*** (1965) originally, to induce hallucinatory experiences in a person by means of drugs, especially LSD, but also, and more widely, used metaphorically, meaning 'to produce in a person a powerfully pleasurable (or shocking) sensation'. The slang expression originated in the US. See also **mind-blowing (1966)**.

> 1967 *San Francisco Examiner*: On a hip acid (LSD) trip you can blow your mind sky-high.

> 1970 *Rolling Stone*: Blue blazer, grey flannel pants, shirt and a beautiful scarf with a chunky Mexican turquoise/silver bracelet and ring which blew the white-shirted jury's minds.

body language *n* (1966) the gestures and movements by which a person unconsciously or indirectly conveys meaning. The term is apparently a translation of French *langage corporel*.

> 1983 *Chemical Engineer*: Various types of 'body language'—such as shuffling feet, yawns, glances at watches... and so on—may signal that it's time to call for a break.

born-again *adj* (1961) characterized by (an experience of) new birth in Christ or spiritual renewal; of a Christian: placing special emphasis on this experience as a basis for all one's actions; evangelical. The usage originated in the US, and is associated particularly with the activities of the religious right in that country in the last quarter of the 20th century. It is based on John iii.3: 'Jesus answered and said unto him, Verily, verily, I say unto thee, Except a man be born again, he cannot see the kingdom of God.' It was later widely used metaphorically to suggest the extreme (or fanatical) enthusiasm of the newly converted or re-converted.

> 1961 *Church & People*: Each was a born-again Christian.

> 1977 *Time*: Encouraged by the presence of a born-again Southern Baptist in the White House,... the far-flung residents of the new Bible Belt are loosely lumped together under the name Evangelicals.

> 1982 *Observer*: Nott has never been a true, born-again monetarist.

> 1985 Jonathan Raban: They're a bit born-again about smoking now.

breathalyser *n* (1960) a device for measuring the alcohol content of a breath sample, and used in particular to identify drink drivers. The word was coined from *breath* + *analyser*. The verb *breathalyse*, a back-formation, is first recorded in 1967. Earlier terms for similar devices include *drunkometer* (1934) and *intoximeter* (1950).

> 1960 *Times*: The Breathalyser, an American instrument for measuring the percentage of alcohol in the blood from a breath sample, was put on view . . . yesterday.

> 1967 *Times*: Would it not be sensible to amend the Bill so that the police power to stop and 'breathalyse' people should be limited?

bus *v* (1961) to transport (people) by bus from one place to another, especially in order to encourage or achieve racial integration. The usage is mainly American, and the practice of *bussing* was the cause of considerable controversy in the US in the 1960s (and later).

> 1965 *Economist*: Local authorities should adopt the policy known in the United States as 'bussing'—that is to say, spreading immigrants' children around over a wide area.

byte *n* (1964) a group of eight consecutive bits operated on as a unit in a computer. The word is an arbitrary formation, probably influenced by **bit (1948)** and *bite*.

caftan, kaftan *n* (1965) a wide-sleeved, loose-fitting shirt or dress worn in Western countries, resembling the original garment worn in the Near East. It became a fashion item in the mid 1960s, largely on the back of a vogue for the East and its religions and cultures.

> 1966 *Daily Telegraph*: Caftans, the season's fashion talking point, won murmurs of delight in lightweight silk, hand-painted, in versions both short and long from artist Noel Dyrenforth.

caring *adj* (1966) that cares; compassionate, concerned. From the mid 1970s the adjective was often used specifically with reference to professional social work, care of the sick or elderly, etc., in such phrases as *caring profession, caring society*. See also **carer (1978)**.

> 1966 *Punch*: This was good, caring, committed television, of the kind I am always begging for in these columns.

> 1980 Margaret Drabble: The welfare state itself, and all the caring professions, seemed to be plunging into a dark swamp of uncertainty.

cash dispenser *n* (1967) an automatic machine from which customers of a bank, building society, etc. may withdraw cash, especially from a current account. The synonymous *automated teller machine* is 1970s.

> 1967 *Bankers' Magazine*: Following 'Barclaycash' . . . and the Westminster's 'cash dispenser service' . . . the National Provincial has started up its 'cash cards' dispenser—like the others good for £10 when inserted into a machine located outside a branch.

cassette *n* (1960) a closed container of magnetic tape with both supply and take-up spools, so designed that it needs merely to be inserted into a suitable tape recorder, computer, or video recorder to be ready for use. The invention transformed the cumbersome reel-to-reel tape recorder into something handily portable that could be listened to on the move.

> 1960 *Tape Recording and Hi-Fi Yearbook 1959–60*: One of the new decks . . . is the first British product designed to operate with cassettes.

charts *n* (1963) a list of the records or songs that are most popular or selling best at a particular time. See also **top ten (1958)**.

> 1963 *The Beatles*: More chart-topping discs on the way; more packed audiences to drown the frantic beat with cheering.

> 1967 *Scottish Daily Mail*: Engelbert Humperdinck's six-week-long reign at the top of the charts with *The Last Waltz* has finally been broken by the Bee Gees with *Massachusetts*.

chat show *n* (1969) a television programme in which guests are interviewed by the host. The term is first recorded later than the synonymous *talk show* (1965), but it has weathered somewhat better.

> 1972 *Times*: The apotheosis of the chat show arrives tonight when Muggeridge guests for Parkinson.

chip *n* (1962) a tiny square of thin semi-conducting material, typically silicon, which is designed to function as the base of a large number of circuit components and which can be incorporated with other similar squares to form an integrated circuit. The miniature foundation stone of the late-20th-century information revolution, it was invented in the US in 1958.

> 1965 *Scientific American*: Engineers . . . saw the possibility of producing complete circuits within a silicon chip by forming all the circuit elements by diffusion.

commute *n* (1960) a journey made in commuting, especially to or from one's place of work; the distance travelled. The noun was coined, in the US, from the verb *commute* 'to travel in this way', which is first recorded (again in the US) in 1889. This in turn was based on the notion of buying a *commutation ticket*, US English for *season ticket*. *Commuter*, archetypal 20th-century suburban animal, is first recorded in 1865.

> 1960 *Time*: He frequently test-drives a competitor's car on his commute to Ann Arbor.

computerize *v* (1960) to operate by means of a computer; to install a computer or computers in (an office etc.).

> 1961 *Times*: The businessman will probably . . . think out . . . what areas of his business might be profitably computerized.

consumerism *n* (1960) a doctrine advocating a continual increase in the consumption of goods as a basis for a sound economy. This is an altogether more red-in-tooth-and-claw usage than the previous **consumerism** 'protection of consumers' interests' **(1944)**, but the latter made a comeback in the 1960s and 70s, and at the beginning of the 21st century is the more widely used.

> 1960 Vance Packard: A leading apostle of 'consumerism' . . . pointed out that every recent United States recession had been caused by . . . a failure to see that consumption kept pace with production.
>
> 1962 Eve Godfrey: Consumerism has become the guiding force of our economy.

convenience *adj* (1961) designed for convenience; easy and quick to prepare or use. This was a quality much prized in the middle of the 20th century, when considerable ingenuity and research went into technological methods of reducing the domestic drudgery of earlier years. As the decades passed, however, *convenience* (mainly applied to food) came to connote lack of spontaneity and originality. The usage originated in the US. See also **fast food (1951)**.

> 1961 *Economist*: Even the Thanksgiving turkey has now become a 'convenience' food.
>
> 1965 *Daily Express*: The 'convenience store' is always open in America.

cultural revolution *n* (1966) a cultural and social movement in Communist China, begun in 1965, which sought to combat 'revisionism' and restore the original purity of Maoist doctrine.

> 1966 *Economist*: Lin Piao . . . has loyally used the army as a guinea-pig for the 'cultural revolution' dose of salts with which Mao is now purging the whole country.

Dalek *n* (1963) a type of evil robot appearing in *Doctor Who*, a BBC television science-fiction programme. Its mobile-dustbin appearance and tinny voice intoning 'Exterminate! Exterminate!' made it a cult figure in the 1960s and 70s. It made its debut in the second *Doctor Who* adventure, written by Terry Nation, who allegedly got the inspiration for the name from an encyclopedia volume labelled DAL—LEK (although Nation himself denied that).

damage limitation *n* (1965) the action or process of restricting damage caused by an accident, error, etc., or of attempting to do this. Originally a piece of military jargon, it is in the area of political news management that the term has become widely known.

1987 *Economist*: The damage limitation after the Reykjavik summit, brilliantly managed by the White House staff, went down the plug hole in the flood of post-Iran doubts.

database *n* (1962) a structured collection of data held in computer storage, especially one that incorporates software to make it accessible in a variety of ways. Hence, any large collection of information.

1985 *Sunday Times*: CIR went through its data-base looking for companies interested in investing in new ideas in electronics.

1985 *Ashmolean*: A museum and its records are one vast database.

designer *adj* (1966) denoting goods bearing the name or label of a famous designer, with the implication that they are expensive or prestigious. The usage, which originated in the US, later broadened out, especially in the 1980s, to designate anything fashionable among the smart set (e.g. *designer food*, prepared in minimalist quantities by fashionable chefs). See also **designer drug (1983)**.

1966 *New York Times*: Designer scarves join name-dropping game.

1984 *Times*: Small wonder Perrier is called Designer Water. My local wine bar has the cheek to charge 70p a glass.

1985 Suzanne Lowry: He loves seafood . . . and detests designer dishes.

1989 *Guardian*: Designer stubble of the George Michael ilk has also run its bristly course.

developing *adj* (1961) of a poor country: in the process of developing higher economic, industrial, and social conditions. This was the latest in the litany of 20th-century euphemisms that English came up with to avoid sounding patronizing to poor countries: in this case the previous offender which needed replacing was **underdeveloped (1949)**.

1964 Hla Myint (title): The economics of the developing countries.

1969 Robin Blackburn: Bourgeois economists once talked about the economically 'backward' countries; then 'underdeveloped' was felt to be a kinder adjective. They now prefer to refer to poor capitalist countries as 'developing nations'.

digital *adj* (1960) designating (a) recording or broadcasting in which the original waveform is digitally coded and the information in it represented by the presence or absence of pulses of equal strength, making it less subject to degradation than a conventional analogue signal. The method was originally used for making high-quality audio recordings, but at the end of the 20th century it was being phased in as a broadcasting medium.

1960 *Institute of Radio Engineers, Transactions on Electronic Computers*: The nature and features of digital recording.

1978 *Gramophone*: It would be a great pity if this opportunity for a 'quantum leap' in audio standards were spoilt by the emergence of several conflicting, incompatible digital discs.

1999 *Radio Times*: ITV is only on digital terrestrial.

disco *n* (1964) an abbreviation of **discotheque (1954)** which rapidly superseded the full form in general use. In the 1970s the word, which originated in the US, came to denote also a style of pop music frequently played in discos, characterized by a heavy bass beat.

1964 *Playboy*: Los Angeles has emerged with the biggest and brassiest of the discos.

1965 *New York Times*: A couple of scantily clad girls swiveled and undulated to the disco-beat.

1975 *Time*: Though New York City's blacks and Puerto Ricans have been doing the Hustle for years, its current vogue among people of all colors and ages has coincided with the explosion of 'disco' sound—rhythm and blues with a strong Latin beat.

DJ *n* (1961) an abbreviation of **disc jockey (1941)**. It is first recorded in print in 1961, but previous references to it in the spelling *dee-jay* (1955) show that it had been around well before that.

1965 *Daily Telegraph*: The BBC is plainly fascinated by the phenomenon of the disc jockey, now abbreviated to DJ.

dove *n* (1962) someone who advocates negotiations as a means of terminating or preventing a military conflict, as opposed to one who advocates a hard-line or warlike policy. The usage originated in the US, based on the stereotype of the dove as a bird of peace. It is usually contrasted explicitly with **hawk (1962)**.

> 1962 *Saturday Evening Post*: The hawks favored an air strike to eliminate the Cuban missile bases . . . The doves opposed the air strikes and favored a blockade.

> 1966 *Listener*: The term 'hawks and doves' . . . was put into circulation by Charles Bartlett, President Kennedy's great journalistic confidant, in the course of an apparently inspired account of what took place in the President's own National Security Council at the time of the Cuban missile crisis.

dreadlocks *n* (1960) a Rastafarian hairstyle in which the hair is allowed to grow without combing, and forms into matted 'locks' which hang down from all over the head. The abbreviated *dreads* is first recorded in 1977.

eco- *prefix* (*1969*) an abbreviation of *ecological* or *ecology*. *Eco-* had occasionally been used before in the formation of technical terminology (e.g. *ecospecies*, *ecotype* (1920s), **ecosystem (1930s)**, *ecosphere* (1950s)), but its wide-ranging career in non-specialist vocabulary began in the late 1960s, as the environmentalist movement got into its stride. Among the earliest recorded formations of this new phase were *eco-activist*, *ecocatastrophe*, and *ecocide*.

> 1969 *Time*: Last week eco-activists staged a 'Damn DDT Day' in San Francisco's Union Square.

> 1970 *Natural History*: I've been an ecofreak for 30 years.

ego-trip *n* (1969) an activity, period of time, etc. devoted entirely to indulging in one's own interests or in self-expression.

> 1969 *It*: They're using the music as a vehicle for character and personality building. I don't think they're half as much a musical ego-trip as people imagine.

endangered *adj* (1964) of an animal or plant: in danger of extinction. The adjective is used especially in the phrase *endangered species*.

> 1964 *Congress Record*: A partial list of extinct and endangered species of the United States and Puerto Rico is attached.

Euro- *prefix* (1962) conforming to or resulting from European Union (formerly EEC) standards, regulations, etc. The prefix is often used jokingly, sarcastically, or dismissively. The organization was founded (under the Treaty of Rome) in 1957, but Britain did not begin to take serious notice of it until the 1960s (Britain first tried to join in 1963).

> 1965 *Daily Telegraph*: Studies are being made aimed at agreeing on common electrical standards throughout Europe . . . A common electric plug has been devised . . . It is called the 'Europlug'.

factory farming *n* (1964) agriculture organized on industrial lines. It is largely a polemical term, implying cruelly cramped conditions and deprivation of freedom and fresh air. The related *factory farm* dates from the 1890s.

> 1964 *New Statesman*: Boycott factory farm food? . . . Boycott factory farmers? . . . The essential thing is to amend the Protection of Animals Act (1911) to cover factory-farming techniques.

flares *n* (1964) flared trousers. Intermittently fashionable during the last four decades of the 20th century, they were at other times the object of derision. The term originated in the US.

> 1964 *New York Post*: Belted coats, skimmers, flares, demi-fits, the 'in' silhouettes for dress and casual wear!

> 1985 Suzanne Lowry: The rest of the male world sported peach cord flares.

flower people, flower children *n* (1967) members of a subgroup of hippies in the late 1960s and early 70s who wore or carried flowers as symbols of peace and love.

Their philosophy, if such it could be called, was termed *flower power* (1967). They were widely ridiculed for their unworldliness and condemned because of their reputation for drug-taking, sexual promiscuity, etc.

> 1967 *Guardian*: Beat-reared, Greenwich-nurtured teenagers are running away... to be flower people.

> 1969 *Listener*: The political innocence of the Hornsey flower children.

> 1969 Nik Cohn: As fads go, Flower Power was less than impressive... London was content mostly to ape California. Everyone wore kaftans and beads and bells. Everyone spoke in hushed tones of San Francisco and Monterey, of acid and Love and the Maharishi.

focus group *n* (1965) a group of people chosen to be representative of the population as a whole or of a specific subset of the population, and brought together to take part in guided discussions about consumer products, political policies, etc., so that their attitudes and opinions can be studied. In the 1990s, it became a leading target of those who saw marketing techniques driving principles out of politics.

> 1997 *Times*: The party chairman... insisted on testing the poster with focus groups of floating voters.

game show *n* (1961) a television light-entertainment programme in which celebrities or members of the public compete in a game or quiz, often for prizes. The term, and the concept, originated in the US.

> 1961 *Saturday Evening Post*: The set announced, 'It's Time to Say When!' and after a commercial, the first of the day's 'game shows' began.

gender *n* (1963) the sex of a human being, from the point of view of the social and cultural, as opposed to the biological, distinctions between the sexes. The word is often used before a noun.

> 1963 Alex Comfort: The gender role learned by the age of two years is for most individuals almost irreversible, even if it runs counter to the physical sex of the subject.

> 1986 *Financial Times*: It was most important... that schools could intervene in and modify the education of a child regardless of race, gender or class background.

generation gap *n* (1967) an (undesirable) difference in outlook and understanding between older and younger people. No doubt the difference had existed before, but it took the youth-oriented 1960s to take sufficient notice of it to coin the term *generation gap*. It went on to inspire *gender gap* (1977).

> 1967 *Boston Globe*: He acknowledged that the 'generation gap' is difficult both for the younger and the older generations.

genetic engineering *n* (1969) alteration of the DNA of a cell for the purpose of research, as a means of manufacturing animal proteins, correcting genetic defects, or making artificial improvements to plants and animals. The term, with its built-in contrast between life-processes and metal-bashing, remains an uneasy one at the start of the 21st century, largely because of the seed of doubt sown by that word 'improvements'.

> 1969 *New Scientist*: The day may be approaching when genetic engineering may make it possible to make a plant to order.

> 1971 *Guardian*: Human genetic engineering aimed at the elimination of genetic diseases.

global village *n* (1960) a term popularized by Marshall McLuhan (1911–80) for the world in the age of high technology and international communications, through which events throughout the world may be experienced simultaneously by everyone, so apparently 'shrinking' world societies to the level of a single village or tribe.

> 1960 Carpenter & McLuhan: Postliterate man's electronic media contract the world to a village or tribe where everything happens to everyone at the same time: everyone knows about, and therefore participates in, everything that is happening the minute it happens. Television gives this quality of simultaneity to events in the global village.

golden handshake *n* (1960) a gratuity given as compensation for dismissal or compulsory retirement. Later semi-facetious coinages which it inspired include *golden handcuffs* (1976) and *golden parachute* (1981).

> 1960 *Economist*: There is little public sympathy for the tycoon who retires with a golden handshake to the hobby farm.

hawk *n* (1962) someone who advocates a hard-line or warlike policy. The usage originated in the US, based on the idea of the hawk as an aggressive bird. It is usually contrasted explicitly with **dove (1962)**.

> 1967 David Boulton: The committee seems to have become immersed immediately in a struggle between doves and hawks.

hype *n, v* (1967) (to publicize with) deceptively inflated advertising or promotion. The word originated in the US. It is often taken to be short for *hyperbole*, but it can probably be traced back to an earlier US slang usage, meaning 'to short-change', whose origins are unknown.

> 1967 Norman Mailer: The hype had made fifty million musical-comedy minds; now the hype could do anything.

> 1969 Nik Cohn: Hype is a crucial word. In theory it is short for hyperbole. In practice, though, it means to promote by hustle, pressure, even honest effort if necessary, and the idea is that you leave nothing to chance. Simply, you do everything possible. Hype has become such an integral part of pop that one hardly notices it any more.

identikit *n* (1961) a composite picture of a person whom the police wish to interview assembled from features described by witnesses. It transformed the business of alerting the public to suspected criminals: in place of a vague verbal description or a dubious drawing, Frankensteinish montages began to appear in newspapers and on television. The word is a blend of *identity* and *kit*.

> 1961 *Observer*: About forty police forces in this country are now testing an American device called an 'Identi-Kit', which is used to translate witnesses' descriptions of a person into visual terms.

in *adj* (1960) in the slang of the 60s, fashionable, sophisticated.

> 1960 *Spectator*: A personable young strippeuse at Vegas (as we 'in' people call Las Vegas).

> 1965 *Melody Maker*: Record companies release more discs in the belief that folk is the new 'in thing'.

> 1970 *Times*: The in-crowd calls [Casablanca] 'Casa', and I offer the information here for anyone who can use it to advantage.

-in *suffix* (1960) used originally to designate a communal act of protest by blacks in the US against racial segregation (in that case the ultimate model was **sit-in (1937)**); subsequently it indicated any group protest or large gathering for some common purpose, especially as held by students. See also **teach-in (1965)**.

> 1960 *Newsweek*: Into the already-roiled waters of the South, Negroes will wade this summer in a campaign to break down segregation at public beaches—a wade-in counterpart to the wide-spread lunch-counter sit-ins of recent weeks.

> 1963 *Time*: The 'pray-in' at churches.

> 1965 *New York Times*: There have been sit-ins, lie-ins, stand-ins, eat-ins, shop-ins, sleep-ins, swim-ins, and sing-ins.

> 1968 *Listener*: There's a kind of cathartic quality about Danny la Rue that is a tremendous relief after weeks of trying to admire the Rowan and Martin Laugh-In.

> 1971 *Guardian*: A student sleep-in began last night.

inner city *n* (1968) the central area of a city, especially regarded as having particular problems of overcrowding, poverty, etc. The term originated in the US.

> 1968 *Saturday Review* (US): The twin concepts of decentralization and community control of the schools developed in response to the failure of schools in the inner city.

intelligent *adj* (1969) of a device or machine: able to vary its behaviour in response to varying situations and requirements and past experience; specifically (especially of a computer terminal), having its own data-processing capability; incorporating a microprocessor.

> 1986 *Keyboard Player*: An intelligent masterkeyboard . . . allows control, via MIDI, of up to eight synthesizers in all registrations.

interactive *adj* (1967) of or being a computer or other electronic device that allows a two-way flow of information between it and a user, responding immediately to the latter's input.

> 1981 *Event*: Interactive video, TV screens equipped with computer-linked press-buttons for instant Q&A verdicts on the show—asked in the studio and answered in your own home.

interface *n* (1962) a means or place of interaction between two systems, organizations, etc.; a meeting-point or common ground between two parties, systems, or disciplines. The usage arose out of the earlier (19th-century) scientific sense, 'a surface forming the boundary between two portions of matter or space'. The noun and its associated verb 'to come into interaction' (first recorded in 1967) have become particular targets for attack by those on the look-out for pretentious jargon.

> 1962 Marshall McLuhan: The interface of the Renaissance was the meeting of medieval pluralism and modern homogeneity and mechanism.

> 1968 *Lebende Sprachen*: Before turning to a discussion of how this management system . . . interfaces with functional organization let us try to define what we mean by project management.

into *prep* (*1969*) interested or involved in; knowledgeable about. This was the 'in' preposition of the late *1960*s and early *70*s, much resorted to by those wanting to sound 'cool'.

> 1969 *Rolling Stone*: I tend to like the stuff the rock groups are doing because they're creative and original, and that's something I'm very much into.

> 1971 *New Yorker*: First I was into Zen, then I was into peace, then I was into love, then I was into freedom, then I was into religion. Now I'm into money.

-ism, -ist *suffixes* (1965) denoting unfair or bigoted discrimination on the stated grounds. The prototype is **racist (1932)**, but it was not until the 1960s that the suffixes began to take on a life of their own. First in the new field was **sexist (1965)**, but soon every anti-bias grouping was jumping on the bandwagon (see also **ageism (1969)**). Another burst of new coinages (often frivolous or debunking) was prompted by the political correctness of the 1980s.

> 1992 *Out*: Why must we look like what society dictates is fetching? Because we live in a looks-ist world.

> 1994 *Guardian*: I have the right to challenge sizeism and bodyism alongside racism, sexism and ageism.

jet lag *n* (1969) the delayed effects, especially temporal disorientation, suffered by a person after a long flight on a (jet) aircraft.

jumbo jet *n* (1964) a large jet airliner with a seating capacity of several hundred passengers. The abbreviated *jumbo* is first recorded in 1966.

> 1966 *New Statesman*: The competitors . . . need only a small handful of jumbos . . . on the popular long-distance routes.

laser *n* (1960) a device that is capable of emitting a very intense, narrow parallel beam of light. The word was formed from the initial letters of *light amplification by the stimulated emission of radiation*, on the model of the earlier *maser* (1955) (in which the *m* stands for *microwave*). Originally treated as the name of a particular kind of maser (*optical maser*) emitting visible light, *laser* in due course became the general term for all devices of this kind, whatever the wavelength of the emitted radiation.

> 1963 *Monsanto Magazine*: A laser beam can generate intense heat—10,000°F. or higher—in a small area.
>
> 1967 *New Scientist*: With the laser-guided bomb, the large bombers might be able to drop their loads over the target area from high altitudes with greater assurance of putting them on target.

lib *n* (1969) a colloquial shortening of *liberation* in the sense 'emancipation', a usage which developed in the early 1960s, largely in the context of the struggle of US blacks for civil rights. It was taken up by other groups pressing for new freedoms, and it was these to which the abbreviation *lib* attached itself—first *women's lib*, then others. The somewhat trivializing effect of the short form was a strong factor in the later search for alternative terminology (see **women's liberation (1966)**). See also **libber (1971)**.

> 1969 *Time*: 'My twelve-year-old son has been hearing a lot about Women's Lib lately,' says Ruth.
>
> 1970 *Los Angeles Free Press*: Gay Lib Front meets . . . The Pope hopes that all Gay organizations—Old line, Gay lib, motorcycle, and social—will join in the demonstration.

lifestyle *n* (1961) a way or style of living. Originally this was a specialized term used by the Austrian psychologist Alfred Adler to denote a person's basic character as established early in childhood which governs their reactions and behaviour, and first recorded in this sense in 1929. The much broader modern sense (particularly as used in the jargon of marketing) betrays, in the eyes of cynics, the late 20th century's obsession with style at the expense of substance.

> 1961 *Guardian*: The mass-media . . . continually tell their audience what life-styles are 'modern' and 'smart'.
>
> 1990 *M & M*: Al Fares is the only serious upmarket lifestyle magazine in the Middle East.
>
> 1995 *Independent*: The latest lifestyle choice for the vibrant elderly is the 'retirement village', an American invention pitched somewhere between Club Med and Brookside.

lotus position *n* (1962) a bodily position in Yogic exercises which is said to resemble a lotus blossom (which is symbolic in Hindu and Buddhist thought). The term is a translation of Hindi *padmasana*, which had been turned into English as *lotus posture* as long ago as the 1880s. *Lotus position* was the version that caught on during the revival of Western interest in Eastern mystic religions in the 1960s.

> 1968 *Guardian*: Sitting in the lotus position . . . concentrating upon one's navel and repeating the mystic syllable, 'Om, Om'.

love beads *n* (1968) a necklace of coloured beads worn by the hippie generation of the late 1960s and early 70s as a symbol of universal love.

> 1973 Berkeley Mather: Weirdo fringed shirts, headbands, love beads . . . as unsavoury a bunch of love children as I have ever seen.

maxi- *prefix* (1961) denoting things, especially articles of clothing, that are very long or large of their kind. A reduction of *maximum*, it was no doubt modelled on **mini- (1919)**. The *maxiskirt* appeared in the mid 1960s in reaction to the **miniskirt (1965)**, and was followed by the *maxidress* and *maxicoat*, intensely fashionable in the late 60s and early 70s.

> 1966 *Times Educational Supplement*: There will be Lady X in Rutland realizing with a gasp of horror that she is wearing the same maxi-skirt as Lady Y.
>
> 1970 Robert Lowell: The girl's maxi-coat, Tsar officer's, dragged the snow.

midlife crisis *n* (1965) an emotional crisis occurring in midlife, characterized by the feeling that one is growing old or that life is 'passing one by'.

> 1965 Elliott Jaques: Less familiar perhaps, though nonetheless real, are the crises which occur around the age of 35—which I shall term the mid-life crisis—and at full maturity around the age of 65.

mind-blowing *adj* (1966) breathtakingly astonishing or astounding. Essentially it is the expression *blow someone's mind* (see **blow (1965)**) turned into an adjective. It originated in the US.

> 1967 *Jazz Monthly*: While the music lasted little of this was evident; the spectacular mind-blowing ferocity of it all simply carried the group through.

> 1974 Helen McCloy: A mind-blowing mustard yellow for the woodwork and on the walls a psychedelic splash of magenta and orchid and lime.

mini *n* (1961) an abbreviation of *minicar*, a term used in the 1940s as a name of a type of three-wheeled car made by the British firm Bond. *Mini* itself was first used in 1959 as part of the proprietary name, *Mini-Minor*, of a small car manufactured originally by the British Motor Corporation. By 1961 this had been shortened to *Mini*.

> 1961 *Engineering*: The Mini's astonishing success is due purely and simply to good engineering.

mini *adj* (1963) very small, tiny. The colloquialism is either an abbreviation of *miniature* or an adjectival use of the prefix **mini- (1919)**, and was probably inspired by the noun **mini (1961)**.

> 1966 *Daily Telegraph*: M. Redlus insists: 'My minis will be the most mini in Europe but they'll be decent.'

> 1967 *Word Study*: There's nothing mini about their wages.

> 1967 *New Scientist*: The current preoccupation with 'mini-ness' has now extended into the realm of . . . microbiology.

minimal *adj* (1965) a term used in the arts to denote an approach characterized by the elimination of elaboration. It was applied specifically, in the 1960s, to abstract painting and sculpture eschewing expressiveness and using simple geometric shapes, and in the 1970s to music based on simple elements, often repeated several times with minute variations. The related *minimalism* and *minimalist* are first recorded in the late 1960s.

> 1965 Richard Wollheim: Such a gesture . . . would provide us with an extreme instance of what I call minimal art.

> 1969 *Manchester Guardian Weekly*: Tony Smith, usually taken as the original minimalist sculptor . . . is well represented by large sculptures.

> 1985 *Radio Times*: In the 1960s [Steve Reich] began exploring the musical effects of repeated musical patterns that incorporate gradual changes over an extended period. The style came to be called *minimalism*.

miniskirt *n* (1965) a very short skirt. This was the archetypal 1960s garment, symbolizing at once the exuberance of the baby-boom teenagers and the sexual permissiveness with which the decade has become associated. The French fashion designer André Courrèges is credited with its invention.

> 1965 *Economist*: The Fashion House Group of London dumbfounded the . . . audience of American buyers quite as much by the sight of the British aggressively selling as by their mini-skirts and kooky outfits.

mission statement *n* (1967) a formal summary of the aims and values of a company, organization, or individual. This piece of business jargon, which originated in the US, is often ridiculed as portentous and pious.

> 1992 *Industry Week*: The departmental management developed a mission statement that talked of meeting the company's information needs in a timely and cost-effective fashion.

monetarist *n* (1961) someone who advocates tighter control of the money supply as an important remedy for inflation. The word was originally coined as an adjective around 1914, with the general sense 'having a monetary basis'. The noun *monetarism*, denoting the theory or policies of monetarists, is first recorded in 1969. The theory became fashionable in the 1970s and conventional wisdom in the 80s (when it was implemented by a number of Western governments). One of its main proponents was the US economist Milton Friedman.

> 1963 *Economist*: To control inflation by curtailment, as prescribed by the 'monetarists'.

> 1969 *Newsweek*: The combination of Stansian horse-and-buggy finance with Friedmanian go-go monetarism.

mouse *n* (1965) a small hand-held device which is moved over a flat surface to produce a corresponding movement of a cursor or arrow on a computer's VDU, and which usually has fingertip controls for selecting a function or entering a command. It was named from its shape, and particularly its lead, which resembles a mouse's tail.

> 1965 English & Engelhardt: Within comfortable reach of the user's right hand is a device called the 'mouse' which we developed for evaluation . . . as a means for selecting those displayed text entities upon which the commands are to operate.

nanny state *n* (1965) government institutions and practices of the Welfare State collectively, perceived as being overprotective, interfering, or excessively authoritarian, and as stifling initiative. A term first recorded in a *Spectator* article by the Conservative politician Iain Macleod (writing under the name 'Quoodle'), it came into its own in the 1980s, when one of the Thatcher government's main obsessions was rolling back the nanny state.

> 1965 Iain Macleod: The London County Council is dying, but the spirit of the Nanny State fights on.

> 1983 *Washington Post*: The British, we are incessantly told, have now rejected the 'nanny state' and regard the social worker as a boring pest.

no problem (1963) used as a polite disclaimer to an (explicit or implicit) suggestion that one has been troubled. It originated in the US.

> 1973 Martin Amis: Finally, every time I emptied my glass, he took it, put more whisky in it, and gave it back to me, saying 'No problem' again through his nose.

nuke *v* (1962) to attack or destroy with nuclear weapons. The term originated as US military slang, from the noun *nuke* 'a nuclear weapon' (1959).

> 1967 *Look*: I remember in Saigon how disturbed General Westmoreland was after talking to a group of American editors . . . who told him they favored 'nuking' (A-bombing) China.

number-cruncher (1966) a colloquial term for a machine with the capacity for performing arithmetical operations of great complexity or length. The derivative *number-crunching* is first recorded in 1971.

> 1966 *New Scientist*: The Flowers report recommended the setting up of some 'regional centres' each with a large 'number-cruncher' to take the bulk-computing load off more local machines.

> 1971 *Scientific American*: Here's a calculator that speaks your language. You can customize its keyboard, memory size, display, programs and peripherals to suit your number-crunching tasks.

orchestrate *v* (1969) to arrange or organize surreptitiously so as to achieve a desired (but in practice often artificial-seeming) effect. A favourite late-20th-century metaphor (based on the literal sense 'to combine harmoniously, like instruments in an orchestra', which dates from the mid 19th century), it now teeters on the edge of being a cliché.

> 1969 *Daily Telegraph*: Russia and America yesterday ratified the treaty banning the spread of nuclear weapons. They chose the same day by a diplomatic agreement typical of the way the two super-Powers are 'orchestrating' their moves in this front.

> 1975 *New York Times*: Three busloads of foreign journalists were brought to the staging camps on an officially sponsored visit. The enthusiasm that greeted them was as carefully orchestrated as is the march itself.

pager *n* (1968) a radio device that emits a sound when activated by a telephone call, used to contact a person carrying it. It was based on the verb *page* 'to have a person called by a page', which is first recorded in 1904.

> 1968 *Guardian*: There are already . . . in this country devices called radio pagers. You carry in your pocket the pager, which is linked by radio connection to your telephone. When the telephone rings, the pager blips, and you can answer the call by speaking into the pager. As things stand the pager is illegal.

paparazzo *n* (1961) a freelance photographer who pursues celebrities to take their pictures. The word comes from the name of an intrusive press photographer in

Federico Fellini's film *La Dolce Vita* (1959) (the name was supplied by the writer of the film's scenario, Ennio Flaiano, who in turn got it from *Sulle Rive dello Ionio* (1957), Margherita Guidacci's translation of George Gissing's travel book *By the Ionian Sea* (1901), in which a restaurant-owner is called Coriolano Paparazzo). It is mainly used in the plural form *paparazzi*.

> 1977 *Maclean's Magazine*: If Margaret was troubled by the publicity or the paparazzi that followed her during her New York stay, she certainly didn't show it.

peace dividend *n* (1968) a (financial) benefit from reduced defence spending; a sum of public money which may become available for other purposes when spending on defence is reduced. The term originated in the US, and the first supposed provider of such largesse was the ending of the Vietnam War. In practice such hopes proved illusory, and the term vanished from the scene until the late 1980s. The ending of the Cold War saw its revival—a temporary one, since once again governments seemed to find ways of spending just as much on weapons as before.

> 1968 *Fortune*: In Washington, the magic phrase is 'the Peace Dividend'... The fact is that peace dividends will neither materialize so quickly nor amount to so much money as many people think.

> 1995 *Economist*: When the Soviet Union began to collapse in 1990, many people predicted a huge and long-awaited 'peace-dividend'.

peace process *n* (1965) negotiations towards the peaceful settlement of an established conflict. In the 1970s the term came to be associated with US Secretary of State Henry Kissinger's *shuttle diplomacy*. In the 80s it was much used in the context of Middle East peace negotiations, and in the 90s it was inherited by the attempts to bring peace to Northern Ireland.

> 1975 *Economist*: They claim that he has no idea where Mr Kissinger's piecemeal peace process is leading, beyond the short-sighted hope that acquiescence in it will at least buy time.

> 1994 *Financial Times*: Mr Major has won plaudits for his handling of the peace process.

permissive society *n* (1960) a society in which sexual freedom is tolerated. The term was a hostile label attached to Western society of the 1960s and 70s, particularly by those who found that there was altogether too much sex going on. See **permissive (1956)**.

> 1968 *Listener*: This dreadful dilemma of the puritan in a permissive society.

> 1970 Germaine Greer: The permissive society has done much to neutralize sexual drives by containing them.

phone-in *n* (1968) a live radio or television programme during which listeners telephone the studios to ask questions or express their views. The term originated in the US. It was first used in 1967 in the sense 'a protest in the form of mass telephone calls of complaint', but this usage did not survive long.

> 1968 *Time*: He proposed reducing transit fares for San Franciscans over 65 to 5¢ and, on a subsequent TV 'phone-in', said he would try to get buses closer to the curb at pickup.

porn *n* (1962) a colloquial abbreviation of *pornography*. The usage hit the streets with the large-scale expansion in the pornographic book and magazine trade in the 1960s. The alternative *porno* is first recorded (as a noun) in 1968, but it never caught on to the same extent.

> 1962 *John o' London's*: The central character and narrator, the Captain, is a seedy but not at all unsympathetic individual who makes a precarious living by writing 'porn'.

> 1964 *New Society*: 'There's nothing odd about our customers,' the porn shop assistant said.

prime time *n* (1964) the time of day when a radio or television audience is expected to be at its largest; a peak listening- or viewing-period. The term originated in the US.

> 1964 *Variety*: For the first time in years, WNBC-TV has copped the number one rating position in prime time, in the highly competitive N.Y. market.

1976 *Billings* (Montana) *Gazette*: Jaclyn Smith is one of the gals who's huckstered in TV commercials a committee studied along with prime-time programs to determine the image given women on the small screen.

profile *n* (1961) a (characteristic) way of presenting oneself to the world. It is typically used in the phrase *low profile*, first recorded in 1970.

1970 *Guardian*: The United States . . . has repeatedly committed itself to keeping its profile low.

1972 *Times*: The most complicated question is the profile the Army should adopt at the start of Ulster's 'marching season'.

quark *n* (1964) any of a group of sub-atomic particles (originally three in number) conceived of as having a fractional electric charge and making up in different combinations the hadrons, but not detected in the free state. The term was coined as a nonsense word by James Joyce ('Three quarks for Muster Mark!', *Finnegan's Wake* (1939)), and applied to the fundamental particle by its discoverer, the US physicist Murray Gell-Mann.

1965 *New Scientist*: Just as atoms are composed of particles (protons, neutrons and electrons) so may the heavy particles themselves be made up of combinations of simpler entities, called 'quarks'.

rap *v*, *n* (1965) (originally and especially among African-Americans) (to engage in) a special type of improvised repartee, or more generally, impromptu dialogue or discussion. A single instance of the verb *rap* in the sense 'to converse' is recorded in 1929, but there is no evidence of continuity of usage between then and the 1960s. The notion of improvised speech led on later to **rap** 'music with improvised words' **(1979)**.

1965 Eldridge Cleaver: In point of fact he is funny and very glib, and I dig rapping (talking) with him.

1977 *Zigzag*: 'Dum Dum Boys' opens with a 'whatever happened to me mates' rap.

satellite television *n* (1966) originally, the use of an earth-orbiting satellite to relay a television signal from one country to another (e.g. across the Atlantic), from where it could then be broadcast in the conventional way. When the prospect of individual subscribers receiving television signals directly from a satellite was discussed, the term *satellite-to-home* was often used ('What about direct satellite-to-home broadcasting? . . . Perhaps the only way in which the federal government could expect to keep abreast of the developments in communications technologies would be to set up a Department of Communication', *Economist* (1967)). But when theory became commercial reality, in the mid 1980s, although the official term was *direct broadcasting by satellite*, or *DBS* for short (first recorded in 1981), *satellite television* (or *satellite broadcasting*, or just plain *satellite*) was what most people called it.

1966 *BBC Handbook*: The BBC's first satellite television transmissions were shown in 1962.

1989 *Which?*: There are also several monthly magazines with a mix of technical information and features about the films and other programmes on satellite and cable.

scenario *n* (1962) a predicted sequence of events. The metaphor (based on the word's earlier sense 'outline of the plot of a film, play, etc.') was by the 1970s in danger of becoming a cliché (Robert Burchfield, editor of the *Supplement to the Oxford English Dictionary*, noted 'The over-use of this word in various loose senses has attracted frequent hostile comment').

1962 Herman Kahn: The scenario begins by assuming a crisis; everybody is on edge. A Soviet missile is accidentally fired.

1971 *Observer*: Several of the computer 'scenarios' include a catastrophic and sudden collapse of population.

self-destruct *adj* (1966) denoting a mechanism enabling a missile or other device to destroy itself under certain conditions. The verb *self-destruct* is first recorded in 1969.

> 1966 R. W. Taylor: There's a double safeguard in a self-destruct system that would operate automatically in case of navigational error.
>
> 1969 *Daily Colonist* (Victoria, British Columbia): This message will self-destruct in 10 seconds but the printed message is the one that lives on.

serial *adj* (1961) of a person, action, etc.: habitual, inveterate, persistent, or sequential. The initial application (in American English) was to a murderer, and it continues to be used mainly with reference to criminals who repeatedly commit the same offence (e.g. *serial rapist*). The commonest collocation is probably **serial killer (1981)**. In the 1990s the usage branched off in a new, facetious direction.

> *a*1961 S. Kracauer: [He] denies that he is the pursued serial murderer.
>
> 1986 *Sunday Times*: It is in the United States . . . that serial killings have become a crime epidemic.
>
> 1992 *Economist*: The shah, the diary proves, was a serial adulterer.
>
> 1993 *Independent on Sunday*: Behind the barbed-wire in Southern California, 'active retirees' become serial golfers, swimmers, gymnasts.

sex change *n* (1960) a change of sex brought about artificially by surgical means, treatment with hormones, etc. The term had been used before by biologists to denote a natural gender-reversal ('These results . . . , while providing virtual proof of sex-change from male to female in a section of the male population, point also to the probable occurrence of two types of males in *P[atella] vulgata*', *Nature* (1946)), but once journalists and their headline-writers had got their hands on it, it was virtually lost to them. The papers also pioneered an adjectival use, denoting someone who has undergone such a change.

> 1960 *Twentieth Century*: Sex-change may well seem, as *The Times* said, 'unprepossessing' as a subject for comedy.
>
> 1984 *Daily Telegraph*: A sex-change Kiss-a-Gram girl stepped into the Marlborough Street dock yesterday clad in a see-through bra, black knickers, and fishnet stockings with suspender belt.

sexist *n* (1965) someone who advocates the idea that one sex is superior to the other (usually, that men are superior to women) or discriminates against members of the supposed inferior sex. The adjective *sexist* is first recorded in 1968, as is the noun *sexism*, denoting the idea or the discrimination. The coinage, based on **racist (1932)**, had before long inspired a range of other *-ists* and *-isms* denoting various sorts of discrimination (see **-ism, -ist (1965)**).

> 1965 P. M. Leet: When you argue . . . that since fewer women write good poetry this justifies their total exclusion, you are taking a position analogous to that of the racist—I might call you in this case a 'sexist'—who says that since so few Negroes have held positions of importance . . . their exclusion from history books is a matter of good judgment rather than discrimination.
>
> 1968 Caroline Bird: There is recognition abroad that we are in many ways a sexist country . . . Sexism is judging people by their sex where sex doesn't matter.
>
> 1971 *Publishers' Weekly*: The Women's National Book Association panel during NBA Week on 'sexism' in children's books.

shuttle, space shuttle *n* (1969) a manned space vehicle with wings enabling it to land like an aircraft and be used repeatedly. The usage was actually coined by John Wyndham in a fictional context in 1960 ('The acceleration in that shuttle would spread you all over the floor'), but not applied to a real vehicle until the end of the decade. It came into its own in the 1980s, when a series of such vehicles was launched by the US to carry out a range of space operations. The first flight, of a shuttle named 'Columbia', took place in 1981.

> 1969 *New Scientist*: Another shuttle plying on a regular basis between Cape Kennedy and this large space laboratory.
>
> 1981 *Daily Telegraph*: The American space shuttle landed on a dry lake bed in California's Mojave Desert yesterday to complete the maiden flight of the first re-usable rocketship.

single *adj* (1969) designating a person who is bringing up a child or children without a marital partner. It is used mainly in the terms *single parent* and *single-parent family*, standard politically correct vocabulary until, towards the end of the 20th century, it was realized that *single* might seem to discriminate against the unmarried (*unmarried mother*—first recorded in 1834—was the term *single parent* had been invented to replace), so *lone parent* was pressed into service instead.

> 1969 Jetse Sprey: Stigmatization of the single-parent family, and especially of single parents, does occur.

> 1976 *Women's Report*: This, coupled with the fact that more women are voluntarily becoming single mothers by refusing to have their babies adopted, has caused the government to set up a Cabinet Committee on Family Affairs.

sitcom *n* (1964) a contraction of *situation comedy* 'a television or radio comedy programme in which the humour is derived from the reactions of a regular set of characters to a range of situations' (first recorded in 1953). The term originated in the US.

> 1964 *Life*: Even Bing Crosby has succumbed to series TV and will appear in a sitcom as an electrical engineer who happens to break into song once a week.

skyjack *v* (1961) to hijack (an aeroplane); a favourite ploy of terrorists from the 1960s onwards. The word was formed from *sky* + *hijack*. The derivative *skyjacker* is also first recorded in 1961.

> 1961 *New York Mirror*: Pan Am Jet skyjacked to Havana.

> 1982 *Daily Telegraph*: The skyjackers . . . were said to have threatened crew members.

sleaze *n* (1967) sordidness, sleaziness. The word is a back-formation from *sleazy* 'sordid', which is first recorded in 1941. The application to 'financial or other corruption' evolved in the early 1980s (see **sleaze (1983)**).

> 1967 *Listener*: For all its brazen sleaze, Soho is a pretty fair working model of what a city neighbourhood should be.

software *n* (1960) the programs and procedures required to enable a computer to perform a specific task, as opposed to the physical components of the system. The term was modelled on **hardware (1947)**.

> 1960 *Communications Association Computing Machinery*: Nearly every manufacturer is claiming compatibility with all other equipment via such software as Cobol.

street-wise *adj* (1965) familiar with the outlook of ordinary people in an urban environment; cunning in the ways of modern urban life. The word originated in the US.

> 1981 *Daily Telegraph*: Their [i.e. young blacks'] values place a premium on being 'street-wise', . . . that is, being able to survive in the rough and tough world of the streets.

surgical *adj* (1965) designating swift and precise military attack, especially from the air. This notorious piece of military doublespeak, conferring the illusion of dispassionate accuracy on murderous mayhem, originated in American English.

> 1965 T. C. Sorensen: The idea of . . . a so-called 'surgical' strike . . . had appeal to almost everyone first considering the matter, including President Kennedy.

> 1971 *Harper's Magazine*: Even the language of the bureaucracy—the diminutive 'nukes' for instruments that kill and mutilate millions of human beings, the 'surgical strike' for chasing and mowing down peasants from the air by spraying them with 8,000 bullets a minute—takes the mystery, awe, and pain out of violence.

switched on *adj* (1964) aware of all that is considered fashionable and up to date. Slang.

> 1964 *House and Garden*: I . . . want . . . to open a department store which caters for switched-on people.

take-away *adj, n* (1964) designating cooked food sold to be eaten away from the premises of sale. The word is first recorded as a noun, denoting a shop selling such food, in 1970, and denoting a take-away meal in 1982.

> 1964 *Punch*: Posh Nosh . . . was serving take-away venisonburgers.
>
> 1981 Michael Hardwick: Proprietor of . . . a small string of burger eateries and takeaways.
>
> 1990 Ruth Rendell: He hadn't made a fortune in order to sit in his house eating takeaways and watching videos.

teach-in *n* (1965) an informal debate (often of some length) on a matter of public, usually political, interest, originally between the staff and students of a university. Hence, a conference attended by members of a profession on topics of common concern. The term, which originated in the US, was modelled on **sit-in (1937)** and the like (see **-in (1960)**).

> 1965 *Times*: This free-for-all debate . . . was called by the ugly new jargon name of 'teach-in'—a concept recently invented at Harvard, which has crossed the Atlantic.
>
> 1965 *Economist*: Universities all over the country [i.e. USA] have conducted informal 'teach-ins' on Vietnam, running from eight in the evening to eight the following morning.

teeny-bopper *n* (1966) a girl in her teens or younger, especially one who is a fan of pop music and follows the latest fashions.

> 1966 *Telegraph* (Australia): The teenybopper is aptly named because her two distinguishing features are her teeny size and her cool boppy with-it attitude to life.

telecom *n* (1963) an abbreviation of *telecommunication* (first recorded in 1932). In present-day usage (on the model of *telecommunications*) it is mainly plural, the singular form having been monopolized by the name of *British Telecom*, a British telecommunications company separated from the Post Office in 1981.

> 1964 Douglas Macarthur: By 'telecom' I was directed to use the Navy and the Air Force to assist South Korean defenses by whatever use I could make of these two arms.

termination *n* (1969) a euphemistic term for an induced abortion.

> 1969 *Time*: Women denied a legal abortion commonly seek termination elsewhere.
>
> 1973 *Times*: The pregnant women walking about the hospital ward were all in for abortions. Or terminations, as they called them—a much nicer word.

theme park *n* (1960) an amusement park organized round a unifying idea or group of ideas. Both the concept and the term were originally American. They were exported to Europe in the late 1960s, but did not catch on in a big way until the 1980s (when *theme* began to take on a new life of its own as an adjective—see **theme (1983)**).

> 1960 *American Peoples Encyclopedia Year Book*: While most established parks and kiddielands were profitable, the theme parks, seeking to duplicate Disneyland's success, were often in trouble.
>
> 1989 *Holiday Which?*: Local conservationists are even more horrified by a new proposal—including a Disney-style theme park—covering 1,000 acres.

Third World *n* (1963) the countries of the world, especially those of Africa and Asia, which during the Cold War were aligned with neither the Communist nor the non-Communist bloc; hence, the underdeveloped or poorer countries of the world, usually those of Africa, Asia, and Latin America. *Third World* is a translation of French *tiers monde*, a term formulated by the French demographer Alfred Sauvy (1898–1990) in the mid 1950s. (The corresponding *First World* and *Second World*, though never widely used, denote respectively the West and the Communist bloc.)

> 1963 *Economist*: Relations between Europe and the third world nowadays.
>
> 1964 *Economist*: The ingredients common to most 'third world' countries (poverty, ignorance, love-hate of the former colonial powers).

tights *n* (1965) a woman's or girl's one-piece stretchable garment covering the legs and body up to the waist, worn in place of stockings which were impractically revealing beneath the fashionable **miniskirt (1965)** (the demise of stockings and suspenders was greeted with relief by women, with regret by men). The term was used at the end of the 19th century for an undergarment taking the place of knickers and stockings, but the 1960s usage almost certainly comes from the tights worn by dancers, actors, etc.

> 1965 Peter O'Donnell: Modesty wore . . . a full black skirt, with black stretch tights.

together *adj* (1969) a colloquialism meaning 'composed, self-assured' or 'free of emotional difficulties or inhibitions'.

> 1971 *New Yorker*: A young lady of twenty-two who's been through what Twiggy has been through has got to be a very together person to survive.

topless *adj, adv* (1964) of a garment: not covering the breasts; hence, of a woman: naked or almost naked above the waist; bare-breasted. The application to places where bare-breasted women work (e.g. as waitresses) is first recorded in 1967. There is an isolated instance of the word on record from the 1930s referring to men's swimwear ('With another bathing-suit season at hand, local lawmakers are aiming their ordinances at males on the score of topless suits rather than at underclad females', *Time* (1937)), but the application to women is a child of the 1960s.

> 1964 *San Francisco Chronicle*: Saigis introduced San Francisco's first topless bathing suit for women.

> 1966 *Observer*: The appearance of topless waitresses.

tower block *n* (1966) a multi-storey block of flats (or sometimes offices). This was the 1950s' and 60s' solution to the problem of high-density housing, later so reviled that *tower block* became a dirty word. It is sometimes shortened to just *tower*.

> 1967 A. J. Marshall: The newest and nicest tower block is Centre Point.

track record *n* (1965) known facts about past achievements or behaviour taken as a guide to future performance. The metaphor, which originated in the US, is drawn from the athletics track, where the term denotes literally 'the performances achieved by a particular athlete in the past'.

> 1965 *Life*: Wilder has had a series of extremely successful pictures . . . We were betting on his track record that this one would be too.

transcendental meditation *n* (1966) a method of relaxation and meditation based on the theory and practice of yoga popularized in the West by the Maharishi Mahesh Yogi. It was in vogue in the late 1960s and early 70s, on the back of a general enthusiasm amongst the youth of the West for Eastern mysticism.

> 1966 C. F. Lutes: The system on which Maharishi's teaching is based—a simple method of transcendental meditation . . . —is indeed systematic and produces measurable and predictable results and is therefore scientific.

traumatic *adj* (1962) distressing, emotionally disturbing. This is a generalized use of the psychiatric term, denoting severe emotional damage, which dates from the late 19th century.

> 1962 Aldous Huxley: Memories of traumatic events in childhood.

> 1977 Edward Heath: Whatever the outcome, the impact on the United States of the decade of war in Vietnam was traumatic.

trendy *adj, n* (1962) fashionable, up to date, following the latest trend. It is first recorded as a noun, 'a trendy person', in 1968. From the beginning, it was a two-edged term: it can be used admiringly, but there is often also a suggestion of slavish and uncritical pursuit of the latest vogue.

> 1962 *Punch*: I saw the headline 'The Trendiest Twin Set'.

> 1968 Joan Fleming: She was well in with what is now called the Chelsea set . . . , there are trendies and *personae non gratae* amongst them.

> 1972 *Lancet*: Pathobiology (a trendy name for general pathology) seems to be a fashionable subject in the United States.

turn off *v* (1965) a slang verb meaning 'to put off, repel'. The related noun, *turn-off* 'something or someone that repels you', is first recorded in 1975.

> 1965 *Harper's Bazaar*: Humperdinck turns me off.

> 1975 *New York Times*: Patrons dined on *cervelle Grenobloise*. 'Sounds better in French,' said the chef... 'Brains is a turn-off.'

turn on *v* (1965) a slang verb meaning 'to arouse interest, enthusiasm, or sexual response'. The related noun, *turn-on* 'something or someone arousing or exciting', is first recorded in 1969.

> 1965 *Harper's Bazaar*: Bach really turns me on.

> 1967 Joseph Hayes: The excitement in her eyes deepened. 'You turn me on, man.'

> 1969 *Telegraph* (Brisbane): I think I'm more of a turn-on now than I ever was when I was trying to conform to that curvy image.

twist *n* ***the twist*** (1961) a dance to pop music in which the hips are gyrated. Earlier dances were named 'the twist' in the 1890s ('They're ready an' willin', An' fair at Kadrillin', But my little Flo does the twist', *Sunday Times* (1894)) and the 1920s ('"The Twist", created by M. Camille de Rhynal... is designed to cultivate gliding and swaying movements', *Daily Telegraph* (1928)), but the term did not catch on then as in the 1960s. It is also first recorded as a verb in 1961.

> 1961 *Guardian*: I have read recently that a new dance has been introduced in America called 'The Twist'... It is a week with only one new film, a small loud monstrosity called 'Hey, Let's Twist'.

unisex *adj* (1968) characterized by a style (of dress, appearance, etc.) that is designed or suitable for either sex. *Unisex clothing* was pioneered by the French designer André Courrèges.

> 1968 *Life*: With-it young couples... are finding that looking alike is good fashion as well as good fun. The unisex trend was launched by... the teen-agers.

Valium *n* (1961) a proprietary name (registered in the US in 1961 and in Britain in 1962) for the drug diazepam, used especially as an anti-anxiety agent, hypnotic, and muscle relaxant. The origin of the name is unknown. Along with *Librium* (1960), Valium was notorious as the dependency sedative of the 1960s.

> 1972 *Guardian*: She had taken an overdose of Valium after getting drunk the night before.

VDU *n* (1968) an abbreviation of *visual-display unit*, a device for displaying on its screen data stored in a computer, and usually incorporating a keyboard for manipulating the data. Within a dozen years the television-like screens had become an unremarked part of the office environment. *Visual-display unit* itself is first recorded in 1968 too, but the term *visual display*, denoting the display of computer information via the screen of a cathode-ray tube, dates back to the early 1950s.

> 1968 *British Medical Bulletin*: The data-terminal... may consist of a 'video display unit' (VDU), in effect the combination of a television-like display tube with a keyboard.

> 1976 *Liverpool Echo*: Hardware consists of an ICI 1900 mainframe linked to mini-computers with disc storage, local printers and VDUs.

vox pop *n* (1964) popular opinion as represented by informal comments from members of the general public, especially when used for broadcasting; statements or interviews of this kind. The term is from Latin *vox populi* 'voice of the people'.

> 1964 Hall & Whannel: In television... we could include... the use of the brief survey of popular opinion on any topic by means of the posed question (the so-called 'vox pop').

Wasp *n* (1962) a member of the American white Protestant middle or upper class descended from early European settlers in the US. The term is more often than not derogatory. For its etymology, see the following quote.

> 1962 E. B. Palmore: For the sake of brevity we will use the nickname 'Wasp' for this group, from the initial letters of 'White Anglo-Saxon Protestants'.

wholefood *n* (1960) unrefined food containing no artificial additives. The original connotation was to some extent food for crankies, but the term gradually joined the mainstream.

> 1960 *Mother Earth*: We should like to hear from further growers who may have available supplies of wholefood, especially winter salads, parsnips [etc.].

> 1978 *Peace News*: If you are interested in wholefoods, running a shop collectively and a political awareness of food please contact us.

window *n* (1965) a period outside which the planned launch of a spacecraft cannot take place if the journey is to be completed, owing to the changing positions of the planets. The usage broadened out in the 1970s to 'a (limited) period of opportunity'.

> 1967 *New York Times*: The Soviet and American vehicles flew to Venus close together because both were fired during one of the periodic 'windows' for such shots.

> 1985 *Sunday Times*: Regional bank bosses know that...they must rush to acquire their neighbours, to make the most of their window of opportunity.

women's liberation *n* (1966) the liberation of women from subservient social status and all forms of sexism; also (usually with capital initials) a militant movement with these aims. The shortened form *women's lib* is first recorded in 1969 (see **lib (1969)**). The abbreviation, in particular, became a target for trivializers, and within a decade or so supporters had largely abandoned it in favour of *feminism* (a late-19th-century coinage). See also **women's movement (1902)**.

> 1966 *New Left Review*: Fourier was the most ardent and voluminous advocate of women's liberation and of sexual freedom among the early socialists.

you're welcome (1960) a polite formula used in response to an expression of thanks. It is prevalent particularly in US English, and is sometimes criticized as a rote response, particularly when used by service-industry employees. See also **have a nice day (1971)**.

> 1960 *Times*: The coloured lift attendant in South Carolina who had that attractive way of saying, almost singing, 'You're welcome' whenever we thanked her.

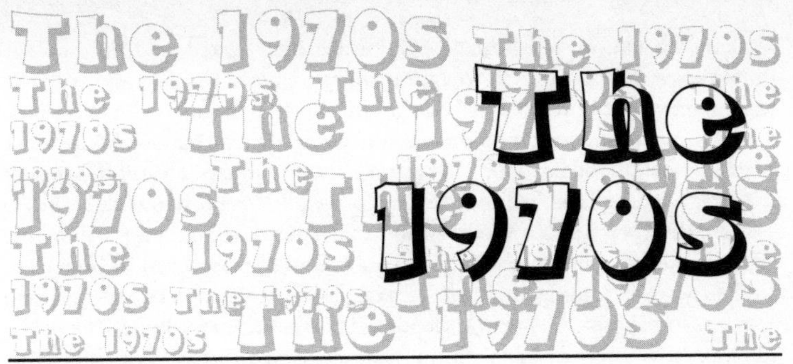

The 1970s

There are party decades and hangover decades. After the exuberance of the 1920s came the gloom of the 30s. And now, in the 1970s, the reaction to the Swinging Sixties set in. At the end of the century the decade tended to be looked back on without affection by those who had lived through it, memorable mainly for not being the 60s. The Western world received a check to its long post-war run of prosperity, largely precipitated by the rapid rise in oil prices in the early years of the decade, and inflation and unemployment walked abroad. The leader of the world's most powerful nation was forced to resign in disgrace: an episode summed up in the single word *Watergate*. And Abba bestrode the popular entertainment scene.

Our collective confidence took a series of knocks. We were destroying our environment; new diseases were appearing to which we had no answer (*Lassa fever, legionnaires' disease*); and even though we had reached the moon, we did not seem quite to know where to go from there. Against this background, terrorism inexorably extended its tentacles.

The growing realization of what we were doing to our planet found its response in *environmentalism*. The 70s were the first *green* decade. *Ecofreaks* 'fanatical environmentalists' appeared, scattering their *smiley faces* (round cartoon-like representations of a smiling face) about them. The *counter-culture* (a radical culture rejecting current social norms) of the *New Age* preached the virtues of *alternative technology*. The *energy crisis* of the early 1970s forced us all to take the *gas guzzlers* 'cars that consume large amounts of fuel' seriously, and search for *renewable* sources of energy. *Doomwatch* was in fashion, and *CFCs* made their ominous debut, with their threat of *global warming*. We learnt that we must recycle, and the first *bottle banks* sprouted in the streets. Even sounds could be pollutants: *noise pollution*. We condemned *speciesism* 'discrimination against certain animal species', embraced *bioethics* 'the ethical aspects of biology', and discovered the existence of a whole new geopolitical region: the *South* (the world's less advanced nations). When it all got too heavy, we could just *bliss out*.

What sort of society were the *baby boomers* (products of the post-World War II baby boom) helping to create? One in which the *poverty trap* (in which working left one worse off than being on benefits) lurked, and the *bag lady* (a homeless woman) started to appear in city centres, but one also with the urge to *gentrify*, to preserve its *heritage*, and to sleep on *futons*. One in which long-anonymous *carers* found a name, and many of their charges acquired new ones: *crumblie*, *wrinklie* (both 'old person'). One in which we learnt to live with *full-frontal* nudity, and had to find time for *quality time* with our children.

But if there was one phenomenon above all that marked out the 70s it was the gender issue. The 60s feminist campaign against sexism began to bear fruit; women were becoming *liberated*. *Sexual politics* could not be ignored, and *women's studies* were well up the agenda at universities and colleges. The *libbers* pursued their guerrilla war with the *male chauvinist pigs* (see **male chauvinism (1936)**). The *gender gap* was closing, and expectant fathers were demanding *paternity leave*.

Not the least of the effects of the feminist revolution was on the English language. The revolutionaries found sexist assumptions ingrained in the very fabric of the lexicon, particularly in the ambisexual use of *man* and the various masculine personal pronouns. Why should a woman who chaired a meeting be referred to as a *chairman*? How could anyone justify alluding to human history as the history of *man*, or of *mankind*? Was it not discriminatory to say 'If anyone wants to leave, *he* should do so now'? We were asked to kindly adjust our vocabulary.

The chairman could become the *chairperson*, and likewise the spokesman could become the *spokesperson*. The neutral element *-person* spawned scores of new formations, many of them patronizingly facetious. It remained in limited use at the end of the century, although other more euphonious solutions have often been found preferable (*chair* for *chairman*, *fire-fighter* for *fireman*). Polemical coinages such as *herstory* (for *history*) have for the most part remained marginal. The answer to the subtler problem of the masculine pronouns remains in the balance. Orthographic tricks such as *s/he* are of no relevance to the spoken language. Formulations like *he or she*, or *she or he*, become tiresome if often repeated. The most promising candidate as a non-sex-specific pronoun remains *they*, which has actually been used in this role, particularly in the environment of indefinite pronouns such as *somebody* and *anyone*, since at least the 16th century ('If... a psalm escape any person, or a lesson, or else if they omit one verse or twain', *Pilgrimage of Perfection* (1526)), and can be quoted from eminent writers from then to the present day ('Nobody else... has so little to plague them', Charlotte Yonge (1853); 'Nobody does anything well that they cannot help doing', John Ruskin (1866)), but which continues to irk the self-appointed language police.

Insistence on or conformity to such non-sexist usage was a major force behind the growth of *politically correct* vocabulary, which had its full efflorescence in the 1980s.

Also in anticipation of the 80s, the 70s were a decade greatly exercised by money, and the language of capitalism, the terminology of the *bean counters* (accountants and financial statisticians), made considerable strides. Corporate manoeuvrings produced *buy-outs*, *unbundling*, *asset-stripping*, and *golden handshakes*. No doubt there was some *creative accounting* going on, and perhaps even some *laundering* of funds. We could pick up our cash from an *automated teller* or a *cashpoint*, or simply use *plastic money*—a *debit card*, perhaps—or even pay by *direct debit*. In the UK, buyers and sellers had to cope with the vocabulary of a new currency: was it to be *pee* or *pence*? Meanwhile, economists and financiers bemused us with talk of *PSBR*, *supply side*, *petrodollars*, and *index-linked granny bonds*.

Those in work could perhaps take advantage of *flexitime*, or experiment with *job sharing*. But the 70s were not the happiest of times in the workplace: it was the decade of *industrial action* and *flying pickets*, culminating in the UK in the 'Winter of Discontent'. Many lost their jobs, and found out all about the *job centre* and the *giro cheque*. The market in new euphemisms for 'firing an employee' was brisk: *dehire*, *deselect*, *outplace*, *release*. Sacking half the workforce was *downsizing*.

The major change in the UK's political and economic circumstances was its joining of the European Economic Community in 1973. This ushered in a period in which English was increasingly beset by European jargon. We grew familiar with the *green pound* (an EU accounting unit for agricultural commodities), *E-numbers*, wine *lakes*, and the mysterious *snake* (a narrow range of fluctuations for exchange rates). In future there would be the prospect of *EMU* 'economic and monetary union' and the *single currency*, the *ECU* 'European Currency Unit' and the *euro* (already under active discussion), not to mention a continuing flow of often hostile or mocking *Euro-* (1962) compounds.

Closer to home in Britain, the troubles in Northern Ireland were taking a grip, and we had to add *plastic bullet* and *rubber bullet*, *car bomb* and the verb *kneecap*, *no-go area* and *Provo* 'Provisional IRA' and *Bloody Sunday* to our vocabulary. The prospect of *proximity talks* 'diplomatic negotiations conducted through intermediaries' was well in the future. On the wider political scene it was a polarized time, with the *hard left* (or *loony left*) in the ascendancy, *Militant Tendency* active in the Labour Party, and *Thatcherism* on the horizon. In the US the concept of *spin* was invented, which would permeate politics round the world in the final quarter of the 20th century.

The computer continued its march towards the centre of our lives, bringing with it copious amounts of new terminology, at first arcane, now commonplace: *floppy disk* and *hard disk*, *microprocessor* and *window*, and the dreaded *virus*. We acquired *personal computers* or *word processors*, and to print the result of our labours, the *dot matrix*, the *daisy wheel*, and later the *laser printer*. We could sit at our *workstation* in our *paperless* office, communicate via the *Ethernet* (a local-area computer network), and hope the whole system did not *crash*; or perhaps, with the help of the computer, we could simply *telecommute* from home. *User-friendly touch screens* facilitated our transactions, and we had barely heard of *hacking* and the need for *data protection*.

And to cater to our recreational needs, there was the pioneering computer game *Space Invaders.*

Towards the end of the decade the mass-market video arrived, and *couch potatoes* could use their *Betamax* (an early video format) to record their favourite *miniseries* or *docutainment* programme, or to watch *action replays* of the latest sporting *megastars* in action. *Teletext* services such as *Ceefax* were coming on stream, *electronic mail* was arriving, and music buffs had the prospect of being able to play *compact discs* on their *music centres.* And what sort of music would they be listening or dancing to? If they were young, it would very likely be *heavy metal, punk rock* (inspiration of the characteristic youth look of the decade—spiky coloured hair and leather clothes with chains, safety pins, etc.), *New Wave, rap,* or possibly *salsa.*

It was the era of *hot pants* (women's very brief shorts) and *leg-warmers, Doctor Martens* and *flip-flops, bomber jackets* (short zippered jackets) and *bustiers* (short close-fitting tops), *loon pants* (widely flared trousers), *skinny* sweaters (tight-fitting), and *Afghan coats. Trainers* graduated from the jogging track to the high street, and the *trouser suit* (1939) made a big comeback.

The upwardly mobile could plump for *nouvelle cuisine*, cook their chicken in a *chicken brick* (an earthenware container), join the race for *Beaujolais nouveau* (the latest vintage of Beaujolais wine), go green with a *Vegeburger,* or yellow with a *piña colada* (a cocktail made from pineapple juice and rum). The downmarket choice was *pub grub, junk food,* or a *Big Mac.*

And the craze of the decade? *Streaking.*

action replay *n* (1973) a playback (at normal speed or in slow motion) of a recorded incident in a sports match etc., especially immediately after the action occurs. This far-reaching development of the video age allowed television spectators (and in due course spectators at the ground, via a large screen) to cheat real time and enabled incidents (and officials' decisions about them) to be microscopically examined. The terms *instant replay* and simply *replay* are also used (the noun *replay* had been used in the audio field since the early 1950s).

> 1974 *Cleveland* (Ohio) *Plain Dealer*: The scoreboards will be placed on each side and the instant replay screens at each end.
>
> 1977 Jim Laker: The action replay can be of great help . . . in showing the reason for a batsman's dismissal.

alternative *adj* (1970) applied to a lifestyle, culture, etc. regarded by its adherents as preferable to that of contemporary society because it is less conventional, materialistic, or institutionalized, and often more in harmony with nature. The usage grew out of **alternative society (1969)**.

> 1970 Anthony Sampson: Cyclops has died. Strange Days has died. Grass Eye and Zig Zag ail. The alternative Press is in trouble all round.
>
> 1982 *New Zealand Listener*: There is another non-rigid non-school with what in today's language we could call an alternative life-style.
>
> 1983 *British Medical Journal*: One of the few growth industries in contemporary Britain is alternative medicine.

alternative technology *n* (1972) (a) technology designed to conserve natural resources and avoid harm to the environment, especially by harnessing renewable energy sources such as wind- or solar-power.

> 1991 *Whole Earth Review*: Computers are not alternative technologies. They are energy consumptive and lock a person into the system of Earth destruction.

asset *n* (1977) a resource available to an armed force; a piece of military hardware. The chilling bureaucracy of war: a lethal weapon becomes an item on a balance sheet. The euphemism originated in the US.

> 1977 *Aviation Week & Space Technology*: U.S. Air Forces Europe . . . plans to increase its air assets greatly in this central region of the North Atlantic.

back to basics (1975) a catchphrase applied to a movement or enthusiasm for a return to fundamental principles (e.g. in education) or to policies reflecting this. It originated in the US, and did not impinge much on British consciousness until 1993, when it was adopted as a slogan by the Conservative Party ('It is time to get back to basics: to self-discipline and respect for the law, to consideration for others, to accepting responsibility for yourself and your family, and not shuffling it off on the state', John Major, Conservative Party Conference (1993)). Numerous fallings from grace amongst government ranks soon enabled opponents to turn the phrase back on those who had sponsored its use.

> 1977 *National Observer* (US): The current 'back to basics' movement, the campaign to give the highest priority to the teaching of the fundamentals of reading, writing, and arithmetic.
>
> 1994 *Vanity Fair*: 'Back to Basics' has so far involved three resignations, nine girlfriends, one close male friend, two violent deaths and two . . . 'love children'.

Big Mac *n* (1970) a proprietary name (registered in the US in 1973, with claim of use since 1957) for the largest in a range of hamburgers sold by McDonald's fast-food outlets.

> 1970 *Forbes* (New York): [McDonald's] tested big burgers—today's big seller—for years before adopting the Big Mac.

biotechnology *n* (1972) the branch of technology concerned with modern forms of industrial production utilizing living organisms, especially micro-organisms, and their biological processes. This represented a reapplication of a term which had originally (see **biotechnology (1947)**) been applied to what would now more usually be called 'ergonomics'.

> 1972 (title of periodical): Biotechnology and bioengineering symposium.
>
> 1982 *Times*: Biotechnology appeared to have staked out half a dozen major industries, each of which would be transformed by new manufacturing processes based on cell culture, genetic engineering, or the catalysing powers of enzymes.

boat people *n* (1977) refugees who leave their country by boat. The term was originally applied to refugees from Vietnam and other South-East Asian countries who fled by putting to sea in small boats, rafts, etc.

> 1977 *Chicago Tribune*: Repressive rule in the south has created a new classification of refugees, 'the boat people'. These are the thousands of families of Vietnamese . . . who push off in leaky boats and rafts into the South China Sea.

bonk *v, n* (1975) to have sexual intercourse (with). This British colloquialism did not really take off until the mid 1980s, when it was discovered and gleefully exploited by tabloid headline-writers ('Bonking Boris', in reference to the German tennis player Boris Becker's sex life, created a big alliterative impression in 1987). It was probably a metaphorical extension of *bonk* 'to hit' (first recorded in 1931), on the model of *bang*. The noun *bonk* 'an act of sexual intercourse' is first recorded in 1984.

> 1975 *Foul*: Rita is currently being bonked by the entire Aston Villains defence!
>
> 1984 McConville & Shearlaw: 'They're not even bonking any more.' . . . Entirely cross-sexual, with women being just as likely to say they bonk as are men . . . 'Did you have a good bonk last night?'
>
> 1986 *Daily Telegraph*: Fiona . . . has become so frustrated that she has been bonking the chairman of the neighbouring constituency's Conservative association.

bulimia *n* (1976) an emotional disorder, occurring chiefly in young women, in which binges of extreme overeating alternate with depression and self-induced vomiting, purging, or fasting, and there is a persistent over-concern with body shape and weight. The word is ultimately from Greek *boulimia* 'great hunger', which was formed from the intensive prefix *bou-* (originally from *bous* 'ox') and *limos* 'hunger'. English had used it as a medical term (usually in the form *bulimy*) since at least the late 14th century, denoting extreme or pathological hunger, especially in the insane, but this usage (in full *bulimia nervosa*) recognizes a newly diagnosed psychological illness, in many ways the reverse of *anorexia nervosa* (a term which dates from the 1870s). The derived *bulimic* is first recorded as an adjective in 1977 and as a noun in 1980. See also **anorexic (1907)**.

> 1976 *Scientific American*: After about two years a second phase [of anorexia], called bulimia, usually develops, in which the victim alternately fasts and gorges herself.
>
> 1980 *Washington Post*: Bulimics may not exhibit the outward signs of starvation that are the hallmark of the anorexic.
>
> 1985 *Woman's Own*: She developed another slimmer's disease—bulimia nervosa. 'For four months I stuffed myself with food then purged myself.'

carer *n* (1978) a person whose occupation is the care of the sick, aged, disabled, etc. The term is also applied to someone who looks after a disabled or elderly relative at home, often at the expense of her or his own career. It is a modern specialization of *carer* 'one who cares', which dates back at least to the 17th century. The related adjective *caring* (as in *caring professions*) is first recorded in 1976 (see **caring (1966)**).

> 1982 *Times*: More money should be spent on the carers—those people, mainly women and mainly unpaid, who look after old and handicapped relations.

CFC *n* (1976) an abbreviation of *chlorofluorocarbon* (first recorded in 1947), any of a class of compounds of carbon, fluorine, and chlorine whose presence in the atmosphere is thought to cause damage to the ozone layer. They were widely but quietly used as refrigerants and aerosol propellants and in the plastics industry for several decades, and it was not until doubts surfaced about their safety that their name became at all well known (usually in the abbreviated form).

> 1989 *Daily Telegraph*: Shoppers are told that meat and eggs are packaged in CFC-free containers.

chairperson *n* (1971) a chairman or chairwoman: usually intended as an alternative that avoids specifying the sex of the office-holder. For some reason, this was the main coinage around which the controversy about non-sex-specific *person* raged in the 1970s (see **person (1971)**). Opponents attacked it on political and aesthetic grounds. Subtler arguers claimed that in practice it was only applied to women, and that men were still called *chairmen* (although actually that was not always so—see the second example below). Seekers of the middle way advocated the use of the genderless *chair* ('Martha Layne Collins . . . is to serve as chair of the Convention', *New Yorker* (1984)), a usage which dates back to the 17th century.

> 1971 *Science News*: A group of women psychologists thanked the board for using the word 'chair-person' rather than 'chairman'.

> 1984 Sue Townsend: Dear Chairperson, Arthur, it is with the deepest regret that I offer my resignation as vice-chairperson of the Elm Ward Labour Party.

collateral damage *n* (1975) destruction or injury beyond the intent or expectation of an aggressor, usually occurring in a civilian area surrounding a military target. The term is commonly used as a euphemism for 'accidentally killing civilians'. This piece of US military jargon reached a wider audience during the Gulf War, and thereafter embarked on a new, metaphorical career.

> 1975 *Aviation Week*: Low-and-moderate yields also would be developed to replace Pershing 1-A nuclear warheads for greater military effectiveness and less collateral damage.

> 1991 *Washington Post*: Weapons of such precision that military targets can be detected, isolated and killed almost without collateral civilian damage.

> 2001 *www.citybeat.com*: More Americans than ever before own homes—67.1 percent in early 2000—but the boom included collateral damage. Across the nation, tragic stories have emerged from what might seem a positive development.

compact disc *n* (1979) a disc on which sound or data is recorded digitally as a spiral pattern of pits and bumps underneath a smooth transparent protective layer and reproduced by detecting the reflections of a laser beam focused on the spiral. By the end of the 1980s such discs had largely replaced LPs and tapes as the main medium of audio recording. The widely used abbreviation *CD* is also first recorded in 1979. See also **CD ROM (1983)**.

> 1979 *New Scientist*: Although the Compact Disc (CD) system indubitably works as claimed and could offer an attractive alternative to today's grooved records . . . CD is sure to receive far hotter competition from Japan than the compact cassette.

> 1984 *What Video?*: My musical examples came from what is still one of the best examples of CD recording around.

couch potato *n* (1979) someone who spends leisure time passively or idly sitting around, especially watching television or videotapes. The term was reputedly coined by Tom Iacino as a pun on US slang *boob-tuber* 'television addict', from *boob tube* 'television' (the potato being a type of tuber), but maybe it simply arose by association with *vegetable* 'inert person'. Either way, its neat encapsulation of vacuous indolence ensured its success in the censorious 1980s. It was registered as a proprietary term in the US in 1984, with claim of first use in 1976.

> 1979 *Los Angeles Times*: The Humboldt State Marching Lumberjacks . . . and the Couch Potatoes who will be lying on couches watching television as they are towed toward the parade route.

date rape *n* (1975) rape of a woman by a man she is dating or with whom she is on a date. The term originated in the US.

1991 *New York Times*: Most date rape cases come down in the end to Her versus Him.

debit card *n* (1975) a plastic card issued by an organization, giving the holder access to an account, via an appropriate computer terminal, especially in order to authorize the transfer of funds to the account of another party when making a purchase etc., without incurring revolving finance charges for credit. The term originated in the US. Compare **credit card (1952)**.

deconstruct *v* (1973) to subject to deconstruction, a strategy of critical analysis associated with the French philosopher Jacques Derrida (1930–2004), directed towards exposing unquestioned metaphysical assumptions and internal contradictions in philosophical and literary language, and emphasizing the meaning of words in relation to each other rather than to referents in the real world; to analyse and reinterpret in accordance with this strategy, which was both influential and controversial (i.e. reviled) in the last quarter of the 20th century. Both *deconstruct* and *deconstruction* are first recorded in an English translation of Derrida's work.

1976 G. C. Spivak: Ricoeur delivers hermeneutic interpretations of several texts that Derrida deconstructs.

1979 *London Review of Books*: We are not in favour of the current fashion for the 'deconstruction' of literary texts, for the elimination of the author from his work.

dependency culture *n* (1973) a social or political climate in which people rely on money or services provided by the State. The term is applied particularly, and disapprovingly, by right-wing theorists to reliance on State benefits by the unemployed or poor, viewed as robbed by this largesse of the motivation to provide for themselves or to improve their situation.

1992 *Economist*: During the boom years of the mid-1980s . . . conservative works chronicling the growth of a black dependency culture in America's ghettos multiplied.

doomwatch *n* (1970) observation intended to avert danger or destruction, especially of the environment by pollution or nuclear war. The term was suggested by the name of a BBC television series first broadcast in 1970 ('BBC-TV's new scientific soap-opera, *Doomwatch*, has been fortunate in its first selection of topics to warn us about', *New Scientist* (1970)). The derived *doomwatcher* is first recorded in 1971.

1970 *Guardian*: The Government Chemist . . . tested 50 tins of tuna bought throughout the country . . . Mr Prior said: . . . 'We shall be getting on with this—this Doomwatch, if you like to call it that.'

1978 *Nature*: As WMO sees it, hard evidence does little to support many of the disaster hypotheses of the doom-watchers . . . There is one major exception: the problem of increasing CO_2 in the atmosphere.

downsize *v* (1979) to reduce the size of. The word originated in the US; it has been widely used as a euphemistic cover for reducing the size of an organization by dismissing employees. It was not an entirely new usage, but a generalization of the slightly earlier *downsize* 'to design or build a car of smaller size', which came out of the energy crisis of the early 1970s.

1982 *Fortune*: Right now he's 'downsizing' the company, and hopes to achieve 1982 cost savings of about $600 million.

electronic mail *n* (1977) the sending of non-spoken information between individuals over a telecommunication network to a selected location or locations where it is stored for subsequent retrieval, typically via a personal computer. The term is also applied to the information sent. By the end of the 20th century it was much more commonly referred to by its abbreviation **e-mail (1982)**.

1977 *Science*: An electronic mail system is becoming practical today, because of the wide availability . . . of electronic communication channels.

environmentalism *n* (1972) concern with the preservation of the environment, especially from the effects of pollution; the politics or policies associated with this.

> 1972 *Science News*: The arguments in the United States over environmental problems have not yet reached these basic levels, even though environmentalism got its first major impetus there.

euro *n* (1971) a name proposed for the monetary unit of the European **single currency (1970)**, based on the prefix *Euro-*, and officially accepted by the European Commission in December 1995. It began circulating alongside the national currencies of eleven countries of the European Union (not including the UK) in 1999, and replaced those currencies in 2002.

> 1971 *Guardian*: How would you feel about paying your bills in Euros..? 'Euro' is the name . . . thought the ideal one for a European currency.

> 1999 *Observer*: 'Do euros mean I have to make different arrangements when I go on holiday?' 'No, everything you've been doing before, you can still do—at least for the next three years.'

Exocet *n* (1970) a proprietary name for a kind of rocket-propelled short-range guided missile of French manufacture, used especially in tactical sea warfare. French *exocet* means literally 'flying fish'. The term did not become familiar to lay audiences until the Falklands War of 1982, when the Argentinians used Exocets against British forces.

> 1983 *Annual Register 1982*: On 4 May HMS Sheffield, a type 42 destroyer, was sunk by a French-made Exocet air-to-sea missile.

floppy disk *n* (1972) a small, flexible plastic disc with a magnetic coating used as an inexpensive, lightweight, moderate-capacity storage device for computer information. After some initial uncertainty, *disk* became the standard spelling in British as well as American English. Compare **hard disk (1978)**.

> 1972 *Computer Design*: Century Data Systems has introduced the CDS-100 'floppy disc' drive, a portable storage device that utilizes a single, removable, disc cartridge as the recording medium.

flying picket *n* (1974) a British term for (a member of) a group of striking workers who picket premises or organizations other than those at which they are employed, especially one which travels from another area to a striking site or sites in order to reinforce local pickets.

> 1984 *Times*: 138 pits are on strike or are 'picketed out' by flying pickets from . . . militant coalfields.

F-word *n* (1973) a euphemistic formulation, American in origin, for referring to the word *fuck* in circumstances where it would be taboo. As other once embargoed items (e.g. *shit*) have emerged from the closet, it has gradually replaced the previous circumlocution **four-letter word (1934)**. In the late 1980s the pattern produced a flurry of lookalikes, both serious (*C-word* for *cunt*) and polemical (*L-word* for *liberal*, used by those for whom *liberal* is a dirty word: 'Hillary is a liberal (the bad L-word)', *Independent* (1993)), and also facetious (see the second quote below).

> 1973 *New York Times Book Review*: I ain't got time to be outraged about these books. I dismiss them. The kids use the expression 'f-word', the 'f-word', when they want to talk about it without saying it. Well, I say, 'f-word' them books, and 'f-word' the pretentious writers who write them.

> 1995 *Daily Telegraph*: Others describing such an incident might have used an f-word—'feckless' or, in extremes, 'a foozler'. Benaud opted for: 'What a shemozzle!'

-gate *suffix* (1973) an ending denoting an actual or alleged scandal (and usually an attempted cover-up), in some way comparable with the Watergate scandal of 1972 onwards. It is added (on the model of *Watergate*) to the name of the place where the scandal occurred, or somewhere linked with it (e.g. *Dallasgate*); to the name of a person or organization implicated in it (e.g. *Muldergate*); or to something connected with it (e.g. *Winegate*). Probably the most notorious example was *Irangate* (1986), a scandal involving allegations that profits from US arms sales to Iran had been diverted to aid anti-government guerrillas in Nicaragua.

1973 *Saturday Review World* (US): Inevitably, the brouhaha of Bordeaux became known as Wine-gate.

1975 *Modern People*: Shocking Dallasgate revealed.

1978 *Observer*: The South African Government easily defeated . . . an attempt . . . to force its resignation over 'Muldergate'—the Information Department scandal.

1987 *Daily Telegraph*: [Oliver] North will be asked about his accepting the gift of a security gate at his home, a sub-plot that has become known as Gategate.

gentrify *v* (1972) to renovate or convert (housing, especially in an inner-city area) so that it conforms to middle-class taste; also, to make (an area) middle-class. The verb is usually used disparagingly, with the implication of swamping genuine working-class culture with effete bourgeoiserie. The noun *gentrification* soon followed.

1972 J. I. M. Stewart: The humbler dwellings . . . were well-groomed rather than neat, and their little gardens had been gentrified as effectively as had their low parlours.

1973 *Times*: The switch to owner-occupation has shifted overcrowding to the north of the borough which already suffered acutely before the 'gentrification' process began.

1977 *New York Times*: Newcomers are 'gentrifying' working-class Islington and should be resisted, not welcomed.

global warming *n* (1977) a long-term gradual increase in the earth's temperature, thought to be caused by various side-effects of modern energy consumption such as the augmented **greenhouse effect (1929)**.

1977 *Economist*: Even a doubling of carbon dioxide could be serious: a global warming of nearly three degrees centigrade, and possibly over eleven degrees in parts of the Arctic.

1989 *Nature*: A Senate resolution calling on the United States to take the lead in setting up an international convention to slow global warming.

green *adj* (1971) relating to or supporting environmentalism, especially as a political issue; belonging to or supporting an ecological party. The term is also used more loosely to mean 'environmentalist, ecological'. The association of the colour green with the environmentalist lobby, especially in Europe, dates from the early 1970s in West Germany, notably with the *Grüne Aktion Zukunft* 'Green Campaign for the Future', and the *grüne Listen* 'green lists (of ecological election candidates)', both of which emerged mainly from campaigns against nuclear power stations. Its initial manifestation in English was as part of the name of *Greenpeace*, an international organization which campaigns in support of conservation and the protection of the environment. Members or supporters of an ecological party, or more broadly those committed to environmentalism or ecology, came to be known as *greens* (1978).

1972 Robert Keziere: A bringing-together of the peace and environmental movements . . . Greenpeace seemed like a concept that might create such an alliance.

1978 *Economist*: European politics are turning green; or so the ecologists would have us believe . . . The Greens are more likely to take votes from the Social Democrats and the Liberals than from the Christian Democrats.

1979 *Now!*: The rebuff to 'green', environmentalist ideals is displayed by the drop in the Centre Party's vote from 24 to 18 per cent.

1985 *Sunday Times*: The 5,000-strong Ecology Party swapped its 'too middle class' name for the Green Party at its annual conference in Dover yesterday.

1986 *New Socialist*: If the government's greens . . . get their way, then the pollution from Drax B may yet be cleaned up.

hacking *n* (1976) the use or programming of a computer as an end in itself, for the satisfaction it gives. Someone who does this is called a *hacker* (also first recorded in 1976). The term was reputedly first used at the Massachusetts Institute of Technology. The back-formed verb is first recorded in 1983. In the early 1980s the word developed the more sinister connotation of breaking electronically into others' computer systems (see **hacker (1983)**).

> 1976 Joseph Weizenbaum: The compulsive programmer spends all the time he can working on one of his big projects. 'Working' is not the word he uses; he calls what he does 'hacking'... The compulsive programmer, or hacker as he calls himself, is usually a superb technician.

> 1983 G. L. Steele: At MIT, I would sometimes work nights for a month at a time. Now that I am married, I find that I can hack only in spurts.

hang *v* ***let it all hang out*** (1970) a slang expression, originating in the US, meaning 'to be uninhibited or relaxed'.

> 1978 Robert Westall: When my parents quarrel, they... fight in hoarse whispers. But like a lot of upper-middles... Derek and Susan let it all hang out.

happening *adj* (1977) exciting, lively, trendy, up-to-the-minute, hip; that is, 'where the action is'. The slang expression originated in the US, based on the notion of 'what is happening now'.

> 1977 Cyra McFadden: Who could live anywhere else? Marin's this whole high-energy trip with all these happening people.

> 1990 *Radio Times*: My kind of day is a Saturday when we've had a totally happenin' week on Children's BBC.

harassment *n* (1975) the subjecting of a person to aggressive pressure or intimidation through unwanted sexual advances. When originally conceptualized by feminists, the offence was termed *sexual harassment*, to distinguish it from other forms of harassment, but so preponderant is the usage that by the 1990s plain *harassment* (almost always stressed, *à la* US English, on the second syllable) was widely understood to mean 'sexual harassment'.

> 1975 *New York Times*: Sexual harassment of women in their place of employment is extremely widespread.

> 1993 *New York Times Book Review*: The increasing emphasis on woman's essential weakness and man's essential bestiality that underlies many of the current debates about rape, harassment and pornography.

hard disk *n* (1978) a computer disk that is rigid and has a large storage capacity, as distinct from the smaller-capacity **floppy disk (1972)**.

have a nice day (1971) used as a conventional formula on parting. It originated in the US, and is considered (and in some quarters reviled) as the archetypal American parting shot. See also **you're welcome (1960)**.

> 1971 Dorothy Halliday: The admonitions of the freeway from the airport are wholly American: Keep off the Median... Have a Nice Day.

heritage *n* (1970) used, often as an adjective, in the context of preserving or exploiting local and national features of historical, cultural, or scenic interest, especially as tourist attractions. By the 1980s the usage had proliferated to such an extent that it seemed to jaundiced observers that its idea of a packaged, touristic past had all but supplanted history. Its status was further enhanced in the 1990s when Britain appointed its first Secretary of State for the National Heritage, responsible for such areas as the arts, museums, and sport.

> 1970 *Nature*: The idea of the 'heritage highway', a route which links places in the life of national figures... seems to me to be a sort of motorized nature trail.

> 1986 *Financial Times*: Cadw has struck a blow for the entire heritage industry.

> 1988 *Breakfast Time* (BBC): If you're interested in history, or heritage, as we're supposed to call it today, you can have a good day out today, as all the National Trust properties are open for free.

high-tech *adj, n* (1972) short for *high-technology*, denoting the production or utilization of highly advanced and specialized technology (first recorded in 1964). The term is also applied specifically to a style of architecture and interior design that imitates the functionalism of industrial technology.

> 1972 *Last Whole Earth Catalog*: It's the only high-tech home I've found at all lovable.

> 1978 Kron & Slesin: Some people call this phenomenon 'the industrial style', but we call it 'high-tech'. High-tech . . . is a term currently used in architectural circles to describe buildings incorporating prefabricated . . . building components.

> 1980 *New Age* (US): A pocket calculator, a very high-tech gadget.

industrial action *n* (1971) action such as a strike, a go-slow, working to rule, etc., taken by industrial or other workers. It is useful as a cover-term, but there was almost certainly also a euphemistic impulse behind its coinage, avoiding the rebarbative *strike*. It was an obvious target for jokes about the inappropriateness of the word 'action'.

> 1971 *Times*: *The Times* regrets that, in common with other national newspapers, it will probably be unable to publish tomorrow because of industrial action.

Islamophobia *n* (1976) hatred or fear of Islam or Muslims. The term's profile did not begin to rise until the mid 1990s, when terrorist activities associated with Islamic fundamentalism started to impinge on the West.

> 1995 *Times*: I suspect that Islamophobia, under the guise of fundamentalist scaremongering, is being deliberately promoted in the overseas media.

job centre *n* (1972) a government office that lists and advertises current job vacancies in an area. As well as a sprucing up (see the quote below), Britain's labour exchanges got a new name (*labour exchange* dates from the 1860s): *job centre* is down-to-earth but snappy.

> 1972 *Times*: Forget about the Government employment exchanges . . . think about the bright, new offices with a new image and a sign outside saying *job centre*.

junk food *n* (1973) food that appeals to popular (especially juvenile) taste but has little nutritional value. The term originated in the US.

> 1973 *Washington Post*: How many children are going to fill up on junk foods and be too full to eat a nutritious lunch now?

kneecap *v* (1975) to shoot (someone) in the knee (or leg) as a form of punishment. The practice is associated with Northern Ireland, where it has been used against those who incurred the wrath of a terrorist organization.

> 1975 *Observer*: Ulster's gunmen have found they can get hold of Government cash by giving victims a 'knee-capping'—their grim colloquialism for a bullet in the legs . . . Kneecapping . . . has replaced tarring and feathering as the province's most common form of terrorist punishment . . . 'This so-called kneecapping is really a misnomer, because the kneecap itself is rarely touched.'

learning difficulties *n* (1975) difficulties experienced by a schoolchild in learning one or more subjects to the level of proficiency expected of his or her contemporaries, especially because of social problems or mental or physical handicap. This piece of educationists' jargon was intended to replace earlier synonyms (e.g. *backward*, *educationally subnormal*) which had become taboo (although in due course their schoolmates reportedly taunted such children in the playground with 'LD! LD!').

level playing field *n* (1979) a state or condition of parity or impartiality; fair play. The expression originated in the US. By the 1990s it had become a cliché, especially in the world of politics.

> 1988 *Independent*: The US side is opposed to subsidies, arguing they want 'a level playing field' if Canadians are allowed more access.

> 1995 *Accountancy*: They are still not providing a level playing field in terms of opportunities for women.

libber *n* (1971) a campaigner for a particular political freedom. A derivative of **lib (1969)**, in practice, when used on its own it is taken to mean 'women's liberationist'.

> 1971 *Telegraph* (Brisbane): Women's libbers are preparing to do battle with the police in Baltimore.

1973 *Times*: The Female Woman sorts out . . . the contemporary confusion of ideas about the sexes which the Libbers have . . . worse confounded.

loony left *n* (1977) the extreme left wing of a political party, especially the Labour Party, viewed as being extremist or fanatical. It was a favourite bugaboo term of the political right in the late 1970s and 80s, intended to make the voters' flesh creep. The left sometimes responded with *loony right* ('"Red Dawn", described widely as of the loony-right and paranoid, was not a very good movie', *New York Times Magazine* (1985)), but it lacked the alliteration that made *loony left* a success.

1977 *Economist*: The views of the loony left are well known in the democratic world.

1987 *City Limits*: The press has branded Deirdre Wood a 'loony lefty'.

marginalize *v* (1970) to render or treat as marginal; to remove from the centre or mainstream; to force or confine (an individual, social group, activity, etc.) to the periphery of any sphere or influence or operation. Originally a sociologists' term (perhaps adapted from French *marginaliser*, which occurs in this sense slightly earlier), it was taken up enthusiastically by various interest groups and liberation movements, and became one of the main social buzzwords of the 1980s.

1978 *Dædalus*: That Rousseau was self-taught . . . seemed to discredit and marginalize him all the more.

1987 Caryl Phillips: Society, taking its lead from the media and its politicians, begins to reject a whole class and marginalizes them in the job market.

megastar *n* (1976) an exceptionally famous, well-publicized, or successful superstar, especially in the world of entertainment.

1990 *She*: Sometimes, when I'm doing my shows, I [i.e. Edna Everage] see people in the audience slipping from their seats into a kneeling position and I say, 'Get up! Off your knees! Back into your seat!' After all, I'm just a megastar, no more than that.

me generation *n* (1978) applied to the people of the 1970s to characterize their supposedly obsessive preoccupation with personal fulfilment and self-gratification during that decade. Later the expression was re-applied to the people of the 1980s to characterize their supposed selfishness and materialism.

1978 *Journal of Technical Writing & Communication*: The 'me generation' is obsessed with self.

1985 *Sunday Telegraph*: At more than 60 American campuses, apartheid has suddenly inflamed the 'me generation' that was thought to be too materialistic to care.

mole *n* (1974) a secret intelligence agent who gradually achieves a position deep within the security defences of a country or organization. The term is also used more broadly to denote anyone within an organization or in a position of trust who betrays confidential information. The metaphor has been traced back as far as the 17th century (the underlying idea of someone burrowing away in the dark is a fairly obvious one), and certainly *mole* was used in an espionage context earlier in the 20th century ('I also have certain moles at my command . . . When the Cirque Doré mobilizes itself it has many eyes and ears', John Buchan (1925)), but its modern currency is due to its use by the British author of spy fiction John le Carré (see the first quote below for his account of its origins).

1976 John le Carré: A 'mole' is, I think, a genuine KGB term for somebody who burrows into the fabric of a bourgeois society and undermines it from within.

1984 *Times*: Clearly therefore, we suggest, this points to a 'mole' within British Telecom Prestel headquarters.

moment *n* ***at this moment in time*** (1972) now. This windy circumlocution became notorious in the 1970s and 80s.

1973 *Guardian*: The usual stuff about meaningful confrontations taking place . . . at this moment in time.

mover and shaker *n* (1972) a person who influences events, especially events of importance in the world. The expression has its origin in a line from 'Ode' (1874) by the English poet Arthur O'Shaughnessy (1844–81): 'Yet we are the movers and shakers Of the world for ever, it seems.' (The poem was set to music by Elgar as *The Music Makers* (1912). Its prevailing mood of wistful regret contrasts strangely with the thrustfulness of the expression for which it is now mainly remembered.) It is sometimes reversed to *shaker and mover*, and as it came into commoner use in the 1980s it was often shortened to simply *shaker*. It is usually used in the plural.

> 1972 Fletcher Knebel: The rich movers and shakers . . . always manage to manipulate the Congress for their own benefit and screw the rest of us.

> 1988 *Sunday Times*: Puttnam, 1963 edition, a 22-year-old proletarian meteor photographed by . . . David Bailey as one of a portfolio of Sixties shakers like Paul McCartney and Michael Caine.

network *v* (1976) to make use of one's membership of a 'network' of colleagues, friends, acquaintances, etc., usually on an informal basis, and especially for the exchange of information etc., or for professional or other advantage. The usage originated in the US.

> 1979 *Working Woman*: The way networking works in real life for both men and women goes something like this: when you need help, someone you have known over a period of time, for whom you have done services and favors of friendship, takes your need as the opportunity to return them.

> 1980 M. S. Welch: This book will show you how to network.

New Age *n* (1971) a cultural movement covering a broad range of beliefs and activities and characterized by a rejection of modern Western-style values and culture and the promotion of a more integrated or holistic approach in areas such as religion, medicine, philosophy, astrology, and the environment. The term, with its messianic overtones, was first used as long ago as the 1840s, and crops up from time to time in 19th- and early 20th-century theosophical and mystical writings, but it was the 1970s that saw its institutionalization. It is often used adjectivally.

> 1971 David Spangler: Findhorn strengthens this movement, sometimes called the 'New Age movement', and becomes a cornerstone of the universal foundation of new, inspired confidence.

> 1987 *Sunday Express Magazine*: Most of them listen to New Age music—waves lapping, whales calling, amplified heartbeats and so on. None of them listen to the Beach Boys.

new world order *n* (1977) the global balance of power following the end of the Cold War. As a general and somewhat poetically vague term for a transformed dispensation of human existence, *new world order* can be traced back as far as 1848, and by the 1890s it was being used in a more specifically political sense, denoting a new set of conditions, principles, laws, etc. governing world affairs. The shattering events of World War I provoked another peak in usage ('From Ladd's time to the present there has been a rapid increase of interest in plans for a new world order for the purpose of maintaining peace', F. C. Hicks (1920)), but probably its greatest impact has been its most recent one, as a coded reference to the triumph of the US and the West over the Communist world.

> 1977 *US News & World Report*: His basic aim: Build a new world order based on a U.S. commitment to moral values rather than an 'inordinate fear of Communism'.

> 1991 George Bush: And now, we can see a new world coming into view. A world in which there is a very real prospect of a new world order.

no-go area *n* (1971) an area to which entry is impossible or forbidden for specified people, groups, etc.

> 1971 *Guardian*: For journalists and others, the Bogside and Creggan estates are 'no-go' areas, with the IRA in total effective control.

> 1972 *Guardian*: The Duke of Norfolk has decreed the Royal Enclosure at Ascot a 'no-go' area for the miniskirted or hotpanted lass.

nouvelle cuisine *n* (1975) a style of originally French cooking that avoids traditional rich sauces and emphasizes the freshness of the ingredients and attractive presentation. The term is a borrowing from French, literally 'new cooking'. This was introduced in 1974 by the two French food critics Henri Gault and Christian Millau. Nouvelle cuisine was pioneered by the French chefs Paul Bocuse, Jean and Pierre Troisgros, and Michel Guérard (who introduced his own variation called *cuisine minceur*). Intensely fashionable in the late 1970s, it was subsequently reviled for merely painting pictures on a plate and leaving eaters in need of a square meal.

> 1978 Conran & Hobhouse: These three-star chefs have between them changed French cooking radically. The new style . . . which they have developed together over the years is called Nouvelle Cuisine, and its principles are that food should have a 'lyrical lightness'.

page three girl *n* (1975) a scantily-clad or nude female model whose picture appears as a pin-up in the popular press. The term was originally applied specifically to such a girl regularly featured on page three of the British tabloid *The Sun* (and the term *Page Three* was registered as a proprietary name by *The Sun*'s owners). The breakthrough display of nipples in a mass-market newspaper brought *The Sun* great commercial success in the 1970s and 80s.

> 1975 *Sun*: Lovely Jackie Brocklehurst makes her bow today as a super *Sun* Page Three girl.

passive smoking *n* (1971) the inhalation of smoke involuntarily from the tobacco being smoked by others, considered as a health risk. The term may be a translation of German *Passivrauchen*. The related *passive smoker* is first recorded in 1976.

> 1971 R. G. Richardson: Some studies give attention to the fact that non-smokers cannot avoid inhaling smoke when breathing smoky air, the so-called 'passive smoking'.

paternity leave *n* (1973) temporary absence from work granted to a man in the period up to and following the birth of his child.

> 1975 *Times*: The Greater London Council . . . agreed tonight that fathers on their staff should normally be allowed up to five days paternity leave.

person *n* (1971) used in place of *man* in a range of compound forms in order to avoid an invidious exclusion of women. It is mainly found in the titles of jobs and offices that can be held by either sex, but it is also used more widely in various fanciful and often allegedly amusing combinations (e.g. *henchperson*). Initially the earnest political correctness of some advocates of the usage made it the butt of heavy-handed humour, resulting in such nonce coinages as *Personchester* and *personhole cover*, but by the end of the 20th century it had been more or less comfortably absorbed into the language. Its plural is almost invariably *persons* rather than *people*. See also **chairperson (1971)**, **spokesperson (1972)**.

> 1971 *Scientific American*: If there is any doubt at the counter, let him show the salesperson this ad.

> 1972 *Listener*: Two young black women will almost certainly join Representative Shirley Chisholm in Congress . . . putting up the number of black 'Congresspersons' to at least 14.

> 1973 *Listener*: Chairperson Mitchell and her henchpersons looked at the way education brainwashes girls.

> 1976 *Oxford Times*: Builders' merchants require yardperson.

> 1976 *Journal of the Royal Society of Arts*: The exercise known amongst marketing men, or should I say marketing persons, as market segmentation.

personal computer *n* (1976) a computer designed for use by an individual, especially in an office or business environment. The term is commonly abbreviated to *PC*, which is first recorded in 1978.

> 1976 *Byte*: You can do such modelling . . . using the personal computer as a central element.

> 1982 *Computerworld*: Then the next year the PC (Personal Computer) came out and you saw that for $3,000 you could do the same thing you had paid all that money for.

plastic money *n* (1974) credit cards, debit cards, etc. as a method of payment. The colloquialism originated in the US. It was later shortened to simply **plastic (1980)**.

politically correct *adj* (1970) conforming to a body of liberal or radical opinion, especially on social matters, characterized by the advocacy of approved causes or views, and often by the rejection of language, behaviour, etc. considered discriminatory or offensive. The term, which originated in the US, is often used derisively by those who do not espouse such views. The expression is recorded as long ago as the late 18th century in the neutral sense 'correct from a political point of view' ('"The United States", instead of the "People of the United States", is the toast given. This is not politically correct', John Wilson (1793)), but as a term in its own right it had to await the liberalization of the 1960s and its backlash. The now frequent abbreviation **PC** is first recorded in 1986, the noun *political correctness* in 1979.

> 1970 Toni Cade: A man cannot be politically correct and a chauvinist too.
>
> 1986 *Los Angeles Times*: The key to this was found not in her message songs—like many of her ilk, she tends toward smug political correctness.
>
> 1991 *Village Voice* (New York): I've been chided by a reader for using the word *gringos* and informed that *European American* is politically correct.

proactive *adj* (1971) of a person, policy, etc.: that creates or controls a situation by taking the initiative or by anticipating events (as opposed to responding to them). The adjective has also been used latterly to mean 'innovative, tending to make things happen'. Its typical habitat is management or business jargon. It was coined from *pro* and *reactive*, perhaps with a subliminal memory of the earlier psychology term *proactive*, denoting a mental process that affects a subsequent process.

> 1971 A. J. R. Reiss: Citizens usually bring matters to police attention ... The police department deals with such requests as a reactive organization ... The police also acquire information by intervening in the lives of citizens on their own initiative. In this capacity, they serve as a proactive organization.
>
> 1985 *Globe & Mail* (Toronto): If you are the proactive and innovative individual we are looking for ... we invite you to submit a resume in confidence.

pro-choice *adj* (1975) in favour of upholding a woman's legal right to choose whether to have an abortion. The term originated in the US, and is first recorded as a noun, denoting a 'pro-choice' policy. It is essentially a euphemism for 'pro-abortion'.

> 1975 *Ms*: The legal battles ... have virtually all been decided in favour of pro-choice.
>
> 1986 *Parliamentary Affairs*: 'Pro-life' senators opposing those allied with the 'pro-choice' movement.

pro-life *adj* (1976) opposed to inducing abortions. Originally US, the term is first recorded in the derivative *pro-lifer*, denoting an anti-abortionist. It is one of the more obnoxious weasel-words thrown up by late-20th-century polemical word-coiners, implying as it does that those who wish women to be able to have abortions are against life. Out of the same stable, but less successful, was *pro-family* ('Some "pro-family" activists ... noisily pressed their antiabortion and "morality" platform', B. Frishman (1984)). Those opposed to this stance counter-coined with *anti-choice*, first recorded in 1978 ('What hypocrisy to call such anti-humanitarian people "pro-life". Call them what they are—antichoice', *Ms*).

> 1976 *National Observer* (US): Carter ... had misled proabortionists and prolifers.
>
> 1979 *Time*: As the oldest of eleven children (all married), I'd like to point out our combined family numbers more than 100 who vote only for pro-life candidates.

punk rock *n* (1971), **punk** *n* (1974) a loud, fast-moving style of rock music characterized by aggressive and deliberately outrageous lyrics and performance. Its most high-profile exponents were the band, The Sex Pistols. In the later 1970s punk developed in Britain into a youth cult whose adherents, *punk rockers* (1976), rejected middle-class values and standard pop culture and dressed in a provocative style (e.g. with spiky day-glo hairstyles and leather clothing with chains, safety pins, etc.). The original *punk* in *punk rock* came from the mainly US adjective *punk* 'worthless, rotten'.

> 1971 *Creem*: [Rudi Martinez is] doing the knee-drop, and the splits and every other James Brown move. He's the only one in punk-rock who's still got 'em and he's makin' a comeback.

> 1976 *Sunday Times*: Punk-rockers hate Mick Jagger (also, Led Zeppelin, Yes and Genesis) as much as they hate critics . . . Punk will fade. Its apologists are ludicrous.

quality time *n* (1977) time spent in giving someone one's undivided attention in order to strengthen a relationship, especially between a parent and child. The expression is a symptom of the manically busy last quarter of the 20th century in Western culture, when both parents usually went out to work and a special phrase had to be coined to denote time spent relaxing with their children.

> 1977 *Business Week*: The time they spend with their children is 'quality time, not quantity time,' say the mothers, echoing the claim of many executive fathers, and the children's home life is frequently more stimulating.

quango *n* (1973) a semi-public administrative body outside the civil service but financed by the exchequer and having members appointed by the government. The word is an acronym, but its elements are disputed: it is commonly explained as standing for *quasi-autonomous national government organization*, but this is not independently recorded before 1976, and it is considerably pre-dated by *quasi-nongovernmental organization* ('In recent years there has appeared on the American scene a new genus of organization which represents a noteworthy experiment in the art of government . . . We may call it the quasi nongovernmental organization', *Annual Report of the Carnegie Corporation* (1967)). Either way, its connotations are usually negative, suggesting placemanship and the exercise of undemocratic authority.

> 1973 Christopher Hood: It was the Americans who first drew attention to the importance of what they have labelled the 'grants economy', the 'contract state' and the 'quasi-non-government organisation' (Quango).

> 1979 *Daily Telegraph*: Anthony Barker of Essex University, describes the gathering as his act of atonement for having, he claims, invented the word quango . . . 10 years ago.

rap *n* (1979) a style of popular music developed by New York blacks in the 1970s in which words, usually improvised, are spoken rhythmically and often in rhyming sentences over an instrumental backing. *Rapper* and the related verb *rap* are also first recorded in 1979. The usage developed from **rap** 'improvised repartee' **(1965)**.

> 1979 *Billboard*: The Philadelphia-based rapper, Kurtis Blow, will soon record a 'Christmas Rapping' 12-inch record 'with holiday appeal'.

> 1982 *Face*: There is even a Rap single of 'Mama' available.

reality television *n* (1978) (a television genre consisting of) programmes that focus on non-fictional subject matter, primarily with the aim of providing entertainment rather than information. At first it concentrated mainly on the role of the 'fly-on-the-wall' documentary, following ordinary people around as they went about their quotidian tasks allegedly unaffected by the presence of the camera. Its surge in popularity in the 1990s, however, was based on placing people ('celebrities' as well as members of the public) in stressful or embarrassing situations and seeing how they would respond.

> 1978 *Newsweek*: The pilot episode shows a Washington, D.C., surgeon treating two severely burned children (one of whom dies) and, later, playing poker and driving his Jeep. 'This will be reality television,' promises NBC programming head Paul Klein. 'No actors will ever be used.'

> 2000 *New Scientist*: Viewers get jaded very quickly and want to see reality TV that degrades and demeans participants—for their entertainment, like a modern-day Roman circus.

right-on *adj* (1970) in accordance with received radical opinion of the time; also, more broadly, modern, trendy. The colloquialism originated in the US as a development of the exclamation *right on!* denoting full agreement or approval (' "Only in a capitalist society could art be turned to profit." "Right on",' *Melody Maker* (1970)), which is first recorded in 1925.

> 1970 *Time*: In Boston, Homans is known as a 'right-on lawyer'—he defends blacks, war protesters and poor people.
>
> 1976 *Spare Rib*: I had just read *Sappho was a Right-On Woman* by Sidney Abbott and Barbara Love.

safe sex *n* (1973) sexual activity in which precautions are taken (e.g. wearing a condom) to ensure that the risk of spreading sexually transmitted diseases, especially Aids, is minimized. It is also termed, less ambitiously, *safer sex*.

> 1990 *Mediamatic*: Part-parody, part safe-sex education, her presentation uses a combination of home movies, slides, vignettes.
>
> 1995 *Daily Telegraph*: John Bowis, the impressively girthed health minister, was in a Soho café for the launch of 'Cruise Cards', promoting 'safer sex'.

sell-by date *n* (1973) a date marked on food packaging to indicate the latest recommended date of sale, especially for perishable goods. The phrase is widely used metaphorically in such phrases as *past its sell-by date*, denoting obsolescence.

> 1973 *Which?*: Most of the date stamps will be 'Sell by . . . ' dates.
>
> 1987 *Daily Telegraph*: Socialism: the package that's passed its sell-by date.

sexual politics *n* (1970) the principles determining the relationship of the sexes. The term was coined by the feminist campaigner Kate Millett, and used by her as the title of a 1970 book.

> 1970 Kate Millett: The prospect of radical change in sexual politics . . . So we proceed to the counter-revolutionary sexual politicians themselves—Lawrence, Miller and Mailer.

Silicon Valley *n* (1974) an area in which industries associated with information technology are concentrated. The name was applied originally and specifically to the Santa Clara valley, southeast of San Francisco, where many leading US microelectronic firms are located. It was inspired by the use of silicon in making computer chips. A parallel area of Scotland, roughly between Glasgow and Edinburgh and containing IT towns such as Livingston, Cumbernauld, and Glenrothes, was nicknamed 'Silicon Glen'.

single currency *n* (1970) a currency proposed for use by the member states of the European Union (in full the *single European currency*), specifically one based on the **euro (1971)** and implemented in 1999. The term *single currency* is actually first recorded in 1900, but in a much more generalized application.

> 1975 *Economist*: Hopes for a single European currency by 1980 now look absurdly optimistic.
>
> 1995 *Independent*: So, the top political heads of Europe have concluded that the new single currency should be named after a prefix.

Sloane Ranger *n* (1975) an upper-class and fashionable but conventional young person, especially a female one who lives in London. The term replaces the *Lone* of *Lone Ranger* (a well-known hero of western stories and films) with *Sloane* (part of the name of *Sloane Square*, on the border of Belgravia and Chelsea, London, in or near which many such people live). It was coined by Martina Margetts, a sub-editor on *Harpers and Queen*, introduced to a wider world by the style writer Peter York in an article in that magazine in October 1975, and further defined by him and Ann Barr in the *Official Sloane Ranger Handbook* in 1982 (where the colloquial *Sloanie* is first recorded). It is often also shortened to simply *Sloane*.

> 1975 Peter York: The Sloane Rangers . . . are the nicest British Girl . . . The Sloane Rangers always add tone. They never put on prole accents, like self-conscious Oxford boys in the sixties . . . Once a Sloane marries and moves to Kennington and starts learning sociology through the Open University, she is off the rails . . . Sloane Ranger pet hates . . . incense, Norman Mailer.

> 1982 Barr & York: Sloane Rangers hesitate to use the term 'breeding' now (of people, not animals) but that's what background means... 'A Sloanie has a pony' is... ingrained in the Sloane mind.
>
> 1986 *Listener*: She has to be literally beaten by her mother into marrying Cary Elwes-Guildford—who resembles a low-grade Sloanie with a taste for whores and bad liquor.

smart *adj* (1972) of a weapon or other device: capable of some independent and seemingly intelligent action. The adjective is used especially in *smart bomb*, a powered missile which is guided to its target by an optical system. See also **smart card (1980)**.

> 1972 *Guardian*: Three out of four [missions] have been using 'smart' bombs.
>
> 1977 *Scientific American*: When smart traffic signals become ubiquitous and are linked to a control center, the traffic cop at the intersection will become obsolete.

spin *n* (1978) a bias or slant on information, intended to create a favourable impression when it is presented to the public. The term originated in the US, and is often in such phrases as *put a positive spin on*. The metaphor appears to come from baseball (or possibly pool), where spin is imparted to the ball to make it travel in the desired direction. It is a key term in late 20th- and early 21st-century news management, in which **spin doctors (1984)** are always keen to put the most favourable gloss on a story and journalists equally intent on removing it.

> 1978 *Guardian Weekly*: The CIA can be an excellent source [of information], though, like every other, its offerings must be weighed for factuality and spin.
>
> 1979 *Washington Post*: American spokesman Jody Powell gave a press briefing and put a negative spin on the talks.

spokesperson *n* (1972) someone authorized to speak on behalf of another person, group, or organization. The term was created as a non-sex-specific alternative to *spokesman* and *spokeswoman*, and has been one of the more successful and long-lived of such coinages (see also **person (1971)**).

> 1972 *Guardian*: The spokesperson (non-sexist term) for UCWR complained that she had been 'physically assaulted by a university administrator'.
>
> 1981 *Economist*: As a feminist fillip Miss Joan Lestor... has been made spokesperson for women's rights and welfare.

stealth *adj* (1979) denoting a branch of technology concerned with rendering aircraft hard to detect by radar, or an aircraft designed in accordance with this. The usage originated in the US. It is first recorded in 1979, but prefigured in 1975: 'Advanced Research Projects Agency has funded studies on high-stealth aircraft through USAF Aeronautical Systems Div.', *Aviation Week & Space Technology*. The futuristic and menacing shape and all-black coloration of the B2 *stealth bomber* (developed in great secrecy and used in the Gulf War) caught the public imagination.

> 1981 *New Scientist*: In the air the US will go ahead with the B1 bomber and will develop the 'Stealth' bomber, an aircraft that will employ as yet unperfected technology to make itself invisible to enemy radar.

streaking *n* (1973) the action of running naked in a public place. It was a craze of the early 1970s which began on US college campuses and has left its legacy in the occasional unclothed invader of sports grounds. *Streaker* is also first recorded in 1973, and the verb *streak* (a back-formation) in 1974.

> 1973 *Time*: Another statistic in a growing Los Angeles-area fad: streaking... Streakers generally race nude between two unpredictable points.
>
> 1974 *Runner's World Magazine*: During the winter of 1958–9 a group of us 'streaked' all over Berkeley.

street credibility *n* (1979) status or reputation amongst one's peers in the world of urban street youth culture. The shortened form *street cred* soon appeared (see **cred (1981)**).

1979 *Sounds*: Levine has real street credibility (not like some wimp who wears Mary Quant's latest range, went to public school and then tells the world he's as street level as the Cockney Rejects).

supermodel *n* (1977) a highly successful and internationally famous fashion model.

1992 *Sun*: Supermodel Claudia Schiffer has ditched her boyfriend to wed Prince Albert of Monaco, it was claimed last night.

surrogate *adj, n* (1978) a woman whose pregnancy arises from the implantation in her womb of a fertilized egg or embryo from another woman. The term is used adjectivally mainly in *surrogate mother*, but also sometimes applied to relatives of the woman who stand in an analogous position towards the child. The related noun *surrogacy*, hitherto rarely used in the general sense 'the position of a surrogate', is first recorded in 1982.

1978 *Times*: The demand for surrogates remained strong... Despite potential legal problems, some have already opted for surrogate mothers.

1982 Walters & Singar: The objections to surrogacy based on fears of financial exploitation... are very real.

televangelist *n* (1973) an evangelical preacher who uses the mass media, and particularly television, to promote especially fundamentalist doctrine. The term (and its derivative *televangelism*, first recorded in 1980) did not come into widespread use until the 1980s, when a range of sexual and financial scandals hit the headlines involving leading US televangelists such as Jim Bakker and Jimmy Swaggart. It is a blend of *television* and *evangelist*.

1987 *Independent*: With mutual hatreds now so vividly exposed, the 'televangelists' may find it difficult in future to retain the support of their flocks.

text message *n* (1978) a written message transmitted electronically. The term (now often simply *text* (2000) for short) arose in the US in the late 1970s in the context of computer networks, but it really came into its own in the 1990s, with the emergence of mobile phones capable of sending and receiving keyed messages. *Text messaging* (first recorded in 1982) became the fashionable mode of instant written communication, and spawned its own particular brand of highly condensed vocabulary (e.g. *CUL8R* 'see you later', *FYI* 'for your information', *NE1* 'anyone'). The verb *text*, in the sense 'to communicate (with) by means of a text message', is first recorded in 1998.

2000 *Independent*: Text messaging is now one of the most popular ways for a teenager to ask out that special someone... on a first date.

2001 *Press & Journal* (Aberdeen): Such was the host's concern that at 2am she sent a text message to one of her friends telling her what had happened and asking for assistance.

2001 *Leicester Mercury*: I texted my mother and my friends when I got my results.

Thatcherism *n* (1979) the political and economic policies advocated by Margaret Thatcher (b. 1925), British politician, leader of the Conservative Party from 1975 and Prime Minister 1979–90, especially as contrasted with those of earlier Conservative leaders. The main tenets of Thatcherism are generally held to be monetarism, privatization, and self-help. The noun and adjective *Thatcherite* is first recorded somewhat earlier, in 1976.

1976 *Economist*: Tory constituency rooms were by 1974 fuller of anti-Butler Thatcherites than Mr Heath dreamed.

1979 *Times*: The party was fighting off the shrill divisiveness of Thatcherism, with its simple monetarist policies.

touchy-feely, touchie-feelie *adj* (1972) a usually dismissive epithet applied to people given to the tactile expression of feelings (e.g. by touching and hugging), motivated by emotion rather than intellect. The term arose, in the US, out of the encounter groups of the 1960s, whose members often sought psychological benefit through close physical contact with each other.

> 1995 *Daily Telegraph*: We Greens are quite touchy-feely types. But because you go to a Green Party Conference it doesn't mean you want to be hugged all the time.

trainer *n* (1978) a soft running shoe without spikes; a training shoe (the term *training shoe* itself is first recorded in 1973). They started off as athletes' equipment but by the 1980s they were fashion items, particularly among teenagers.

> 1982 *New Society*: Skinny teenage boys in the ubiquitous parkas, jeans and trainers.

user-friendly *adj* (1977) easy to use; designed with the needs of users in mind. The term was originally used with reference to computers, but its range of application soon broadened out. This use of *-friendly*, too, quickly found imitators (e.g. *citizen-friendly* (1982)).

> 1979 *Interfaces*: User friendliness is a term coined by Harlan Crowder to represent the inherent ease (or lack of ease) which is encountered when running a computer system.
>
> 1984 *Listener*: No TV show (not even the news) could close without reference to this user-friendly family of dolls.

virus *n* (1972) a computer program or section of programming code which is designed to sabotage a computer system by causing itself to be copied into other parts of the system, often destroying data in the process. It was originally a science-fiction term; the real thing did not appear until the early 1980s, when the word *virus* was adopted for it.

> 1972 David Gerrold: You know what a virus is, don't you? . . . The VIRUS program does the same thing.
>
> 1984 Fred Cohen: We define a computer 'virus' as a program that can 'infect' other programs by modifying them to include a possibly evolved copy of itself . . . The concept was first introduced in this seminar by the author, and the name 'virus' was thought of by Len Adleman.

whistle-blower *n* (1970) someone who reveals (discreditable) secrets about an organization, especially one to which he or she belongs. The term originated in the US, based on the expression *blow the whistle* 'to expose wrongdoing', which is first recorded in 1934.

> 1970 *New York Times*: When they reflect more fully on how well the majority leader handled a whistle-blower and protected their interests.

word processor *n* (1970) a keyboard device incorporating a computer programmed to store, amend, and format text that is keyed in, a printer to print it automatically, and usually also a screen to display it. In the coming decades it was to revolutionize many aspects of text production and render old typesetting and secretarial skills redundant. Also first recorded in 1970 is *word processing*, denoting the storing and organizing of texts by electronic means, especially using a word processor.

> 1970 *Administrative Management*: In 1970 . . . ITEL . . . introduced its 'Word Processor' . . . 'Word processing', a concept that combines the dictating and typing functions into a centralized system.
>
> 1984 David Lodge: A roomful of secretaries . . . would wait patiently beside their word-processors, ready to type . . . his latest reflections.

zero tolerance *n* (1972) non-acceptance of antisocial and especially criminal behaviour, typically by strict and uncompromising application of the law. This political slogan of the law-and-order lobby originated in the US and spread to Britain in the 1990s.

> 1982 *Christian Science Monitor*: Beyond its 'zero tolerance' for drug abuse, the Navy also wants to root out another problem, alcohol abuse.
>
> 1997 *Daily Telegraph*: The Labour leader pledged his support for 'zero tolerance' schemes pioneered in New York.

The 1980s

The 1980s are chiefly remembered for money. Not only was there a lot of it about in the Western economies: those who had it relished it, boasted about it, consumed conspicuously with it, even worshipped it. To be *seriously* rich was no trivial matter. It was the decade of *dosh* 'money' (1953). The financial sector contributed generous amounts of new vocabulary to the English language, as did the changes in society brought about by the considerable rearrangements of wealth.

Politically, deregulation was in the air. Patience with post-war state controls was wearing thin, and people were ready to pass the levers of power into the hands of a right-wing government that would allow (or promise) more scope for individual initiative (in Britain, the Conservative Thatcher government had come into office in 1979, and by the end of 1980 the American electorate had voted the Republican Ronald Reagan into the presidency). In the world of high finance, this meant a clearing away of restrictions on how the money men were permitted to operate, and on the sort of fiscal schemes and manoeuvrings they could indulge in. As far as the British stock market was concerned, the climactic moment was the *Big Bang* of October 1986, which removed a whole range of previous restrictive practices. All the novel phenomena required names, and the fertile brains of financiers (at home with a menagerie of bulls, bears, and stags) obliged with an array of outlandish metaphors that have come to symbolize the decade: *dawn raid* and *white knight*, *golden hello* and *golden parachute*, *greenmail* and *grey market* and *swaption*. Readers of the financial and business columns of the newspapers would puzzle over *arbs* and *derivatives*, new acronyms like *EFTPOS* and *EPOS*, *PEP* and *PIN*, new concepts such as *ethical* investment and *internal markets*. In the Far East the *tiger* (or *dragon*) economies of Hong Kong, Singapore, South Korea, and Taiwan were cranking themselves up, and from Japan came the notion of *zaitech* (corporate investment in financial markets). Payment increasingly meant *plastic*, with the prospect of being able to *swipe* your *smart card*. Britain now had *pound coins*, but hard cash was further threatened by *telebanking*. The bubble of economic euphoria was burst on *Black Monday* (19 October 1987), when share prices around the world hit the floor. Was it just a *blip*, or was a long recession on the way? Only the 1990s would tell.

People who had a lot of money in their pocket were intent on spending it—and not discreetly. If you had it, you flaunted it; it was the era of *conspicuous consumption* (1899), of *loadsa* money. The quintessential figure of the decade was the *yuppie*, the high-earning 25–30-year-old business executive, lawyer, stockbroker, etc. with the smart car, the *mobile phone* (1945) (or *cellphone*), and the *Filofax* (1931) (or *personal organizer*). The raison d'être of the coinage was a *lifestyle* (1961), and it was to be the first of a rash of such lifestyle coinages. The lexical fashion fad of the 1980s left a legacy of *buppies* 'black yuppies', *dinkies*, and *woopies* 'well-off older people', not to mention non-acronyms such as *empty-nester. Stressed-out thirty-somethings* relaxed in *wine bars*, *shopaholics* shopped till they dropped, the *chattering classes* chattered, *foodies* held olive-oil tastings, and *power-dressing* was the fashion statement that mattered. The tabloids entertained their readers with tales of *bimbos* 'attractive but empty-headed young women' (1920) and *himbos* 'male bimbos', *bimbettes* 'adolescent bimbos' and *toy boys*.

But if the rich got richer in the 1980s, the poor also got poorer. The supposed benefits of *trickle-down* (1944), by which economic improvements eventually reach the less well-off, were slow to show themselves. The *underclass* (1918), a class of the poor and disadvantaged, was growing; *cardboard cities*, where the homeless slept in cardboard boxes, were appearing. While politicians were berating the **dependency culture (1973)**, growing unemployment swelled the numbers on *income support* and attending *job clubs*. No employee seemed safe from the dreaded *UB40*, the card issued to unemployment benefit claimants in Britain. This was the world not of the sharp suit but of the *shell suit* (a type of tracksuit commonly associated with the lower classes). The happy partying of the early part of the decade had given way to the sound of *lager louts* breaking glass.

The political mantras of the decade were *privatize* (1970) (see **privatization (1959)**) and *monetarist* (1963). In Britain, Margaret Thatcher proclaimed the *enterprise culture* and the joy of *marketization* 'exposure to market forces'. Her government (bone-*dry* by the middle of the decade, having been purged of *wets*) pursued the *feel-good factor*, but managed to upset Middle England with the *poll tax* (officially named the *community charge*). The *leaderene* (a mocking title applied to Mrs Thatcher) gained a reputation for *handbagging* 'verbally assaulting' all who tried to thwart her. Meanwhile, self-destructive tendencies within the Labour Party led the *Gang of Four* (Roy Jenkins, David Owen, William Rodgers, and Shirley Williams) to break away and form the *SDP* 'Social Democratic Party' (later combined with the Liberals to become the *Liberal Democrats*); its main contribution to the English language during its brief career was *fudge and mudge* (denoting prevarication). Television arrived in the British parliament, and with it the strange practice of *doughnutting* 'clustering round a parliamentary speaker to give an impression of a large and attentive audience'. *Emily's list* (from an acronym based on 'early money is like yeast') set out to increase the number of women MPs. Ominously, the terms *sleaze* and *spin doctor* appeared for the first time in the political lexicon.

On the international scene, the 80s got into their stride with the Falklands War (1982), the winning of which (despite the obfuscation of *Haigspeak*, the tortured vocabulary of US Secretary of State Alexander Haig) did wonders for Margaret Thatcher's electoral prospects (the so-called *Falklands factor*). The conflict's lexical legacy (*Argie*, an insult word for Argentinians; an unpleasant new use of *gotcha*; and the verb *yomp*) was for the most part mercifully short-lived.

The nuclear stakes were being raised by *SDI* (the 'Strategic Defense Initiative', popularly known as *Star Wars*), a futuristic scheme for defence against Soviet missiles on which the US saw fit to spend the profits of *Reaganomics* (the economic policies of Ronald Reagan). The deployment of cruise missiles in Britain led to the establishment of *peace camps* (encampments of peace protesters), and there were chilling forecasts of *nuclear winter*, but disarmament diplomacy continued, adding *build-down* 'reduction of nuclear armaments', *START* 'Strategic Arms Reduction Talks', and *zero option* 'the giving up of all nuclear missiles on both sides' to its bizarre lexicon. The Soviet monolith was breaking up, a process which propelled the terms *glasnost* and *perestroika* temporarily into the English language. The satellite states of eastern Europe grasped their independence (Czechoslovakia in a *velvet revolution*), and by the end of the decade it was clear that the forty-year Cold War was over—and that the West had won it.

In the 1980s, *cyberspace* infiltrated the interstices of the everyday world. Computer technology leaped ahead, enriching the English language with *dongle* (a device enabling a copy-protected program to run) and *toggle* (a key for switching between operations). Only an ageing minority were not, it seemed, *computerate*, and able to cope with *booting*, *downloading*, and *dragging*, recognize an *icon* or a *spreadsheet*, or use a *laptop*, a *palmtop*, or a *touchpad*. While the grown-ups were *teleworking* (working from home via a computer link), the kids could play *Pac-man* or *Game Boy*. *Hackers* were becoming a problem, but there were now *vaccines* to counter the threat of viruses. Increasingly, though, the computer's most pervasive influence on the modern world lay in the area of communication. It was the decade which saw the beginnings of the *Internet* and the *information superhighway*, of *e-mail* and the *telecottage* (a communal computer resource), of *domains* (areas within a computer network) and *newsgroups* (computerized discussion groups). The days of *snail mail* were numbered. The era of the *virtual* was coming.

The media was transforming itself on all fronts. *DBS* (satellite television) arrived, and *dishes* (or in a few cases *Squarials*—square (or strictly diamond-shaped) aerials) sprouted all over the country. *Infotainment* was on offer, and *rolling news* (complete with *sound bites*). Alternatively, if you had a *camcorder*, you could make your own *video nasty* (but preferably not a *splatter* movie—one featuring graphic violence). Sounds were portable in the shape of *ghetto-blasters* and *Walkmans*, and the enticing *jewel boxes* (plastic cases) of CDs filled the record-shop shelves. *Chatlines* and *helplines* reflected a revitalized telephone industry. In the increasingly competitive world of print journalism, reporters *doorstepped* their victims and indulged in *feeding frenzies* (voracious competition for news stories). It was not a decade for the shy and retiring: the representative media figure was perhaps the *shock jock* (a talk-radio host specializing in provocation and abuse).

Environmental concerns grew ever more powerful, as the extent of human depredations became increasingly evident. We embraced the concept of *biodiversity*, eagerly bought *eco-friendly* and *cruelty-free* products, nodded over the necessity for a *carbon tax*, and supported the construction of *wind farms*. From its fringes (*eco-terrorists* and *New Age travellers*) to its solid middle-class centre, the environmental movement was a force to be reckoned with.

One of the key facts of the decade was *Aids*. Unknown at its beginning, by 1989 its terminology was familiar wherever English was spoken: *buddy* 'Aids patient's helper', *HIV*, *PWA* 'person with Aids' (some areas of the world had a different name for it: *slim* in Africa, for instance). The official answer was *safe sex* (1973): not an easy concept to popularize at a time when the media were obsessed by *bonking*. Nevertheless, *Femidoms* (intravaginal contraceptive sheaths) and *dental dams* (to prevent infection during oral sex) were added to the prophylactic armoury. (For purely contraceptive purposes there was the *abortion pill* or, if it was too late for that, the reviled *abortuary*—a polemical term for an abortion clinic.) Other diseases lined up to attack us: *ME* (or *yuppie flu*), *repetitive strain injury*, *sick-building syndrome*. Then there was all that *technostress* to deal with. Nor did our animals escape: cattle succumbed in droves to the dreaded *BSE* (colloquially *mad cow disease*), and suddenly beef was off the menu.

A prolific and vibrant youth culture produced a myriad new dances and styles of music (many of them of *hip-hop* origin). There was *moshing* (involving violent body contact), *body-popping* (characterized by robotic, jerking movements), and *moonwalking*, *break-dancing*, *dirty dancing* (involving close-range hip gyrations), and *slam dancing* (with deliberate violent collisions) (there was also *lap dancing*, but that was not the same sort of thing at all). It was the decade of *acid house*, *raves*, and *warehouse parties* (for dancing to pop music), of *goths* (with dark clothes and make-up) and *greboes* (with long hair and anarchic musical tastes) and *thrash metal* (a very fast punk-influenced type of heavy metal), of the *lambada* and the *bhangra* beat (from Brazil and the Punjab respectively). *Garage* took on a whole new meaning—'a soul-influenced New York variety of house music'. It was a culture that got its highs from *ecstasy* (or *Es*, or *Adam*). *Designer drugs* were the fashion of the decade, *Prozac* the favourite happy pill, and *crack* the new market leader.

Youth slang shuffled its approval words with enough dexterity to keep adults guessing. One moment it was *crucial*, the next *wicked*. *Brill*, *fabby*, *gnarly*, *massive*, *mega*, *radical*, and *tubular* all had their turn at one time or another.

Meanwhile, *PC* language made further strides. Pets became *animal companions*, prostitutes *sex workers*, and to avoid charges of *ableism*, any deviation from the norm had to be described in terms of being *challenged. Fattist* or *sizeist* comments were to be severely discouraged. Even in a *post-feminist* age, *person* was still alive and well and producing offspring: *waitperson.* The *New Man* proudly made his debut (although alas within a decade he would have transformed himself into a *New Lad*).

abled *adj* (1981) able-bodied; not disabled. This was a polemical coinage, formed in contradistinction to *disabled*, and often used euphemistically as the second element in compounds (particularly *differently abled*) seeking to avoid the negative associations of *disabled*.

> 1981 *Washington Post*: The disabled vary like the abled. Some are terminally ill, some are teen-agers paralyzed by car accidents.

> 1990 *Amateur Stage*: All the young members of this group suffer from cerebral palsy but insisted 'We are not disabled, we are differently abled'.

acid house *n* (1988) a type of house music (see **house (1986)**) with a very fast beat, a spare, mesmeric, synthesized sound, and usually a distinctive gurgling bass noise. The term is also applied to the youth cult associated with this music, characterized by a vogue for warehouse parties (dances held in large venues), a revival of psychedelia, and the taking of hallucinogenic drugs. *Acid* may well be the slang term for LSD (see **acid (1966)**), although many cultists claimed that it came from the record *Acid Trax* by Phuture (in the slang of Chicago, where this music originated in 1986, *acid burning* was slang for 'stealing', and the music relies heavily on 'sampling', a polite word for stealing musical extracts).

> 1988 *Observer*: Drugs fear as the 'acid house' cult revives a Sixties spectre . . . 'Acid house' started in four London clubs . . . In the past month it has 'taken off', spreading to other clubs throughout the country.

Aid *n* (1984) used as the second element in the names of events etc. organized to raise money for particular charitable causes. The original one was *Band Aid*, based on the name of the rock music group formed by Bob Geldof in October 1984 to raise money for famine-relief in Ethiopia. It was followed by *Live Aid* and many others.

> 1984 *Times*: *Do They Know It's Christmas*, [a record] on which Boy George, Sting, George Michael, members of Duran Duran, Status Quo, and U2 appear under the joint name of Band Aid.

> 1985 *Times*: The failure of Live Aid to penetrate the poorer countries is unlikely to affect adversely the amount of money it makes.

> 1985 *Times*: The fashion world is smouldering with gossip about Fashion Aid, which takes off like a rocket at the Albert Hall tonight.

Aids, AIDS *n* (1982) an acronym formed from the initial letters of *acquired immune deficiency syndrome* (also first recorded in 1982), denoting an illness (often if not always fatal) in which opportunistic infections or malignant tumours develop as a result of a severe compromising of the body's immune system, which is itself caused by earlier infection with a retrovirus, **HIV (1986)**, transmitted in sexual fluids and blood.

> 1982 *Morbidity & Mortality Weekly Report* (US Centers for Disease Control): CDC defines a case of AIDS as a disease, at least moderately predictive of a defect in cell-mediated immunity, occurring in a person with no known cause for diminished resistance to that disease . . . The infant had no known contact with an AIDS patient.

> 1985 *Daily Telegraph*: A cancer clinic in the Bahamas has been ordered to close . . . after two patients . . . were given serum infected with HTLV-III, the deadly virus which causes Aids.

A-list *n* (1984) a (notional) roster of the most celebrated or sought-after individuals (often in the context of their desirability as guests and the prestige they confer on the events they attend); hence, a social or professional elite. The term originated in the US, and is often used adjectivally to denote pre-eminence and prestigiousness. The possibilities of a hypothetical hierarchy are also occasionally explored further down—e.g. *B-list* and (the dregs) *Z-list*.

> 1990 *Sunday Times*: Even so, in the trade's terms, it was an A-list event, graced by such luminaries as Derek Cooper, Paul Levy and Lady Arabella Boxer.

anorak *n* (1984) a boring, studious, or socially inept young person (caricatured as typically wearing an anorak); especially, one who pursues an unfashionable and solitary interest with obsessive dedication. The colloquialism, which equates the wearing of an anorak with nerdiness, is British.

> 1995 Jayne Miller: The Beatles have become almost an obsession. I try to get out-takes and rare records, I'm almost anorak level about it—getting really excited if I can hear John Lennon cough.

Argie *n, adj* (1982) (an) Argentinian. It is decidedly a term of contempt, used initially in the context of the Anglo-Argentinian conflict over sovereignty of the Falkland Islands (1982) and occasionally revived subsequently by British tabloid headline-writers (e.g. for Anglo-Argentinian soccer matches).

> 1982 *Daily Telegraph*: We yelled at the Argies.

> 1982 *Private Eye*: It is my proud privilege to loan the ship to the British Government for use in our heroic crusade against the Argie hordes.

> 1998 *Sun*: *Sun* prayer mats can't foil Argies.

awesome *adj* (1980) marvellous, wonderful, stunning. The slang usage originated in and is mainly restricted to US English. It is a meaning that has dribbled down from the original 'awe-inspiring' via 'remarkable' (which dates from the early 1960s), part of the perennial search for new ways to enthuse, and further ammunition for the 'English-going-to-the-dogs' faction.

> 1982 *Guardian*: It's so awesome, I mean, fer shurr, toadly, toe-dully!

> 1986 *Making Music*: I just know it'd be an awesome band.

balti *n* (1984) a type of cooking from northern Pakistan, characterized by highly spiced dishes typically served in wide metal pans (*balti* means literally 'bucket' in Urdu) accompanied by nan bread. Restaurants serving this cuisine (known as *balti houses*) began to appear in Birmingham in the early 1980s (an area to the south of Birmingham city centre became known colloquially as the 'Balti Triangle'), and had spread nationwide in Britain by 1990.

> 1984 *Curry Magazine*: Can anyone tell me what Balti is?... Some unusual dishes on the menu are Curried Quail, Balti chicken or meat.

> 1987 *Good Food Guide 1988*: Highlights are the superb balti dishes, cooked and served in blackened iron pans.

Big Bang *n* (1986) a colloquial name for the deregulation of the London Stock Exchange on 27 October 1986, when a number of complex changes in trading practices were put into effect simultaneously. People had been working their way towards the metaphor (which is of course based on the name of the theory of instantaneous creation of the universe—see **big bang (1950)**) for some years (for instance, 'It is argued that a "big bang" approach, with all changes in Stock Exchange rules taking place on a single day..., would allow firms to make rational plans', *Financial Times* (1983); and again, 'The removal of the minimum commissions guaranteed to the 250-member firms of the [Stock] Exchange is now likely to happen in one go—by what is known as the "big bang" approach', *Times* (1984)).

> 1986 *Sunday Express*: After the Big Bang tomorrow, the City will never be the same again... From tomorrow,... the distinction between brokers and jobbers disappears.

biodiversity *n* (1987) diversity of animal and plant life, as represented by the number of extant species. The term was reportedly proposed by Walter G. Rosen in 1986. Diversity of life forms is seen as essential to keeping the machinery of the earth going—as many farmers who embraced monoculture in the 1960s later came to realize.

> 1987 *Nature*: Here biodiversity increases with the introduction of understory vegetation.

blip *n, v* (1983) a temporary movement in statistics, usually in an unexpected or unwelcome direction; hence any kind of temporary problem or hold-up. As a verb, *blip* is used to denote figures suddenly rising on a graph. The underlying idea is of a blip or sudden peak on a radar trace. The usage emerged from financial jargon into the public domain in Britain in 1988, when the Chancellor of the Exchequer, Nigel Lawson, reportedly announced that a large increase in the Retail Price Index was just a 'temporary blip'.

> 1989 *Listener*: Nigel Lawson's dilemma is the Conservative Party's also. Is the first tremor on its happy political landscape merely 'a blip', as the Chancellor has called the storm that has gradually engulfed him?

> 1989 *New York Times*: Prices moved higher during overnight trading, and blipped a shade higher still following the release of the G.N.P. figures.

boot *v* (1980) to prepare (a computer) for operation by causing an operating system to be loaded into its memory from a disc or tape, especially by means of a fixed sequence of instructions; also, to cause (an operating system or a program) to be loaded in this way. The word is an abbreviation of the synonymous *bootstrap* (1953), the underlying idea of which is that the first-loaded instructions pull the subsequent ones up 'by their bootstraps'. It is often used with *up*.

> 1986 *Courier-Mail* (Brisbane): If you boot up your system without the keyboard being plugged in, you will see an error message.

> 1986 *What Micro?*: Once you boot up and run the new Mac one difference is immediately apparent.

Botox *n* (1986) a proprietary name for a preparation of botulinum toxin which is injected into a muscle to cause temporary paralysis, either as part of the treatment of various medical conditions or in the cosmetic treatment of facial wrinkles, especially frown lines and crow's feet. At first it was a term known only to medical science, but in the mid 1990s, as word of the substance's supposedly miraculous rejuvenative qualities spread, it was (almost literally) on everyone's lips, and lost no time in transmuting into a verb (first recorded in 1994).

> 2002 *Daily Telegraph*: Men tend to have much deeper lines on their foreheads, so Botox is the perfect treatment for them.

> 2003 *Food & Travel*: The inner lagoons and beaches are as tranquil and unruffled as a Botoxed brow.

break-dancing *n* (1982) a style of dancing popularized by US blacks, often individual or competitive, and characterized by a loud insistent beat to which dancers perform energetic and acrobatic movements, sometimes spinning around on their backs on the pavement or floor. It was pioneered during the late 1970s by teams of black teenage dancers in the south Bronx, New York City. The original literal meaning was dancing to fill the 'break' in a piece of rap music.

> 1983 *Daily News*: They are young street dudes, nearly all of them black, anywhere from 10 to 23 years old, and what they are doing is a new style of dancing known as 'breaking' or 'break dancing'. It is the first new dance phenomenon in the cities in more than a decade.

BSE *n* (1987) an abbreviation of *bovine spongiform encephalopathy* (also first recorded in 1987), a fatal neurological disease of cattle characterized by behavioural disorders including unsteady gait and nervousness. It was first identified in Britain in 1986, and is thought to have been caused by feeding infected animal products to cattle. Its jaw-cracking name was usually either abbreviated to *BSE* or colloquialized to **mad cow disease (1988)**. The term *human BSE* (1990) was used originally to designate Creutzfeldt-Jakob disease (*CJD*), and latterly more specifically new variant CJD (see **nvCJD (1996)**).

> 1987 *Economist*: Bovine spongiform encephalopathy (BSE) twists the tongues of vets and wrecks the brains of cows.

> 1993 *Guardian*: If man is susceptible to BSE, then at least 8 million adults are likely to have eaten enough to get Creutzfeldt-Jakob Disease.

camcorder *n* (1982) a portable video camera incorporating a built-in video recorder. The word is a blend of *camera* and *recorder*. The earlier term *videocamera* (first recorded in 1978) does not imply a recording facility.

> 1982 *Economist*: Manufacturers of video tape recorders . . . have agreed that these 'camcorders' will all use the same standard 8mm. video tape.

cashback *n* (1988) a facility offered by retailers (especially supermarkets) by which a customer can withdraw a limited amount of cash when making a credit or debit card purchase, the amount of which is added to the bill. It is an adaptation of the earlier usage, 'an incentive to buyers by which in return for purchasing something they receive a cash refund' (first recorded in 1973).

> 1993 *Daily Mail*: Nearly one in ten now gets cash elsewhere, often from a supermarket. For example, Sainsbury's has a cash-back scheme, which allows you to add extra to your bill if you pay by debit card.

CD ROM *n* (1983) a compact disc (see **compact disc (1979)**) on which text or data is stored and which is used as a read-only memory. It revolutionized the publishing business, making it possible to offer large reference works and commercial databases from which a maze of information is available at the touch of a computer key.

> 1983 *Electronics*: The CD ROM, which is expected to hit the market next year, can hold 525 megabytes of formatted data.

cellphone *n* (1984) a hand-held or mobile radio-telephone providing access to a cellular radio network. It remains the preferred term for a *mobile phone* in US English.

> 1984 *Cellular Busines*: The Cellphone is available now with a suggested price of $1,995.

> 1989 *Satellite Times*: There were only about half a dozen others . . . taking trans-Atlantic phone calls on a cellphone.

challenged *adj* (1985) disabled, handicapped. The usage originated in North America. It became one of the highest-profile politically correct euphemisms of the 1980s, inspired by replacing the negative connotations of 'handicap' with a more positive notion of rising to a challenge. It was, however, easily mocked: alongside serious usages like *physically challenged* and *mentally challenged* came facetious coinages such as *vertically challenged* 'short', *follicularly challenged* 'bald', and *hymenally challenged* 'non-virginal'.

> 1985 *New York Times*: The disabled skiers, whom Mr. Kennedy prefers to call 'physically challenged', achieve speeds on difficult runs that would be daunting to most competitors.

> 1995 *Freedom: Canada's Guide for the Disabled*: Sources suggest that there may be well over four million people in Canada considered as challenged due to a wide variety of disabilities.

> 1996 *Good Food*: Celebrity chefs . . . take centre stage and teach the culinarily-challenged to cook.

chattering classes *n* (1985) a social group consisting of articulate members of the educated middle class, typically seen as holding liberal opinions (notably opposition to the Thatcher government of the 1980s) and given to debating social, political, or cultural issues amongst themselves. The expression is a British colloquialism, and usually used with dismissive contempt (generally by someone who might him- or herself be regarded as belonging to the group). It was reportedly coined by the journalist Frank Johnson in the early 1980s, and popularized by Alan Watkins in *The Observer*.

> 1987 *Daily Telegraph*: Does anybody really care who is elected Chancellor of the University of Oxford? Only the chattering classes are exercised.

chill *v* (1985) to pass time idly; to hang around, especially with other members of a group. It originated in the US, and is usually followed by *out*. It is a development of the earlier slang *chill* (*out*) 'to relax, calm down, take it easy', which is first recorded in 1979.

> 1985 J. Simmons et al.: Now the Adidas I possess for one man is rare Myself, homeboy, got fifty pair Got blue and black 'cause I like to chill And yellow and green when it's time to get ill.

> 1988 *New Musical Express*: The perfect Xmas prezo would be to spend it at home 'chilling out' . . . with the Schoolly family.

crack *n* (1985) a potent highly addictive crystalline form of cocaine made by heating a mixture of it with baking powder and water until it is hard, and breaking it into small pieces which are inhaled or smoked for their stimulating effect. The term originated in US slang. Since the late 1980s it has been widely used in the fuller form *crack cocaine*, especially in official parlance. It refers both to the fact that the hard-baked substance has to be 'cracked' into small pieces for use, and to the 'cracking' sound the pieces make when smoked. *Crackhead* for someone who habitually takes or is addicted to crack cocaine is first recorded in 1986.

> 1985 *San Francisco Chronicle*: The cocaine freebase, the purest and most dangerous form of coke, goes by a number of street names—crack, rock, pasta, basa—and is smoked in a pipe rather than snorted.

> 1986 *US News & World Report*: Crack . . . has rocketed from near obscurity to national villainy in the past six months.

> 1986 *Time*: A recent survey . . . indicates that . . . more than half the nation's so-called crackheads are black.

cred *n* (1981) credibility, reputation, status amongst one's peers. The word was originally used in the phrase *street cred*, a shortening of **street credibility (1979)**, but gradually the emphasis shifted from the sharp world of urban street culture to mere fashionability or 'hipness', and the *street* was quietly dropped. Later still *cred* came to be used adjectivally, meaning 'fashionable, trendy'.

> 1981 *Guardian Weekly*: A couple of expressions have only come my way in the last month or so. One is 'street wise' and the other 'street cred'.

> 1985 *International Musician*: I know that walking down main street with an oboe in hand does nothing for the street cred.

> 1986 Bob Geldof: 'Cred' was achieved by your rhetorical stance and no one had more credibility than the Clash.

> 1991 *Hot Air*: Annie Nightingale's got the most cred show in the air . . . Tune in and groove.

cyberspace *n* (1982) the notional environment within which electronic communication takes place, especially when represented as the inside of a computer system; space perceived as such by an observer but generated by a computer system and having no real existence; the space of virtual reality. The term was coined by the science-fiction writer William Gibson, and first used by him in a short story in 1982. He based it on **cybernetics (1948)**. It became the progenitor of a wide range of *cyber-* compounds in the 1980s and 90s, relating to computer-mediated electronic communications, the use of the Internet, and virtual reality—for example, *cybernaut*, *cyberart*, *cyberhippy*, *cyberlawyer*, *cyberworld*. See also **cybercafé (1994)**.

> 1984 William Gibson: Molly was gone when he took the trodes off, and the loft was dark. He checked the time. He'd been in cyberspace for five hours.

> 1993 *Guardian*: The search for a kidnapped girl from a small town in California has leapt into cyberspace as her picture criss-crosses the world's computer networks, databases and electronic mail systems.

dawn raid *n* (1980) a swift operation effected early in stock-market trading whereby a stockbroker obtains for his or her client a markedly increased shareholding in a company (often preparatory to a take-over) by clandestine buying from other substantial shareholders. The practice was an early example of the financial piracy of the 1980s.

> 1981 *Bookseller*: Following his 'dawn raid' last July, which gained him 29·4 per cent of BPC, Robert Maxwell . . . clearly plans to secure and consolidate his control of the group.

designer drug *n* (1983) a drug synthesized to mimic a legally restricted or prohibited drug without itself being subject to such restriction. The term is also used more broadly to denote any recreational drug with an altered structure. It imports the 'fashionability' implications of **designer (1966)**.

1983 *Sacramento Union*: Thirty-four people have died in the last four years after using 'designer drugs', heroin look-alikes concocted in underground laboratories and hitting the streets one step ahead of government regulations.

dinky *n* (1986) an acronym coined (on the model of **yuppie (1982)**) from the initial letters of *double* (or *dual*) *income, no kids*, denoting either partner of a usually professional working couple who have no children (*yet*, as the final *-y* is sometimes interpreted) and are characterized, especially by advertisers and marketers, as affluent consumers with few domestic demands on their time and money—in other words, the perfect target. The term originated in North America. The abbreviated *dink* is first recorded in 1987 (the surprise registered in the final quote below is no doubt due to the fact that *dink* is also US slang for 'penis', 'twerp', and 'Communist Vietnamese soldier'). Similar but less successful coinages in the lifestyle-acronym-mad mid 1980s included *oink* 'one income, no kids' and *tinkie* 'two incomes, nanny, and kids'.

1987 *Observer*: People who will live in Docklands are empty nesters, dinkies, two incomes, two cars.

1987 *New York*: When a friend referred to two young professionals as 'a couple of dinks', it was a bit surprising . . . Double Income, No Kids.

download *v* (1980) to transfer (especially software) from the storage of a larger computer system to that of a smaller one.

1982 *Which Computer?*: The existing software . . . will be down-loaded onto the new machine.

dry *n* (1983) a politician, especially a member of the British Conservative Party, who advocates economic stringency and individual responsibility, and uncompromisingly opposes high government spending. The term is used mainly in specific contrast with **wet (1980)**.

1984 *Times*: It is hard to see economic dries such as Mr. Ridley buying the channel tunnel arguments now.

eco-friendly *adj* (1989) not harmful to the environment; also applied to products manufactured with explicit regard to the environment.

1989 *Daily Telegraph*: The only way that eco-friendly products are going to take off is for them to be presented by manufacturers and retailers as high tech and modern.

ecstasy *n* (1985) a colloquial name for the hallucinogenic drug 3,4-methylenedioxy-methamphetamine, inspired by its effect on the user. It originated in the US. The drug was widely used on the rave scene from the later 1980s onwards as a provider of energy for all-night dancing, despite the occasional fatality linked with it. The name is often abbreviated to *E* (1988).

1987 *Times*: Police impounded £10,000-worth of a drug known as 'ecstasy' yesterday . . . the first time it has been found in Britain.

E-fit *n* (1988) an electronically produced photofit picture, typically used in the identification of criminals. The word is a blend of *e* for 'electronic' and *photofit* (1970), denoting a composite photograph made up of individual facial features.

1995 *Daily Telegraph*: The suspects were identified to police from computer-enhanced photofits, or E-Fits, of the two men.

e-mail, email *n, v* (1982) an abbreviation of **electronic mail (1977)** which by the middle of the 1980s had established itself as the standard term. It is first recorded as a verb in 1987.

1982 *Computerworld*: ADR/Email is reportedly easy to use and features simple, English verbs and prompt screens.

1986 *Times*: Electronic mail—now known universally as e-mail. The partnership of word processor and e-mail almost eliminate [sic] the need for paper.

1994 *Loaded*: For Sonic Youth we would first e-mail them at serv@cornell.edu.

empower *v* (1986) to make (a person or group) stronger and more confident, especially in controlling their life and claiming their rights. A pre-echo of what might be called this 'pregnant' sense can be found in the writings of William Penn in 1690 ('Who empowered them as their work witnesseth'), but as a widespread usage it is definitely a child of the 1980s.

> 1986 Christopher Lasch: Communitarianism... rejects the kind of liberalism that seeks to 'empower' exploited groups by conquering the state.
>
> 1991 *Utne Reader*: While Afrocentrism helps empower blacks, it labels homosexuality a 'deviation' that weakens black culture.

enterprise culture *n* (1980) a model of capitalist society which specifically emphasizes and encourages entrepreneurial activity and speculation, financial self-reliance, etc.

> 1980 *Economist*: Sir Keith [Joseph] himself would agree that industrial policy now begins and ends with the treasury: an economic policy designed to foster the 'enterprise culture'.

fatwa, fatwah *n* (1989) an edict or statement issued (as if) by a religious authority, especially one pronouncing a death sentence or calling for some other form of extreme punishment. The Arabic word was borrowed into English in its original sense, 'an edict issued by a Muslim juridical authority', as long ago as the 17th century, but it failed to make much impression until in 1989 the Ayatollah Khomeini, religious leader of Iran, issued such a ruling sentencing the British novelist Salman Rushdie to death for publishing *The Satanic Verses* (1988), a book which many Muslims considered blasphemous and highly offensive. As a result it quickly extended itself metaphorically in various directions.

> 1989 *Guardian*: When the Catholic archbishop came out against Noriega, and fatwahs against him were read out in church, the church services in the middle class suburbs turned into political demonstrations against the regime.
>
> 1995 *Saturday Night*: In 1974, when the splendid Hank Aaron hit his 715th dinger, overtaking the Babe's career record of 714 homers, he suffered something like a fatwa, requiring police protection against the many death threats he received.

feel-good factor *n* (1984) a feeling of satisfaction and well-being derived from a particular object, circumstance, etc. The term was originally US, but came to be used particularly in British political jargon in the late 1980s and the 90s to denote a feeling of well-being and (financial) security prevailing in a nation, believed to lead to increased consumer spending and satisfaction with the government in power. The ultimate model for the usage is *Doctor Feelgood*, a hypothetical doctor who readily prescribes mood-enhancing drugs, such as amphetamines, for recreational use; he was made famous in a US hit song of 1967.

> 1984 *Industry Week*: The 'feel good' factors are the same in Japan as in the United States because human nature is inherently the same East and West.
>
> 1987 *Business Week*: Thatcher is benefiting from the 'feel good' factor among voters.

foodie *n* (1982) someone who is (obsessively) interested in food; a gourmet. Foodies were the product of the post-war revolution which made it possible in Anglo-Saxon countries to regard food as an object of enthusiasm and study rather than as a necessary evil. The term was popularized by the publication of Ann Barr and Paul Levy's *The Official Foodie Handbook* in 1984.

> 1982 *Harpers & Queen*: Foodies are foodist. They dislike and despise all non-foodies... The [colour] supplements encouraged the foodie movement.
>
> 1982 *Observer*: We foodies know her better as the author of the Penguin volume, 'An Invitation to Indian Cooking'.

Generation X *n* (1989) a generation of young people perceived to be disaffected, directionless, or irresponsible, and having no part to play in society; a 'lost generation'. The term can be traced back to the early 1950s, and featured as the title of a 1964 science-fiction novel by Charles Hamblett and Jane Deverson, but it did not gain wide currency until the appearance in 1991 of Douglas Coupland's *Generation X: tales for an accelerated culture.* A member of the generation is known as a *Generation Xer*, or simply as an *Xer.* See also **slacker (1994)**.

> 1989 *Toronto Star*: What if this Generation X turns around collectively and comes to the conclusion they can't sit around waiting, and instead . . . start their own businesses.
>
> 1992 *Playboy*: Xers like their infotainment. The average Xer logs 23,000 hours in front of the TV before reaching the age of 20. They learned all they need to know about politics from Oliver Stone's JFK.
>
> 1994 *Rolling Stone*: Maybe it's the pandemic shrug of Generation X, the futility felt by the young when analyzed to death by self-styled experts, carpet-bombed by music videos and wired to 157 channels with nothing on.

ghetto-blaster *n* (1981) a large portable stereo radio (and cassette player), especially one on which pop music is played loudly. The term originated in the US. There was a vogue amongst inner-city youths, and especially blacks, in the US around 1978–82 for carrying around such radios with the volume turned up to danger level—whence the name. An even less politically correct alternative was *third-world briefcase.*

> 1983 *Daily Mirror*: A beat throbbing from a ghetto-blaster—a giant, portable stereo system.

glasnost *n* (1986) a declared Soviet policy from 1985 of greater openness and frankness in public statements, including the publication of news reflecting adversely on the government and political system; greater freedom of speech and information arising from this policy. The Russian word *glasnost* (literally 'the fact of being public') is recorded in dictionaries from the 18th century, but in the more general sense of 'publicity'. It was used in the context of freedom of information in the Soviet State by Lenin, and called for in an open letter to the Soviet Writers' Union by Aleksandr Solzhenitsyn in 1969, but did not become a subject of serious public debate in the Soviet Union until an *Izvestiya* editorial requested letters on the subject on 19 January 1985. Its use by Mikhail Gorbachev on 11 March 1985 in a speech accepting the post of General Secretary of the CPSU subsequently led to its being associated particularly with his policies. With the benefit of hindsight, it was one of the first significant cracks in the wall of Communism, which was to collapse in Eastern Europe before the end of the decade. See also **perestroika (1986)**.

> 1986 *New York Times*: Exposes of corruption, shortages and economic problems appear virtually daily in the [Soviet] press. It is a change that became evident after Mikhail Gorbachev came to office last March and called for more 'glasnost', or openness, in covering domestic affairs.

glass ceiling *n* (1984) an unofficial or unacknowledged barrier to personal advancement, especially of a woman or a member of an ethnic minority in employment. The term originated in the US.

> 1984 *Adweek*: Women have reached a certain point—I call it the glass ceiling. They're in the top of middle management and they're stopping and getting stuck.

gotcha (1982) originally, a triumphalistic banner headline celebrating the sinking of the Argentinian battleship *General Belgrano* during the Falklands War, printed by the *Sun* newspaper (4 May 1982, first edition only). It achieved instant notoriety for its apparent glorying in the death of Argentinian sailors, and came to be used as shorthand for the vulgarity and moral vacuity of tabloid culture. It was a specific application of a representation of the colloquial pronunciation of (*I have*) *got you*, first recorded (in the form *gotcher*) in 1932 and usually used in the sense either 'I have caught or destroyed you' or 'I have understood you'.

> 1983 Robert Harris (title): Gotcha! The Media, the Government and the Falklands Crisis.
>
> 1994 George Bain (title): Gotcha! How the Media Distorts the News.

green shoots *n* (1989) signs of economic recovery. The usage (based on the clichéd metaphor of new growth on a plant) was brought to public notice in Britain when the

Chancellor of the Exchequer, Norman Lamont, attempting to raise the spirits of the faithful at the 1991 Conservative Party Conference in the depths of the recession, said, 'The green shoots of economic spring are appearing once again.'

> 1992 *New Republic*: Every week in the last four months of 1991 was marked by predictions from one minister or another that the recession was about to end. The 'green shoots' of recovery were now showing.

> 1995 *Independent*: I'm absolutely brassed off with all this talk of green shoots and clear blue water.

hacker *n* (1983) someone who uses their skill with computers to try to gain unauthorized access to computer files or networks. This colloquial term evolved from **hacking** 'the use of computers as a hobby' **(1976)**. By the middle of the decade the back-formed verb *hack* was being used in this sense, usually accompanied by *into*.

> 1983 *Daily Telegraph*: A hacker . . . yesterday penetrated a confidential British Telecom message system being demonstrated live on BBC-TV.

> 1985 *Times*: The equipment needed can be used quite legitimately . . . But it can also be used to hack into other people's computers.

heroin chic *n* (1986) a glamorization of the culture and appearance of heroin users, characterized especially by the use of very thin, wan fashion models.

> 1986 *Sunday Times*: Keith Richard, Jack Bruce and Eric Clapton have been among the more celebrated victims of the myth of heroin chic.

> 2005 *Courier-Mail* (Queensland): Increasing numbers of designers are turning away from the heroin chic of years past to embrace a fuller-figured healthy model.

hip-hop *n* (1982) a youth subculture, originating amongst the black and Hispanic population of New York City, which comprises elements such as rap music, graffiti art, and break-dancing, as well as distinctive codes of dress and speech; also, the music associated with this subculture, characterized by often politically inspired or motivated raps, delivered above spare electronic backing, and harsh rhythm tracks. The word was formed alliteratively from *hip* 'fashionable, cool' and *hop* 'dance'.

> 1984 *Washington Post*: Like breakdancing, rap and hip hop in general flourished at street level despite overexposure in too many 'breaksploitation' films and a virtual end to exposure in the media.

HIV *n* (1986) an abbreviation of *human immunodeficiency virus*, either of two retroviruses (HIV-1, HIV-2) which cause Aids. The fact that the *V* stands for *virus* is often overlooked, resulting in the tautological *HIV virus*.

> 1986 *Capital Gay*: An international committee on viral names has been looking into the problem, and was rumoured to have agreed on 'human immune deficiency virus' (HIDV or HIV).

> 1987 *Daily Telegraph*: One of the two blood donors had been found not to be carrying the HIV virus, but the other could not be traced.

house *n* (1986) a type of pop music, originally created by disc jockeys in dance-clubs, which typically features the use of drum machines, sequencers, sampled sound effects, and prominent synthesized bass lines, in combination with sparse, repetitive vocals and a fast beat. It probably took its name from the *Warehouse*, a nightclub in Chicago where this music was first popularized around 1985. See also **acid house (1988)**.

> 1986 *Q*: Washington has Go-Go, The Bronx gave the world hip-hop and Chicago, that toddlin' town, steps forward with House Music.

> 1988 *New Statesman*: The pirates hype . . . the neo-disco known as house.

icon *n* (1982) a small symbolic picture of a physical object on a VDU screen, especially one that represents a particular option (e.g. a small picture of a pen representing the word-processing option) and can be selected to exercise that option. Towards the end of the decade the *icon* was punningly joined by the *earcon*, denoting a symbolic sound representing an option (based on a reinterpretation of *icon* as *eyecon*).

> 1982 *Computerworld*: Star's screen displays black characters on a white background. These are known as icons on the Star and are equivalent to the familiar physical object in an office.

information superhighway *n* (1985) any of a number of projected or actual national high-speed, high-capacity telecommunications networks linking homes and offices and permitting the transmission of a variety of electronic media, including video, audio, multimedia, and text. The metaphor is based on the idea of a multi-lane road for high-speed traffic (the literal sense of US *superhighway*, which is first recorded in 1925). It is often abbreviated in US English to *I-way*.

> 1993 *New York Times*: One of the technologies Vice President Al Gore is pushing is the information superhighway, which will link everyone at home or office to everything else—movies and television shows, shopping services, electronic mail and huge collections of data.

Internet *n* (1986) originally applied to a set of linked computer networks operated by the US Defense Department, and hence to the global computer network which evolved out of this, providing a variety of information and communication services to its users, and consisting of a loose confederation of interconnected networks which use standardized protocols. Both these usages represent a specific application of *internet* 'a set of linked networks' (first recorded in 1974), which in turn is a shortening of the synonymous *internetwork*.

> 1986 *Network World*: The electronic mail net runs over Internet, an international network of networks operated by the Department of Defense.

> 1997 *Times*: Where most tourist services on the Internet can only provide text and picture data on places of interest, InferNet is going one step better and including an accurate scale map of locations as well.

killing field *n* (1980) a place of warfare or unrest involving heavy loss of life, especially as a result of massacre or genocide. The term is usually used in the plural. It was popularized as the name of the film *The Killing Fields* (1984), about the massacre of three million Cambodians under Pol Pot's Communist Khmer Rouge regime in the mid 1970s.

> 1983 *New York Times*: Foreign tourists could be flown in to see both the monument and a sample of Mr. Pol Pot's killing fields.

> 1995 *Focus*: The tens of thousands of ritualised revenge-killings that have in recent times transformed Haiti into a killing field.

laptop *adj, n* (1984) (a computer) small and light enough to be used on one's lap. The coinage was modelled on *desktop* (1968), denoting a computer small enough to be accommodated on a desk. It was followed by the even tinier *palmtop* (1987).

> 1984 *Fortune*: Led by Tandy's four-pound Radio Shack Model 100 . . . the lap-tops are selling briskly.

> 1984 *Byte*: Laptop portables such as Gavilan were stealing the show.

life *n* ***get a life*** (1983) start living a fuller or more interesting existence. The slang expression is used as a scornful admonition to someone whose way of life is viewed as unacceptably empty, dull, or 'sad' (e.g. nerds, anoraks, or trainspotters).

> 1995 *Internet World*: 'Get a Life' messages periodically appear—usually in impolite terms—advising *Star Trek* enthusiasts that they could be spending their time better elsewhere.

liposuction *n* (1983) a technique of cosmetic surgery in which particles of excess fat (Greek *lipos* 'fat') are loosened and then removed by being sucked through an incision using a vacuum pump. It was hailed as the fatties' magic bullet: weight loss without the stress of dieting.

> 1986 *Choice*: With liposuction bruising and rippling in the skin can occur where skin is very lax or excessive fat is removed.

loyalty card *n* (1986) an identity card issued by a retailer to its customers so that each individual transaction can be recorded as part of a consumer incentive scheme under which credits are amassed for future discounts each time a purchase is made.

1993 *Bookseller*: Publishers' restrictions do not, for example, allow us to issue a Dillons customer loyalty card.

1995 *Which?*: Loyalty cards may be popular, but rather than having to join special clubs to get savings, we think it's better if all customers can see cuts on shelf prices.

mad cow disease *n* (1988) a colloquial, mainly British name for **BSE (1987)**, reflecting with black humour its effect on the behaviour of cattle suffering from it. The coinage produced a brief flutter of more or less frivolous lookalikes, such as *mad chicken disease*, and was widely borrowed in translation in countries which banned British beef (e.g. *vache folle* in French).

1996 *Private Eye*: In the West Country it is common knowledge that 'mad cow disease' was present at epidemic levels long before it was 'discovered' by Maffia [i.e. Ministry of Agriculture, Fisheries, and Food] vets in Kent in 1985.

ME *n* (1982) an abbreviation of *myalgic encephalomyelitis* (first recorded in 1956), a disease of unknown cause but usually occurring after a viral infection, and characterized by headaches, fever, localized muscular pains, extreme fatigue, and weakness. It, or its diagnosis, became prevalent during the 1980s, and, partly because of the mystery surrounding it, it went under a number of alternative names, including *post-viral (fatigue) syndrome*, *chronic fatigue syndrome*, *Iceland disease* (from an outbreak in 1948–49 in Akureyri, northern Iceland), and *yuppie flu* (1988).

1990 *Health Now*: It is widely taken throughout Brazil as an antidote to stress and is potentially a very valuable supplement for increasing energy levels of ME sufferers.

1990 *Chicago Tribune*: For many years, [ME] has been called 'yuppie flu', because most of the estimated 1 to 5 million who suffer from the disorder are affluent professional women from 25 to 45.

mega *adj* (1982) huge, enormous. This colloquial transformation of the prefix *mega-* 'very large' into an adjective in its own right originated in the US. Signs of the change can be discerned in the 1960s, but in these early examples it is usually difficult to distinguish the adjective from the prefix, other than typographically (it is printed as a separate word). It is not really until the 1980s that it emerges as a fully fledged adjective, capable of being used after the verb *be* and expanded in semantic range: it can mean 'hugely successful or celebrated', and it is also widely used as an approval word, meaning 'excellent, great'. In addition it is used as an intensifying adverb.

1982 *Guardian*: Valspeak is . . . the funnest, most totally radical language, I guess, like in the whole mega gnarly city of Los Angeles.

1987 *New Musical Express*: It's a crap record but I had to have it. Look at it. Isn't it mega? What a great sleeve!

1999 *Independent*: A celeb, who in spite of mega achievements, is thought by everyone to be a total pillock.

mobile *n* (1986) see **mobile phone (1945)**.

moonwalking *n* (1980) an exaggeratedly slow action, dance, or method of proceeding which resembles the characteristic weightless movement of walking on the moon. The term was applied specifically in the late 1980s to a style of dancing popularized by US entertainer Michael Jackson, involving appearing to move forwards while in fact sliding backwards.

1980 *Christian Science Monitor*: One hang balloon thrill is 'moon walking': heating the balloon until you are almost weightless and then hopping across the landscape as if gravity were a figment of Sir Isaac Newton's imagination.

1988 *Los Angeles Times*: Kids think they were the first ones to come up with moonwalking and poplocking.

netizen *n* (1984) a (habitual or keen) user of the Internet. The word is a blend of *net* and *citizen*.

1996 *Daily Telegraph*: Several Web sites have set up Valentine's Day pages to put love-lorn netizens in touch.

New Man *n* (1982) a man who rejects sexist attitudes and aims to be caring, sensitive, and non-aggressive and to take a substantial role in his household's domestic routine. He was a product of 1970s feminism who for a historical moment in the 1980s was widely taken as a role model, but who as the decade moved on came more and more to be regarded as a wimp. See also **laddish (1991)**.

> 1985 *Chicago Tribune*: Does the New Woman Really Want the New Man?... The answer, as you might guess, is a frustrated no.

NIMBY, nimby *n* (1980) an acronym formed from the initial letters of 'not in my back yard', a slogan expressing objection to the siting of something unpleasant, such as nuclear waste, in one's own locality (although by implication not minding if it is dumped on someone else in consequence). It was reputedly coined by Walter Rodger of the American Nuclear Society. The derivative *nimbyism* is first recorded in 1986.

> 1980 *Christian Science Monitor*: A secure landfill anywhere near them is anathema to most Americans today. It's an attitude referred to in the trade as NIMBY—'not in my backyard'.

> 1988 *Economist*: Over 90 Tory backbenchers, including some keen Thatcherites, have joined a parliamentary group dedicated to Sane Planning: doublespeak for 'not-in-my-back-yard', or nimbyism.

noughties *n* (1989) the decade from 2000 to 2009. The word seems to have been separately invented several times in the late 1980s and early 1990s, but it was not until late in the 90s, when an urgent need to name the next decade began to be felt, that its profile was significantly raised. As the millennium approached interest increased, competitions were held, and large numbers of suggestions were bandied about. Among the more popular were *noughts*, *oughties*, and *zips*, but after the dust had settled, it became clear that *noughties* was the name most widely in use (despite or because of its double entendre). A combination of *nought* 'zero' with the model *twenties*, *thirties*, etc., it was no doubt also partly inspired by the *naughty nineties* (indeed, it is often spelled *naughties*).

> 2001 *Sunday Times*: The Noughties celebrity face has a line-free forehead and bee-stung lips.

nuclear winter *n* (1983) a period of extreme cold and devastation that has been conjectured to follow a nuclear war, caused by an atmospheric layer of smoke and dust particles shutting out the sun's rays.

> 1983 Carl Sagan: We considered a war in which a mere 100 megatons were exploded, less than one per-cent of the world arsenals, and only in low-yield airbursts over cities. This scenario, we found, would ignite thousands of fires, and the smoke from these fires alone would be enough to generate an epoch of cold and dark almost as severe as in the 5000-megaton case. The threshold for what Richard Turco has called The Nuclear Winter is very low.

PC, pc *adj, n* (1986) an abbreviation of **politically correct (1970)** and of *political correctness* (1979).

> 1986 *New York Times*: There's too much emphasis on being P.C.—politically correct.

> 1992 *Economist*: Subjects like science and engineering where the ravages of PC are unknown (or, at least, rare).

perestroika *n* (1986) the reform of the Soviet economic and political system, first proposed at the 26th Communist Party Congress in 1979 and actively promoted under the leadership of Mikhail Gorbachev from 1985. The word means literally 'restructuring' in Russian. See also **glasnost (1986)**.

> 1986 *Washington Post*: If words can define an era, then *perestroika* is the catchword here before Tuesday's opening of the Communist Party Congress as Soviet leader Mikhail Gorbachev enters a decisive phase of his leadership.

personal organizer *n* (1985) a portable folder or wallet containing loose-leaf sections for storing personal information (such as appointments and addresses). The **yuppie (1982)** was lost without one. In Britain, it was usually known by the proprietary name **Filofax (1931)**. In due course computer technology caught up with pen and paper, and the term came to be re-applied to a pocket-sized microcomputer or software for a personal computer, providing similar functions to the loose-leaf folder.

> 1985 *Los Angeles Times*: These busy people all rely on personal organizers—compact, three-ring binders designed to keep track of various aspects of one's life.

PIN *n* (1981) an abbreviation of *personal identification number*, a number allocated by a bank etc. to a customer for use with a cash card. It is mainly used in the phrase *PIN number*; the full form was never widely enough employed for the tautology to be apparent.

> 1982 *Daily Telegraph*: It will be his or her responsibility to ensure that the PIN is kept secret, but what of prying eyes at the checkout?

plastic *n* (1980) a shortening of the earlier **plastic money (1974)**, which referred to the material of which such cards are made, but also alluded to plastic's connotations of artificiality and meretriciousness.

> 1980 *Time*: Visa and MasterCard users will now have to pay more for using plastic.

> 1988 *Which?*: To use plastic in a cash machine, you need a personal identification number (PIN).

poll tax *n* (1985) the term in general use in Britain for the local tax officially known as the *community charge* (1985), levied between 1989/90 and 1993. It is an ancient term, meaning literally 'per-capita tax' (*poll* is an old word for 'head'). It, or its earlier variant *poll-money*, had been in use since the 16th century, and it carries with it connotations of public unrest and anti-tax riots which the Conservative government introducing this latest version was anxious to avoid—hence the bland authorized name *community charge*. In the event, it got the riots anyway. See also **council tax (1991)**.

> 1985 *Times*: It is the dreaded poll tax that I am referring to.

> 1988 *Annual Register 1987*: Particular emphasis was placed on the poll tax as a way of forcing local councils to become fully 'accountable' to all their electors.

power dressing *n* (1980) a style of dressing for work and business intended to convey an impression of efficiency and confidence. The term was applied particularly to clothing adopted by some women to fit in with the ruthless business ethic of the 1980s, characterized by the use of shoulder-pads to create a more masculine-looking outline.

> 1989 *Dimensions*: Power dressing for executive women is dead. No-one wants a square-cut, double-breasted jacket with aggressive shoulders now.

Prozac *n* (1985) a proprietary name for the antidepressant drug fluoxetine hydrochloride. It was the wonder-drug happy pill of the late 1980s, but was more soberly regarded in the 1990s following reports of side-effects such as excessive assertiveness and aggression.

> 1993 *Spy*: Prozac can make a hormone-addled young adult less sensitive, more confident, less homesick, and able to have a good time at parties.

rave *n* (1989) a large, originally often illegal party or event, with dancing to fast electronic pop music, and sometimes associated with the recreational use of drugs such as LSD and ecstasy. The term (an extension of *rave* 'lively party' (1960)) is also applied to electronic dance music of the type played at such events. Raves were usually held in rural locations such as fields and large barns, their location kept secret until the last moment to avoid the attentions of the police. The related *raver* 'someone who attends a rave party' is first recorded in 1991.

> 1991 *New Musical Express*: When you're at a rave there's 10,000 ravers going mental—you can't beat the energy.

> 1991 *Sun*: If you want to dress for success on the rave scene you'll need a proper selection of pukka gear . . . Heat can't escape through the material and the raver comes out of the club feeling like a roast chicken.

1992 *Economist*: To the uneducated ear, rave music is a bone-jangling din, hurtling along at up to 200 beats a minute.

road rage *n* (1988) violent anger caused by the stress and frustration of driving a motor vehicle. The term is used particularly in connection with acts of violence committed by one motorist against another which are provoked by the supposedly objectionable driving of the victim. It is the foremost example of a rash of *rage* coinages in the late 1980s and 90s, reflecting the frustration and barely suppressed aggression of late-20th-century urban life: others include *trolley rage* (affecting supermarket customers), *phone rage*, and *golf rage*.

1995 *Guardian*: A driver was jailed for 18 months yesterday for a 'road rage' attack after which a pensioner died.

1995 *Independent*: Courts should be given power to order 'rage counselling' for aggressive motorists.

Semtex *n* (1985) a malleable, more or less odourless plastic explosive, manufactured in several grades and known largely through its use by terrorists. Its name was given to it by its manufacturers, probably based on *Semtín*, the village in Eastern Bohemia, Czech Republic, where it is made, plus the initial syllable of *explosive* or *export*.

1988 *Daily Telegraph*: The Czechs were replying to a Foreign Office request for help in fighting terrorism and in tracing the growing consignments of Semtex reaching the IRA from Col Gaddafi of Libya.

serial killer *n* (1981) someone who murders repeatedly, often with no apparent motive and usually following a characteristic predictable pattern of behaviour. The application of *serial* to murderers dates from at least the early 1960s (see **serial (1961)**), but the term *serial killer* came into prominence in the US in the mid 1980s in the wake of a number of notorious cases, notably the crimes eventually traced to Theodore Bundy and John Wayne Gacy.

1990 *ArtForum*: Part of the calculated dementedness of the antisitcom *Married with Children* is the star family's surname, the same as that of notorious serial killer Ted Bundy.

shopaholic *n* (1984) a compulsive shopper. It was a phenomenon that arose out of the credit boom of the early 1980s. The suffix *-aholic*/*-oholic* 'compulsive consumer or buyer' enjoyed something of a boom then too: other roughly contemporary but mainly short-lived coinages include *clothesaholic*, *creamaholic*, and *nutaholic*.

1984 *Washington Post*: [The rumour] that Diana is a 'shopaholic'... was described as 'absolute rubbish'.

sleaze *n* (1983) corruption involving politicians or government officials. The term is either a back-formation from *sleazy* 'sordid, disreputable', or a semantic extension of the earlier **sleaze** 'sordidness, sleaziness' **(1967)**, first recorded in 'The sleaze factor', a chapter heading in the book *Gambling with History* by the US journalist Laurence Barrett. It remained current during the Reagan administration of the 1980s, usually in that phrase *sleaze factor*, and moved to the UK towards the end of the decade, when a number of scandals began to engulf the Conservative government. Many involved financial corruption (e.g. the so-called **cash for questions (1994)** affair, in which several MPs accepted payment for asking particular questions in the House of Commons), but the term was also applied to sexual scandals involving MPs, something of a return home for *sleazy*, which originally often connoted sexual squalor.

1988 *Courier-Mail* (Brisbane): Mr Meese... had become the outstanding symbol of the so-called 'sleaze factor' which has bedevilled the Reagan administration.

1995 *Daily Telegraph*: Although Tory disunity and uncertainty about Britain's economic prospects are undoubtedly the main reasons underlying voter discontent with the Government, the 'sleaze factor' is almost certainly making an independent contribution.

smart card *n* (1980) a plastic bank card or similar device with an embedded microprocessor, used in conjunction with an electronic card-reader to authorize or provide particular services, especially the automatic transfer of funds between bank accounts. The term originated in the US.

> 1988 *Times*: The beauty of the algorithm . . . is that it can be built into hardware that will fit even on 'smart cards', and enables the identity of end-users to be checked in less than a second.

sound bite *n* (1980) a brief extract from a recorded interview, speech, etc., usually edited into a news report on account of its aphoristic or provocative quality. The term, which originated in the US, is also applied to a phrase or sentence intended by its speaker to be quoted in this way. It came to prominence in the 1988 US presidential election campaign, and has come to be shorthand for the superficiality of late 20th- and early 21st-century political discourse.

> 1980 *Washington Post*: Remember that any editor watching needs a concise, 30-second sound bite. Anything more than that and you're losing them.

spin doctor *n* (1984) a political press agent or publicist employed to promote a favourable interpretation of events to journalists. The term originated in the US. *Doctor* comes from the various figurative uses of the verb *doctor* (ranging from 'to patch up, mend' to 'to falsify'); on *spin*, see **spin (1978)**. Such an individual is sometimes also called (in the US) a *spin meister* (1986).

> 1984 *New York Times*: They won't be just press agents trying to impart a favourable spin to a routine release. They'll be the Spin Doctors, senior advisers to the candidates.

> 1995 *Guardian*: The party's spin doctors were alarmed to hear the BBC was covering the speech and delighted to hear that it had not 'made' the news bulletin.

> 1998 *Sunday Times*: Head-hunters have spent two months trying to find an ideal candidate for the new strategic post as the Queen's 'spin doctor'.

stalk *v* (1988) to harass or persecute (a person, especially a celebrity) with unwanted and obsessive attention. The persecutor is known as a *stalker*.

> 1988 *Newsday*: The worst place to look for insight into a celebrity stalker . . . is the celebrity stalker himself.

> 1990 *Daily Mail*: A fan . . . stalked . . . star Stephanie Zimbalist for 18 months, writing 200 letters threatening: 'I'll get you'.

> 1994 *Coloradoan* (Fort Collins): The attacks on Kerrigan and Seles, and the stalking of other women, are alarmingly looking more like a trend than isolated incidents.

Star Wars *n* (1983) a nickname, based on the title of a popular science-fiction film released in 1977, for the 'Strategic Defense Initiative', a US project to develop and deploy satellite-mounted devices (e.g. lasers) to destroy enemy missiles in flight.

> 1985 *Radio Times*: President Reagan believes his 'Star Wars' defence initiative may end the threat from nuclear weapons.

street cred *n* (1981) see **cred (1981)**.

swipe *n* (1983) an electronic device for reading information magnetically encoded on a credit card, identity card, etc., usually incorporating a slot through which the card is passed. The term originated in the US, and often occurs in the phrase *swipe card*, denoting a card for use in such a device. It is first recorded as a verb, denoting the passing of a card through such a device, in 1986 (*wipe* is used synonymously).

> 1983 *American Banker*: A direct debit system that links a 'swipe' card reader and PIN . . . pad to an electronic cash register.

> 1986 *Chain Store Age*: When a cashier accepts payments by a VISA credit card, for example, he presses the VISA button on the CAT and swipes the card through the automatic card reader.

Teflon *n, adj* (1983) originally, a proprietary name (registered in the US in 1945 by Du Pont) for polytetrafluoroethylene, a type of thermoplastic resin with a very low coefficient of friction. The name did not become widely known until the substance began to be used for non-stick pans in the 1960s, and in the 1980s it came to be applied bemusedly to politicians whose reputation remains undamaged by scandal or misjudgement, or who manage to deflect criticism on to others, so that nothing 'sticks' to them. The usage began as a specific reference to Ronald Reagan, US President 1981–89, whose ability to sail unscathed through all difficulties earned him the epithet *Teflon (coated) President.*

> 1983 Patricia Schroeder, Congress Record: After carefully watching Ronald Reagan he is attempting a great break-through in political technology—he has been perfecting the Teflon coated Presidency. He sees to it that nothing sticks to him.

> 2004 *www.xlab.co.uk*: This week was meant to be Tony Blair's toughest as prime minister, but, in true Teflon Tony style, he's come through it totally unscathed.

theme *adj* (1983), **themed** *adj* (1986) denoting a catering outlet in which all aspects of design and atmosphere are related to a particular unifying theme (e.g. pirates, Merrie England). The concept, and the usage, evolved from the **theme park (1960)**. They later broadened out in application to other areas of retailing.

> 1983 *Times*: A growth segment of the pub trade is emerging . . . theme pubs. Their hall mark is a design concept to create a particularly individual atmosphere (the theme) with varying combinations of restaurant, cocktail bar and normal bar service. Various theme restaurants have emerged in the past five years.

> 1986 *Evening Standard*: Cashier/receptionist reqd. for fashionable themed restaurant in the City.

> 1998 *Christie's leaflet*: Following the highly successful jewellery theme sales held in London in 1997—*Bijoux Français* and *Indian Jewellery*—we are holding a special sale devoted to *Bijoux Signés*.

toy boy *n* (1981) an attractive young man who is 'kept' as a lover by an older person (typically a woman, but the word is also applied to homosexual catamites). The term was a favourite of the British tabloids in the 1980s, which exploited its essentially mocking message to the full.

> 1983 *Financial Times*: At the start he is observed as Caesar's toy boy, stripped for the religious ceremony.

> 1987 *News of the World*: At 48 she is like a teenage girl again—raving it up with four different lovers including a toyboy of 27!

velvet revolution *n* (1989) a non-violent political revolution, especially one in which a totalitarian regime is replaced. The term is a translation of Czech *sametová revoluce*, introduced into English by the series of events in Czechoslovakia which led to the ending of Communist rule in late 1989.

> 1989 *New York Times*: This was a special way of declaring their faith in what has come to be called the velvet revolution, for its gentle, non-violent quality.

> 1990 *Independent*: Now that 'velvet' revolutions are all the rage, *Citizens* never shirks from examining the bloodlust of 1789.

video nasty *n* (1982) a video film depicting scenes of violence, cruelty, or killing. The term rode in on the back of the video rental boom in Britain in the early to mid 1980s, which brought such films into people's homes for the first time.

> 1984 *Listener*: Unless one has seen a video nasty . . . it is difficult to imagine the depths of degradation to which certain producers are willing to sink.

virtual *adj* (1987) denoting an electronic equivalent of something in the real world, generated by computer software. The usage was a development of a computing use of *virtual* which dates from the late 1950s, designating techniques for simulating memory space, disk storage, and operating environments. By the late 1980s computers could simulate real space which people could move about in and react with (e.g. using a helmet containing a screen). This was named *virtual reality*, and the new usage spread out from there. Latterly *virtual* has come to be used still more broadly to denote something imagined rather than physically present.

1992 *Independent*: This spring the Open University is to start a course taught almost entirely on computer networks to explore the possibilities of 'virtual classrooms'.

1998 *Radcliffe Quarterly*: For Ella Fitzgerald, too, cookbooks could offer virtual meals.

2006 *www.vrleeds.co.uk*: A street by street virtual reality tour of the City of Leeds, with hundreds of panoramic images on line. Includes interior tours of tourist attractions.

Walkman *n* (1981) a proprietary name (registered in 1981) for small battery-operated cassette players and headphones capable of being worn by a person who is on foot (hence *walk*...). It was widely used, especially in the 1980s, as a generic term, although strictly speaking the name is the property of Sony, the manufacturers (who a couple of years later registered the name *Discman* for a portable CD player). In the 1990s it was largely replaced by the non-product-specific **personal stereo (1992)**.

1981 *Japan Times*: Sony Walkmans, easy-driving Honda scooters and aluminum household Buddhist altars sold like hotcakes during 1981.

1984 Sue Townsend: They wear red satin side vent running shorts, sleeveless satin vests, white knee socks, Sony Walkman earphones and one gold earring.

wannabe, wannabee *n, adj* (1981) (an admirer or fan) seeking to emulate a particular celebrity or type, especially in appearance or dress. The term originated as US surfers' slang, representing a casual pronunciation of *want to be*. It was popularized in the mid 1980s through its application to the female fans of the US rock star Madonna, many of whom adopted her style of dress and make-up. The concept is a necessary adjunct of the *celebrity culture* phenomenon.

1986 *Washington Post*: A morbid Madonna-wannabe fascinated with tabloid tales of bizarre deaths.

1990 *Sunday Times*: Word travels fast among the young literati and their wannabe friends.

wet *n* (1980) a politician with liberal or middle-of-the-road views on controversial issues; applied specifically (and with derogatory intent) to a member of the Conservative Party opposed to the monetarist policies of Margaret Thatcher. The word is also used adjectivally. See also **dry (1983)**.

1980 *Times*: Mr James Prior, Secretary of State for Employment, is described in one Sunday paper as 'the champion of the Tory wets'... Who...are to be counted among the wets? The answer seems to be anybody who crosses the Prime Minister in fashioning a particular policy.

1981 *Observer*: The term 'Wet' was originally used by Mrs Thatcher, who meant it in the old sense of 'soppy', as in 'What do you mean the unions won't like it, Jim? Don't be so wet.' It meant feeble, liable to take the easy option, lacking intellectual and political hardness. Like so many insults, it was gleefully adopted by its victims, and so came by its present meaning of liberal, leftish, anti-ideological.

1982 *Listener*: In considering the promotion of wet (or wettish) Ministers, she will tell herself that Pope was right.

wicked *adj* (1984) wonderful, marvellous, outstanding. The usage originated in African-American English and street-gang slang, and was adopted by British youth culture in the late 1980s. *Wicked* has been used ironically in US English since early in the 20th century to mean 'remarkably fine or admirable' ('Phoebe and I are going to shake a wicked calf', F. Scott Fitzgerald (1920)), but this 1980s usage is more likely inspired by the parallel use of *bad* as an approval adjective. That is first recorded in the 1890s in African-American English; it proliferated in 1920s jazz slang ('Ellington's jazzique is just too bad', Charters & Kunstadt (1927)), widened into general use in the 70s, and was picked up by the youth culture of the 80s ('We ran into some of the baddest chicks, man, we partied, we had a nice time', Gene Lees (1988)).

1989 *Time Out*: I've been to loads of Acid House parties. We have a wicked time but never, not never, do we take any drugs.

1990 *Daily Telegraph*: The boy looked in wonder at the polyurethane and leather marvel and offered it the coolest of street compliments. 'Well wicked,' he breathed.

Windows *n* (1983) the proprietary name of a graphical computer user interface based on 'windows', defined parts of a VDU display, such as may be allocated to a particular category of information (that sense of *window* is first recorded in 1974).

> 1983 *Wall Street Journal*: Microsoft Corp. introduces its Microsoft Windows package, which is designed to make it easier to juggle several computer jobs simultaneously.

wysiwyg *n* (1982) an acronym (pronounced as if it were spelt *whizziwig*) formed from the initial letters of *what you see is what you get*, a slogan used in the computer industry denoting that what appears on the VDU screen exactly represents the eventual output.

> 1984 *Scientific American*: The resulting interface between the computer and the user would then fall into the class of interfaces known as *wysiwyg*, which stands for 'What you see is what you get'.

yomp *v* (1982) to march with heavy equipment over difficult terrain. The word came into prominence when used by the Royal Marines during the Falklands conflict of 1982. Its origins have never been certainly identified. It has been compared by those familiar with the terminology of rally-driving with *yump* (of a rally car or its driver) 'to leave the ground while taking a crest at speed', which apparently comes from a Scandinavian pronunciation of *jump*, but whether there is any connection has not been confirmed. Its colourful sound and appearance made it popular with journalists and headline-writers in Britain, and it enjoyed some metaphorical usage (see the second quote below), but after a few years it faded from the scene. (The equivalent word in the Parachute Regiment was *tab*, of equally obscure origin.)

> 1982 *Daily Telegraph*: And always in the cold light of the Falklands dawn, the . . . Marines . . . have been ready to 'yomp on' for the next stage of the journey.

> 1983 *Listener*: Mrs. Thatcher may begin yomping . . . around the hustings considerably sooner.

yuppie *n* (1982) a member of a socio-economic group comprising young professional people working in cities, of a type thought of as typifying the ethos of the 1980s: ambitious, go-getting, newly affluent, young, class-free, owing no debt to the past. It is a hybrid word, of US origin, coined probably by grafting an acronym based on *Young Urban Professional* (or *Young Upwardly mobile Professional*) on to a basic model suggested by *hippie*. At first it had rivals in *yumpie* ('The yumpies climbing the ladder of success with great agility can be described as upscaling', *New York Times Magazine* (1984)), based on *Young Upwardly Mobile Professional*, and *yap* ('Phillips' Yaps believe in vigorous self-advancement, jogging and BMWs', *Sunday Times* (1984)), based on *Young Aspiring Professional*, but *yuppie* proved the fittest for survival, and went on to become perhaps the main buzzword of the 80s. Numerous mostly condescending or hostile derivatives were formed from it, including *yuppify*, *yuppyish*, *yuppiedom*, *yuppieism*, and *yuppette*, and it provided the role model for a rash of lookalike words (e.g. *buppie* 'black yuppie', *guppie* 'gay yuppie', also 'green [i.e. environmentally concerned] yuppie', *Juppie* 'Japanese yuppie'). It was probably also the main inspiration behind the general fashion for acronymic lifestyle terms in the mid 80s (e.g. **dinky (1986)**).

> 1982 Joseph Epstein: People who are undecided about growing up: they are college-educated, getting on and even getting up in the world, but with a bit of the hippie-dippie counterculture clinging to them still—yuppies, they have been called, the YUP standing for young urban professionals.

> 1984 *Times*: A new term has been introduced into the American political lexicon . . . It is 'Yuppie', which stands for Young, urban professional people.

> 1984 *Guardian*: The yuppies themselves, in the 25–34 age group, supported Senator Gary Hart in the primaries.

> 1984 *Washington Post*: Yuppiedom does not conduce to a realistic view of the human condition or of American society.

> 1986 *Financial Times*: There is nothing yuppyish about the Folkes Group.

> 1987 *Independent*: What Dickens is describing, I suddenly realised, is yuppification. The trendies were moving in.

The 1990s and 2000s

As the millennium approached, the world seemed a fragmented place. The certainties of 1900 had been blasted by two world wars. At the end of the 1980s the Cold War ice had melted, opening up new possibilities and uncertainties. The stratified, deferential society inherited from the 19th century had given place to the *people's* democracy. A confident, optimistic belief in progress had faded; late-20th-century humanity was cynical about the efficacy of science and technology, and aware of the damage it had done to the world and its other inhabitants. Sensing the ultimate victory of capitalism, Professor Francis Fukuyama had even proclaimed 'the end of history'. And as if all that were not enough, the stoical, stiff-upper-lip British had become a sentimental, touchy-feely nation (if the public reaction to the death of Diana, Princess of Wales was anything to go by).

As Communism's grip on Eastern Europe loosened, nowhere was the outcome more bitter than in Yugoslavia. Civil war broke out in 1991 with the secession of Croatia and Slovenia. It smouldered on to the end of the decade, and introduced the sour euphemism *ethnic cleansing* into the English language. The other major hot conflict of the 90s was the Gulf War (1991), a punitive action by the United Nations to expel Iraqi invaders from Kuwait. A number of US military euphemisms were brought to wider public notice as a result (notably *collateral damage* (1975), *friendly fire* (1925), and *mission creep*), and duly ridiculed. Several years after the war was over, sufferers from *Gulf War syndrome* were still trying to establish that it was caused by conditions they had encountered in Kuwait and Iraq. The military strategists drew the lesson that what was needed to police an increasingly volatile world was a *rapid-reaction force*.

To counterbalance this geopolitical fissiparousness (the number of independent states in Europe went up from 25 in the 1980s to approaching 40 in the late 90s), the European Community was enlarging itself. Under the terms of the 1992 Maastricht treaty, it transformed itself into the *European Union*. Such developments were not to the liking of *Euro-sceptic* (1986) elements within the ruling Conservative Party in Britain. They were encouraged in their doom-laden predictions by *Black Wednesday*, in which Britain was forced ignominiously to abandon its membership of the European Exchange Rate Mechanism.

The humbling of the pound spelled the beginning of the end for the British Conservative government, which had been in power since 1979. Shorn of its reputation for economic competence, and plagued by its own Euro-sceptics, who could exploit its tiny parliamentary majority to try to press their case, it stumbled along on a wave of unprecedented public unpopularity. Beset by accusations of *sleaze* (1983) and scandals such as *cash for questions*, it tried to identify the *green shoots* (1989) of economic recovery and establish *clear blue water* between itself and its political opponents. The electorate, however, was not convinced. In the general election of 1997, the government suffered a crushing defeat. Even MPs who had taken the precaution of the *chicken run* (abandoning a marginal seat for an apparently safer one) could not escape the landslide.

Taking the Tories' place, *New Labour*: a transformed Labour Party which had abandoned its more extreme socialist policies in favour of the *third way*. Under *Blairism*, *tax and spend* was out, *welfare to work* and *tough love* (1981) were in. Having taken the lesson of more than a decade of internecine strife, the new government made sure its supporters stuck close to the party line: to be *off-message* was the greatest crime; any deviation would be spun back into line by the *spin doctors* (1984). Labour had learnt well from the *Clintonites* in the US how to gain and hold on to power.

The get-rich-quick-and-flaunt-it society of the 80s had evaporated in the recession of the early 90s. *Essex man* was no more, and *Essex girl* was keeping a lower profile. It was forecast as the 'caring decade', although *Generation X* (1989), *jobseekers*, and sufferers from *negative equity* probably did not find it so.

Confidence returned with the end of the recession, and Britain reinvented itself as *Cool Britannia*, proprietor of *Britpop*. Revelling in the new prosperity, *chavs* happily flaunted their *bling*. For entertainment, people had *docusoaps* on TV, *Aga sagas* in the bookshops, and *red top* tabloids (e.g. *The Sun* and *The Mirror*) on the news-stands: possible evidence of *dumbing down* (1933) for those in search of it. At work, there was a good chance you would be *hot-desking* (desk-sharing), and the new institution of *dress-down* Friday (when casual clothes may be worn) reached Britain from the US.

The New Man had become the *New Lad*, with his *laddish* behaviour. The female backlash went over the top with *bobbitting*, a *girl power* (1986) solution not even *Viagra* could remedy. The gay community, meanwhile, had to face the new threat of *outing*.

Cybernauts surfed the *World Wide Web* (or the *Web* for short). To be in the swim you had to have your own *website*, *home page*, or *blog*. You would hope to avoid the *spam* and the *mail bombs* (destructively huge e-mails), but the main fear in the *cybercafé* was the dreaded *millennium bug*, which threatened to make the world's computer systems crash when the clocks chimed midnight on 31 December 1999.

Fortunately the paranoia on that occasion was misplaced. But then, on 11 September 2001—*9/11*—the world changed. The attacks by *al-Qaeda* on the New York World Trade Center and other US targets ushered in the 'war on terror'—the campaign by America and its allies to eradicate the perceived threat posed to Western civilization by 'rogue' terrorism-sponsoring states, identified collectively by US president George W. Bush as the *axis of evil*. As its somewhat fraught course proceeded, culminating in the US-led invasion of Iraq in 2003 and the consequent *regime change*, its most notable new contribution to English vocabulary threatened to be such banalities as *freedom fries* and *sex up*. Intent, however, on fiddling while the fires of international conflict and *global warming* (1977) stoked themselves, we pursued ever more enthusiastically the solipsistic path of individualized electronic communication, with our *MP3* players, our *WAP* phones, and our *Wi-Fi*. And in 2004 we discovered the joys of *podcasting*.

Aga saga *n* (1992) a type of popular novel set typically in a semi-rural location and describing the domestic and emotional lives of articulate middle-class characters. The gently mocking term, which seems to have been inspired mainly by the novels of British author Joanna Trollope (b. 1943), exploits the nostalgic association of Aga stoves with lost rural idylls.

> 1994 *Independent on Sunday*: The success of Joanna Trollope's rural novels led to a whole wave of Aga Sagas from publishers hoping to cash in.
>
> 1995 *Daily Telegraph*: When contemporary women writers publish novels about other women of a certain class the critics call them 'Aga Sagas' and throw them on the fire.

alcopop *n* (1995) a carbonated, often fruit-flavoured drink containing alcohol. This controversial marketing development (which actually had its beginnings in the US in the 1970s) involved the alcoholizing of drinks typically consumed by children.

> 1995 *Daily Telegraph*: 'Alcopop' sales fizz as young Britain gets the taste.
>
> 1996 *Independent*: The launch of two new alcoholic fruit drinks looks set to brew up another storm over criticism that the 'alcopops' encourage under-age drinking.

al-Qaeda *n* (1996) a network of Islamic fundamentalist groups, founded in 1988 and associated with the terrorist attacks on the World Trade Center, New York City, and other US targets on 11 September 2001 (see **9/11 (2001)**). Its name in Arabic (*al-qā'ida*) means literally 'the base'. Its originator and leader Osama bin Laden (b. 1957) became the West's leading hate-figure of the early part of the 21st century, and was at the top of the FBI's list of the world's most wanted terrorists.

> 2002 *Times*: Defence sources admitted that the fighting ability of the Taleban and al-Qaeda had been underestimated.

ASBO *n* (1997) an acronym formed from the initial letters of *anti-social behaviour order*, a court order obtainable in Britain by local authorities which places restrictions on the movements or actions of a person who persistently engages in anti-social behaviour. ASBOs were introduced under the terms of the Crime and Disorder Act in 1998 and first applied in 1999.

> 2005 *Daily Post* (Liverpool): Some yobs laugh in the face of Asbos which, in some cases, ban them from doing what is illegal anyway.

axis of evil *n* (2001) a polemical term applied in the US in the wake of the attack on the World Trade Center and other targets in September 2001 (see **9/11 (2001)**) to a group of states identified as harbouring and promoting terrorism aimed at the West or as building up stocks of weapons intended to be used against the West. It was coined by David Frum, a former speechwriter of President George W. Bush, and was first brought to wide public notice in the President's State of the Union address on 29 January 2002. The countries usually picked out for individual identification as members of the 'axis' were Iraq, Iran, and North Korea.

babelicious *adj* (1991) of a person, especially a young woman: extremely sexy. This slang blend of *babe* 'sexually attractive young woman' (1915) and *delicious* was introduced in the sketch 'Wayne's World' on the US television show *Saturday Night Live*, and popularized by the 1992 film *Wayne's World*.

> 1991 Mike Myers & Robin Ruzan: The babelicious movie star.
>
> 1993 *Picture* (Sydney): Babelicious Debbie . . . won the utmost honour of becoming THE PICTURE Wet T-shirt/Luscious Body champion 1993.

benefit tourism *n* (1993) travelling to or within Britain in order to live off social security payments while untruthfully claiming to be seeking work. The polemical usage was introduced in a speech made to the British Conservative Party Conference in 1993 by Peter Lilley, Secretary of State for Social Security. *Benefit tourist* is also first recorded in 1993.

1994 *Independent on Sunday*: Mr Lilley's clampdown on 'benefit tourism' has been attacked by the Government's own social security advisory committee.

1995 *Economist*: As for EU citizens using their right of entry to become 'benefit tourists', on March 20th the High Court upheld Britain's right to deny income support to unemployed EU citizens if they were not seeking work.

Black Wednesday *n* (1992) 16 September 1992, the day on which the UK was forced by adverse economic circumstances to withdraw sterling from the European Exchange Rate Mechanism. It was so called because it was generally regarded as a disaster (and certainly it was an embarrassing piece of mismanagement which permanently wrecked the Conservative government's reputation for economic competence), but Euro-sceptics hailed it with other epithets (such as 'White Wednesday').

1992 *Earth Matters*: The national coffers [are] much depleted after 'Black Wednesday'.

1992 *Economist*: The Bundesbank is thought to have lent the Bank around DM33 billion (£13 billion) through the ERM's 'very-short-term financing facility' on Black Wednesday.

Blairism *n* (1993) the political and economic policies of Tony Blair, leader of the British Labour Party since 1994 and Prime Minister 1997—, characterized by a willingness to combine a concern for social issues with an acceptance of many aspects of market-based economics. Supporters of Blair or his policies have been dubbed *Blairites*, or, in the case of his more fervent or fawning followers, *Blairistas* (1995), a lampooning term modelled on earlier borrowings from Spanish such as *Peronista* (1946) and *Sandinista* (1928).

1994 *Guardian*: A little more exposure to Blairism and evidence that it is not just a leadership phenomenon but running deep in the veins of the party itself, would make the balance of forces much tighter.

1995 *Guardian*: It is well worth re-reading that compromise text, for it meets virtually all the arguments for modernisation advanced by the Blairites, yet remains true to the spirit of Clause 4.

1995 *Independent*: Barrie Clement... makes the same mistake as Tony Blair and the Blairistas by assuming that those who voted for Mr Blair as leader of the Labour Party will now follow blindly wherever he chooses to lead them.

bling *n, adj* (1999) originally, ostentatious or flashy jewellery. The word emerged, apparently as a verbal realization of the visual effect of light being reflected off gems or precious metals, in the slang of rappers and hip-hopsters. It rapidly broadened out in application to denote ostentatious and usually tasteless displays of wealth. In early usage it was often reduplicated to *bling-bling*.

2002 *Independent*: I'm not talking bling-bling stuff that's just about showing wealth; I'm talking about elegant, beautiful work.

2003 *Independent*: All the bling at David's birthday party was simply on loan for the evening.

blog *n* (1999) a shortening of *weblog* (1997), the original term for an Internet website containing an eclectic and frequently updated assortment of items of interest to its author. Someone who writes or maintains such a site is said to *blog* (1999), and may be referred to as a *blogger* (1999). The world of blogs and of their writers and readers, and the mindset associated with them, has been termed the *blogosphere* (2002), a word apparently coined by William Quick.

2001 *Washington Post*: Journalist Jim Romenesko's clearinghouse for media gossip... showed how a personal blog could go pro when the Poynter Institute hired him... to blog full time.

2002 *Salina Journal*: Blogs... contain daily musings about news, dating, marriage, divorce, children, politics in the Middle East... or millions of other things or nothing at all.

2002 *Washington Post*: Welcome to the blogosphere, a rapidly expanding universe where legions of ordinary folks are launching Weblogs—blogs for short—... that feature lots of reader feedback.

bobbitt *v* (1993) to amputate the penis of (especially a husband or lover) in an unpremeditated or vindictive manner, typically as an act of revenge for perceived sexual grievances. The term comes from a 1993 incident in the US (exhaustively reported in the world's media) in which Lorena Bobbitt cut off her husband John Wayne Bobbitt's penis with a kitchen knife in revenge for alleged acts of rape and abuse. It may have been influenced by a punning similarity to *bob it* (i.e. 'cut it short').

> 1993 *Pittsburgh Post-Gazette*: I have heard several people say that 'that no-good so-and-so should be bobbitted' or that 'bobbitting would serve that creep right'.
>
> 1996 *Independent*: One woman scorned bobbitted her boyfriend with a Stanley knife.

Bridget Jones *n* (1998) an independent single woman in her thirties. The usage was inspired by *Bridget Jones's Diary* (1996) by Helen Fielding, a humorous fictional diary recounting the highs and (more usually) lows in the life of a thirty-something female in 1990s Britain.

> 1998 *Independent*: This year's list [of additions to the English language] might indeed have found some words and phrases to endure. Single, unattached women in their 30s risk being called Bridget Jones for years to come.

Britpop *n* (1994) the music of a loose affiliation of independent British groups performing in the mid 1990s (e.g. Blur, Oasis, Pulp, Radiohead, Supergrass), showing influences from a variety of British musical traditions (e.g. mod and punk). The term was originally coined in the mid 1980s as a generic term for British pop music ('Potent Brit Pop from the heart and soul of punk's long-gone Buzzcocks', *Chicago Tribune* (1986)), but in the 90s it came to be applied specifically to a new wave of British music produced as a self-conscious reaction against the prevalence of American musical styles.

> 1995 *Arena*: A call to Select magazine's editor suggesting Suede and their peers were all part of a British reaction to the American grunge movement, and Britpop was born.
>
> 1996 *Independent*: Ex-punky indie-melodicists making it work for themselves in the post-Britpop world.

cash for questions *n* (1994) designating a series of incidents in the mid 1990s in which several Conservative MPs were alleged to have accepted money from private individuals in return for tabling specific questions in the House of Commons. The formula was revived in 1998 to accuse the Labour government of 'cash for access' (i.e. accepting payment for access to government ministers). See also **sleaze (1983)**.

> 1994 *Daily Telegraph*: His comments reflect his concern over the damage to the Tory Party image from the recent 'cash for questions' controversy.
>
> 1996 *Observer*: Cash for questions seems tame stuff compared with the way the eighteenth-century Commons lubricated its business.

chav *n* (1998) a lower-class, typically youthful, British person, especially from the southeast of England, who is characterized by brash and loutish behaviour and the wearing of (real or imitation) designer clothes. Chavs' aggressively consumerist lifestyle became a much commented-on social phenomenon in early 21st-century Britain. The origins of the word itself remain uncertain. The likeliest candidate is perhaps Romani *čhavo*, denoting an unmarried Romani male, but other possibilities have been suggested: *chavvy* 'baby, child', from Angloromani *chavvy* 'child' (perhaps partly via Polari (British gay) slang *chavy* 'child'); Angloromani *charver* or *charva* 'woman, especially a prostitute'; and *Chatham*, the name of the town in Kent where the usage is said to have originated (though that may well be a later rationalization).

> 2004 *Sunday Times*: Older children desire nothing more than to dress, talk and behave like chavs, that is, a youth tribe that prides itself on council-estate chic—man-made fabrics, fake labels and lots of eight-carat gold: think Vicky Pollard in *Little Britain*.

clear blue water *n* (1994) a substantial and noticeable difference in ideology and policy between the British Conservative Party and its political opponents, especially the Labour Party. The metaphor was based on the idea of one boat being clearly ahead of another in a race, with a not very subtle reference to the traditional colour of the

Conservatives. It was first used by the Conservative minister Michael Portillo and quickly became a political cliché.

> 1994 *Observers*: Both Ministers believe that the Conservatives should put 'clear blue water' between themselves and Labour by moving further to the radical Right.
>
> 1995 *Independent*: I'm absolutely brassed off with all this talk of green shoots and clear blue water.

Cool Britannia *n* (1992) a slogan encapsulating a supposed renaissance of pop culture in Britain in the mid 1990s, featuring bands, clothes designers, restaurateurs, etc. fashionable throughout the known world. It is a pun on *Rule Britannia*, and had actually been used in 1967 as the title of a song by the Bonzo Dog Doo Dah Band. By 1998 its appeal was wearing thin, amid accusations that politicians, particularly the new Labour government, were trying to cash in on the coolness.

> 1993 *Sunday Times*: The children of cool Britannia may not know much about trigonometry, but they do know every art term in the book. On the other hand, your average American rock fan probably thinks dada is somebody you can borrow the car from.
>
> 1996 *Independent*: Cool Britannia discovers its style again; tourists are flocking to join in a cultural renaissance.
>
> 1996 *International Herald Tribune*: 'Cool Britannia' is inspiring the Yanks.

council tax *n* (1991) in the UK, a tax levied by local authorities, calculated according to whichever of several bands the estimated capital value of a property falls into, and introduced in 1993 to replace the unpopular *community charge* (1985) (see **poll tax (1985)**).

> 1991 *Daily Telegraph*: Mr Major secured full Cabinet backing yesterday for a new local tax—expected to be called the Council Tax—which will be based on a two-person household, with a discount for a single person living alone.
>
> 1992 *Daily Mail*: The new council tax, designed to replace the community charge, is expected to be based on the 1990 value of properties.

cybercafé *n* (1994) a café where customers while eating and drinking can sit at computer terminals and log on to the Internet.

> 1995 *.net*: Cyberia, the UK's first cybercafe . . . offers a pretty affordable way for anyone to play with the big daddy of Internet connections—if only for half an hour or so.

Dianamania, Dimania *n* (1996) a mass-hysterical reaction to the presence or idea of Diana, Princess of Wales (often colloquially known as 'Di'). The term was latterly applied specifically to the wave of public emotion caused in Britain and elsewhere by her death in a car crash in Paris on 31 August 1997.

> 1996 *Guardian*: Though most reporters were still proclaiming the city gripped by Dimania, there were signs yesterday of princess fatigue.
>
> 1997 *Guardian*: The Christmas holiday period will be the first of two tests of whether the Dianamania was a late-summer madness or a lasting national rite of pasage . . . She may think such stuff is for politicians but, as she is likely to discover when Dimania revives this Christmas, the Queen is running for office.
>
> 1998 *Sunday Times*: Time for a foreign holiday if you are fed up with Dimania—this is only the start of a fortnight of mourning on television.

docusoap *n* (1991) a television genre consisting of (actual or semi-staged) unscripted footage of people going about their ordinary lives and work. It combines the actuality of the fly-on-the-wall documentary with the developing storyline of the soap opera. The usage was anticipated in the US in the late 1970s by *docu-soap opera*, which denoted a dramatized scripted film of actual events.

> 1998 *Daily Telegraph*: Chris Terrill's 12-part docu-soap . . . charted the journey of the Galaxy, a 2000-passenger cruise ship bound for the Caribbean.
>
> 1998 *Independent*: Docusoaps are now beginning to get really serious ratings.

dotcom *n* (1994) an Internet address for a commercial site expressed in terms of the formulaic suffix *.com*, and hence a company which uses the Internet for business, especially one with an Internet address ending in *.com*. Someone employed by a dotcom company has been dubbed a *dotcommer* (1997); and a failed or unsuccessful dotcom is, in the inevitable pun, a *dot-bomb* (1999).

> 1996 *Internet World*: A broad discussion of what's around the corner for dot.coms. What effect will 'dumb-delivery' devices have as they make the Web more accessible to the home market?

> 2000 *Sunday Times*: Cybercrime is on the up—not all dotcom millionares aim to make their fortunes through anything quite as wholesome as a stock-market listing.

> 2000 *Daily Telegraph*: The caricature of the twentysomething dotcommer, . . . working 18 hour days while continually plugged into the net and mobile phone, has already become a cliché.

> 2002 *Personal Computer World*: The number of US dotbombs doubled last year, with at least 537 going bust or closing down compared with 225 in 2000.

DVD *n* (1993) an abbreviation of *digital video disc*, a type of digital recording medium similar in appearance to a CD but with much increased storage capacity. According to its manufacturers, the expansion stands for *digital versatile disc*, but the *v* is now generally taken to mean *video*, probably because the principal reason for developing the disc was to allow a full-length feature film to be stored on one disc.

> 1994 *Variety*: In May of this year, Sony and Philips announced the joint development of a quad density digital video disk—or DVD.

> 1997 *San Francisco Chronicle*: The first DVD players will be hitting the stores this month, priced from $599 to $1000.

DWEM *n* (1990) an acronym formed from the initial letters of *dead white European male*, a contemptuous term applied to famous male historical figures, especially writers, artists, and thinkers, whose work has dominated the curricula of Western schools and universities, and is now challenged by some as discriminatory and unrepresentative, especially sexist, and Eurocentric or insufficiently multicultural. The term originated in the US, and is still mainly used there.

> 1990 *Forbes*: 'PC,' she smiled, using the new campus jargon for opinions that are 'politically correct'. That and 'DWEM' (dead white European male) are, I gather, two of the most common acronyms on campus.

> 1992 *New Republic*: I have usually taken comfort in the obvious response that DWEMs have given us habeas corpus and digitalis, cantatas and penicillin.

emoticon *n* (1990) a representation of a facial expression formed by a short sequence of keyboard characters, usually to be viewed sideways, and used in e-mail etc. to convey the sender's feelings or intended tone. There is a small range of widely recognized and used emoticons (e.g. :-) a smile, ;-) a wink, :-(a frown), but also a well-documented lexicon of more outlandish symbols created out of the basic range of keyboard punctuation marks (e.g. :-* a kiss, :-o, loquacity). The word is a blend of *emotion* and **icon (1982)**.

Essex girl *n* (1991) a humorously derogatory British term applied to a type of young woman, supposedly to be found in and around Essex, and variously characterized as vulgar, unintelligent, promiscuous, and materialistic. The coinage was based on **Essex man** below, but in this case the focus is social rather than political. The archetypal Essex girl garb includes unsubtle gold jewellery, white high-heeled shoes, short tight skirts, and probably, if the rash of politically incorrect Essex girl jokes going around in Britain in the early 1990s are to be believed (see the first quote below), knickers with no elastic.

> 1991 *Independent*: How does an Essex girl turn the light on afterwards? She kicks open the car door . . . Essex Girl jokes are told on the radio; they are faxed around between offices.

> 1993 *Independent*: You can parade in shiny and pricey skin-tight leggings. You can be jazzed up with Essex-girl gold jewellery for weekends.

Essex man *n* (1990) a derogatory British term used to denote a supposed new type of Conservative voter, to be found especially in London and the southeast of England in the late 1980s, typically characterized as a brash, self-made young businessman who benefited from entrepreneurial wealth created by Thatcherite policies. A touchstone of Tory electoral success in the 1980s was held to be the regular return of Conservative members to Parliament by newly enriched working-class voters in a number of Essex seats (e.g. Basildon and Harlow) which had hitherto been solidly Labour.

> 1990 *Sunday Times*: The mass of the tribe has changed: the life and soul of the new Conservative Party, and the bedrock of its support, is Essex man.
>
> 1994 *Guardian*: Essex Man has returned to his two-up two-down in Billericay and loadsamoney has been silenced under loadsadebts.

ethnic cleansing *n* (1991) the purging, by mass expulsion or killing, of one ethnic or religious group by another. A chilling euphemism introduced into English by courtesy of the inter-ethnic conflict within the area formerly known as Yugoslavia, which started in 1991, and particularly associated with the bitter fighting between the Bosnian Serbs and the Bosnian Muslims. A translation of Serbo-Croat *etničko čiščenje*.

> 1994 *Imprimis*: The world still seems helpless to stop ethnic cleansing in Bosnia.
>
> 1995 *Times*: The area has a large number of towns and villages, many emptied of Muslims and Croats in three years of ethnic cleansing.

European Union *n* (1991) a federation of (originally western) European states, established by the Maastricht Treaty in 1992, which is co-extensive with the European Community, and whose members send representatives to the European Parliament. The abbreviation *EU* is first recorded in 1993.

> 1991 *World Press Review*: But only diehard Euro-skeptics believe that the European Union part of this scenario will never see the light of day.
>
> 1995 *Daily Mirror*: Despite what the anti-European politicians say, are we willing to accept being part of Europe, how much do we know about the EU and should we get closer to the European dream?

FAQ *n* (1991) an acronym formed from the initial letters of *frequently asked questions*, denoting a computer text file containing a list of questions and answers relating to a particular subject, especially one giving basic information on a topic to users of an Internet newsgroup.

> 1994 *Independent*: 'Respect other people's time and bandwidth' means, among other things, checking the 'FAQ' (Frequently Asked Questions) document before posting a query.
>
> 1997 *Linux Journal*: Are there FAQs about setting up Netscape 2.02 with Linux? After you unzip Netscape where do you put the files?

fashionista *n* (1993) an often derogatory term for someone employed in or otherwise gaining a living from the fashion industry, as a designer, model, photographer, fashion writer, etc., and also for someone addicted to the buying and wearing of high-fashion clothes. It was coined in America using the Spanish suffix *-ista* '-ist', apparently on the model of earlier borrowings from Spanish such as *Peronista* (1946) and *Sandinista* (1928).

> 1996 *Time Out N.Y.*: A universe of trendy promoters . . . ensures a crowd of beautiful people, suntanned fashionistas and their coattail riders, all air-kissing and cocktailing.

freedom fries *n* (2003) a polemical alternative name proposed in the US for *French fries* (i.e. chips) as a sign of America's grave displeasure with France for declining to support its invasion of Iraq in 2003 (the French themselves were widely characterized as 'cheese-eating surrender-monkeys'). It was coined by Republican Representative Bob Ney (and soon followed by *freedom toast* for *French toast*). The renaming of foodstuffs in times of international conflict is far from new: during World War I, for example, *sauerkraut* became *liberty cabbage* in the US.

> 2003 *cnn.com*: Neal Rowland, the owner of Cubbie's [a restaurant in Beaufort, North Carolina], now only sells his fried potato strips as 'freedom fries'—a decision that comes as Americans watch French officials back away from support for possible war in Iraq.

gastropub *n* (1996) a public house which specializes in serving high-quality food.

> 1996 *Evening Standard*: Will stale pork pies and reheated bangers ever be axed from pub menus? The rise of the gastropub suggests that, one day, they might.

GM *adj* (1992) an abbreviation of *genetically modified*, denoting foodstuffs that contain or consist of genetically altered plant or animal material. *Genetically modified* is first recorded as a technical term in the biological sciences in 1970, but its application by producers and marketers to foods and consequent wider lay usage are a 1990s phenomenon. By the end of the decade it was a bogey term, evoking thoughts of Frankenstein.

> 1999 *Sunday Times*: Dr Stanley Ewan of Aberdeen University . . . measured their internal organs and found the stomach walls of the rats fed GM potatoes were grossly distended.

golden goal *n* (1994) the first goal scored during extra time in a soccer match, which ends the match and gives victory to the scoring side. The concept was introduced to try to forestall the 'penalty shoot-out' as a way of deciding unresolved matches in a knock-out competition.

> 1994 *Daily Mirror*: FIFA general secretary Sepp Blatter said yesterday that a system of sudden-death would be introduced in extra-time, with a goal—the 'golden goal'—ending the match.

Google *v* (1999) to search for information on the Internet using the Google search engine. Google was launched in September 1998, its name a conscious echo of *googol*, a mathematical term for ten raised to the hundredth power, with reference to the huge amount of information contained on the Internet (the difference in spelling is reputedly due to an error made by its founders when registering the name). Its rapid rise to market leadership is signalized by the name's transformation into a verb (which can be both intransitive and transitive, with the object of the search as the object of the verb).

> 1999 *Re*: Hi Guys! in alt.fan.british-accent (Usenet newsgroup): Has anyone Googled?

> 2001 *New York Times*: I met this woman last night at a party and I came right home and googled her.

grunge *n, adj* (1991) (in) a style of appearance or dress characterized by loose-fitting, layered, often second-hand clothes, ripped jeans, and heavy boots, favoured by fans of grunge music and also briefly appropriated by the retail fashion industry. The use of *grunge* with reference to informal music has been claimed since the late 1960s, and there is recorded evidence of it from the early 70s, but it seems not to have become a specific term until the beginning of the 90s, when it was applied to a style of rock music characterized by a raucous guitar sound which was developed by a number of mainly Seattle-based US groups. The term soon spread from there to the appearance of its fans.

> 1993 *Chicago Tribune*: Still, designer grunge is a concept that doesn't play well in Seattle where the real grunge community wears a 'uniform' of layered, worn clothing.

> 1994 *Rolling Stone*: The group is discussing what it's like to be seen as grunge kids in the reality of post-Nirvana Aberdeen.

Gulf War syndrome *n* (1991) a disorder of the nervous system alleged to have been contracted by soldiers serving in the Gulf War of 1991. The causes (and indeed the existence) of the disorder are still disputed: suggested agents include the anti-nerve-gas medication given to troops destined for the Gulf, and harmful chemicals encountered on active service there. The condition has also been referred to as *desert fever, Desert Storm syndrome* (from the code name of the Allies' land campaign in the Gulf War), and *Persian War syndrome*.

> 1992 *USA Today*: Hundreds of gulf war veterans . . . are reporting various illnesses they say are the result of service in the Persian Gulf. Dubbed 'gulf war syndrome', symptoms range from hair loss, fatigue and muscle aches to dizzy spells and shortness of breath.

1996 *Week*: Nicholas Soames, the Armed Forces Minister, has announced a full inquiry into Gulf War Syndrome and apologised for unknowingly misleading Parliament over the extent to which troops had been exposed to harmful pesticides during the Gulf War.

home page *n* (1993) a document created in a hypertext system (especially on the World Wide Web) which serves either as a point of introduction to a person, institution, or company, or as a focus of information on a particular topic, and which usually contains hypertext links to other (related) documents. Compare **website (1994)**.

1993 *R & D*: At startup, Mosaic provides the user with a home page that contains a number of information links with which the user can begin his exploration.

1995 *Guardian*: Edward Kennedy was the first senator to establish a 'home page' on the Internet giving two way access to the public.

HTML *n* (1992) an abbreviation of *Hypertext Markup Language*, a specification for generating World Wide Web pages which enables the viewing software to display text, images, and other resources and to execute links to other such pages; it also allows the user to create and print out documents.

1994 *Computer Weekly*: HTML has 'tags' to tell your browser how to lay out the text it is receiving—'text' that can include images, sounds and even live, digital video.

http *n* (1992) an abbreviation of *hypertext transfer protocol* (sometimes also interpreted as *hypertext transport protocol*), the term applied to a protocol that supports the retrieval of data on a computer network, and especially of HTML documents on the World Wide Web. It became familiar in the 1990s as the initial element in Web addresses.

2000 *Guardian*: To transport the data, a new protocol was invented called HTTP (Hypertext Transfer Protocol). But TCP/IP and other protocols date back to the 1970s.

identity theft *n* (1991) the dishonest acquisition of personal information in order to perpetrate fraud, typically by obtaining credit, loans, etc. in someone else's name.

1991 *Boston Globe*: The Social Security Administration in Boston . . . agrees that identity theft can be quickly stopped. 'If you can document someone else is using your Social Security number, we'll give you a new number.'

jobseeker *n* (1993) in Britain, an unemployed person required to demonstrate efforts to find work in order to qualify for government benefits. The semi-euphemistic *jobseeker* for 'unemployed person' is first recorded as long ago as 1942, but this specific application stems from the introduction of the so-called *Jobseeker's Allowance* in 1993 (see the first quote below).

1993 *Guardian*: Similarly, the unemployed are now 'jobseekers', entitled to Jobseeker's Allowance provided they first sign a Jobseeker's Agreement.

1995 *Independent*: Pilot projects of workfare . . . could be launched after the Jobseeker's Bill becomes law.

laddish *adj* (1991) indulging in uncouthly macho behaviour and attitudes. The inspiration for the term was perhaps the British so-called *New Lad* (1991), a (young) man who embraced sexist attitudes and the traditional male role as a reaction against the perceived effeminacy of the **New Man (1982)**. By the middle of the 1990s girls were wanting to join in, and the female *ladette* (1995) was born.

1991 *Face*: We're all cackling in laddish glee. Things are looking up.

1997 *Independent*: A ladette is best described as a young woman who is confident, assertive, drinks a lot and is as rude and crude as any lad.

metrosexual *n, adj* (1994) a term coined by the journalist Mark Simpson to denote a (heterosexual) man whose lifestyle, spending habits, and concern for personal appearance are likened to those considered typical of a fashionable, urban, homosexual man. It combines *metropolitan* and *sexual* in a punning reference to *heterosexual*. Somewhat later near synonyms were *just gay enough* and *gay-adjacent*.

1994 Mark Simpson in *Independent*: One sharply dressed 'metrosexual' in his early 20s . . . has a perfect complexion and precisely gelled hair, and is inspecting a display of costly aftershaves.

2004 Bernice Kanner: Many . . . straight men know the difference between volumizing conditioners and botanical ingredients. They are not gay or bisexual so much as 'metrosexual'.

millennium bug *n* (1995) the anticipated inability of certain computer software to deal correctly with dates later than 31 December 1999, which threatened to bring computer systems worldwide crashing to a halt at the arrival of the millennium (in the event, nothing untoward happened). It was also sometimes referred to as the *millennium bomb.*

1995 *Chicago Tribune*: To fix software that carries the millennium bug, the code must be run through a decompiling program that converts the computer code into languages like Cobol.

1996 *Times*: The Internal Revenue Service envisages taking 300 man-years to defeat the 'new millennium bug'.

Millennium Dome *n* (1997) a very large structure in the shape of a flattened dome constructed on the Greenwich Peninsula, SE London, to house a national exhibition celebrating the millennium in 2000. The name is often shortened contextually to simply *the Dome.* The project was attacked widely during the course of its building on such varied grounds as its expense, the banality of its proposed contents, and the self-aggrandizing tendencies of its political master Peter Mandelson. Those who visited its exhibition largely found it disappointing, and when it closed on 1 January 2001 it had made a heavy financial loss. After lying idle for some time, it was announced that the Dome would become a 20,000-seater arena, and it is planned to hold some Olympic events there in 2012.

1997 *Earthmatters*: Part of [the Millennium Experience] is going to be showing what our environment will be like, how we can sustain it, and how new technologies will shape our housing, our energy, transport and so on. We need the Millennium Dome and the rest of the Experience to present those things with the originality and the panache they deserve.

1998 *Observer*: An earlier scene had shown Draper walking Dainton around the Dome. 'Isn't it marvellous,' gushes Draper. 'Waste of money,' counters Dainton.

mission creep *n* (1991) a gradual slippage in political or strategic objectives during the course of a military campaign, often resulting in an unresolved conflict or open-ended commitment. The term originated in the jargon of the US military, but its usefulness as a euphemism soon recommended it in other contexts.

1994 *Guardian*: 'When you tell one lie, and then you have to tell another, and then another . . . what's that called?' 'Mission creep.'

1998 *DM News*: Database projects are notorious for 'mission creep'. What starts as a manageable, focused development effort somehow evolves into a multimillion, multiyear systems project that tries to be everything to everybody.

MP3 *n* (1996) an abbreviation denoting a computer file standard used for the compression of audio sequences (by a factor of about 12) for the purpose of digital storage and transmission. In its full form it is *MPEG-1, Audio Layer III* (*MPEG* being short for *Moving Picture Experts Group*, the name of the committee that originally devised such standards). Originally a piece of fairly abstruse jargon, the term became much more widely known and used at the end of the 20th century as more and more people used the technology to download compressed music from the Internet and play it on their multimedia computers.

1998 *Wired*: Some legal MP3 music is floating around the web; in time, this may become the indie-rock distribution channel of choice.

Muggle *n* (1997) in the writings of J. K. Rowling (b. 1965), the British author of children's fantasy fiction, a person who possesses no magical powers. The word was apparently coined from the colloquial *mug* 'a fool' (although it should be pointed out that in US slang, *muggle* can mean 'a marijuana cigarette'). It has gone on to enjoy some metaphorical use for someone who lacks a particular skill or skills, or who is regarded as inferior in some way.

> 1999 *Computer Weekly*: Our new senior DBA starts on Monday. She's a muggle. No IT background, understanding or aptitude at all.

mullet *n* (1994) a hairstyle, worn especially by men, in which the hair is cut short at the front and sides and left long at the back. It was popularized by the US hip-hop group the Beastie Boys, but its moment of stylishness was brief, and by the late 1990s it had become the epitome of tonsorial naffness. The origins of the term are unclear. It appears to have been the same Beastie Boys who coined it, but what they based it on is a matter of dispute: possibilities advanced (some of them by the Boys themselves, apparently to muddy the waters) include the fish-name; an obsolete verb *mullet* meaning 'to dress hair with a mullet', a type of tweezers (from French *molet*); and *mullet-head*, meaning 'a stupid person'.

> 1998 *Sunday Mirror*: The Mullet... If you have one, then a word in your ear: Scissors.

name and shame *v* (1990) to disclose publicly a person's or institution's (perceived) wrongdoing or failure. The usage is of North American origin. Such disclosures were a popular move in the morally self-righteous 1990s.

> 1993 *Vancouver Star*: Juveniles should be named and shamed, not protected, so that they and their parents may be held responsible.

> 1998 *Mirror*: Jack Straw... is a strong advocate of tough punishments for juvenile drug offenders—including naming and shaming them, and fining their parents.

negative equity *n* (1992) the indebtedness that occurs when the market value of a property falls below the outstanding amount of a mortgage secured on it, representing a reversal of the favourable (and expected) situation in which a property is a valuable asset. The term has been in use since the 1950s in US financial jargon in broad application to assets generally. This specific British use arose out of a situation in which house prices, inflated by the boom of the 1980s, suddenly tumbled with the recession of the early 90s, catching out many people who had bought at the top of the market.

> 1993 *Guardian*: The proportion of house owners with negative equity rose by a fifth over the past year as prices in some regions continued to fall.

New Labour *n* (1992) the British Labour Party as it is after the internal reforms initiated by Neil Kinnock (party leader 1983–92), and carried through by John Smith (party leader 1992–94) and Tony Blair (party leader 1994–, Prime Minister 1997–). The changes affect both its constitution and internal workings (e.g. the introduction of 'one man one vote' for decision-making within the party) and its policies (characterized by a move towards the political centre; see **third way (1990)**). The use of *new* to suggest a radical political departure or change of direction is far from new (for example, the programme of social and economic reform in the US planned by the Roosevelt administration of 1932 onwards was termed the *New Deal*), and the term *New Labour* itself first came to prominence in 1989 to denote a breakaway wing of the New Zealand Labour Party. See also **Blairism (1993)**.

> 1995 *Independent*: The Labour front bench's prevarication over rail renationalisation has only added to the mistrust felt by rank and file trade unionists towards Mr Blair and 'New Labour'.

> 1997 *Mail on Sunday*: Rebel MP Tam Dalyell—thorn in the side on New Labour's pro-devolution campaign—said he would refuse to bow to threats to oust him before the next General Election.

9/11 *n* (2001) a shorthand way of referring to the terrorist attacks on the World Trade Center in New York City and the Pentagon in Washington on 11 September 2001. It is the numerical version of *September 11*, which often performs the same function. There is some evidence for its use in this role as early as the very same day, and English was quick to accommodate it in various grammatical guises (e.g. '9/11 victims'). It caught on in Britain (despite its reversal of the standard British date formula—'9/11' would normally be interpreted as '9 November') and elsewhere, even being applied metaphorically to other similar events (a headline in the Spanish newspaper *El Mundo* on 12 March 2004, following terrorist bombings in Madrid, translates as 'Our September 11—A Day of Infamy'). The same model was used to produce 7/7 in the wake of the terrorist attacks on London's transport system on 7 July 2005 (fortuitously, the order of day and month made no difference).

nvCJD (1996), **vCJD** (1997) *n* abbreviations of, respectively, *new variant CJD* and *variant CJD*, names given to a degenerative disease of the human brain similar to Creutzfeldt-Jakob disease (*CJD*—the abbreviation is first recorded in 1975) but differing from it in earlier onset and in certain early psychiatric and sensory symptoms. It is thought to be causally linked to **BSE (1987)**, and initially was unofficially termed *human BSE* (1992).

> 1999 *Daily Express*: Already 40 people have died from new-variant CJD.
>
> 2003 *Independent*: Other diseases such as variant-CJD, linked with BSE in cows, . . . are transmitted through food.
>
> 2003 *Times*: A link has been established between gelatine and vCJD.

off-message *adj, adv* (1993) departing from a planned or intended message. The term is applied specifically to a politician who departs from the official party line. It originated in the US, but was taken up enthusiastically in Britain, especially by the media managers of New Labour, for whom loyal adherence to the script (being 'on message') is an acid test of political soundness and promotability.

> 1993 *Washington Post*: The president essentially went 'off-message'. He moved from topic to topic . . . and promoted his economic plan only in passing.
>
> 1997 *Daily Telegraph*: A colleague said there had been a serious conflict among ministers because the commitment was '100 per cent off-message'.
>
> 1998 *Private Eye*: The Lib Dems' off-message response to planned benefit cuts.

out *v* (1990) to expose the undeclared homosexuality of (especially a prominent or public figure), originally mainly as a tactical move by gay-rights activists. The term originated in the US. It is a verbal use of the adjective *out*, which is first recorded in the sense 'acknowledged openly as a homosexual' (i.e. 'out of the closet') in 1979.

> 1995 *Maclean's*: 'I consider outing a supreme act of moral cowardice,' he said. 'In no case I am aware of have the outers offered counselling or support to the person they are outing.'
>
> 1996 *Face*: It's typical of Garber's style that Vice Versa is packed with juicy anecdotes about the sex lives of celebrities. She 'outs' dozens as bi—instead of exclusively straight or gay.

people's *n* (1997) designating something thought of as relating to, belonging to, or including all the ordinary members of the population, as opposed to an establishment élite. It was a concept that took off in Britain in the wake of the death of Diana, Princess of Wales, when the unexpectedly effusive public expressions of grief supposedly demonstrated, among other things, that it was the rank and file of Britain, not their rulers or the great and the good, who would determine the nature and extent of the nation's response. The term has its roots in the 19th century (an educational institution called the 'People's Palace' was opened in London in 1887), but since the 1930s it has been associated mainly with Communist regimes; this new usage is more mystical than political.

> 1997 *Daily Telegraph*: The continuing myth that Tony Blair coined the phrase 'The people's Princess'. . . [It] was actually the title of the chapter about Diana in Anthony Holden's 1993 book about the House of Windsor, *The Tarnished Crown*.
>
> 1997 *Independent on Sunday*: If the Palace is to be converted into a 'living gallery' or 'people's palace', it would be closed to the public for state occasions.
>
> 1997 *Guardian*: They were joined by 'ordinary' people chosen as a cross-section of the nation, at the 'People's Banquet'.

1999 *Evening Standard*: The Government's proposals for an interim Chamber appear something of a dog's breakfast, including... the appointment of up to 20 'people's peers'.

personal stereo *n* (1992) a small battery-operated cassette player and headphones capable of being worn by a person who is on foot. The generic term has largely come to replace the earlier trade name **Walkman (1981)**. It is first recorded in 1992, but was probably in use well before then (the synonymous *personal hi-fi* is first recorded in 1985).

1992 *Which?*: If you want your children to keep their music to themselves during the holidays, a personal stereo is the ideal gift.

phish *v* (1996) to perpetrate a fraud on the Internet in order to glean personal information (e.g. credit card details) about individuals, especially by impersonating a reputable company. The word is a respelling of *fish*, the underlying idea being of 'angling' for information. Its ultimate model was perhaps *phreak* (1972), a blend of *phone* and *freak* denoting someone who makes phone calls illegally without payment, but the phenomenon of *ph* as an *f* with attitude really began to take off in the early 1990s (e.g. in *pharm* for a place where genetically modified plants or animals are grown). A more highly targeted version of the practice, in which one specific organization is attacked, has been termed *spear phishing* (2004).

1996 *Re*: Get on aol from off aol in alt.online-service.america-online (Usenet newsgroup): You could go phishing for passwords (not that i do it... or recommend it).

2003 *Sunday Telegraph*: Have you been 'phished'? My brother was, just last week.

podcasting *n* (2004) the making available of a digital recording of a radio broadcast or similar item on the Internet for downloading to a personal audio player or a computer. The most popular and fashionable of such players in the early 21st century was the iPod, introduced by the Apple company in 2001—whence *podcasting*.

2005 *Wired*: Even beer megacorporation Heineken is getting in on the action. The brewer has started making podcasts of pop DJs available on its Web site as part of a promotional campaign. Given that podcasting didn't exist nine months ago, this adoption curve is impressive. Podcasting—unregulated, low-cost, on-demand radio—is heading for a tipping point.

Power Ranger *n* (1993) the proprietary name of a plastic toy figure resembling a character from the US children's television series *Mighty Morphin Power Rangers*. These American teenagers are regularly summoned to change into masked kung-fu heroes to do battle with the evil Space Aliens and other villains.

1994 *Guardian*: The key to the toys' success is television. The characters are all tied in to a series about a group of teenagers able to 'morph' into crime-fighting Power Rangers.

1995 *Sugar*: Snap up one of these fab Power Ranger key-rings.

pukka *adj* (1991) excellent, of the highest quality; fashionable. This was a fashionable British approval word of the 1990s, based on the earlier *pukka* 'genuine', and associated particularly with the trendy young chef Jamie Oliver. It was also sometimes used as an adverbial intensifier.

1991 *Independent*: I'm going to France soon..., so I'll look well pukka trendy.

1996 *Observer*: Girls mug girls for jewellery or pukka clothes.

rainbow nation *n* (1992) a multiracial nation, especially one in which all races live in harmony and equality. The term has been applied particularly to South Africa in the post-apartheid era.

1994 Nelson Mandela: We shall build the society in which all South Africans, both black and white, will be able to walk tall,... assured of their inalienable right to human dignity—a rainbow nation at peace with itself and the world.

regime change *n* (1990) the removal of a hostile foreign government, especially by military force. The expression, in its more neutral and obvious sense 'replacement of one governing administration by another', can be traced back to the 1920s, but this euphemistic twist was introduced by the spin-meisters of the late 20th century. It came to particular public notice with the controversy over the motivation for the US-led invasion of Iraq in 2003.

> 1990 *International Security*: The U.S. government tacitly acknowledged that the struggle to promote regime change [in Nicaragua] had shifted from the military to the political-electoral terrain.

> 2002 *Sun* (Baltimore): Iraq's use of gas in that conflict is repeatedly mentioned . . . as justification for 'regime change' in Iraq.

respect *n* (1990) used, originally in African-American English, to denote regard or esteem, without deference on the part of the speaker, but often an indication that he or she accepts or approves of the person or thing spoken of. It is often used interjectionally.

> 1990 *Face*: At one huge rave last summer, the DJ announced, 'Respect is due to the visuals', and everyone broke out in a massive round of applause.

> 1992 *Face*: For services to British fashion, this season's FACE award winner: Lionel Blair. Respect!

SARS *n* (2003) an acronym formed from the initial letters of *severe acute respiratory syndrome*, the name of an infectious disease, caused by a coronavirus, that affects the respiratory system and can in some cases be fatal. An outbreak in China beginning in late 2002 provoked fears of a worldwide pandemic.

sex up *v* (2003) to make more 'sexy', in the sense 'alluring, likely to attract interest'. *Sex up* meaning literally 'to increase the sexual content of' dates from the early 1940s, but this metaphorical application came to prominence in the early 21st century thanks to reports of its use to characterize the treatment given by the British government in 2003 to a document purporting to be an accurate assessment of Iraq's military capability, and in particular of its possession of 'weapons of mass destruction'. It was generally taken to imply more than a hint of exaggeration, if not plain dissimulation.

> 2005 *Observer*: Sir John Scarlett, head of MI6, has been accused of trying 'to sex up' a report by the Iraq Survey Group, the body charged with finding weapons of mass destruction after Saddam Hussein was toppled.

slacker *n* (1994) someone, particularly a member of the current generation of young adults, perceived to lack a sense of direction in life. The usage was inspired by the 1991 film *Slackers*, featuring a former student unable to move beyond the student lifestyle and lacking any ambition. Compare **Generation X (1989)**.

> 1995 *Wired*: The tone is set by graphic artists and wannabe musicians and common-or-garden slackers off to drink cheap beer on Dad's money.

> 1995 *Guardian*: 'It's certainly a reaction to the slacker thing, which was so "anti-style",' says Paul Tunkin, promoter of the London club Blow Up.

spam *v*, *n* (1994) to flood the Internet with tedious or inane postings, especially sending the same message or advertisement to large numbers of newsgroups. Such a message is termed a *spam*. The term originated in the US. It was based on the tinned-meat brand name (see **Spam (1937)**), but the reason for the application is unclear: some have linked it with the *Monty Python* sketch in which Spam appears with every item on a restaurant menu, others with the notion of Spam hitting the fan and filling the surrounding environment.

> 1995 *Everybody's Internet Update*: The alt.current-events.net-abuse Usenet newsgroup is the place to discuss spamming and other obnoxious advertising.

speed dating *n* (2000) a process by which people seeking romantic relationships attend organized events at which they have a short conversation with each of several potential partners. The idea, and the term, originated in the US Jewish community, and some events still focus on people belonging to a particular ethnic or cultural group.

2004 *Evening Standard*: Britain's first naked speeddating event will take place in Brighton next month.

surf *v* (1993) to move from site to site on (the Internet), sampling the contents. The usage is probably an extension of the earlier metaphorical application of *surf* to hopping from channel to channel on the television.

1994 *Guardian*: It costs 20 times as much to 'surf' the world-wide Internet in Germany as it does in the US.

third way *n* (1990) an alternative mode approximately midway between two prevailing and antagonistic systems. Originally applied to the Swedish policy of neutrality between East and West, in the 1990s it became a buzzword in the US and Britain for those advocating a new radical centrist approach, breaking the mould of conflict between political parties of the left and right.

1990 *Independent*: Our capitalists and communists have always, out of hand, condemned the Third Way, or socialist alternative to Stalinism.

1998 *Observer*: The third way Brazilian style might not just offer a way forward for Brazil but some lessons for us in Britain.

trailer trash *n* (1993) people who live permanently in caravans or mobile homes and are regarded as being common, antisocial, unsightly, feckless, or otherwise beyond the pale of civilization. The usage is mainly restricted to the US, and is based on the American *trailer* 'mobile home'.

1993 Lowe & Shaw: Getting the permission's the hard bit, getting past all the narrowminded people who don't want trailer trash down the road.

Trustafarian *n* (1992) a young person from a wealthy background who affects the lifestyle and attitudes of the inner-city ghetto. The British term is a contemptuously humorous blend of *trust fund* (frequently such people's means of support) and *Rastafarian*.

1994 *Guardian*: Here, for instance, is the home of 'Trustafarians'—rich white kids who subscribe to the notion of West London bohemia—and here, for the older generation, is a politically correct mix of creeds, colours and ideologies.

UKIP *n* (1994) the acronymic name of the United Kingdom Independence Party, a British right-wing political party founded in 1993. The central pillar of its policy is the extrication of the United Kingdom from the European Union.

vCJD *n* (1997) see **nvCJD (1996)**.

Viagra *n* (1998) the proprietary name of a drug used for treating male impotence by stimulating penile blood flow. Manufactured by the Pfizer company, its active ingredient is sildenafil citrate. Its apparent success led, unsurprisingly, to a stampede of hopeful purchasers.

1998 *Daily Telegraph*: The drug works by stimulating blood flow and is reportedly effective on women as well as men. Many people who are not impotent are thought to be trying Viagra to see if it improves their sex lives. Viagra has few notable side-effects except mild headaches in some people.

1998 *Sunday Times*: Frank Dobson, the health secretary, insists that the NHS will prescribe Viagra only to men who have 'sound clinical reasons' for taking the drug.

WAP *n* (1997) an acronym based on the initial letters of *wireless application protocol*, a specification supporting the transfer of data (especially for Internet access, including text and images) to and from a hand-held wireless device, especially a mobile phone with a suitable display panel. This was a key modality for the much heralded 'third generation' that would take mobile technology on to a new plane of transcendency at the end of the 20th century.

2000 *Daily Telegraph*: By the end of this year, almost all mobiles will be WAP-phones.

Web *n* (1994) a shortened version of **World Wide Web (1990)**.

1994 *American Scientist*: The first components of the system were working by 1991, but the Web did not begin to spread outside the high-energy physics community until 1993.

1995 *New York Times*: Some people believe the Web is the most important advance in publishing since the printing press.

webcast *n* (1995) a live broadcast transmitted over the Internet. The transmission of such broadcasts is known as *webcasting* (1995).

1996 *Guardian*: It's risky to claim a first, but Purina is on safe ground with the first Webcast of the birth of an endangered rhino.

weblog *n* (1997) see **blog (1999)**.

website *n* (1994) a document or set of linked documents, usually associated with a particular person, organization, or topic, that is held on a computer system and can be accessed as part of the **World Wide Web (1990)**. Compare **home page (1993)**.

1994 *.net*: Pore over fascinating trivia on The Death of Rock 'n' Roll, a . . . Web site that provides detailed information on rigamortis rockers who are prematurely pushing up the daisies.

1996 *Interzone*: They experience difficulty in separating their website lives from their real lives, and find the freedom of the former infinitely preferable to the limitations of the latter.

Wi-Fi *n* (1999) a name given to any of a range of standards, especially 802.11b, for high-speed wireless transmission of data over a relatively small range, enabling the downloading of audio, video, and data without the need for cables. It was based on *hi-fi*, with the *wi-* imported from *wireless* (the claim that it is short for *wireless fidelity* seems to be a later rationalization). It is a proprietary term in the US.

2003 *Daily Telegraph*: Individuals with Wi-Fi equipped laptops roam the streets looking for 'open' wireless systems.

WMD *n* (1991) see **weapon of mass destruction (1937)**.

World Wide Web *n* (1990) a visually based system for accessing information (text, graphics, sound, video) by means of the Internet, which consists of a large number of 'documents' tagged with cross-referencing links by which the user can move between sources. Originally intended as a tool by which particle physicists might exchange information, by 1993 it had been taken up far more widely, and by the end of the 20th century, computer addresses prefixed by the abbreviation *www* had become an everyday sight. See also **Web (1994)**.

1990 Tim Berners-Lee & Robert Cailliau (title): WorldWideWeb: Proposal for a HyperText Project.

1994 *Guardian*: The World Wide Web . . . is poised to create an egalitarian new cybersociety for all, regardless of creed, colour or class.

1995 *Internet World*: As a WWW site administrator, or Webmaster, becomes comfortable with the site's basic functionality, more advanced features can be added.

1998 *Radio Times*: You'll find more to interest you at the fascinating Windrush website (www.bbc.co.uk/education/windrush).

Index

A

abled 208
A-bomb 113
abominable snowman 60
absenteeism 60
abstract 37
abuse 160
acid 160
acid house 208
ack-ack 85
acronym 113
action replay 185
addict 11
adrenaline 11
adult 139
adviser 37
aerial 11
aerodrome 11
aerosol 60
affirmative action 85
African-American 160
Afro-Caribbean 139
Aga saga 230
ageism, agism 160
aid 113
Aid 208
Aids, AIDS 208
air 60
air-conditioning 85
air force 37
air hostess 85
air-lift 113
airline 37
airliner 11
airport 37
air raid 37
air-raid precautions 85
alcopop 230
algorithm 85
alien 113
A-list 208
allergy 37
al-Qaeda 230
alternative 185
alternative society 160
alternative technology 185
Alzheimer's disease 37
American dream 85
angry young man 139
anorak 208
anorexic 11
antibiotic 113
anti-matter 139
apartheid 114
appease 85
appeasement 38
Argie 209
arms race 85
art nouveau 12
artificial intelligence 139
Aryan, Arian 85
ASBO 230
assembly line 38
asset 185
astronaut 60
asylum seeker 139
atom bomb 114
atomic bomb 38
atomic energy 12
atomic power 38
atonal 60
attitude 160
audio 38
automation 114
autopilot 86
avant-garde 38
awesome 209
axis of evil 230

B

babelicious 230
baby-sitter 86
back to basics 185
backlash 139
backroom boy 114
bacteriological warfare 60
ballyhoo 12
balti 209
banana republic 86
bathing beauty 60
battery 86
Beatlemania 160
beatnik 140
beautician 61
beauty parlour 12
beauty queen 61
beauty salon 61
beauty shop 12
Belisha beacon 86
benefit tourism 230
benzedrine 86
big bang 140
Big Bang 209
Big Brother 114
big business 12
Big Mac 185
bikini 114
billet 86
bingo 86
biodegradable 161
biodiversity 209
biotechnology 114, 185
birth control 38
birthday card 12
bit 115
black hole 161
black market 86
black-out 87
black out 39
black power 161
blackshirt 61
Black Wednesday 231
Blairism 231
Blighty 39
Blimp 87
bling 231
blip 209
blitz 115
Blitzkrieg 87
blog 231
blow 161
blues 39
B.O. 87
boat people 186
bobbitt 231
body bag 140
body language 161
bodyline 87
body odour 87
boffin 115
Bolshevik 39
bomb 13, 115
bomber 39
bonk 186
boot 210
born-again 161
Botox 210
boutique 140
boy scout 13
bra 88
brain-washing 140
brassière, brassiere 13
brave new world 88
bread-line 13
break-dancing 210
breathalyser 161
Bren gun 88
Bridget Jones 232
brinkmanship 141
Britpop 232
broadcast 61
BSE 210
bubble-gum 88
buck 13
bulimia 186
burger 88
bus 162
business lunch 61
by-pass 61
byte 162

C

caftan 162
camcorder 210
cameraman 14
camouflage 39
canned 14
carer 186
caring 162
car park 61
cashback 211
cash dispenser 162
cash for questions 232
cassette 162
cat 61, 88
cathode-ray tube 14
CD ROM 211
cellphone 211
central heating 14
CFC 186
chain store 39
chairperson 187
challenged 211
charisma 141
charts 162
chat show 162

chattering classes 211
chauffeur 14
chav 232
cheesecake 88
chemical warfare 39
chill 211
chip 163
cinema 14, 39
city centre 14
civil defence 88
classified 115
clear blue water 232
climax 40
clip-joint 89
clone 14
closed shop 15
closet 141
CND 141
cocktail cabinet 89
cocktail party 61
coffee bar 141
coke 15
Coke 15
cold turkey 62
cold war 115
collaboration 116
collateral damage 187
collective farm 62
colour-bar 40
coloured 89
colour prejudice 15
colour supplement 89
colour television 62
columnist 62
combine harvester, combine 62
commando 116
commentary 62
commercial 89
commitment 116
common market 141
Commonwealth 40
commute 163
compact disc 187
complex 15
comprehensive 116
computer 116
computerize 163
concentration camp 15
conga 89
conscientious objector 40
conservation 62
conspiracy theory 15
consumerism 117, 163
convenience 163
conventional 142
conveyor belt 15
cool 89
Cool Britannia 233
cornflakes 16
cosmetic 63
cosmic rays 63
cosmonaut 142
couch potato 187
council tax 233
counselling 117
count-down 142
coupon 40
crack 212
crash 40
cred 212
credit card 142
crew cut 117
crisp 63
crooner 90
cruise missile 142
crumpet 90
Cubism 40
cultural revolution 163
curvaceous 90
cybercafé 233
cybernetics 117
cyberspace 212

D

Dalek 163
damage limitation 163
data 118
database 164
data processing 142
date rape 187
dawn raid 212
D-Day 41
deadline 63
death ray 41
debit card 188
deconstruct 188
defence 90
demo 90
demob 63, 90
denial 41
deoxyribonucleic acid 90
dependency culture 188
depression 16
Depression 90
designer 164
designer drug 212
détente 16
deterrent 142
developing 164
Dianamania 233
dig 91
digital 164
Dimania 233
dinky 213
director 41
disc jockey 118
disco 164
discotheque 142
disinformation 143
disposable 118
dissident 118
dive-bomb 91
DJ 164
DNA 118
documentary 91
docusoap 233
do-it-yourself 143
donor 41
doomwatch 188
dotcom 234
double helix 143
dove 165
download 213
downsize 188
dreadlocks 165
dreadnought 16
drop-out 91
dry 213
dumb down 91
Durex 91
DVD 234
DWEM 234
dysfunctional 91

E

East 143
eco- 165
eco-friendly 213
ecosystem 92
ecstasy 213
E-fit 213
ego-trip 165
electric blanket 92
electrify 16
electrocute 16
electronic 16
electronic brain 118
electronic mail 188
electron microscope 92
eleven plus 92
e-mail, email 213
emoticon 234
empathy 17
empower 214
end 92
endangered 165
engaged 118
enterprise culture 214
environment 143
environmentalism 189
equal opportunity 63
escalation 92
escalator 17
espresso 118
Essex girl 234
Essex man 234
establishment 63
estrogen 64
ethnic 119
ethnic cleansing 235
euro 189
Euro- 165
European Union 235
evacuate 92
evacuee 92
exclusive 17
executive 17
existential 92
existentialism 119
Exocet 189
expansionism 17
expressionism 17
extrovert 41

F

fab 144
face-lift 93
face-lifting 64
factory farming 165
fall-out 144
family planning 93
family values 42
fantastic 93
FAQ 235
Fascism 64
fashionista 235
fast food 144
fat cat 64
fatwa, fatwah 214
fax 119
feel-good factor 214
fellow-traveller 93
fifth column 93
film 18
film star 42
Filofax 93
final solution 119
firing squad 18
fission 93
flak 93
flapper 64
flares 165

floating voter 18
floppy disk 189
flower people, flower children 165
flying bomb 119
flying picket 189
flying saucer 119
focus group 166
foodie 214
foreplay 64
four-letter word 93
fraternization 120
freedom-fighter 120
freedom fries 235
free world 144
Freudian 42
fridge 65
friendly 65
frig 65
front line 42
fruit machine 94
fuck off 65
führer, fuehrer 94
fundamentalism 65
fusion 120
futurism 18
F-word 189

G

Gallup poll 120
game show 166
gamesmanship 120
gamma ray 18
garage 18
gas chamber 120
gas mask 42
gastropub 236
-gate 189
gay 94
gender 166
gene 42
generation gap 166
Generation X 214
genetic engineering 166
genetics 18
genocide 121
gentrify 190
geriatrics 19
Gestapo 94
ghetto-blaster 215
G.I. 94
girl guide 19
glamour boy 94
glasnost 215
glass ceiling 215
global village 166
global warming 190
GM 236
gobbledygook 121
golden goal 236
golden handshake 167
Google 236
goon 95
Goon 144
goose-stepper 65
gotcha 215
grass 95
grass roots 42
Great War 42
green 190
green belt 95
greenhouse effect 65
green shoots 215
groove 95
groovy 95
ground zero 121
group therapy 121
group 145
grunge 236
guesstimate 95
guided missile 121
guinea-pig 66
Gulf War syndrome 236

H

hacker 216
hacking 190
half-life 19
hallucinogenic 145
hang 191
happening 191
harassment 191
hard disk 191
hardware 121
have a nice day 191
hawk 167
health farm 66
heavy water 95
hep-cat 95
heritage 191
heroin chic 216
heterosexual 66
hi-fi 145
high-tech 191
hijack 66
hip 19
hip-hop 216
hippie, hippy 145
hit parade 145
hitch-hike 66
HIV 216
hobbit 95
holiday camp 122
holism 66
Hollywood 66
Holocaust 145
home page 237
homosexual 43
hood 96
Hoover 67
hopefully 96
hormone 19
hospitalize 19
hostess 96
house 216
house arrest 96
housey-housey 96
H.P. 122
HTML 237
http 237
Hun 43
hunger march 19
hydrogen bomb 122
hype 167

I

ice cube 67
icon 216
id 67
identification card 19
identikit 167
identity card 19
identity theft 237
image 146
imperialism 43
in 167
-in 167
include someone out 96
industrial action 192
industrial relations 20
inferiority complex 67
information superhighway 217
information technology 146
infrastructure 67
inner city 167
insecure 96
instant 43
insulin 67
integration 122
intelligence quotient 68
intelligence test 43
intelligent 168
intelligentsia 20
interactive 168
interceptor 96
interdisciplinary 96
interface 168
Internet 217
into 168
introvert 43
I.R.A. 68
iron curtain 68
iron lung 97
Islamophobia 192
-ism 168
isolationism 68
isotope 43
-ist 168

J

jazz 44
jeans 146
jeep 122
jet engine 122
jet lag 168
jet set 146
jingle 97
jive 97
job centre 192
jobseeker 237
join up 44
jukebox 97
jumbo jet 168
junk food 192

K

kaftan 162
killing field 217
kitchen sink 146
Kleenex 68
kneecap 192

L

L 97
laddish 237
ladies' 44
land 44
laptop 217
laser 168
learning difficulties 192
Lebensraum 20
legend in one's lifetime 44
Leninist 44
lesbian 68
level playing field192
Levi's, Levis 69
lib 169
libber 192
libido 20
life 217
lifestyle 169
like 147

liner 20
liposuction 217
liquidate 69
listener 69
listener-in 69
live 97
Loch Ness monster 97
logo 97
lone 123
long-playing 69
loo 123
loony left 193
lotus position 169
love beads 169
loyalty card 217
LP 123
LSD 147
luxury 98

M

machismo 123
macho 69
mad cow disease 218
male chauvinism 98
mall 147
manic depressive 20
marginalize 193
market 69
Marmite 20
marriage bureau 124
marriage guidance 98
massage parlour 21
mass murder 44
maxi- 169
ME 218
means test 70
Meccano 21
media 70
mega 218
megastar 193
megaton 147
me generation 193
meltdown 147
mercy 70
meritocracy 147
metrosexual 237
microwave oven 148
midlife crisis 169
millennium bug 238
Millennium Dome 238
mind-blowing 169
mini 45, 170
miniaturize 124
minimal 170
miniskirt 170
ministry 45
mission creep 238
mission statement 170
mobile 218
mobile phone 124
mod con 98
model 21
modem 148
mole 193
moment 193
monetarist 170
moonwalking 218
moron 45
motel 70
motor-bike 21
motorcade 45
motorway 21
mouse 171
mover and shaker 194
movie 45
MP3 238
Ms 124
muck-raker 21
muesli 98
Muggle 238
mullet 239
multiracial 21
Munich 98
mushroom 46
mustard gas 46
Muzak 99

N

name and shame 239
nanny state 171
napalm 124
napoo, napooh 46
narcissism 21
National Service 46
national serviceman 125
National Socialism 99
National Socialist 70
naturist 70
Nazi 99
negative equity 239
neon 22
nerd 148
netizen 218
network 194
neurosis 22
neutron 71
never-never 71
New Age 194
New Deal 99
New Labour 239
New Man 219
news bulletin 71
newscaster 99
news flash 22
news management 148
Newspeak 125
newsreel 46
new technology 148
new town 46
new world order 194
niet 148
NIMBY, nimby 219
no-go area 194
no man's land 22
non-alignment 149
non-U 149
no problem 171
noughties 219
nouvelle cuisine 195
nuclear 46, 125, 149
nuclear winter 219
nucleus 46
nudism 71
nuke 171
number-cruncher 171
nvCJD 240
nylon 99

O

Odeon 100
Oedipus complex 47
oestrogen 71
off-message 240
on-line 149
opinion-former 22
orchestrate 171
organic 125
Oscar 100
out 240
outsider 125
oven-ready 149

P

pacifism 22
paedophile 126
paedophilia 22
pager 171
page three girl 195
palace revolution 22
Palestinian 23
panties 23
paparazzo 171
paper handkerchief 23
paramilitary 100
paratroops 126
park 47
parking meter 100
Parkinson's law 149
passive smoking 195
paternity leave 195
PC, pc 219
peace dividend 172
peaceful coexistence 72
peace offensive 47
peace process 172
pecking order 72
pedophile 126
pedophilia 22
penicillin 72
people's 240
people's republic 47
Pepsi-Cola 23
perestroika 219
permissive 149
permissive society 172
person 195
persona 47
personal computer 195
personal organizer 219
personal stereo 241
personnel department 126
phish 241
phone-in 172
photocopy 72
photogenic 72
Photostat 47
physiotherapy 23
pill 149
pilot 23
PIN 220
pin-up 126
pizza 100
plane 23
plastic 24, 220
plastic explosive 24
plastic money 196
platinum blonde 100
plug 24
plutonium 126
podcasting 241
pogrom 24
poison gas 47
polio 101
politically correct 196
poll 24
poll tax 220

polyester 73
polythene 101
pop 73
population explosion 150
porn 172
posh 47
post-impressionism 48
postmodern 126
poverty line 24
P.O.W. 48
power dressing 220
Power Ranger 241
power station 24
PR 127
prefab 101
prestigious 48
prime time 172
prison-camp 73
privatization 150
proactive 196
pro-choice 196
production line 101
profile 173
profiteer 48
program 127
programme 73
progressive 24
Prohibition 73
pro-life 196
promotion 73
propaganda 25
property-owning democracy 74
protest 150
Prozac 220
psyche 48
psychedelic 150
psychoanalyse 48
psychoanalysis 25
psychological warfare 127
publicize 74
public relations 48
pukka 241
punk rock, punk 196

Q

quality time 197
quango 197
quantum 49
quantum theory 49
quark 173
queer 74
questionnaire 25
quiche 127
quick-frozen 101
Quisling 127

R

race relations 49
racialism 25
racialist 49
racist 101
radar 127
radio 25
rainbow nation 241
rap 173, 197
rationalize 74
rationing 49
rat-race 101
rave 220
raygun 102
ready meal 150
reality television 197
recession 74
recreational 150
recycle 74
red 49
redbrick 128
reflation 102
refugee 49
regime change 241
reinforced concrete 26
remote control 26
repress 26
request 75
resistance 102
Resistance 128
respect 242
right-on 197
road rage 221
robot 75
rock 128
rock and roll, rock 'n' roll 151
rocket 50
role 50
role model 151
Rolls-Royce 26
runway 75

S

sabotage 50
sacred cow 50
safe sex 198
sanctions 50
SARS 242
satellite 102
satellite television 173
scenario 173
scene 151
schizophrenia 50
science fiction 75
scooter 50
scramble 128
secret weapon 102
segregation 26
self-destruct 173
self-determination 51
self-service 51
sell-by date 198
Sellotape 128
Semtex 221
send 102
senior citizen 102
serial 51, 174
serial killer 221
service charge 75
sex 75
sex appeal 75
sex change 174
sex discrimination 51
sex drive 51
sexist 174
sex object 51
sex symbol 51
sexual politics 198
sex up 242
sexy 76
shadow cabinet 26
shell shock 52
shopaholic 221
shorthand typist 27
shuttle 174
silent 52
silent majority 151
Silicon Valley 198
single 175
single currency 198
sitcom 175
sit-in 103
sixty-four dollar question 128
skid row 103
skiffle 151
skyjack 175
slacker 242
sleaze 175, 221
sliced bread 151
slim 103
Sloane Ranger 198
smart 199
smart card 221
smog 27
snog 129
soap opera 103
social mobility 76
social security 27
social services 103
social worker 27
software 175
sonic boom, sonic bang 152
sophisticated 129
S.O.S. 52
soul 129
sound barrier 103
sound bite 222
soundtrack 76
soviet 52
Soviet 76
space age 129
spacecraft 103
spaceman 129
space shuttle 174
spacesuit 76
space-time 52
space vehicle 129
spam 242
Spam 103
-speak 152
speed dating 242
speeding 27
spin 199
spin doctor 222
spin-dry 76
spiv 104
split personality 52
split the atom 27
spokesperson 199
sputnik 152
square 130
Stalinism 76
stalk 222
standardize 27
Star Wars 222
stealth 199
stereophonic 76
storm troops 52
strategic 152
stratosphere 27
streaking 199
streamline 28
streamlined 52
street cred 222
street credibility 199
street-wise 175
striptease 104
student 28
studio 52
sub 53
suffragette 28
summer time 53
summit 152
sun-bather 77
Sunday supplement 28
superman 28
supermarket 104
supermodel 200
superpower 130
supersonic 104
supremo 130
surf 243

surgical 175
surrealist 77
surrogate 200
swastika 105
swinging 153
swipe 222
switched on 175

T

tabloid 53
tabloid journalism 28
tactical 153
take-away 175
take-over 130
talkie 53
tank 53
tanker 28
tape record 29
tape recorder 105
taxi, taxi-cab 29
teach-in 176
tear gas 53
Technicolor 53
teddy bear 29
Teddy boy 153
teenage 77
teenager 130
teeny-bopper 176
Teflon 222
telecom 176
televangelist 200
televise 77
television 29
termination 176
terrorist 130
test-tube baby 105
text message 200
thalidomide 153
Thatcherism 200
them and us 154
theme 223
theme park 176
thermonuclear 154
third degree 29
Third Reich 105
third way 243
Third World 176
Third World War 131
throw-away 77
tights 176
together 177
toiletries 77
topless 177
top ten 154
totalitarian 77
touchy-feely, touchie-feelie 200
tower block 177
town planning 29
toy boy 223
track record 177
tractor 30
traffic jam 53
traffic light 77
trailer trash 243
trainer 201
tranquillizer 154
transcendental meditation 177
transistor 131
transplant 154
transvestite 78
traumatic 177
trendy 177
trip 154
Trustafarian 243
T-shirt 78
tube 30
turn off 178
turn on 178
TV 131
twist 178
twit 105
tyrannosaurus 30

U

U 154
UFO 155
UKIP 243
unconscious 54
undercarriage 54
underdeveloped 131
underpants 105
underprivileged 106
unilateral disarmament 78
unisex 178
United Nations 131
unquote 106
up-tight 106
user-friendly 201

V

vacuum cleaner 30
Valium 178
vCJD 240
V.D. 78
VDU 178
velvet revolution 223
vet 30
Viagra 243
video 106, 155
video nasty 223
videotape 155
viewer 106
V.I.P. 106
virtual 223
virus 201
vitamin 54
V-1 131
vox pop 178
voyeur 30
voyeurism 78
V sign 132
V-2 132

W

Walkman 224
wannabe, wannabee 224
WAP 243
war crime 30
war to end war 78
war trial 132
Wasp 178
weapon of mass destruction 106
Web 244
webcast 244
weblog 244
website 244
welfare 30
welfare state 132
West 132
western 54
wet 224
whistle-blower 201
white collar 54
white supremacy 31
wholefood 179
wicked 224
Wi-Fi 244
wimp 79
wind of change 31
window 179
Windows 225
wireless 31
-wise 132
witch-hunt 107
with it 155
WMD 244
woman's magazine 54
women's liberation 179
women's movement 31
word processor 201
world war 31
World Wide Web 244
wysiwyg 225

X

X 155
X chromosome 55
Xerox 156

Y

Y chromosome 55
yomp 225
you're welcome 179
youth club 133
yuppie 225

Z

zero tolerance 201
zip, zip fastener, zip fastening, zipper 79